Holy Places of the Buddha

Holy Places of the Buddha

Crystal Mirror Series
Volume Nine

CRYSTAL MIRROR SERIES

1-3. *Footsteps on the Diamond Path*
4. *Guru Padmasambhava and Buddhism in Tibet*
5. *Lineage of Diamond Light*
6. *The Three Jewels and History of Dharma Transmission*
7. *Buddha, Dharma, Sangha in Historical Perspective*
8. *Light of Liberation: A History of Buddhism in India*

Library of Congress Cataloging-in-Publication Data

Holy Places of the Buddha
p. cm.—(Crystal mirror series : v 9)
Includes bibliographical references and index.
ISBN 0-89800-244-3
1. Gautama Buddha—Shrines—India. 2. Buddhist shrines—India. 3. Temples, Buddhist—India. I. Dharma Publishing. II Series.
BQ633.H65 1994 294.3'435'0943197dc20 94-2497 CIP

Frontispiece: Śākyamuni Buddha and the Sixteen Great Arhats
Photographs on pp. xxxi, 2, 16, 32, 40, 45, 74, 75, 82, 113, 117, 119, 128, 131, 166–167, 187, 239, 250, 281, 283, 287, 291, and 349 courtesy of John C. and Susan L. Huntington; pp. 104 and 122 by A. Cunningham, from ASI Reports 1862–1864. Photographs on pp. 18 and 20 courtesy of Ewalda Buiting.

Director and general editor of the Crystal Mirror Series: Tarthang Tulku. Introduction by Tarthang Tulku (Kun-dga' dge-legs Ye-shes-rdo-rje) Research, compiling, and manuscript preparation for *Holy Places of the Buddha* by Elizabeth Cook.

Typeset in Adobe New Aster with New Aster Outline titles and initials. Printed and bound in the U.S.A. by Dharma Press U.S.A.

10 9 8 7 6 5 4 3 2 1

Contents

Illustrations and Maps

Preface

After I came to India as a refugee in 1959, I resolved to visit the great pilgrimage sites of the Buddha's homeland. The Enlightened One himself indicated that practice at these holy places had special power to deepen faith in the Dharma and benefit all beings, and it was clear that in those troubled times special help was needed. In 1961 I made my first pilgrimage. Since then I have returned to the major sites several times.

On my first pilgrimage journey, I was very fortunate to be able to follow the pilgrimage map prepared earlier in this century by dGe-'dun Chos-phel, for in those early days it was not easy to find one's way without guidance. Apart from Afghanistan or Sri Lanka, it has been my good fortune to have visited almost every place that this excellent master described.

In 1989, when I returned to India for the first time in more than twenty years, my destination was the most sacred of all the pilgrimage sites of India: Bodh Gayā, the place where the Lord Buddha attained enlightenment. The occasion was the Ceremony for World Peace, sponsored by the Tibetan Nyingma Meditation Center. These ceremonies have been held annually ever since, and today they offer the opportunity for thousands of pilgrims to gather and join together in heartfelt prayer. There are now smaller ceremonies at Lumbinī and

Sārnāth as well, two more places sacred to the Buddha. I am very pleased that these ceremonies appear to have stimulated a broad interest in these ancient centers of pilgrimage.

Within our own community, the opportunity for students to travel to India to participate in the Peace Ceremonies has awakened a strong interest in Dharma history and the practice of pilgrimage. Several times students have stayed on after the ceremonies to visit other sacred sites such as the ruins of Nālandā University, the cave temples at Ajaṇṭā and Ellora, and the Great Stupa at Sāñcī. The benefits they experienced through their journeys were an important factor in deciding to prepare this new volume in the Crystal Mirror Series, a guide to major places of pilgrimage in India and sites historically important to Buddhism.

In preparing this volume, we have sought to locate each site, indicate historical events associated with it, describe the features that a pilgrim would find there, and indicate how the site figured in the transmission of the Dharma. There are many places we could not identify or describe in detail, but we have tried to present sites of importance for anyone interested in the Dharma, including locations sanctified by the presence of the Buddha, places associated with Mahākāśyapa, Śāriputra, and other direct disciples and with such great Māhayāna masters as Nāgārjuna and Asaṅga. We have included sites associated with important events, the cave temples at Ajaṇṭā and Ellora, and the great Buddhist universities.

We are aware that what we have presented here is only a modest introduction, based on the information to which we presently have access. We encourage others to explore further, and in the future we would like to extend our own research. We offer this present compilation in the hope that it will be of value for those planning to visit these sites and useful for anyone eager to deepen his or her appreciation for the Buddha, the Dharma, and the Sangha.

Viewed with the mind of a tourist, the holy places of the Buddha can be interesting, even fascinating, but for the serious student, their significance operates at a deeper level. For those who cultivate an attitude of respect and appreciation, pilgrimage can be a powerful and richly rewarding practice. The more the traveler knows about the places being visited, the more he or she will be able to open the heart to the Three Jewels. If this volume helps to foster such appreciation, it will have fulfilled its purpose.

I would like to acknowledge the staff of Dharma Publishing, whose work has made this book possible, as well as everyone else who participated in its production.

This book is dedicated to all Buddhists who respect and continue the tradition of Dharma and Sangha. May their good intentions produce good results, and may their activity on behalf of the Dharma flourish without interruption until saṁsāra itself comes to an end.

Maṅgalaṁ Jayantu

Kun-dga' dge-legs Ye-shes rdo-rje

Odiyan, January 1994

Introduction

More than 2,500 years ago, on the plains of northern India, an event occurred that transformed the course of human history. Seating himself beneath a pipal tree at the site known today as Bodh Gayā, Siddhārtha Gautama, the prince of the Śākyas, vowed not to arise until he had found the answer to the ultimate mysteries and enduring sorrows of human existence. After a night of heroic struggle and profound insight, he attained his aim. He arose from his seat under the Bodhi Tree as the Buddha Śākyamuni, the Enlightened One of this world age. During the centuries after the Buddha's enlightenment, hundreds of millions of individuals have found transcendent insight and peace by following his example and teachings.

After his unparalleled accomplishment, the Buddha spent the rest of his life traveling in India and elsewhere, sharing the fruits of his realization. At Sārnāth he turned the Wheel of the Dharma for the first time, presenting teachings followed by all Buddhist traditions. On the Vulture Peak at Rājagṛha, he turned the Wheel of the Dharma a second time, proclaiming the truth at the heart of all appearance. At Śrāvastī, his principal residence for more than twenty years, the Enlightened One shaped the form of the Sangha, and at Vaiśālī, where he put an end to an outbreak of plague, he gave many important Mahāyāna Sūtras, including key Third Turning teachings. Sāṁkāśya became renowned as the place where the Buddha descended to earth after visiting the heaven realms to teach his mother the Abhidharma, and Kauśāmbī was honored as the site where he spent two rainy season retreats.

Sanctified by the presence and activity of the Buddha, these holy places were venerated by his followers. First and foremost was Bodh Gayā, for it was here that the great transformation took place. But there were other sites central in the life of the Blessed One as well: Lumbinī, the place of the Enlightened One's birth; the bank of the Nairañjanā River, where he bathed and took nourishment on the day preceding his enlightenment; and Kuśinagara, where he entered into nirvāṇa. Through the centuries, members of the Sangha built stūpas and monuments at these sacred sites. Through acts of devotion and veneration, they renewed their faith and let the blessings of the Buddha enter their hearts, healing the sufferings and confusions of saṁsāra.

Revered for more than fifteen hundred years, the holy places of the Buddha in India eventually fell victim to neglect, and in some cases their very existence was forgotten. But today, almost all of them have been identified. Many are once more active Dharma centers and can be visited by anyone who wishes to trace the steps of the Buddha. There are other sacred sites to visit as well: centers founded and made glorious by the community that continued the teachings of the Great Sage after he had passed into nirvāṇa.

The Buddha himself proclaimed the importance of practice at these locations. Forseeing that in these dark times of the kāliyuga the Dharma would fall into decline, he counseled his followers to respect the holy places of the past and to journey there to pay homage to the Buddha and Sangha. He advised that they sit in meditation, visualizing the Buddha, letting the Three Jewels enter their hearts, and praying with devotion that the teachings be preserved.

In these uncertain times, it is important that we follow this counsel, honoring the ancient places of pilgrimage, repairing the monuments erected there, and revitalizing them as centers for Dharma transmission. When we gather at sacred sites to invoke and honor the Triple Gem through prayer, meditation, and offerings, we clear the way for compassion and enlightened understanding to manifest in the world.

The merit created by such actions will be of inestimable value in the difficult times to come, when famine and disease, natural disasters, war, and disputes among people of good will will increase. In the future, inner calm will be nearly unknown, and chaos will truly prevail. The human lifespan will shorten, disputes and fighting will breed negativity that pollutes the heart and mind, and peace on earth will seem like a fairy tale. In those desperate times, when miracles and blessings alone have the power to counter the gathering forces of darkness, practice at sacred sites will be one of the few ways still available for inviting the compassion of the enlightened lineage. By creating the conditions for such practice today, we can offer untold benefits to the future.

Knowledge of Dharma: Foundation for Appreciation

To prepare our hearts and minds for pilgrimage, we can remind ourselves of the nature of the Buddha and the priceless value of his teachings. Keenly aware of human suffering and its causes, the Compassionate One taught the means for transforming the pain of saṁsāra into the joy of liberation. He taught the antidotes to hatred, attachment, and delusion and the ways that emotional obscurations manifest and can be overcome. He revealed how to take control of time and appearance, how to benefit others, and how to practice selfless generosity and compassion.

The Buddha taught the Four Truths: suffering, its origins, its cessation, and the path that leads to cessation. When the

Buddha turned the Wheel of the Dharma for the first time at Sārnāth, he presented the Four Truths in three different aspects. A fourth dimension of the Four Truths, taught to those with higher realization, became the basis for turning the Wheel of the Dharma for a second and a third time. Explaining with precision how to cultivate a focused mind and train in clarity, the All-Knowing One pointed out the obstacles that come as practice intensifies and explained how to deal with them. He demonstrated through his own being the nature of enlightenment and the signs of its attainment. Revealing how to turn each action and thought toward the Dharma, he opened the path of the Bodhisattva, who works unceasingly to lead all beings to liberation.

Knowing that the Great Sage did all this for our welfare, how can our hearts not swell with gratitude? It is said that just as Rāhula was the child of the Buddha's body, the disciples who turn to the teachings through hearing are the children of his speech, while those transform their being in response to his silent inner voice are the children of his heart. Though the voice of the Dharma may still be weak within us, we too can count ourselves as members of the Enlightened One's family, sustained and brought to maturity by his example and counsel, his loving kindness and boundless compassion.

The Blessed One explained repeatedly that he could only point the way to liberation: Those who wished to escape from saṁsāra would have to take responsibility for their own transformation. His teachings are like a map drawn by a traveler returning from a distant land: at once an invitation and a challenge. To accept this challenge is not easy, for human beings are creatures of saṁsāra, conditioned to saṁsāric standards for action, saṁsāric ways of seeing, and saṁsāric understanding. To break through this conditioning requires strong discipline and perseverance. This is why the Buddha emphasized the importance of conduct as the foundation for all realization. The clear and detailed rules for behavior that he offered for the monastic Sangha, collected in the Vinaya teachings, provide a firm basis for overcoming conventional ways of acting. For those who could not enter the monastic community, he set forth the basics of an ethical way of life, rooted in insight that transcends the limits of saṁsāra and escapes its snares. Those who practice in accord with these rules constitute the greater Sangha. Their special qualities make them protectors of the Dharma and guides for all who seek an end to suffering and sorrow.

Once the foundation of moral conduct is in place, it becomes possible to experience directly the awakening shared by the Buddhas of the past, present, and future: the vision of the cosmos and understanding of enlightened nature that ultimately inspires all followers of the Dharma. Through meditative realization, all who follow the path can prepare themselves to share in this vision and to engage in the dynamic action it evokes.

As a flawless path toward such awakening, the Blessed One in his kindness taught the six pāramitās: giving, morality, patience, effort, meditation, and wisdom. Each of the pāramitās can itself be understood as manifesting six pāramitās, and each of these in turn manifests a wide range of inner qualities. Coordinated with the practices known as the thirty-seven wings of enlightenment and the eightfold path, the pāramitās are practiced differently at each of the five stages of the path. At the third stage of the path, ten different levels of Bodhisattva practice are initiated, and at the tenth of these stages it becomes possible to speak of the perfection of the practice of the pāramitās. Here the two obscurations—kleśavaraṇa and jñeyavaraṇa—are completely transcended. The ordinary human mind, which collects the residues of the obscurations and makes them into the contents of ordinary existence, is overcome, transformed into enlightened nature.

The Buddha taught that the source of this ultimate realization is Prajñāpāramitā—the wisdom that passes beyond saṁsāric conceptualization. Symbolically, Prajñāpāramitā is the mother of the Buddhas. It becomes accessible through the practice of the six perfections, which transcend the virtues of the saṁsāric level and find full expression at the highest stages of the Bodhisattva path. Thus, the exemplars of Prajñāpāramitā are the eight great Bodhisattvas, beings for whom the Buddha manifests as rays of light illuminating all of space and time.

The Transmission of the Teachings

It is a marvel beyond praise that the Buddha found ways to present these most refined of teachings to ordinary human beings. Without his unparalleled skill as a teacher, his realization could never have become a force for transforming saṁsāra into nirvāṇa. The power we sense at places of pilgrimage is linked to this inexplicable transformation, and our presence at such places invites us to dwell on its inexpressible wonder.

The Sūtras in which the teachings of the Buddha are collected usually start with a description of the occasion on which the Sūtra was taught: the location, the principal disciples of the Buddha in attendance, the patron who sponsored and requested the teachings or the individuals whose questions led the Buddha to discourse on a particular topic, and the subject matter of the discourse. Reflecting on these elements, we can cultivate delight in the splendor of the circumstances and awe at the powers of the Buddha that made the teachings possible.

Aware of the countless needs of those trapped in the web of saṁsāra, the Buddha presented teachings on 84,000 topics: subjects so enormous in their scope that they surpass the ability of human beings even to think about them. His teachings operated at many levels simultaneously, and he manifested the inner essence of the Dharma in countless ways, communicating flawlessly to beings caught in various forms of consciousness and mistaken ways of being. He addressed all the inhabitants of the three realms: not just human beings but gods, nāgas, animals, and all other sentient beings.

Manifesting countless forms and activities to communicate the Dharma and share its blessings, the Compassionate One taught verbally, through actions of the body, and through subtle communications on the level of energy; through visual images, symbols, and gestures; through music, art, and appearance. At times he made his influence felt indirectly, inspiring others to speak or ask questions through the power of his meditation; at other times those in his vicinity heard within his silence the teachings they required. For gods and demigods, humans, animals, hungry ghosts, and creatures of the hell realms, he manifested the Nirmāṇakāya, his external form. For those who had already attained advanced stages of realization, he manifested the Sambhogakāya, his inner form. And for those who attained the highest realization, he manifested the Dharmakāya, his innermost form, inseparable from the nature of all that is.

No matter how many beings gathered to hear the Buddha, each of them heard every single word with perfect clarity, in his or her own language. The meaning was absolutely clear and directly relevant; the images used were sweet as nectar, inspiring a wish to learn more. The voice of the Buddha was soothing, and even though the audience gathered around the Blessed One in a great circle, each person perceived the Buddha as facing him or her directly. All who heard, understood; all who understood knew how to practice; all who practiced attained results, and all who attained results set forth firmly on the path of liberation. Those who heard the Buddha abandoned all interest in the concerns of ordinary mind and turned naturally to the practice of the Dharma, taking on spontaneously the discipline the Buddha prescribed.

At whatever level the Buddha taught, his special qualities assured that the teachings were effective. As they took his words and his example to heart, his disciples found that every aspect of their lives reminded them of the teachings and served to reveal their importance, while the teachings themselves gave life inner coherence and meaning. The mantras, the prayers, and the philosophical teachings all supported one another, and the rules for conduct helped show this interconnection and apply it in every part of life.

The Historical Lineage of Dharma Transmission

Because the teachings presented by the Buddha made such a deep impression on those who heard them, it was easy for his disciples to recall each detail of what had been said. The more clearly the Sangha realized how saṁsāric mind acts as a kind of thief or devil, obscuring awareness and realization, the more firmly they held to the teachings as the one sure antidote to ignorance and delusion, and the more firmly they resolved to transmit them onward with perfect accuracy.

The responsibility for such transmission fell to the Arhats, disciples of the Buddha whose mastery of saṁsāra let through them cut through the emotional obscurations that block the full capacities of the mind. Their concentration (samādhi, Tib. ting-nge-'dzin), perfected through their attainments and strengthened still further through the practice of specific dhāraṇīs, allowed the Arhats to recall the words of the Enlightened One perfectly and pass them on without error.

After the Parinirvāṇa of the Buddha, the great Arhats assembled in the First of the Great Councils to recite the teachings and assure their accurate transmission. Sixteen Great Arhats renounced nirvāṇa in order to remain in the world and protect the Dharma. As responsibility for care of the Sangha passed from Mahākāśyapa and Ānanda, direct disciples of the Buddha, to a succession of patriarchs, the inner lineage of the teachings was also successfully preserved.

Eventually, as the Dharma spread throughout all parts of society and to other cultures, the risk arose that the teachings might become distorted. At the time of the Third Council, held several hundred years after the Parinirvāṇa of the Buddha, the different branches of the teachings were written down to safeguard against this danger.

According to the Theravādin tradition of Southeast Asia, the Buddha taught in Pāli, and this has become the canonical written language of the Theravādin school, which preserves the Sūtras of the First Turning and the Vinaya teachings. In the Mahāyāna view, however, the Buddha did not speak only one language, but rather made himself understood in whatever language his listeners—whether humans, devas, rakṣāsas, or yakṣas—could understand. However, the Mahāyāna schools generally preserved the written teachings in Sanskrit, the traditional language for the highest philosophical and spiritual teachings throughout India.

The transmission of the Buddha's teachings reached its high point in about the seventh and eighth centuries of the common era. During this period, Nālandā and the newly built universities—Odantapurī, Vikramaśīla, and Somapurī—were flourishing; the Vinaya, the Sūtras, and the Tantras were all being extensively studied, together with the commentaries of such great Mahāyāna masters as Nāgārjuna and Asaṅga and the masters known as the Six Charioteers. It was then that Tibet reached out for the Dharma and made great efforts to obtain and translate the Buddha's teachings.

Tibetan masters assembled enormous libraries in bSam-yas and other monasteries near Lhasa, with a wealth of texts collected from Nālandā, Bodh Gayā, Vikramaśīla, and elsewhere that rivaled the finest collections of India. The written and oral lineages of the Sūtras, the Vinaya, the Tantra, the Abhidharma, and the commentarial śāstras were all preserved intact as transmitted by the great Vidyādharas and others. By the twelfth century, when the light of the Dharma began to wane in its homeland, the teachings had already been translated and preserved in Tibet. In the twelfth and thirteenth centuries, Tibet's leading scholars began to assemble these texts into authoritative editions that practitioners and scholars have relied on ever since.

Today Buddhist texts are preserved in three major canons —Pāli, Chinese, and Tibetan, with the Tibetan Canon being the most extensive compilation of Mahāyāna teachings. Earlier this century some thirty or forty volumes of Sanskrit texts that had been preserved in Tibet were brought back to India; together with Sanskrit manuscripts preserved in Nepal and occasional texts and text fragments found elsewhere, these are the only remnants of the Sanskrit transmission.

The Tibetan Canon contains over one hundred volumes of teachings by the Buddha. Yet this vast storehouse of knowledge, so various in style and manner, in range of topics and application, is only a small fragment of the teachings presented by the Great Compassionate One for the sake of all beings. It is said in the Sūtras that if all the Buddha's teachings were written in a small hand on palm leaves in the traditional manner, it would take five hundred elephants to carry them. Unfortunately, over the centuries most of these priceless treasures have been lost.

Tracing the Dharma through History

The Dharma in India flourished for well over a millennium. During that time countless monasteries, temples, and universities were founded to transmit its blessings and its knowledge. Texts preserved in Tibet and elsewhere, the accounts of Buddhist historians and pilgrims, and the results of archaeological investigations allow us to reconstruct many of the events of this era. We know in considerable detail the development of different schools: where they flourished, what teachings they developed, and what studies, practices, and texts they emphasized. We know where great centers for Dharma were founded and can identify many of the Dharma kings and patrons who cared for the centers founded by the Buddhist Sangha. We know what the great pilgrimage sites looked like at various times in history, what monuments were founded there, and how the Sangha grew through time.

Still, there are major gaps in our knowledge. The strength of the Sangha varied over time, depending in part on the support it received from various rulers and dynasties. Two of India's greatest sovereigns, Aśoka and Kaniṣka, were both ardent patrons of the Dharma, and the kings of the Pāla dynasty, who controlled the ancient homeland of the Dharma from the eighth through the eleventh centuries, offered strong support that allowed Mahāyāna centers to flourish. But at other times and under other rulers, the Dharma did not enjoy similar patronage, and for these periods our knowledge is fragmentary.

In the twelfth century, the fortunes of the Dharma in India entered into a period of prolonged decline that continued until this present century. Wave after wave of Muslim invasions, followed by centuries of Muslim rule, did serious harm to Buddhist centers and effectively put an end to the monastic Sangha. Gradually Brahman or Śaivite masters took over the old Buddhist sites and either let them fall into decay or converted them into centers for their own tradition. Due to centuries of neglect and the loss of dynastic records, it is not always easy to trace what happened at different pilgrimage sites. The changes to the land and landscape over the centuries make this doubly difficult. Even today, after many decades of archaeological research, the location of some Buddhist centers is still not certain.

Fortunately, the close Dharma connection that developed between India and Tibet kept open a channel for transmission of the teachings. Such great masters as Padmasambhava, Vimalamitra, Śāntarakśita, and Buddhaguhya initiated this exchange in the eighth century. Indian paṇḍitas came to Tibet to share their knowledge and also to study with Vairotsana, Cog-ro Klu'i-rgyal-mtshan, rMa Rin-chen-mchog, Ka-ba dPal-brtsegs, and other Tibetan masters. For centuries, Tibetans in turn spent many years studying at the great centers, where they became quite familiar with the history of the Dharma.

Thanks to these centuries of intimate interaction, Tibetan historians were able to preserve important historical records and data. There are some forty to fifty authentic religious histories available in Tibet. A few are well known in the West, such as the history of the Dharma in India by the sixteenth century historian Tāranātha. Others are still largely unknown. As they are studied and compared to the information passed on in the Sūtras and śāstras and the oral transmission lineages, and as the resulting data is classified and organized in various ways, our knowledge seems certain to increase.

Places of Pilgrimage

Much has changed on this planet since the time when the Buddha walked the earth. Still, when we visit the sacred sites of the Dharma, our imagination can return us to those ancient times. The more we know about the teachings, the more fully we can bring the presence of the Buddha and the great masters alive in our hearts.

For anyone who wishes to appreciate the full significance of pilgrimage, it is vital to learn about the Buddha. A good starting point is to read the Lalitavistara-sūtra, published in English as the *Voice of the Buddha*, as well as other canonical accounts of the life of the Blessed One. The more we understand who the Enlightened One actually was and what he accomplished, the more a naturally deepening devotion will allow us to open our hearts to the blessings that places of pilgrimage have to offer. Through the great compassion of the Enlightened One, we may discover that even in the midst of the kāliyuga, even when our eyes see only ruins and decay, the sacred places of the Dharma offer a taste of peace: peace of mind and peace on earth; the peace of nirvāṇa and the peace of enlightenment.

The age of the Buddha is gone, and we cannot relive it. Yet pilgrimage is a way to bring to life in our own hearts the incomparable realization of the Tathāgata. Despite the passing of the centuries and the enormous turmoil that these places have known, their power is still available. Though the land has suffered greatly, and the buildings are largely in ruins, the land remains, as do the rivers, the skies, and the sun overhead. Despite what has been lost, the holy places are still worthy of our deepest respect.

Places of pilgrimage are places where enlightenment is at home in the world. If you have the opportunity for a pilgrimage, open your senses to what you experience at such sacred sites. Prepare yourself through reading, study, reflection, and meditation. When your experience deepens your faith or understanding, share what you have learned with others, so that in your own small way you can help make the presence of the enlightened lineage accessible to the modern world.

Imagine how wonderful it would be if India could recover its own heritage of spiritual realization, as embodied in the sacred sites of the Dharma. Imagine the benefits if Buddhist lands turned their full attention once more to the places where the Dharma had its origin. Imagine how the West could benefit if it began to discover the knowledge that practice at places of pilgrimage can help restore.

Seeing this potential, our responsibility to the future is clear. Even the most fantastic experience available in saṁsāra cannot compare to glimpsing the truth of enlightenment. Once we know this for ourselves, we have a duty to share that understanding. Even if we cannot achieve realization ourselves, we can support and promote the realization of others.

What else that we might accomplish in this transitory life could be of equal significance?

Because there is so much to be gained from such practice, we encourage all Westerners to pay tribute to the sacred places of the Dharma and express our wish that all Tibetans who follow the Dharma also honor the holy places. Such acts of reverence and appreciation will benefit our Nyingma lineage and also all schools of Buddhism, for all followers of the Dharma share the same origins, and we can all show our respect to the holy places in the same way.

It is said that drop by drop even the whole vast ocean can be emptied. In the same way, we can each contribute to emptying saṁsāra of suffering beings. The tears of compassion that we shed can help keep the enlightened lineage alive; the devotion we manifest can bring its blessings to future generations. Beyond our human pursuits and concerns, the power of the Buddhas, the Bodhisattvas, and the great masters is pure and accessible. Those who walk where they walked have the chance to experience this directly.

Although the teachings that the Buddha offered the world transcend time and place, we are embodied beings, and our physical presence at the places where the Enlightened One taught and practiced and where the Dharma flourished for centuries evokes a special power. Even on a mundane level, visiting such sites helps us understand how vast the Dharma is, how remarkable its institutions and rich its history. For those of you who have the opportunity to tour these places, we wish you all success in your spiritual journey.

Holy Places
of the Buddha

Dharma Publishing

Part One

Eight Great Places of Pilgrimage

The Practice of Pilgrimage

In walking in the footsteps of the Buddha, the pilgrim experiences, however briefly, the thrust toward enlightenment that gives rise to an endless procession of Buddhas.

There are four places, Ānanda, that a devout person should visit and look upon with feelings of reverence. What are these four places?

"'Here the Tathāgata was born!' This, Ānanda, is a place that a devout person should visit and look upon with feelings of reverence.

"'Here the Tathāgata became fully enlightened in unsurpassed, supreme Enlightenment!' This, Ānanda, is a place that a devout person should visit and look upon with feelings of reverence.

"'Here the Tathāgata set rolling the unexcelled Wheel of the Dharma!' This, Ānanda, is a place that a devout person should visit and look upon with feelings of reverence.

"'Here the Tathāgata passed away into the state of nirvāṇa in which no element of clinging remains!' This, Ānanda, is a place that a devout person should visit and look upon with feelings of reverence.

"These, Ānanda, are the four places that a devout person should visit and look upon with feelings of reverence. And truly there will come to these places, Ānanda, devoted monks and nuns, laymen and laywomen, reflecting: 'Here the Tathāgata was born! Here the Tathāgata became fully enlightened in unsurpassed, supreme Enlightenment! Here the Tathāgata set rolling the unexcelled Wheel of the Dharma! Here the Tathāgata passed away into the state of nirvāṇa in which no element of clinging remains.'

"And whoever, Ānanda, should die on such a pilgrimage with his heart established in faith, at the breaking up of the body, after death, will be reborn in a realm of heavenly happiness." —*Mahāparinibbāna-sutta*

With these words, spoken in a grove near Kuśinagara shortly before his final breath, the Buddha emphasized the value of pilgrimage and directed his disciples to visit four significant sites. These four sites, which commemorate the essential events in the life of an enlightened being, are:

LUMBINĪ, birthplace of Siddhārtha, Prince of the Śākya clan.

BODH GAYĀ, where six years after he departed from home, Siddhārtha dispelled all remnants of illusory existence and demonstrated the attainment of complete, perfect enlightenment in the shade of the Bodhi Tree.

SĀRNĀTH, site of the Buddha's first teaching and the first manifestation of the Sangha, the community that exemplifies the blessings of practicing the path to enlightenment.

KUŚINAGARA, where the Buddha entered Parinirvāṇa, completely passing away from all forms of worldly existence.

The four places named by the Buddha became known as the Caturmahāpratihārya, the Four Great Wonders. These are the places where all Buddhas of the past have been born, demonstrated the attainment of enlightenment, set the wheel of the Dharma in motion, and entered Parinirvāṇa, and all Buddhas in the future will perform the same actions at these very places. Defining distinct stages of spiritual awakening, these four central holy places are close to the hearts of all who aspire to realize the Buddha's teachings.

The Auspicious Occasion and Right Juncture

All Buddhist traditions teach that Śākyamuni Buddha is but one in a succession of perfectly enlightened beings who have appeared in the unfolding of universes throughout unending time. The Buddhist vision of cosmic time measures time in kalpas, inconceivably long aeons defined by the birth and passing away of countless world-systems similar to our own. Some kalpas are dark; within them no Buddhas will be born to light the way to liberation. Our present aeon, the Bhadrakalpa, is known as the Fortunate Aeon, for within it one thousand Buddhas will appear.

According to the Bhadrakalpika Sūtra, Śākyamuni is the fourth Buddha of our present aeon. His birth and enlightenment were the outcome of innumerable lifetimes dedicated to virtue and truth. In perfecting the six great virtues (giving, morality, patience, vigor, concentration, and wisdom), he consistently dedicated his life to the welfare of others and followed in the footsteps of Buddhas before him. The merit resulting from his actions culminated in his final birth, in which he became a Buddha.

The Buddha's birth as a human being celebrates the great opportunity and the unique juncture. A human birth is the great opportunity, for, of the five possible destinies of sentient beings (gods, humans, animals, pretas, and inhabitants of the hells), only the human realm offers the necessary conditions for attaining enlightenment. Although beings continually pass away and are reborn in endless cycles of birth and death, birth as a human being is extremely rare. The Buddha taught that a human birth is as difficult to obtain as the possibility of a sea turtle thrusting its head through a single ox yoke floating on the vast ocean. When birth as a human being occurs at the same time that a Buddha's teaching is known, this auspicious convergence of opportunity and circumstance is known as the unique juncture.

Generating the thought of enlightenment is even more precious and rare; carrying it through to fruition is an act of superhuman courage and determination. That the Buddha could shatter the bonds of illusion and bring enlightened knowledge into the world was a supreme accomplishment; that he could set this knowledge in motion through his teachings and transmit it to others was the unique accomplishment of a Buddha. Having demonstrated the full potential of human being and provided the means for others to emulate his example, the Enlightened One gave his final teaching. Passing into Parinirvāṇa, he demonstrated the truth of impermanence and communicated the beauty of a life lived in full awareness of the nature of reality and being.

The Pilgrim's Path

Inspired by admiration and devotion, the path of pilgrimage attunes the aspirant to the body, speech, and mind of the Buddha, enabling them to participate in the Buddha's enactment of birth, enlightenment, teaching, and the complete passing from sorrow, all raised to the point of perfection through the acts of the Buddha. For those who appreciate that the Buddha's actions illuminate the quest for knowledge and fulfillment, pilgrimage is a physical and symbolic returning to the center, a way of realizing the central meaning of the Buddha's life and teachings. In undertaking such a journey, whether bodily or through the power of visualization, pilgrims transform their understanding by reflecting deeply on the view, decisions, and resolve that open wide the path to realization.

Pilgrimage enacted with devotion turns the mind toward knowledge and parts the barriers erected by self-doubt and fear; admiration for those who showed the way to attainment awakens vision, generating love for all beings and an earnest wish to contribute to their happiness. Within this wider vision, pilgrimage takes on the quality of prayer; fusing a deep inner communion with the outer form of devotion, pilgrimage becomes a celebration of human potentiality, a way to participate in the līla, the cosmic play of the fully awakened ones. In walking in the footsteps of the Buddha, the pilgrim experiences, however briefly, the thrust toward enlightenment that gives rise to an endless procession of Buddhas. With heart established in faith, the pilgrim returns from this journey to a world transformed into a stage for accomplishment.

Significance of the Stūpa

In his enlightenment, the Buddha manifested the transforming power of the Dharma, attracting beings from all heavenly realms. At the request of Brahmā, lord of the most sublime of these realms, the Buddha determined to teach the knowledge that leads beyond all forms of suffering and opens the way to fulfillment and peace. After teaching for forty-five years and transmitting the Dharma to thousands of disciples, the Buddha passed away and his body was cremated. The remains of ashes and bone, venerated as relics, were collected into a single vase. When the clans and kingdoms represented at the cremation each claimed their share of the relics, the relics were divided into eight portions and distributed, each kingdom sharing equally. As the Buddha had requested, his relics were enshrined in special reliquaries known as stūpas. In all, ten stūpas were erected to commemorate the Buddha's

Parinirvāṇa: eight over the relics, one over the vase that first held the relics, and another over the embers from the cremation fire.

Accounts of the Buddha's life mention that long before Śākyamuni, stūpas had been built to enshrine the relics of previous Buddhas. It is said that when Prince Gautama of the Śākya clan renounced his kingdom to secure for all beings relief from the sufferings occasioned by the knowledge of old age, sickness, and death, he journeyed first to a stūpa dedicated to the Buddha Kāśyapa, the Buddha before Śākyamuni. When Śākyamuni became a Buddha, he demonstrated to his disciples the form a stūpa should take by folding his robe to create the base, placing his inverted almsbowl atop the robe to represent the heart of the stūpa, and placing his umbrella on top of the bowl to represent the spire.

Intended as a receptacle for relics and offerings, the stūpa symbolizes bodhicitta, the awakened potential for realization. The shape of the stūpa not only represents the deep structure of enlightened mind, it also transmits the power of enlightenment to those who honor its presence. Since the time of the Buddha, followers of the Buddha's way have circumambulated stūpas to invoke the blessings of the Enlightened Ones for curing disease, answering prayers, heightening awareness, and relieving obstructions to spiritual practice.

Pilgrimage in History

Although the stūpas enshrining the relics of the Buddha Śākyamuni were highly venerated and visited by pilgrims for many centuries thereafter, little is known of the practice of pilgrimage immediately after the Buddha's Parinirvāṇa. At some point the sites considered central places of pilgrimage increased from four to eight. The four new sites included were Rājagṛha, where the Buddha tamed the maddened elephant Nālagiri; Śrāvastī, the site of a momentous event known as the

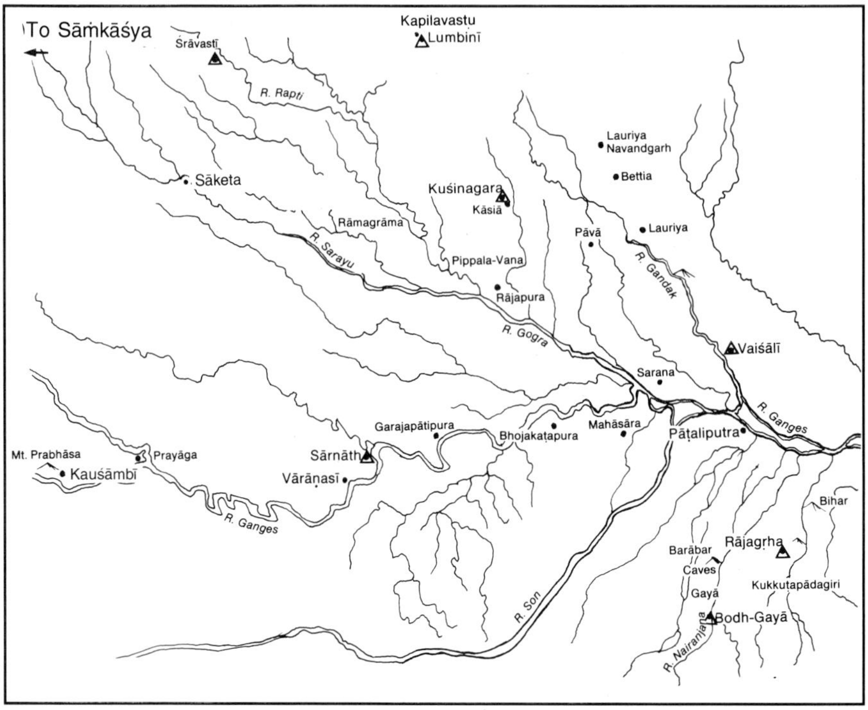

The Ganges Basin, with sites of the Eight Great Wonders

Miracle of the Pairs; Vaiśālī, where monkeys offered the Enlightened One a gift of honey; and Sāṁkāśya, where the Buddha descended from the heaven realms after teaching the Dharma to his mother. These eight places, known as the Aṣṭa-mahāprātihārya, or the Eight Great Wonders, were essential to the itinerary of pilgrims from all parts of Buddhist Asia.

The Aśokāvadāna (accounts of Aśoka) relates that soon after Aśoka's conversion to Buddhism, he asked the Sarvāsti-vādin master Upagupta to show him the places consecrated by the presence of the Buddha and his disciples. For 256 days Upagupta accompanied Aśoka on a grand pilgrimage of India, pointing out the places that the Buddha had blessed with his presence and the locations of specific actions. At each site Aśoka commanded the building of stūpas; at some places he also erected pillars inscribed with commemorative descriptions or exhortations to virtuous conduct.

Tradition holds that Aśoka collected the Buddha's relics from seven of the eight original stūpas and divided them into 84,000 portions, vowing to erect a stūpa for each portion throughout his kingdom, one for every atom of the human body. (At that time, it was considered that a human body was composed of 84,000 atoms.) Each stūpa built either enhanced the power of an existing holy place or established a new place of homage.

Although time and human ravages have damaged or destroyed many of these stūpas, discoveries of numerous stūpas that date to the time of Aśoka verify that Aśoka made a substantial effort to locate and mark all the holy places in his realm. Scholars and art historians now largely agree that the pilgrim's path to the eight holy places was well-established as early as one hundred years after the Parinirvāṇa, and the monuments built by Aśoka at the major pilgrimage sites have confirmed the strength of this tradition.

Records of Pilgrimage

A pilgrimage to the holy places of the Buddha was always arduous, even for those who lived in India. And yet through the centuries after the Buddha's Parinirvāṇa, a steady stream of pilgrims came not only from all parts of India, but also from Śrī Laṅkā, Central Asia, China, Burma, Śrī Vijaya (modern Indonesia), and Tibet. For those traversing the great northwest mountain ranges or braving the fearsome seas, the journey took great endurance and courage. It was not unusual to spend years traveling to worship at the holy places.

The writings of Chinese pilgrims who made their way to India are the only extant eyewitness accounts of events in India and Central Asia between the fifth and seventh centuries. The most widely known of the Chinese travelers are three monk-scholars who kept detailed journals of their travels: Fa-hien, who traveled to India in the early fifth century, and the seventh-century pilgrims Hsüan-tsang and I-tsing. During the eighth century, Tibetans also began traveling to India to obtain teachings and lineages and to meditate in places imbued with spiritual power; additional information concerning the holy places could be gleaned from as yet untranslated Tibetan sources.

Many died on such a pilgrimage; a few chose to spend the rest of their lives in the heartland of the Dharma. Of the Chinese pilgrims, it has been estimated that only two percent of those who embarked for India ever returned to China. Those who did return brought with them teachings that profoundly influenced the course of Buddhism in China. Fa-hien spent fourteen years on pilgrimage through Central Asia, India, and Śrī Laṅkā. I-tsing and Hsüan-tsang (both of whom studied at Nālandā, the great Buddhist university near Rājagṛha), traveled for twenty-four and sixteen years respectively.

Tibetans who made the difficult journey through the Himalayas to India often spent at least ten to twenty years away from their native land. During this time they learned the Dharma from India's great masters and received the transmission of the Mahāyāna and Vajrayāna lineages. While the names of those who returned have come down to us in the histories of the lineages they brought back to Tibet, it is clear that the journey claimed the lives of many more.

Iconography of Pilgrimage

The eight holy places were represented by artists of old, who carved scenes associated with them in bas-reliefs on the gates and railings of stūpas and temples. Examples of these reliefs can be seen today at Bhārhut and Sāñcī. A second-century stone slab (now housed in the Mathurā Museum) pictures a group of five of the Eight Great Wonders, and a fifth century stele (now in the Sārnāth Museum) illustrates all eight in an integrated composition. The development of this iconography brought pilgrimage into the realm of symbology, where it could take deep root in the human consciousness. As a prominent art historian recently noted, once the depiction of events associated with the eight holy places was standardized and shaped into a single portable icon, the pilgrimage could travel with the devotee rather than the devotee traveling to the pilgrimage.[1]

Symbolizing the way to enlightenment, depictions of the Eight Bodhi Stūpas[2] represent the interior transformation associated with the acts of the Buddha and with the pilgrim's path. Each has its distinct iconographical form, and each form has been replicated for millenia in Buddhist lands. Historically, as Buddhism has entered each new culture, masters transmitting the Dharma have taught the value of pilgrimage, erected stūpas, and developed pilgrimage paths as a consecration of the land and a support for devotion. The iconography of pilgrimage heightened awareness of deeply ingrained knowledge of the Buddha's life and teachings. Devotion linked with knowledge deepened and expanded the pilgrimage experience.

For Western Buddhists, who tend to be less familiar with this knowledge, studying and reflecting on the Buddha's life and teachings has special value. Although little remains to be seen at many of the sites described in this book, the holy places still have much to teach us. It is helpful to appreciate the centuries of devotion to enlightenment the holy places represent and to understand the transformative power expressed in the art and architecture of Buddhist India. If we can evoke the quality of this devotion and experience its

1. John Huntington. "Pilgrimage as Image: The Cult of the Aṣṭamahāpratihārya, Part I," in *Orientations* 18:4 (April 1987), pp. 55–68.

2. Birth, Descent from Tuṣita, Victory, Manifestation, Overcoming Illusion (Māra), Enlightenment, Turning the Wheel of the Dharma, and Parinirvāṇa.

benefit in our lives, it may be possible to reach a better understanding of humanity and open new dimensions of knowledge and compassion. In *World Peace Ceremonies, Bodh Gayā,* Tarthang Rinpoche wrote:

"In our world so influenced by aggression and reliance on military power, the Buddha offers a much needed alternative. The Dharma provides more certain protection than the weapons of violence; it teaches the power of peace, supported by the persistent strength of virtue.

"Meditation and practice at holy places can guide us toward a truly worthwhile way of life. For a time, we distance ourselves from the known and familiar. Open and receptive, we can offer body and mind to the Buddhas and Bodhisattvas and find in complete surrender a treasury of inner riches. From a fuller understanding of our being, we generate a confidence grounded in knowledge. Confidence opens the door to enlightened states of being and supports our steps on the path to complete realization."

Whether we visit the actual sites or begin an internal pilgrimage to awaken their significance in our hearts and minds, following the Buddha's injunction to "visit and look upon these places with reverence" confers merit and deepens understanding. By awakening devotion, reflecting on the significance of the life of the Buddha, and making offerings to holy places, Buddhists everywhere can recreate the great pilgrimage in their hearts and bring its vision and meaning alive in our world today.

Lumbinī

After taking seven steps,
he speaks with a voice like Brahmā's:
"The destroyer of old age and death
has come forth, the Greatest of Physicians."
Looking fearlessly in all directions,
he pronounces these words rich in meaning:
"I am the Leader of the World;
I am the Guide of the World.
This is my final birth."

—*Voice of the Buddha*

Lumbinī, birthplace of Gautama Siddhārtha, the prince who became the Buddha Śākyamuni, is one of the four central holy places of Buddhism. Located in modern Rummindei, Nepal, in the Himalayan foothills, the Lumbinī of the Buddha's day was an elegant garden named for Lumbinī, the mother of Queen Māyā. Here Queen Māyā, stopping to rest on the journey from Kapilavastu to her parents' home in Devadaha, felt the signs of impending birth. Reaching out, she grasped a branch of a plākṣa tree with her right hand and the Bodhisattva, the future Buddha, emerged from her right side. Brahmā, Lord of the Brahmāloka, the highest

A ninth-century relief sculpture of the Birth of the Buddha

heaven, together with an assembly of gods from the heavenly realms came to witness this momentous event. Śakra, Lord of the Trāyastriṁśa Heaven, received the child into his arms and lowered him gently to earth. Lotuses arose under the child's feet as he took seven steps in the four directions, proclaimed his purpose, then stood still while the nāga kings

Nanda and Upananda showered him with warm and cool streams of water. The Lalitavistara-sūtra describes the miracles that attended the Great Being's birth:

"All beings felt their skin shiver with pleasure. A great frightening earthquake made their hair stand on end, and the musical instruments of gods and men sounded without being touched. Simultaneously, everywhere in the three thousand great thousands of worlds, trees of all seasons brought forth perfect flowers and fruits. Thunder was heard in the heavens, and rain fell from a cloudless sky. From the land of the gods came forth all sorts of flowers, garments, ornaments, and perfumed powders; soft fragrant winds began to blow. Every place took on a serene and luminous appearance, free from shadows, dust, smoke, and fog.

"Sweet and prolonged, the great sounds of Brahmā were heard from the heights of the sky. All the splendors of Candra and Sūrya, of Indra, Brahmā, and the Guardians of the World were eclipsed by a light which spread throughout the three thousand great thousands of worlds, sparkling with a hundred thousand colors, producing well-being and joy in the body and mind of each being touched by its rays.

"As soon as the Bodhisattva was born, great pleasure filled all beings. All were delivered from desire, hatred, and ignorance, pride, sadness, depression, and fear. They were freed from attachment, jealousy, and greed, and ceased all actions contrary to virtue. The sick were cured; the hungry and thirsty were no longer oppressed by hunger and thirst. Those maddened by drink lost their obsession. The mad recovered their senses, the blind regained sight, and the deaf once more could hear. The halt and the lame obtained perfect limbs, the poor gained riches, and prisoners were delivered from their bonds. For beings thrown into the Avīci and the other hells, for beings reduced to the condition of beasts devouring one another, and

Overleaf: The tank of Queen Māyā, Lumbinī

Foundations of shrines and stūpas unearthed at Lumbinī

for hungry and thirsty beings in the realm of Yāma, there was relief from suffering and misery."

—*Voice of the Buddha I:132–133*

After the birth, Queen Māyā took her bath of purification in a nearby river fragrant with sweet-smelling oils. In later years, after the enlightenment, the Buddha stopped here on his way to Devadaha and gave the teaching known as the Devadaha-sutta (MN II:214).

Landmarks and Monuments

In the twentieth year of his reign, King Aśoka (c. 273–236 B.C.E.) traveled on a pilgrimage to Lumbinī, then known as Lumminīgāma, or the village of Lumminī (modern Rummindei). Here Aśoka erected stūpas and a tall stone pillar topped by a statue of a horse, which he had inscribed to commemorate Lumbinī as the birthplace of the Buddha. In later centuries, lightning struck this pillar, breaking it in half. Fa-hien, who arrived at Lumbinī in the fifth century C.E., mentions a well constructed on the place where the two nāga kings washed the child after his birth. At the time of his visit, the well was still providing water for the monks living here.

When Hsüan-tsang visited Lumbinī in the seventh century, he saw the broken pillar and the 'river of oil' that flowed by its side, where the Bodhisattva's mother was said to have bathed after his birth. Such a river of unctuous water still exists in the area today. Hsüan-tsang observed the remains of a tree planted where the Bodhisattva touched the ground for the first time. Nearby was a bathing pool once used by the Buddha's kinsmen, as bright and clear as a mirror, with the surface covered with variegated flowers. In Hsüan-tsang's time there were four stūpas close to the pillar marking the places where the four world guardians stood at the time of the Bodhisattva's birth, and a stūpa on the place where Śakra, lord of the gods, received the child into his arms.

Rediscovery of Lumbinī

After the time of Hsüan-tsang, little was chronicled concerning Lumbinī; even the location of the Buddha's birthplace appears to have been forgotten. In 1896, a German archaeologist examining the region discovered the lower part of the broken pillar lying on the ground nearly concealed by brush. The broken pillar still bore Aśoka's inscription, stating that this was indeed the site Aśoka had marked as the birthplace of the Buddha:

"Twenty years after his coronation, King Priyadarśī, Beloved of the Gods, visited this place himself and worshipped here saying, 'Here Buddha Śākyamuni was born'. He had made a stone [capital] representing a horse, and he caused this stone pillar to be erected. Because the one worthy of worship was born here, the village of Lumbinī has been

The pillar Aśoka erected at Lumbinī

declared free of taxes and is required to pay only one-eighth of its produce as land revenue."

—*Aśoka, Rummindei Pillar Edict*

During recent years, excavations have revealed the foundations of stūpas and vihāras (monks' dwellings) at Lumbinī. Next to the bathing pool, pilgrims of the present day may see the temple of Queen Māyā and the now restored Aśokan pillar; to the southeast of the pillar flows the Tillar Nadī, or River of Oil. The temple of Queen Māyā, which sits on a raised plinth, is believed to have been built on the foundation of an earlier temple or stūpa, possibly one of the monuments erected by King Aśoka; its walls bear bas-reliefs depicting the birth of the Buddha. These reliefs were sponsored by the Malla kings of the Nāga Dynasty, who ruled this part of Nepal from the eleventh to the fifteenth centuries. There is also a modern statue of the Buddha as a child, standing with finger upraised, proclaiming the purpose of his birth. Ceremonies commemorating Siddhārtha's birth are held at Lumbinī on the full moon of the month of Vaiśākha (April/May), and celebrants may participate by bathing this statue of the young prince.

Since 1958, when King Mahendra of Nepal donated funds for developing the site, Lumbinī has become a place of international importance. The United Nations supports archaeological excavations in the area; the site of the Buddha's birth attracts pilgrims of all backgrounds and national origins, and Theravādin and Tibetan Buddhists have established permanent monasteries just east of the Lumbinī garden. Although a Lumbinī Development Committee was formed in 1970 and plans exist for further development, progress has been slow; there remains much more that could be done to revitalize this holy place as a spiritual center and a living monument to the rich potential of a human existence.

Plans for Lumbinī emphasize the site's association with peace and compassion. In recent years, groups and individuals have gathered here in increasing numbers to offer prayers

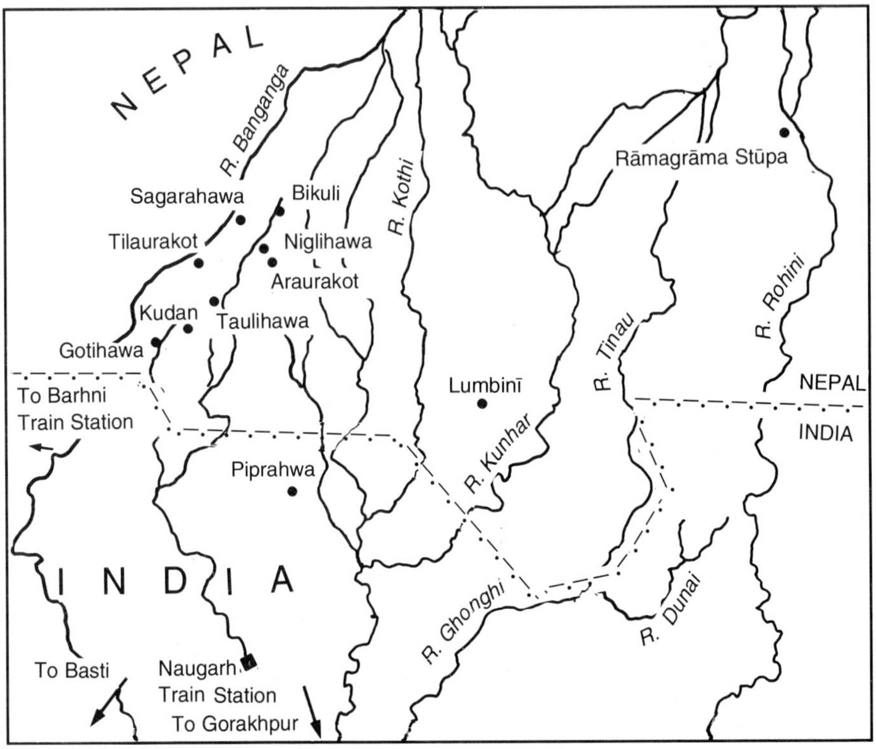

Ruins in the villages of the Nepalese Terai and northern Bihār are all that remain of the ancient Śākyan kingdom.

directed to world peace, harmony, and brotherhood. In January 1993, six hundred lamas, monks, and nuns of the Kagyu school of Tibetan Buddhism held a ten-day Prayers for World Peace ceremony at Lumbinī, led by Ven. Chokyi Nyima of Kathmandu. Two months later, more than nine hundred lamas, monks, and nuns of the Sakya tradition attended a similar ceremony led by H. H. Sakya Trichen. As the momentum for prayer at holy places increases, such ceremonies may be held on a regular basis, for the benefit of beings everywhere.

Kapilavastu

The city of the Śākyas is large and prosperous;
its people are flourishing and abide in happiness.
Śuddhodana, the king, is of pure descent
through both his mother and father,
and has a pure wife . . .
the complete purity of family
appears in the family of the Śākyas.

—Voice of the Buddha

While dwelling in the Trāyastriṁśa Heaven, the Bodhisattva contemplated the clan, family, and land best suited for nurturing the early life of a Buddha. Soon after, Māyādevī, wife of Śuddhodana, king of the Śākyas, dreamed that an elephant white as snow descended from the heavens and entered her right side. The earth shook and a golden light radiated in all directions. The sages of Kapilavastu pronounced the dream auspicious: the queen would bear a son adorned with the marks of a great being.

After the prince was born in the garden of Lumbinī, some miles distant from Kapilavastu, his father King Śuddhodana had the child brought to the palace, where he named him

Siddhārtha, he who has fulfilled his purpose. His family's name was Gautama, indicating his descent from the ancient sage Gotama, father of the lineage of Ikṣvāku that figures prominently in India's ancient chronicles. A week after the prince's birth Queen Māyādevī died and was reborn in the Tuṣita Heaven. Her sister Mahāprajāpatī became the prince's stepmother and devoted herself to the child's care.

Shortly thereafter, the aged sage Asita, noting the events that accompanied Siddhārtha's birth, came to Kapilavastu and asked to see the young prince. Perceiving that the child bore all the marks of a great being, Asita gave his prediction: If Prince Siddhārtha chose the way of the world, he would become a cakravartin king, a virtuous ruler of a vast empire. But if he chose the mendicant's path, he would become a completely enlightened Buddha, an unparalleled guide to liberation. Foreseeing that the child would indeed become a Buddha, Asita wept in sorrow, for he was advanced in years and would not live to benefit from the Buddha's teaching.

As a youth, Prince Siddhārtha excelled in the worldly arts, effortlessly mastering languages, mathematics, science, and the practical skills required of a future king. Throughout this time his father, wishing to keep the prince from any dissatisfaction with worldly life, filled his life with pleasure and protected him from experiencing any discomfort. When the prince became a man, his father urged him to marry, to ensure that the prince would fully engage worldly life. From all the Śākyan maidens, the prince chose Gopā and gained her father's assent to their marriage through a contest of physical strength and skills in the sports of a warrior.

Although Śuddhodana continued to guard the prince from the harsher realities of existence, eventually, as Siddhārtha rode to the royal gardens outside the palace, he perceived four significant sights. The first three revealed the inevitability of old age, sickness, and death, and the fourth, the sight of a mendicant monk, suggested the possibility that such sufferings could be overcome.

Soon after, determined to find a way to end the sufferings of old age, sickness, and death, the prince summoned his charioteer, mounted his horse Kaṇṭhaka, and left Kapilavastu through the eastern gate. Through the night he and his charioteer rode without stopping. Then, having crossed the lands of the Śākyas, the Kroḍyas, and the Mallas, he reached the land of the Maineyas, where he dismounted. Vowing not to return to Kapilavastu until he had attained his purpose, the prince cut his hair, exchanged his princely garments for those of a passing hunter, and sent his charioteer home with his horse to tell of his departure.

Siddhārtha Gautama traveled south to Rājagṛha, capital of Magadha, at that time one of the three most powerful kingdoms in India. After studying with the outstanding teachers of his day, he went west to the banks of the Nairañjanā River, where he practiced austerities for six years before attaining enlightenment under the Bodhi Tree at Bodh Gayā and giving his first teaching at the Deer Park of Sārnāth.

Some time after his enlightenment, the Buddha returned to the city of his youth accompanied by the disciples who formed the early Sangha. As the Enlightened One approached the city gates, his father and countrymen came to greet him. An account of the Buddha's meeting with his father is preserved in the Sūtra known as The Reunion of Father and Son, an extensive teaching on the effects of previous actions. For a time the Buddha dwelled with his disciples in the Nyagrodha Grove outside the city walls, where he taught the Dharma to the assembled Śākyas. Five hundred of his kinsmen became his disciples, including his cousin Ānanda and his son Rāhula; his father the king became a lay disciple along with all of his subjects.

Toward the end of his father's life, the Buddha returned to Kapilavastu; at the king's request, he gave a teaching on what happens after death, known as the Āyuspattiyathākāra-paripṛcchā. After his father's death, Prajāpatī, the Buddha's aunt, and Gopā, his former wife, together with five hundred Śākyan women, became the first bhikṣuṇīs (nuns). So thoroughly did the Śākyas follow the Buddha's teachings of non-harming, that when Virūḍhaka, the vengeful king of Kosala, attacked Kapilavastu, the Śākyas offered no resistance. Virūḍhaka destroyed Kapilavastu and killed most of the Śākyas during the Buddha's lifetime. There is no mention in the Buddhist literature that the city was ever rebuilt.

Pilgrims at Kapilavastu

Although Kapilavastu figures prominently in accounts of the Buddha's life, the city does not seem to have ever been counted among the primary places of pilgrimage. However, in the mid-third century B.C.E., Aśoka included Kapilavastu on his own pilgrimage and erected many monuments commemorating sites of special importance. From the accounts of the Chinese travelers Fa-hien and Hsüan-tsang, written in the fifth and seventh centuries respectively, pilgrims from foreign lands were more likely to travel to this remote area than were Indian bhikṣus.

According to Fa-hien, Kapilavastu was nearly deserted in the fifth century C.E., populated only by a small congregation of monks and about ten families of laypeople. Fa-hien describes the town as a great wilderness, a place where elephants and lions roamed freely and travelers should take great care. However, ruins of King Śuddhodana's palace were still in evidence; Fa-hien notes on one wall of the palace a painting depicting the Buddha's descent from the heavens on the back of a white elephant. Fa-hien saw the nyagrodha tree where the Buddha's stepmother presented him with a robe; the field where the Bodhisattva, as a child, observed farmers plowing the fields; and the place where Virūḍhaka, king of Kosala, massacred the children of the Śākyas.

Fa-hien describes a virtual city of stūpas, each commemorating places significant to the Buddha's life: the place Asita stood when he saw clearly the marks of a great being on Siddhārtha's body; the place Siddhārtha first encountered the reality of old age, sickness, and death; and the place near the eastern gate where the prince departed from Kapilavastu. Additional stūpas stood where Siddhārtha had cast the body of an elephant far beyond the city walls and where his arrow had landed during the Śākyan contest of skill in sports. Penetrating deep into the earth, the arrow's impact created a fountain known for its healing waters. By Fa-hien's time the Fountain of the Arrow had become a well. A large stūpa built by Aśoka commemorated the place where King Śuddhodana greeted the Buddha on his return to Kapilavastu.

In the seventh century, Hsüan-tsang found ten deserted cities in the area around Kapilavastu, all "wholly desolate and ruined," and clearly abandoned for many years. He could not measure the full circumference of Kapilavastu; only the brick walls of the royal precincts were still standing. Although he found the ruins of over one thousand monasteries, only one, maintained by thirty followers of the Saṁmatīya school, was still active.

Hsüan-tsang saw the stūpas Fa-hien had described, as well as vihāras that housed representations of Siddhārtha, his wife, and his son Rāhula. He describes several hundreds or thousands of small stūpas in a field to the northwest, placed there to commemorate the destruction of the Śākyas at the hands of Virūḍhaka. The land around Kapilavastu was rich in sites associated with Buddhas of the past: The pilgrim notes a stūpa marking the birthplace of the previous Buddha Krakucchanda, located a short distance south of Kapilavastu. Another stūpa to the northeast marked the birthplace of the previous Buddha Kanakamuni. Next to it stood a lion-topped pillar erected by King Aśoka bearing descriptions of the events associated with the Buddha Kanakamuni's Parinirvāṇa.

The Search for Kapilavastu

Kapilavastu is pivotal to determining related sites such as the birthplaces of the previous Buddhas described in the Sūtras and the events surrounding the Buddha's departure from home. Yet little is known of Kapilavastu's history after the seventh century. By the nineteenth century the site of the Buddha's youth had been so long neglected that there was no remembrance of its precise location.

After the discovery in 1896 of the Aśokan pillar identifying the location of Lumbinī, researchers used the chronicles of the Chinese travelers to guide their search for the sites the pilgrims had described. But the region around Lumbinī is so rich in ancient ruins that their identification is problematic. Sites unearthed near Lumbinī span the international boundary between India and Nepal, giving rise to several theories concerning which is really Kapilavastu.

Pieces of Aśokan pillars have been found at the Nigalisagar pond near the village of Niglihawa; many probable sites of stūpas and monasteries have been discovered in the area but not yet excavated. At the town of Araurakot, located in Nepal about five miles from Taulihawa, archaeologists found ancient fortifications with traces of a moat and a number of other ruins. This site has been tentatively identified as the birthplace of the Buddha Kanakamuni.

Popular belief associates the birthplace of Krakucchanda Buddha with the nearby towns of Gotihawa and Kudan. In the middle of Gotihawa stands an Aśokan pillar that may have commemorated such an event, but only the lower part remains and it bears no inscription. Some scholars believe that Gotihawa, or possibly Kudan, is the place where King Virūḍhaka slaughtered the Śākyas. But the discovery at Sagarhawa of stūpas, monuments, and bricks bearing pictures of various types of weapons has led others to propose Sagarhawa as a more likely site for the massacre. A clay casket found in one of the stūpas contained bone relics, grains of rice, and precious jewels, which may commemorate the Śākyan warriors.

The specific location of Kapilavastu has proven elusive. In the late nineteenth century, buried remains of a fortified city were found in a forest near the Nepalese village of Tilaurakot. This site, located near the bank of the Banganga River (formerly known as the Bhagirathī River), was proposed as the location of Kapilavastu as early as 1901.

Excavations at Tilaurakot have revealed extensive remains of ancient stūpas, monasteries, and shrines. Seals recently found at Tilaurakot indicate that the remains of two stūpas discovered there were known in Gupta times as the stūpas of Śuddhodana and Māyādevī, the Buddha's father and mother. However, final identification will require more complete excavation and research. Only three layers of the 'palace' are fully excavated: the top layer, which dates to the Kuṣāṇa period; the second level, from Mauryan times; and the lowest level, which may be from the time of the Śākyas. Around this foundation is a fortified rampart about 1,600 × 1,000 feet. If the Tilaurakot site is indeed Kapilavastu, as current evidence appears to indicate, Prince Siddhārtha, mounted on his horse Kaṇṭhaka, passed through the eastern gateway of these very walls in the epic escape from the palace described in the Lalitavistara-sūtra.

However, the town of Piprahwa, a little over fifteen miles from Tilaurakot in the Basti district in Uttar Pradesh, India, has also been proposed as the ancient site of Kapilavastu. Like Tilaurakot, Piprahwa is about nine miles from Lumbinī; extensive remains of stūpas and monasteries identify this region as a Buddhist center. One of the stūpas here is thought to have been built by the Śākyans after the Parinirvāṇa for the purpose of enshrining the relics of the Buddha.

Excavations at Tilaurakot, possibly of the eastern gate of the palace grounds where Prince Siddhārtha left Kapilavastu on his departure from home.

An early excavation of this stūpa in 1898 unearthed a large stone box that contained an inscribed soapstone casket. Excavations carried out in the 1970s revealed that this stūpa was built in several stages; below the level of the casket found in 1898 were two additional chambers made of burned bricks. In each of these chambers the excavators found stūpa-shaped soapstone caskets containing bone relics and several small dishes. The stūpa-shaped caskets were earlier than the casket found in 1898, possibly dating from between the fifth and fourth centuries B.C.E.

An inscription found on terracotta seals discovered in one of the Piprahwa monasteries in the early 1970s connects the building of that particular monastery to the Kuṣāṇa king Devaputra. More than thirty seals were unearthed, some containing the inscription 'Kapilavastu' written in Brāhmī characters that probably date to the first or second centuries C.E.

Rāmagrama

The Lalitavistara-sūtra associates Anumaineya (Maneya), a place near Rāmagrama, with the events that concluded Prince Siddhārtha's home-departure. Traveling throughout the night, the Bodhisattva crossed the land of the Śākyas, the land of the Kroḍyas, and the land of the Mallas. At daybreak he arrived at Anumaineya, a town of the Maineyas. Aśoka is said to have built a large stūpa on the place where the Bodhisattva removed his ornaments and bid his charioteer farewell. Aśoka also placed a smaller stūpa on the spot where the Bodhisattva, renouncing worldly life, had cut off his hair.

The village of Rāmagrama has been tentatively identified with Devadaha, the 'second city' of the Śākyas and the birthplace of Queen Māyādevī, the Buddha's mother. Rāmagrama lies about fifteen miles east of the Lumbinī Grove on the present Jharai River. This location corresponds to the description in the Buddhist texts that places Devadaha east of Kapilavastu on the Rohani River.

The Chinese travelers describe a stūpa at Rāmagrama said to hold the portion of the Buddha's relics allotted to the Koliyas, a tribe related to the Śākyas and connected with the ancestry of the Buddha's mother. Fa-hien recalls a tradition that the stūpa of Rāmagrama was visited by Aśoka on his pilgrimage. Aśoka had already opened the first seven of the original relic stūpas, intending to collect the Buddha's relics and distribute them among 84,000 stūpas. But when he came to open the stūpa at Rāmagrama, he was approached by a nāga, a powerful serpentine being who revered the stūpa and guarded it day and night. Appearing to the king in human form, the nāga convinced Aśoka to leave this stūpa untouched. This event is illustrated in bas-relief on an architrave of the south gate of the great stūpa at Sāñcī. Hsüan-tsang mentions that the nāga still came out at certain times, changed his serpentine body into a human form, and circumambulated the stūpa.

Rāmagrama, far from the main pilgrimage path and the main trade routes, soon fell into obscurity in the years following the Buddha's Parinirvāṇa. A short time before Fa-hien's visit in the early fifth century, pilgrims from distant regions began to come here to pay homage. Distressed to see that there were no monks caring for the stūpa and grounds, one of the pilgrims, seeing that wild elephants were sweeping and watering the area and making offerings before the stūpa, decided to settle here and devote his life to caring for this holy place. So well did he care for the area that tales of his devotion reached the ears of neighboring kings, who sponsored the building of a monastery at Rāmagrama. The kings then asked the pilgrim to take charge of the monastery.

Hsüan-tsang resided at this monastery during his visit; he relates that while the monks were few in number, they showed traveling monks hospitality according to the custom of the Sangha and treated them with the greatest courtesy and generosity. According to Hsüan-tsang, herds of wild elephants still came to that peaceful place, gathered flowers, and scattered them about the area. Hsüan-tsang notes that the stūpa was about a hundred feet tall.

A stūpa that may be the Rāmagrama Stūpa was discovered in 1898; the remains of the stūpa now stand about twenty-eight feet high and are over sixty feet in diameter. It has since been tentatively identified as the original relic stūpa that the nāga prevented Aśoka from opening, although this identification is controversial. There are ruins across the river from the stūpa that could belong to the monastery constructed by pilgrims, as described by Fa-hien and Hsüan-tsang.

Bodh Gayā

Here on this seat my body may shrivel up,
my skin, my bones, my flesh may dissolve,
but my body will not move from this very seat
until I have obtained Enlightenment,
so difficult to obtain in the course of many kalpas.
—Voice of the Buddha

Dwelling on the banks of the Nairañjanā River, Siddhārtha Gautama practiced hardships for six years. Having fasted to the point of death, he could have easily realized the fruit of the ascetic path and gained rebirth in the heavenly realms. At this crucial point, compassion for the sufferings of others renewed Gautama's commitment to enlightenment. Abandoning the practice of hardships, he made a garment from a shroud found in a nearby cemetery and accepted food from the maiden Sujātā. He bathed in the river and ate the food; refreshed and strengthened, he walked with great deliberation toward the place of enlightenment, following in the footsteps of Krakucchanda, Kanakamuni, and Kāśyapa, the three previous Buddhas of our aeon.

In all the world, only one place—the Vajrāsana, the Diamond Throne, the only place firmly rooted to the core of our world-system—could withstand the energies released through the transformative event of a Buddha's enlightenment. While descriptions in the Abhidharmakoṣa-bhaṣya link the Vajrāsana solidly to the earth, within the Mahāyāna traditions the Vajrāsana relates to a more comprehensive vision of space and time. In the cosmology of the Kālacakra Tantra and the Yid-bzhin-mdzod, the Vajrāsana extends far upward above the ground as well as below to the earth's core. Here, shining in space, is condensed a great sun of knowledge—the teachings of all the enlightened ones, carried by an uprising fountain of energy through the infinite vastness of space.

Through the aeons this holy place had attracted a steady stream of sages and renunciates, who had drawn upon its power to illuminate their understanding. Here, seated on the Vajrāsana and shaded by the tree of enlightenment, the three previous Buddhas of our aeon had experienced their great transformation. Following in the footsteps of all the Buddhas before him and renewing the path for Buddhas to come, Gautama approached the Diamond Throne.

Accepting from a grasscutter a gift of kuśa grass, the Bodhisattva Gautama took his place on the Vajrāsana and entered a deep meditation. Rays of light came forth from his body, illuminating the cosmos throughout the ten directions and attracting even the gods to his side. Perceiving his power about to be broken, Māra, Lord of Illusion, rushed to distract Gautama from his purpose. The Bodhisattva touched the earth, calling it to witness the countless lifetimes of virtue that had led him to this place of enlightenment. When the earth shook, confirming the truth of Gautama's words, Māra unleashed his army of demons. In the epic battle that ensued, Gautama's intention prevailed; the power of his compassion transformed the demons' weapons into flowers, and Māra and all his forces fled in disarray.

After the defeat of Māra, the Bodhisattva passed effortlessly through deepening levels of meditation, seeing clearly the arising, duration, and cessation of beings in all times and places. He saw the patterns that rule human lives, limiting freedom and perpetuating suffering. Perceiving the causes of suffering, he also knew its cure; with this knowledge he opened the path to incomparable freedom. As his consciousness widened to encompass realities vast beyond comprehension, Gautama became a Buddha, a perfectly enlightened being. Through his consciousness, freed from all obscurations, flowed the Dharma—direct, unlimited knowledge of reality in all modes of existence.

The earth shook, resounding to this momentous event. Only the Vajrāsana remained unmoved, supporting the Enlightened One's adamantine concentration. In commemoration, this site became known as Bodhimaṇḍa, the Seat of Enlightenment. The region around Bodhimaṇḍa was named Bodh Gayā.

The Buddha meditated at Bodh Gayā for seven weeks after his enlightenment. During the first week the Enlightened One sat motionless beneath the pipal tree, which was thereafter known as the Bodhi Tree, the Tree of the Enlightenment. The second week, the Blessed One traversed the full extent of the cosmos, visiting the three thousand great thousands of worlds, and the third week he gazed steadfastly upon Bodhimaṇḍa, the place of enlightenment. During the fourth week the Buddha walked from the Eastern Sea to the Western Sea.

A great tempest arose during the fifth week; Mucilinda, supreme lord of the nāgas, wrapped the Buddha in his coils to protect him. Throughout the sixth week, the Buddha rested on the bank of the Nairañjanā River, and during the seventh week, he stayed at the foot of the Bodhi Tree. When the merchants Trapuṣa and Bhallika happened by on their travels, they offered the Buddha honey and cakes. Praising their action, the Blessed One gave his first prediction: In the future,

Trapuṣa and Bhallika would both become fully enlightened Buddhas. The Buddha gave the merchants cuttings from his hair and nails, which they took back to their homeland and enshrined in stūpas for the benefit of future generations.

Shortly thereafter, Brahmā, lord of the highest heaven, requested that the Buddha teach the Dharma for the sake of those capable of benefitting from this knowledge. To begin his teaching, the Buddha resolved to seek out the five ascetics who had accompanied him in practicing hardships, for they would be the most prepared to receive the Dharma. Departing from Bodh Gayā, the Buddha went to the Deer Park at Sārnāth where his former companions were residing.

When the rainy season had passed, the Buddha sent his first disciples to travel throughout India and transmit the teachings for the benefit of many. Alone, he passed close to Bodh Gayā on his return to Rājagṛha. Near Uruvilvā, where he had practiced austerities before his enlightenment, the Buddha inspired sixty men and women of the Senāni village to take the lay precepts. At Uruvilvā, the Buddha converted Kāśyapa, the great ascetic, and his two brothers, who abandoned their fire-sacrifices and joined the Buddha's Sangha together with their two thousand disciples.

Veneration of the Bodhi Tree

While the Vajrāsana was the specific site of the enlightenment, the Bodhi Tree, closely linked to the Buddha's accomplishment, became a central focus of devotion early in the history of the Sangha. So important was the Bodhi Tree as a symbol of the rapidly growing religion that it attracted hostilities from supporters of the Brahmanic tradition. One account relates that before Aśoka became a Buddhist, he had the Bodhi Tree cut down and gave the wood to a non-Buddhist ascetic to use in his fire sacrifices. When a new tree sprang forth from the ashes, Aśoka, filled with wonder, offered milk to the remains of the original tree. By morning the tree was as tall as it was before.

Aśoka became a Buddhist shortly thereafter and took up the habit of regularly visiting the tree in repentance for having attempted to destroy it. Aśoka's queen, however, became jealous of the tree and sent a servant to cut it down once again. Again Aśoka bathed the roots with milk, and again the tree restored itself. A descendant of Aśoka is said to have built a stone wall around the tree to protect it from further damage.

Pilgrims sought the Bodhi Tree's seeds and leaves as blessings for their monasteries and homes. The bhikkhuṇī Sanghamittā, daughter of Aśoka, carried a branch of the Bodhi Tree with her to Śrī Laṅkā, where the Laṅkan king Devānaṁpiyatissa planted it in the garden of Mahāmegha, site of the Mahāvihāra, the Great Monastery. Planting the Bodhi Tree reenacted the Buddha's enlightenment, awakening the power of the Dharma in Śrī Laṅkā; the Bodhi Tree prospered, and many new trees grew from its seeds.

The Tibetan historian Tāranātha relates that the great master Nāgārjuna protected the Bodhi Tree from the ravages of elephants by surrounding it with a stone wall encircled by 108 shrines with sacred images. And, when the river damaged the eastern side of the site, Nāgārjuna made a dam from huge blocks of stone carved with images of the Buddha, which became known as the Seven Sages of the Dam. Nāgārjuna is also credited with obtaining relics of the Buddha and enshrining them in the pinnacle of the Mahābodhi monument, empowering the stūpa that crowns the temple.

In the sixth century C.E., Śaśāṅka, a militant Śaivite king of Bengal, attacked and damaged the Bodhi Tree, but Pūrvavarma of Magadha is said to have revived it with the milk of one thousand cows. Visitors to Bodh Gayā have noted that the Bodhi Tree has a remarkable regenerative ability; shoots grow up through the parent tree, so that the tree continually

renews itself. Thus when the 'old' Bodhi Tree fell down in 1876, young trees were already well-established within the parent tree. One of these 'new' trees grew into the great spreading tree that flourishes at Bodh Gayā today.

Bodh Gayā at the Time of Hsüan-tsang

The seventh-century pilgrim Hsüan-tsang provides an invaluable eye-witness account of the site of enlightenment. In traveling to Bodh Gayā, Hsüan-tsang crossed the Nairañjanā (modern Phalgu or Falgun) River and came first to the town of Gaya, often referred to as Brahma Gayā. Hsüan-tsang found only about one thousand families living in Gayā, all non-Buddhist Brahmins considered to be related to a famous ṛṣi, or great sage. A fountain north of the town held holy water reputed to have healing powers.

Southwest of the town, Hsüan-tsang came to Mt. Gayā (Gayāśīrṣa), "with its somber valley, streams, and steep and dangerous crags." (HT II:113) This is where the Buddha taught the Ratnamegha, the Gayāśīrṣa, and the Paramārthadharma-vijaya Sūtras. From ancient times Mt. Gayā had been regarded as a powerful spiritual place; many miracles were said to have occurred here, and the mountain often emanated a divine light. Aśoka had built a stūpa about a hundred feet high on its summit.

A stūpa southeast of Mt. Gayā stood on the birthplace of Kāśyapa, a great ascetic who became an important disciple of the Buddha. To the south of this stūpa were two more stūpas, indicating the place where Gayākāśyapa and Naḍikāśyapa, Kāśyapa's brothers, had performed fire sacrifices before they too became the Buddha's disciples.

Mt. Prāgbodhi, the mountain named Leading to Enlightenment, was located east of the stūpas of the fire-sacrificers.

Left: The Vajrāsana, the Diamond Throne of the Buddha

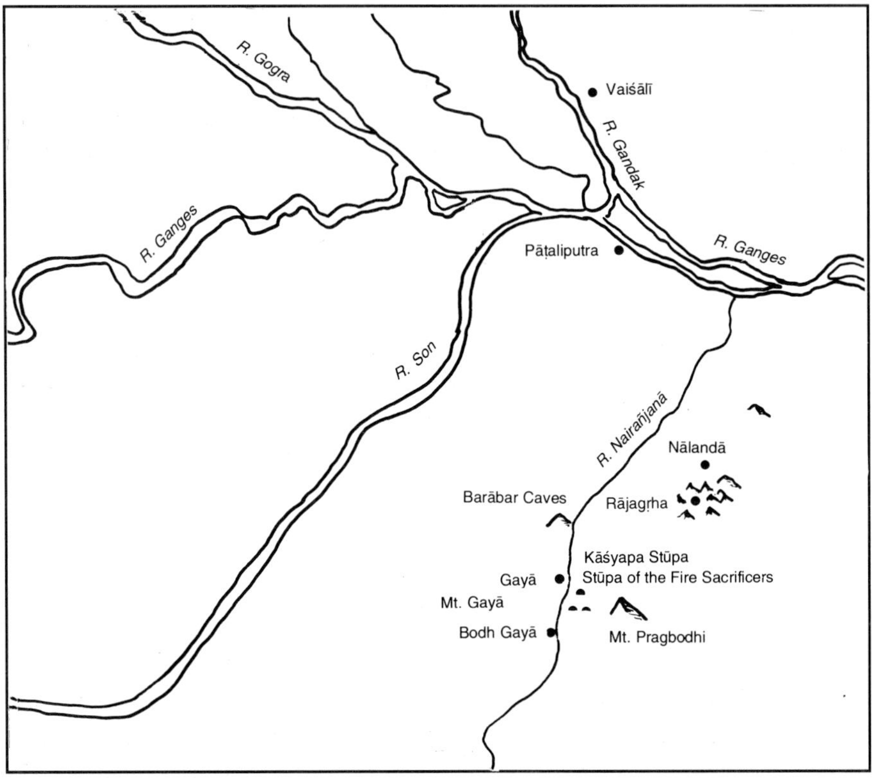

Sites near Bodh Gayā described by Hsüan-tsang

Hsüan-tsang related the tradition that Śākyamuni had considered several sites on this mountain as a possible place for the enlightenment, but each time the earth shook, warning him that this was not the site for his transformation. When Aśoka came to power, he marked each place on this mountain where the Bodhisattva Śākyamuni had walked with small pillars and stūpas. In Hsüan-tsang's time, Mt. Prāgbodhi was still a popular place of pilgrimage.

The site of the Buddha's enlightenment is about four miles from Mt. Prāgbodhi. Approaching Bodhimaṇḍa, Hsüan-tsang noted several Aśokan stūpas; one stood on the place where the grasscutter gave the Buddha kuśa grass for his mat, and another marked the site where a flock of bluebirds had taken wing just before the enlightenment. There were also stūpas on the place where Māra attempted to distract the Buddha from his meditation, and a shrine with an image of Kāśyapa Buddha noted for its special qualities. Stūpas stood where Brahmā exhorted the Buddha to teach, where the Enlightened One had washed his robes, and in every other place associated with events of the Buddha's life.

In the seventh century, there were four entryways to the complex that enclosed the Bodhi Tree: The main gate opened to the east, opposite the Nairañjanā River; the southern gate opened to a flowery bank; the western gate was blocked up; and the northern gate opened to the grounds of a large monastic complex known as the Mahābodhi Vihāra. The grounds of the Mahābodhi Vihāra was filled with stūpas, halls, and living quarters, gifts of royal patrons and the lay Sangha.

Hsüan-tsang described the Bodhi Tree as surrounded by a brick wall "of considerable height, steep and strong." The wall, twenty feet high and about five hundred paces around, was rectangular, longer east to west, and shorter north to south. The area was planted with rare flowering trees, and herbs and shrubs carpeted the ground. The Bodhi Tree was then between forty and fifty feet high, shorter than at the time of the enlightenment. Then, as now, the leaves were shiny all year around, fading on one day only—the anniversary of the Buddha's Parinirvāṇa.

The Mahābodhi Temple

The tall, elegant building that stands at the place of enlightenment is both a temple and a stūpa. Its two lower stories house shrines that have served through the ages as places of homage, ritual practices, and meditation. Its upper portion is crowned by a stūpa complete with a harmikā housing relics of the Buddha. Thus the building is also correctly referred to as the Mahābodhi Stūpa. Here the name Mahābodhi Temple applies to the entire building to distinguish it from the many stūpas built on this site.

The origins of this magnificent building are veiled in obscurity. Hsüan-tsang wrote that Aśoka had built a small structure at Bodh Gayā after his visit to the site around 260 B.C.E. Later, two Brahmins seeking wisdom built a larger temple upon the advice of a deva: "If you wish to plant a superior root of merit, then seek a superior field. The Bodhi Tree is the place for attaining the fruit of a Buddha. Return there, and by the Bodhi Tree erect a large vihāra and excavate a large pool and devote all kinds of religious offerings. Then you will surely obtain your wishes." (HT II:119)

Fa-hien, who visited Bodh Gayā in 409 C.E. and described three monasteries at the site, did not elaborate on the nature of the central monument. He remarked only that a tower (stūpa) had been placed at the site of the enlightenment and at the place where the Buddha gazed on the Bodhi Tree for seven days. While archaeologists believe they may have found some remnants of the base of an original structure, and there is speculation that building or reconstruction may have been done in the Kuṣāṇa period (50 B.C.E.–200 C.E.), this is not firmly established. The date of the great temple's construction and the nature of renovations prior to the seventh century remain unclear.

The first clear reference to a structure at Bodh Gayā is an inscription carved during the Gupta period (fourth to sixth century C.E.) on the inner side of the railing's coping stone, which refers to new plaster and paint for the Vajrāsana-bṛhad-gandhakuṭī, the Great Perfumed Hall of the Seat of Enlightenment. The original throne marking the Vajrāsana may have

The Mahābodhi Temple, Bodh Gayā. —"As long as the sun, the dispeller of darkness, shines with rays diffused in all directions; as long as the ocean is full on all sides with circles of waves curved like the hoods of nāgas; and as long as lustrous slabs of jewels beautify the sides of Mt. Meru, abode of Indra, lord of gods—so long let this temple of the great saint remain everlasting,"
—Inscription of Mahānāman, Śrī Laṅkan bhikṣu, sixth century

also been moved at that time and placed on a new base ornamented with Gupta-style carvings.

In the seventh century, the Mahābodhi Temple as described by Hsüan-tsang was a splendid three-storied building standing 160 or 170 feet high, positioned just east of the spreading Bodhi Tree. (The temple today measures about 160 feet high and is forty-eight feet square at its base.) Its walls, constructed of bluish bricks covered with lime, were highly ornamented and had niches framing golden figures. Its pillars, beams, doors, and windows were adorned with gold and silver inlay and set with pearls and gems.

Silver statues of Avalokiteśvara and Maitreya, each about ten feet high, stood in chamber-like niches to the left and right of the outside gate; within the temple stood a remarkable image of the Tathāgata, said to have been carved by the Bodhisattva Maitreya in the guise of a Brahmin. The statue's chamber was kept lighted day and night.

Śrī Laṅkans in Bodh Gayā

Outside the northern gate of the Bodhi Tree compound was a large monastery built by the king of Śrī Laṅkā, probably around the time of the Gupta emperor Samudragupta (c. 347). It is recorded that the Laṅkan king sponsored the monastery after monks he sent on pilgrimage to Bodh Gayā were poorly received. Upon their return, the monks informed their king that they were not accorded the hospitality traditional for traveling monks because the Dharma of Śrī Laṅkā was not well-known in India. The monks suggested that the king build a monastery at Bodh Gayā as a gesture of Śrī Laṅkā's veneration and support for the Dharma, to which he agreed. A stone inscription at Bodh Gayā records a donation made by the Śrī Laṅkan monk Mahānāman dated 269, which appears to refer to the Gupta year (= 588 C.E.). This inscription indicates that

Śrī Laṅkans had maintained a continuous presence in Bodh Gayā since the monastery's founding.

In the seventh century, the Śrī Laṅkan monastery was occupied by a thousand bhikṣus of the Sthavira tradition. Hsüan-tsang relates that: "They carefully observe the Dharma Vinaya, and their conduct is pure and correct." The monastery consisted of six halls surrounded by a wall thirty or forty feet high. In its construction, "The utmost skill of the artist has been employed; the ornamentation is in the richest colors (red and blue). The statue of Buddha is cast of gold and silver and decorated with gems and precious stones. The stūpas are high and large in proportion, and beautifully ornamented; they contain relics of the Buddha." (HT II:133)

The Seven Major Sites

Of the seven sites at Bodh Gayā commemorating places where the Buddha meditated, only five have been identified with certainty in modern times. The Vajrāsana, the Seat of Enlightenment marked by a stone slab once ornamented with precious stones, is the holiest site, being the adamantine support for enlightenment. The second site, marked by the Animeścalocana Stūpa, a brick structure nearly fifty feet tall, is the place where the Buddha gazed at Bodhimaṇḍa for a week. The third site is the Caṅkramana Shrine, a low platform ornamented with carved lotuses, placed where the Buddha walked up and down during the second week after his enlightenment. The fourth site is the Ratnagraha Shrine, where rays of multicolored light emanated from the Buddha's body as he sat in contemplation. The site of the fifth place, the Rājyatna Tree, is not known. The sixth sacred place is the Asapala Nyagrodha Tree where Sujāta offered the Buddha milk and rice after he ceased his austerities. The seventh is Mucilinda Lake, where the nāga Mucilinda protected the meditating Buddha from a rainstorm by wrapping him in his coils.

In Hsüan-tsang's time, the pool of Mucilinda was located in a wooded grove; the water was dark blue in color, with a sweet and pleasant taste. On its west bank stood a monastery with a statue representing the Bodhisattva emaciated from ascetic practices. To the east of the pool was the place where the Bodhisattva practiced hardships for six years. A short distance to the southwest, a stūpa marked the place where Śākyamuni, having ended his fast, grasped a tree-branch as he emerged from the Nairañjanā River after bathing.

Close by was the place where the Bodhisattva received rice milk from Sujāta and the place where the merchants Bhallika and Trapuṣa offered the Buddha wheat and honey after the enlightenment. A stūpa beside the merchant-offering place indicated where the world-protectors Dhṛtarāṣṭra, Virūḍhaka, Virūpākṣa, and Vaiṣravaṇa each presented the Buddha with an almsbowl, which the Buddha placed one inside the other, then pressed together to form a single bowl.

Central Holy Place of the Sangha

Through the centuries, enlightened beings, Arhats and Bodhisattvas, great masters, scholars, and siddhas have come to Bodh Gayā, usually referred to as Vajrāsana in the histories. In the seventh century, Hsüan-tsang recorded that every year, when the monks ended their three-month observance of the rainy season retreat, they congregated at Bodh Gayā by the "thousands and myriads." For seven days and nights they scattered flowers, burned incense, and sounded music as they walked through the district to honor the sacred sites.

The Vajrāsana, birthplace of realization, has long attracted great siddhas and Vidyādharas as well as lay pilgrims and adherents of the monastic Sangha. In the eighth century, the master Buddhajñāna gained insight into the essence of all the

Left: The Animeścalocana Stūpa stands on the place where the Buddha gazed for a week at Bodhimaṇḍa, the site of the enlightenment.

elements of existence while dwelling for six months north of Bodh Gayā in Kupavana, a forest inhabited by wild animals.

On the roof of the Mahābodhi Temple, the Great Guru Padmasambhava, manifesting as Śākyasiṁha, Lion of the Śākyas, explained the Tantras to the master Dhanarakṣita. At another time, in his wrathful manifestation as Senge Dradog, he defeated five hundred non-Buddhist teachers who sought to refute the Dharma at Vajrāsana in a great contest involving debate and the display of spiritual powers.

Bodh Gayā has long had a close association with masters of the Atiyoga, or rDzogs-chen lineage preserved within the Nyingma tradition. Around the fifth century C.E., dGa'-rab-rdo-rje, the first human Vidyādhara of the Atiyoga teachings, meditated at Śītavana, a charnel ground located northeast of Vajrāsana, and there transmitted his realization to his disciple Mañjuśrīmitra. After his master passed away, Mañjuśrīmitra concealed teachings near the Vajrāsana. These teachings were in time recovered by his disciple Śrī Siṁha. In the eighth century, Śrī Siṁha's spiritual descendant, the great Paṇḍita Vimalamitra, meditated at Bodh Gayā for many years. Tradition identifies a small building on the north side of the Mahābodhi Temple as his residence. This building is also said to have been the home of Nāgārjuna.

During the reign of the Pāla kings (eighth to early twelfth centuries), Bodh Gayā was an important center of learning; novices from all walks of life took vows and studied at the Vajrāsana Monastery. Among them was the master Atīśa, who resided at the Vajrāsana Monastery before becoming the master paṇḍita of Vikramaśīla and working for the Dharma in Tibet. Teachers from Nālandā often came to Bodh Gayā, and Bodh Gayā in turn supplied masters for the universities of Nālandā and Vikramaśīla.

Rāmapāla, a strong king who revitalized the waning fortunes of the Pāla Dynasty, supported forty Mahāyāna and two hundred Śrāvaka bhikṣus at Bodh Gayā. As many as ten thousand Śrāvaka monks congregated at Bodh Gayā on special occasions. During Rāmapāla's rule, the Mahāyāna master Abhayākaragupta served as the upādhyāya (abbot) of Vajrāsana. His contemporary Abhayadatta, describing the lives of India's eighty-four great siddhas, verifies that siddhas often came to meditate at the Vajrāsana and other places of power located nearby. The siddha Lūyipa received teachings from the ḍākinīs at Bodh Gayā; the Kashmīri scholar Ratnavajra traveled here to practice the Mantrayāna, and the siddha Śāntipa meditated here on his way to propagate the Mantrayāna in Śrī Laṅkā.

The Shes-bya-kun-khyab relates that the first Tibetan to visit Bodh Gayā was Akaramatiśīla, sent to India in search of an ancient statue of Avalokiteśvara by the Tibetan king Srong-btsan-sgam-po (d. 650 C.E.). On his return home with the statue and precious relics, Akaramatiśīla stopped at Bodh Gayā to gather leaves and flowers from the Bodhi Tree. Here, as elsewhere in his travels, he collected sand from the bank of the Nairañjanā River where the Buddha had bathed just before his enlightenment. (AT 201).

Additional references to pilgrimages to Bodh Gayā appear in Tibetan writings from the eleventh century onward. As a youth, the scholar and editor Rin-chen-bzang-po came to India and placed offerings at the northern gate of the Mahābodhi Temple. The renowned Nyingma scholar Rong-zom Chos-kyi-bzang-po visited Bodh Gayā, as did Mar-pa lo-tsā-ba, founding father of the Kagyu tradition, and Chag lo-tsā-ba Chos-rje-dpal, known in India as Dharmasvāmin.

In 1261, the master Urgyan-pa, accompanied by numerous disciples, arrived at Bodh Gayā. After he had contemplated the Bodhi Tree for some time, he experienced a tremendous uprising of Bodhicitta, the mind focused on enlightenment. From that time he became a great siddha, master of Sūtra and Tantra.

Waning of Buddhism at Bodh Gayā

As early as 1034, the Ghaznavids, a Turkish tribe established in the land northwest of India, swept unopposed down the Ganges and plundered Vārāṇasī. Buddhists in central and western India began to take refuge in the shrinking Pāla kingdom, where the Dharma still flourished. In the middle of the eleventh century, shifts of power among the Muslim tribes of the northwest brought the Ghūrids to power and set in motion events that led to a series of destructive invasions and eventual occupation of all of northern India. Around 1144 C.E., the Buddhists lost the support of the Pālas, who were supplanted by the Sena kings. Although Bodh Gayā remained a strong center through the reign of the four Sena kings, the later Senas lacked real power in the region; pressured by foreign incursions into their shrinking empire, they had little interest in Buddhism and no energy to protect it.

Inscriptions dated 1035 and 1086 note that there were several Burmese efforts to repair the temple in the eleventh century. The 1086 inscription gives a summary of the temple's history, relating that Aśoka built the temple, Naik Mahanta rebuilt it, and King Sado-Meng restored it. King Mengyi later sent his preceptor Dharmarāja Guṇa to supervise additional restoration, but this project was not completed. The Thera (elder bhikṣu) Varadāsi Naik worked to promote its restoration in 1086. Inscriptions at Prome, Burma, record efforts by the Burmese Kings Kyanzittha and his son Alaungsitthu that led to two missions to rebuild the temple between the late eleventh and twelfth centuries. (Bodh 23)

Invading Muslims, however, made the continuing presence of Buddhist monks at Bodh Gayā impossible. When the Muslim army first entered this area in 1158, most of the monks who had lived at Bodh Gayā sought refuge in Tibet and Nepal, but some remained to rebuild the site between invasions. When the Tibetan monk Dharmasvāmin visited Bodh Gayā in 1234, he found a very large image of Buddha that had been recently walled up to conceal it from Muslim invaders. Monks returned soon after his arrival and resumed their devotional practices, but all other inhabitants had fled the region. Even with these disruptions, the Śrī Laṅkan Sangha appears to have maintained bhikṣus at their monastery in Bodh Gayā through the end of the thirteenth century. During his visit Dharmasvāmin observed that about three hundred Sinhalese bhikṣus were serving as the temple's official keepers.

The Mahābodhi Temple itself was damaged sometime between 1158 and 1590. Near the end of the sixteenth century, devotees of Śiva resettled the long deserted site. It is said that the Muslim government readily granted the site to the Śaivites and recognized their leader as its Mahant (saintly leader). A Śaivite sanctuary was built near the Mahābodhi Temple, and many images were removed from their temple niches and placed within it. (BGT 73)

Even in its neglected state, the magnificent Mahābodhi Temple inspired the creation of Mahābodhi monuments in other Buddhist lands. The earliest, and the one which closely resembles the current temple in Bodh Gayā, appears to have been the Mahābodhi Temple built in Pagan, Burma in the thirteenth century. Three more Mahābodhi Temples were constructed in the fifteenth century, the Schwegugyi Temple in Pegu, Burma, and two in Thailand, one in Chiengmai and the other in Chiengrai. In the sixteenth century, Abhayarāj, a Nepalese Buddhist monk from Patan, inspired by his visit to the great temple in Bodh Gayā, built the Mahabauddha Temple in Patan. (Bodh 102–110)

Recovering a Heritage

In 1812, the Mahābodhi Temple was in ruins. The corner towers were gone, the niches empty, and the surrounding area was covered in rubble and silt. The entire facade of the eastern side had fallen, forming a mound of ruins; the western side of the temple's platform was buried under silt and fallen bricks. Bricks were being taken from the site even then for use in local construction projects. Bagyidaw, king of Burma from 1819–1837, was largely responsible for reawakening interest in restoring Bodh Gayā as a Buddhist site. Although he allotted significant funds for this restoration, obstacles prevented the work from being completed.

When the Burmese left India, the Mahābodhi compound was in the lands of the British government and the Śaivite Mahant. In the 1880s the British government undertook a renovation of the temple and its compound. When the compound was being excavated and cleaned, thousands of artifacts were unearthed, including parts of the hundreds of votive stūpas that had surrounded the temple and a great quantity of tsa-tsas (small images) and seals bearing the Ye Dharma mantra. The compound's smaller monuments were hastily reconstructed from the uncovered pieces, but the lack of care in their reassembly is still obvious when one views the results today.

Controversies arose shortly after the work was completed, when further research indicated that the renovations had not restored the site's original form. To Buddhists in other Asian lands and to others knowledgeable of Buddhist history, there was a clear need for official recognition of the Mahābodhi compound as a Buddhist site and for Buddhist participation in the site's care and maintenance.

As efforts toward this end developed momentum, the Mahant took steps to consolidate his control over the compound by promoting its status as a Hindu shrine. As part of this project he converted the image of the Buddha inside the Mahābodhi Temple into a Hindu deity. About that time, Edwin Arnold, author of *Light of Asia,* visited Bodh Gayā and was so appalled at the condition of the Mahābodhi Temple

Right: Stūpas of the great Arhats in the Mahābodhi compound

that he appealed to the British government to transfer it into the care of the Buddhists.

Inspired by this appeal, Anagarika Dharmapāla, a Śrī Laṅkan Buddhist, sought official permission to restore the site. This campaign, passionately supported by Edwin Arnold's efforts in Śrī Laṅkā, India, and Japan, led to the founding of the Mahābodhi Society in 1891. But although Buddhists in Śrī Laṅkā and Japan were supportive of the Mahābodhi Society's position, the governments concerned took no official action and the British government steadfastly refused to act on the Buddhists' request. Controversy over the site's status persisted; the Buddhist position gained support among European and Indian scholars alike, including the poet Rabindranath Tagore, who appealed to the Hindu sense of justice and propriety to recognize the Mahābodhi compound as a place sacred to all Buddhists.

When India became independent in 1945, the Bodh Gayā issue passed into Indian hands. In the end, it was India, not England, that officially acknowledged the central importance of Bodh Gayā to the Buddhist traditions. In 1949, after sixty years of legal, religious, and political embroilment, the Bihār Legislative Assembly passed the Bodh Gayā Temple Act, entrusting the care of the Mahābodhi Temple and its compound to the newly created Bodh Gayā Temple Management Committee. This act formally recognized the site as a Buddhist holy place and provided that Buddhists and Hindus of every sect are welcome to worship here. A full description of this phase of Bodh Gayā's history can be found in *Buddha Gaya Temple: Its History,* by Dipak Barua (see bibliography).

Care of the temple was formally transferred to the committee in a ceremony held in 1953 and a new phase of renovation began. Gilded images were restored to the niches, and four images of standing Buddhas were placed on the corners of the temple. By 1956, in honor of the Buddha Jayanti Year, the Government of India had made repairs, moved huts encroaching on the temple grounds, installed electricity, and built an international hostel and a modern guest house for visitors. Inner and outer circumambulation paths were constructed and the Lotus Pool renovated. Since that time, adherents of all Buddhist traditions have continued the ancient tradition of supporting restoration and beautification of the great temple and its surroundings.

Today, the large Buddha statue described by Dharmasvāmin again presides over the temple's central shrine; another exquisite image of the Buddha is in the shrine room on the floor above, and statues of Avalokiteśvara stand in chamber-like niches inside the temple on each side of the entrance hall. Other statues from the Mahābodhi Temple are housed in the nearby Śaivite compound, in the Indian Museum in Calcutta, and in the British Museum in London. Additional statues, parts of the ancient sandstone railings, and other artifacts can be seen in the Archaeological Museum located outside the temple compound on the road leading to the Ashok Guest House.

Bodh Gayā Revitalized

Since 1953, Bodh Gayā has been developed as an international place of pilgrimage. Buddhists from Śrī Laṅkā, Thailand, Burma, Tibet, Bhutan, and Japan have established monasteries and temples within easy walking distance of the Mahābodhi compound, and Japanese Buddhists recently donated a large statue of the Buddha for placement just south of the Japanese temple. The site of the enlightenment now attracts Buddhists and tourists from all over the world. At any time during the cooler months between December and March, a visitor to Bodh Gayā can observe a continual stream of Indian and international pilgrims walking the roads or arriving in buses, circumambulating the temple, performing prostrations, and offering prayers in a multitude of languages.

After 1959, when their country was occupied by an army hostile to the Dharma, Tibetans have come to Bodh Gayā in increasing numbers to worship at the site of the Buddha's enlightenment and offer prayers for their teachers, family, and friends still in Tibet. The Dalai Lama celebrated a large ceremony here in the 1980s. Beginning in 1989, monks and lamas of the Nyingma lineage have gathered here from at least six countries to perform the annual Nyagyur Nyingma Monlam Chenmo, Great Aspiration Prayers for World Peace sponsored by the Tibetan Nyingma Meditation Center under the guidance of Tarthang Tulku Rinpoche. A photographic history of the Nyagyur Nyingma Monlam Chenmo is given in *World Peace Ceremony, Bodh Gayā* (Dharma Publishing, 1994), which illustrates nearly all of the art to be seen in the Mahābodhi compound.

For those who aspire to awaken their full potential, Bodh Gayā today is truly a field vibrant with the potentiality of enlightenment. Prayers, devotion, and religious practices offered at this holy place generate manifold blessings. Clearing away the dust accumulated through centuries of neglect, ceremonies and prayers evoke the vital energy of the Buddha's realization. As this energy brightens, illuminating the consciousness of all living beings, Bodh Gayā can shine forth ever more strongly, lighting the path to harmony and peace. Enriched by devotion of Buddhists of all traditions, this holy site is emerging as a powerful inspiration to the modern world, awakening people of all nations to the real possibility of enlightenment.

Art of Bodh Gayā

The carved sandstone railings that line the circumambulation path, some of which date to the first or even the second century B.C.E., represent the earliest surviving art forms at the site of the Buddha's enlightenment. These railings, variously attributed to yakṣa artists or to the master Nāgārjuna, form the enclosure traditionally known as Nāgārjuna's Wall, the Yakṣa Wall, or as Aśoka's Wall. Carved on the railings are medallions containing depictions of Jātaka tales, the life of the Buddha, Sūrya, the sun, various types of unusual animals, yakṣas, and other interesting forms. The railings are of various ages and materials, indications of changes and enlargements that occured during the temple's long history.

The earliest railings may have been part of the enclosure erected by Aśoka. Dismantled during the building of the Mahābodhi Temple, this wall was enlarged and reestablished in the seventh century by Pūrvavarman, king of Magadha. According to the nineteenth century British archaeologist Alexander Cunningham, the footings of this enlarged wall measured 145 × 108 feet. Burmese restorers later repaired the wall, which was damaged during the Turkish raids of the twelfth to thirteenth centuries. The railings were once again removed and repaired during the present century. The wall that now encircles the temple and Bodhi Tree contains some of the original sandstone railings as well as the granite stonework added by later restorations.

Bodh Gayā enjoyed many centuries of royal patronage, which, combined with the contributions of devout pilgrims, supported the creation of an artistic tradition unique in its depictions of qualities associated with enlightened being. Artists of the Gupta period (fourth to sixth centuries), supported by the interest and treasuries of powerful rulers, produced some of the most sublime religious art of all times. Gupta sculptors working in the local black stone created beautiful representations of the Buddha for Bodh Gayā; although some of these statues have been removed to museums in distant lands or elsewhere in India, others can still be seen within the Mahābodhi compound.

Early in the seventh century, representations of the cosmic Buddhas, Great Bodhisattvas, and protective deities associated with Mahāyāna and Vajrayāna practices began to appear

Śākyamuni Buddha, the central image of the Mahābodhi Temple

at Bodh Gayā. Statues of Vajrasattva, Avalokiteśvara, and Tārā joined images of the Buddha Śākyamuni in the niches of the Mahābodhi Temple and on the stūpas in the temple courtyard. An elegant new artistic style developed after the eighth century under the patronage of the Pāla kings. It is likely that Gopāla, the first of the Pāla kings, or his successor sponsored construction of the great entrance gate east of the temple, which was built in the eighth century.

Nearly all the images of the Bodhisattvas and protective deities preserved at Bodh Gayā were carved during the Pāla Dynasty, which lasted into the twelfth century. Among them was the large statue of the Buddha that presides over the Mahābodhi Temple's central shrine, which appears to date to the tenth century. This statue was described by the Tibetan pilgrim Dharmasvāmin, who recorded, "One is never satiated to behold such an image and has no desire to go and behold another . . . even people with little faith when standing in front of the image felt it impossible not to shed tears." (BiogD 67)

Although few of the earliest terracotta and stucco sculptures have survived, the stone images dating from the seventh century offer eloquent testimony that artists made a special effort to represent the sublime qualities of enlightenment at this most sacred site. Nearly all of the statues now restored to their niches on the temple radiate a joyful serenity long associated with enlightened mind. In circumambulating the temple, pilgrims pass below row after row of Buddhas and Bodhisattvas, and absorb into their meditation the forms and symbolic gestures that awaken the full potential of human consciousness. The writings of pilgrims throughout the centuries leave no doubt that among the artistic treasures of hundreds of Buddhist monuments, the art of Bodh Gayā was renowned for conveying the inner joy of enlightenment.

Many of the statues of the Buddha are seated in the Vajrāsana, or full lotus posture, with the right hand touching the ground in the gesture known as bhūmisparśa, or earth-touching mudrā. (Mudrās are symbolic gestures that have religious significance and often identify a specific quality associated with the image.) The earth-touching mudrā recalls the Buddha's victory over Māra, Lord of Illusion, the act of the Buddha that opened the door to full enlightenment.

While the Buddhas of Bodh Gayā are most often sculpted in the bhūmisparśa mudrā, many are represented in the Dharmacakra mudrā, the gesture of Turning the Wheel, or teaching the Dharma. There are also standing Buddhas raising their right hand in the abhayā mudrā, the gesture that dispels fear, or extended in the varadā mudrā, the gift-bestowing gesture, which when made by Buddhas offers the unparalleled gift of enlightenment. Standing at the entrance to the Mahābodhi Temple, one sees each of these four major forms: the large Buddha in bhūmisparśa mudrā seated on the central throne, a smaller Buddha in Dharmacakra mudrā seated above the entryway's exterior, and standing Buddhas on each side of the entrance, the Buddha on the right in abhaya mudrā and the Buddha on the left in the varadā mudrā.

The Bodhisattvas and Tārā, mother of compassion, appear lifelike with their graceful forms and smiling aspects; several are poised on lotus thrones, ready to descend to the aid of beings in need of the healing and compassionate love the Bodhisattvas embody. Blessings radiate from a joyous Vajrasattva holding a dorje and bell in his crossed hands, who manifests the blissful harmony of enlightened wisdom and compassion.

All of Bodh Gayā's statuary is sculpted from stone. A number of art historians and scholars have remarked on the absence of metal images at Bodh Gayā, especially considering the wealth of metal images dating to the Pāla dynasty found in Bihār and eastern India. No trace has been found of the silver images described by Hsüan-tsang, which would long ago have been salvaged for their precious metal. Although it is not likely that the Mahābodhi compound will be excavated further, a more thorough search of the area to the north of the compound, where there were once a number of monasteries, could possibly restore additional treasures to the site of the Buddha's enlightenment.

Sārnāth

Keep in mind this most beautiful wood,
named by the great ṛṣis,
where ninety-one thousand koṭis of Buddhas
formerly turned the Wheel.
This place is matchless, perfectly calm,
contemplating, always frequented by deer.
In this most beautiful of parks,
whose name was given by the ṛṣis,
I will turn the holy Wheel.

—Voice of the Buddha

Sārnāth, located about six miles due north of the ancient city of Vārāṇasī, is renowned as the place where the Buddha gave his first teaching. The name Sārnāth derives from Saraṅganātha, which means Lord of the Deer. Once, in a previous life, the Buddha lived here as the leader of a herd of deer and offered his life to the king in return for his release of a pregnant doe. The king, amazed and humbled by this selfless action, created the Deer Park (Mṛgadava) as a sanctuary for the deer.

The Deer Park, renowned for its peaceful qualities, became a favorite meditation place of the powerful sages, or ṛṣis, of ancient India. Shortly before the birth of Prince Gautama, the devas descended from the heaven realms to announce to the five hundred sages dwelling in the Deer Park the imminent arrival of the future Buddha. Hearing this, all five hundred sages rose in the air and entered nirvāṇa. Their relics fell to earth, consecrating the field known thereafter as Ṛṣipaṭana (Pāli, Isipatana), the Place Where the Ṛṣis Fell.

As the Sūtras record, the Buddha went to the Deer Park of Sārnāth to teach the Dharma to his five former companions: Kauṇḍinya, Vāṣpa, Bhadrika, Mahānāman, and Aśvajit. Seeing him from afar, the five ascetics determined to ignore him, considering that the Buddha had abandoned the path to knowledge. But when the Enlightened One drew near, so radiant was his presence that the five ascetics rose up to pay him homage. Perceiving that he had indeed attained success, the five ascetics asked that he share his knowledge with them.

In the great action known as Dharmacakrapravartana, Turning the Wheel of the Dharma, the Buddha conveyed to his first five disciples the four noble truths, the eightfold path, and the twelve links of dependent origination. First Kauṇḍinya, then each of his four companions, perceived the full significance of the Buddha's teaching, and through their realization established the Arya Sangha, the community of enlightened beings that manifest the efficacy of the Dharma. In this way the Three Jewels—the Buddha, Dharma, and Sangha—came into full view at this holy place. Since that time, Sārnāth and the Deer Park have symbolized teaching and transmission of the Dharma. With the conversion of Yaśas, his friends Vimala, Subāhu, Pūrṇajit, and Gavāmpati, and fifty young men of Vārāṇasī's leading families, the Sangha grew to sixty, and all became Arhats. The Buddha sent these first sixty Arhats out two by two to transmit the Dharma widely.

In later years, the Buddha returned to Sārnāth, where he taught the Buddhapiṭaka-duḥśīlanigraha-sūtra, a teaching on the morality of monks, to an assembly of five hundred bhikṣus. Vārāṇasī, a short distance from Sārnāth, was the site of the Śrīvasu-paripṛcchā, a teaching for the benefit of the merchant Śrīvasu, and the Adhyasayasamodana-sūtra, a teaching on karma for the benefit of sixty Bodhisattvas whose minds were distracted by worldly pleasures. On this occasion the assembly consisted of one thousand bhikṣus and five hundred fully accomplished Bodhisattvas.

Center for Religion, Art, and Education

After the Buddha's Parinirvāṇa, Sārnāth's proximity to Vārāṇasī, a major city and the spiritual heart of India, made it a natural place not only for pilgrimage but also for large monastic centers. Buddhism prospered at Sārnāth under the support of kings and the wealthy middle class; soon the peaceful park developed into a center for art and education as well as religious activities. From the time of King Aśoka, Buddhist patrons through the centuries built stūpas, monasteries, temples, and shrines, which were well maintained up to the Muslim invasion. Sārnāth was a flourishing Dharma center by the second century B.C.E., when the Mahāvaṁsa relates that the elder Dhammasena led a delegation of twelve thousand monks from Sārnāth to Śrī Laṅkā to attend the consecration of the Mahāthūpa in Anurādhāpura.

In Aśokan times, the artisans of Mathurā supplied statuary and ornamentation for the monuments of Sārnāth. When King Kaniṣka renovated Sārnāth's monasteries and built new ones during the first century C.E., the influence of Mathuran art continued. In 87 C.E., the Mathuran monk Bala donated a large Bodhisattva image sculpted in red sandstone. By the third century C.E., however, Sārnāth had developed its own artistic tradition, which reached the heights of aesthetic perfection during the reign of the Imperial Guptas (fourth to sixth centuries C.E.). During the Gupta period the central shrine was enlarged and the Dhamekh Stūpa was refaced in elegantly carved stone.

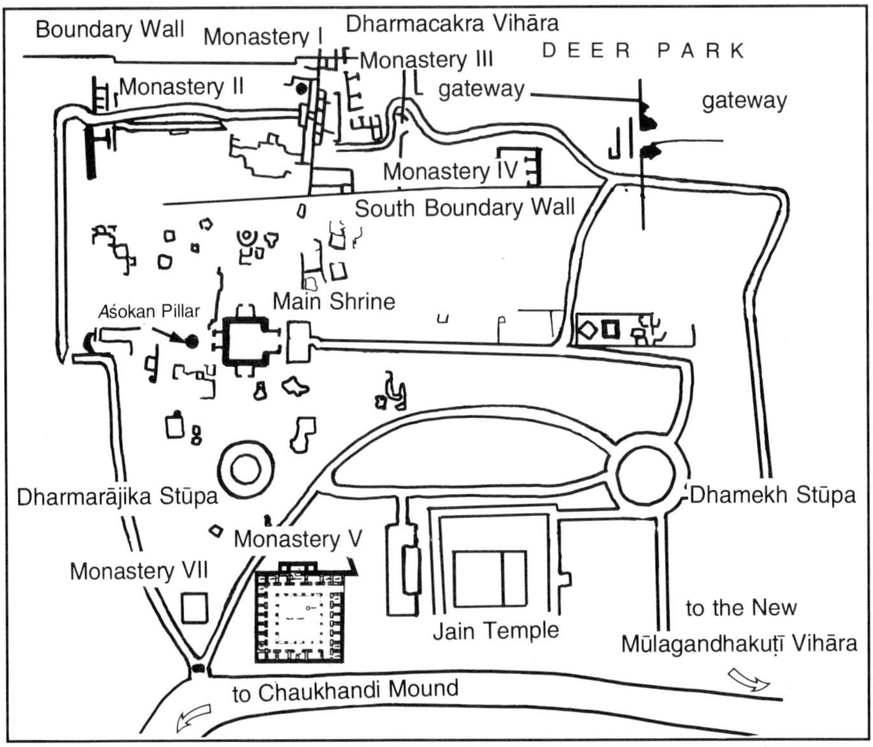

The Deer Park of Sārnāth and its environs

When Fa-hien visited Sārnāth early in the fifth century, he saw two monasteries here and four large stūpas: one on the place where the five disciples rose up to meet the Buddha, another to the north, where the Buddha gave his first teaching, a third where the Buddha gave a prediction concerning the coming of the future Buddha Maitreya, and a fourth, where the nāga Elāpatra asked the Buddha when he would be delivered from his nāga-form.

In the seventh century, the Chinese pilgrim Hsüan-tsang described the stone stūpa at Sārnāth built over the site of the Buddha's first teaching and the pillar bright as jade that stood in front of this site. Stūpas also marked the places where the five hundred Pratyekabuddhas entered nirvāṇa upon hearing of the Buddha's impending birth and where the Buddha's five former companions practiced austerities before the Buddha came to Sārnāth.

For Hsüan-tsang, as for pilgrims through the ages, every step at this sacred place brought to mind the Buddha's living presence. Traces of the footsteps of Buddhas from ages past were visible in a fifty-foot walkway. Stūpas stood at the places where aeons ago Śākyamuni and Maitreya received their predictions of enlightenment. Within the precincts of one monastery alone, there were many reminders of the Buddha's presence and several hundred shrines and stūpas. Here the Tathāgata bathed; here he washed his almsbowl, here he washed his robes, and here are traces of his robes on the rock used for drying. Here the Bodhisattva lived as a six-tusked elephant, here he lived as a bird, here as a king of deer, and here, as a rabbit, he gave his life to feed a starving traveler. For this act the rabbit was placed in the moon, where his selfless generosity could illumine the beings of the world.

Hsüan-tsang recorded that in the seventh century, as now, Vārāṇasī was densely populated. "The families are very rich, and in the dwellings are objects of rare value. The disposition of the people is gentle and humane, and they are earnestly given to study. They are mostly unbelievers, though a few reverence the law of Buddha. The climate is mild, the crops abundant, the trees flourishing, and the underwood thick in every place." (HT II:44)

Where his countryman Fa-hien, who visited Sārnāth in the early fifth century, had described two large monasteries, Hsüan-tsang noted that in the seventh century there were thirty monasteries around the Deer Park, which together contained three thousand monks of the Saṁmatīya tradition. At that time, Sārnāth had become a major center of the Saṁmatīyas, one of the largest of the early eighteen Buddhist schools. Hsüan-tsang also noted a large number of Śaivite ascetics and temples in the city of Vārāṇasī.

Northeast of the city, on the western side of the Varana River, was a hundred-foot-high stūpa built by Aśoka with a pillar erected in front of it. On the pillar's surface, glistening and smooth as ice, the pilgrim discerned the shadowy image of the Buddha. Crossing the river, Hsüan-tsang came to the monastery of Mṛgadava, where lived 1,500 monks of the Saṁmatīya tradition. From his description, the enclosure appears to have been octagonal; its multistoried towers had projecting eaves and finely carved balconies.

Inside the enclosure stood a vihāra two hundred feet high, topped with a gilded carving of a mango fruit. (The mango fruit may have recalled events surrounding the Great Miracle of Śrāvastī.) The vihāra's walls were lined with niches that held golden statues of the Buddha, and a lifesize figure of the Buddha teaching the Dharma was enthroned in its central hall. This may have been the Saddharmacakra-pravartana Monastery, Turning the Wheel of the True Dharma, mentioned in an inscription recording the donation of a manuscript of the Eight Thousand Line Prajñāpāramitā-sūtra to its monks in 1058. The donation of this text indicates that the Mahāyāna was respected and practiced here.

Sārnāth: Memorial to the Dharma

Inscriptions found at Sārnāth indicate that the Dharma flourished here until the end of the twelfth century. The Gāhaḍavāla kings, who ruled from their capital at Vārāṇasī from around 1075–1200 were Vaiṣṇavites, but they or members of their family gave support to at least some of the monasteries at Sārnāth, which were continuously enriched with sculpture through the twelfth century. Inscriptions record that Kumāradevī, wife of the Gāhaḍavāla king Govindacandra, built the Dharmacakra Jinavihāra at Sārnāth in the twelfth century. Another patron sponsored a new casing for the Dharmarājika Stūpa about the same time.

However, during the twelfth century, Sārnāth was attacked several times by Turkish Muslims, who destroyed the monasteries, killed the monks, and sacked the city of Vārāṇasī. One of these attacks was at the hands of Muhammad of Ghūr, who returned home with fourteen hundred camels loaded with treasure. In 1194 his viceroy Kutabuddin completed the area's destruction.

Despite this devastation, intensified by more modern efforts to 'salvage' bricks and stone for landfill and bazaars, Sārnāth remains a wondrous site for the pilgrim of today. A palpable sense of peace pervades the large expanse of mostly level land, once crowned by large monasteries and stūpas. At one end of the site stands the impressive Dhamekh Stūpa, which rises 128 feet above the surrounding well-maintained park. The Dhamekh Stūpa is a solid round tower ninety-three feet in diameter at its base; its foundation, made of large bricks, was until recently largely concealed by a pile of rubble eighteen feet deep. The foundation of this strongly-built monument is said to extend ten feet into the ground. The lower part of the stūpa is octagonal and built entirely of stone; each of its eight sides has niches that once framed life-sized statues. The upper part of the stūpa is made of brick.

The lower stone facing survived until 1794, when most of the stones were removed to build the Jagatganj marketplace, named for Babu Jagat, who ordered the construction. Several sections of the stone facing are still in place, revealing the graceful carving that once ornamented the stūpa. Although Cunningham opened the Dhamekh Stūpa in 1835, no relics were found in its upper chambers.

Two hundred and fifty feet to the west, eighteenth-century excavations unearthed remains of an ancient hemispherical stūpa made of bricks, known as the Dharmarājika Stūpa. Archaeologists consider this stūpa to have been one of the few built earlier than the reign of Aśoka. Railing pillars have been found in the ruins that date to the Śuṅga period, indicating that the Dharmarājika Stūpa may have once been encircled by railings as is the great stūpa of Sāñcī. Inscriptions found here noted that the Dharmarājika stūpa and the Dharmacakra

भारत सरकार
INDIA
भारतीय

Only a small portion of the Dhamekh Stūpa's facing stones survive today. Left, Sārnāth's majestic Dhamekh Stūpa attracts a steady stream of visitors.

monument were repaired by Sthirapāla and Vasantapāla in 1026 C.E. at the request of King Mahīpāla. Like the Dhamekh Stūpa, the Dharmarājika Stūpa was mined in 1794 for materials to build the Jagatganj marketplace; however, in the case of the Dharmarājika Stūpa, the destruction was complete.

Cunningham cites reports that when workers tore down the stūpa, they found a stone casket deep inside, along with cartloads of image-plaques (tsa-tsas) and an image of the Buddha inscribed with the date Samvat 1083 (=1026 C.E.). Inside the casket was a green marble box that contained bone relics, pearls, rubies, and silver and gold earrings. The marble box and its contents were given to the administrator, Jonathan Duncan, but he did not receive the stone casket. When Cunningham later attempted to locate the stone casket, there was no record of it. The image-plaques and the Buddha statue had also disappeared. A search was made for the Buddha image, which was found broken among other stones removed from the stūpa. The statue, which represented the Buddha as teacher, clarified the nature of this site. Tracing the stone casket, Cunningham located an old laborer who remembered that the casket was restored to its original position. Acting on this lead, he finally unearthed the stone casket. (ASI I:114–115)

The demolition and the subsequent discoveries focussed attention on Sārnāth as an important archaeological site. Still, the unique value of this site may have been overlooked and further destruction permitted had not Jonathan Duncan recognized from the artifacts recovered that Sārnāth was an important Buddhist site and generated interest in its immediate preservation. While further excavations clarified Sārnāth's prominence in the religious history of India, this attention came too late to save the Dharmarājika Stūpa; only its foundation remains, an empty testimonial to the great loss that occurred here shortly before this site was protected.

Less than half a mile southwest of the Deer Park Monastery is the Chaukhandi mound, located where Hsüan-tsang described a stūpa three hundred feet high with a reversed-vase dome. The Chaukhandi monument is said to commemorate the reunion of the Buddha with his five former companions, who became his first five disciples. This building was erected during the Gupta period, but the outer bricks were later removed, leaving only the inner mound. Brick walls found in the mound indicate the presence of a large upper structure such as the Chinese pilgrim described, but the site has not been fully excavated. In the sixteenth century, an octagonal tower was built on top of the mound by the Mughal Emperor Akbar; this structure still crowns the Chaukhandi mound.

A vihāra with a chapel was found at the site, along with a bas-relief of the Buddha's Parinirvāṇa. Close by, another temple with a magnificent large frieze was discovered. A large collection of statues was found in a separate area; according to Cunningham, they were apparently concealed here by monks

The Chaukhandi mound, partially excavated, with a more recent octagonal tower

forced to abandon their monasteries during a time of persecution. The bricks of nearly all the buildings unearthed during this first exploration were removed for use in construction. Later excavations revealed as many as four and five layers of buildings, monuments, and shrines built one over the other. In all, around thirty monasteries were found at this site. Nearly every excavation made at Sārnāth revealed traces of destruction by fire. The excavator noted all the buildings had been sacked and burned more than once; blackened bricks can still be seen in the remains. The strong iron fastenings on the facing stones of the Dhamekh Stūpa are probably all that saved the stūpa from being pulled apart and destroyed along with the monasteries.

Excavations at Sārnāth, looking east from the ruins to the western face of the Dhamekh Stūpa. In the background to the left rises the tower of the new Mūlagandhakuṭī Temple.

One of the excavated monasteries was quite extensive, with a large central shrine and as many as 104 rooms for monks. Each room is 8½ × 8 feet, and each has its own door. The ground plan of the monastery is similar to cave monasteries carved out of solid rock at Bāgh and Ajaṇṭā.

Excavations in 1905 revealed a piece of a great pillar erected by Aśoka next to the main shrine. The pillar was broken fairly close to the ground, presumably by lightning, and its base is now surrounded by iron fencing. Some believe this pillar marks the place where the Buddha gave his first teaching; others state that it stands on the spot where the Buddha sent his first sixty disciples to teach the Dharma throughout the land. On the pillar was an edict carved in Brāhmī script at Aśoka's command, directing monks and nuns to refrain from causing dissension within the Sangha.

Aśoka's lion capital, Sārnāth

Two additional inscriptions, carved in the Kuṣāṇa script, date to the time of King Kaniṣka (c. first century C.E.) These inscriptions are preserved in the Sārnāth Archaeological Museum, which was constructed in 1910 to house the treasures unearthed here.

In ancient times the pillar bore a capital with four lions facing the four directions and surmounted by a Dharma wheel. This capital miraculously survived the fall of about forty-five feet. The original capital can now be seen in the Sārnāth Archaeological Museum. Copies were made for other locations as well, including the Indian Museum in Calcutta. Today a representation of this lion capital appears on the official flag of India.

In all, nearly three hundred Buddha images have been uncovered in excavations at Sārnāth, testifying to Sārnāth's importance as an artistic center from Gupta times to the eleventh century. Among them are some of the most beautiful Buddha statues in existence, now well-known to art historians and students of Buddhism through photographic reproductions. Representations of Heruka and Tārā found here indicate that the Vajrayāna was practiced at Sārnāth. Most of these statues, including the famous Buddha statue illustrated on p. xxxii, can still be seen in the Sārnāth Museum.

The specific place of the Buddha's first teaching has not been firmly established. Sites proposed include the Dhamekh Stūpa, the Dharmarājika Stūpa, the Chaukhandi mound, or the Aśokan pillar. A more recent suggestion is the temple site west of the Aśokan pillar; this temple is thought to have been first constructed during the reign of the Mauryan kings (between the third and second centuries B.C.E.).

In 1931, in a ceremony attended by representatives from all Buddhist lands, the Mahābodhi Society consecrated a new temple in the Deer Park and named it the Mūlagandhakuṭī Vihāra after the original home for the Sangha in Sārnāth. (The original Mūlagandhakuṭī Vihāra was built on the spot at Sārnāth where the Buddha spent the first rainy season retreat with his disciples.) Enshrined in the new Mūlagandhakuṭī Vihāra is a statue of the Buddha modeled after one of the statues unearthed at Sārnāth, representing the Buddha in the Dharmacakra mudrā, the gesture of teaching the Dharma. Below it is a chamber containing relics of the Buddha discovered during excavations at Takṣaśilā in the northwest and Nāgārjunakoṇḍa in South India.

The temple has a magnificent large bell donated by the Mahābodhi Society of Japan; on the temple's walls are exquisite frescos depicting the life of the Buddha, painted by a Japanese artist. A Bodhi Tree, grown from a shoot of the Bodhi Tree planted by Sanghamittā in Śrī Laṅkā, rises within a fenced enclosure outside the vihāra. The Bodhi Tree sapling was brought to Sārnāth by Anagarika Dharmapāla, founder of the Mahābodhi Society, who lived for a time in a small monastery next to the new Mūlagandhakuṭī Temple. In a nearby pavilion are statues of the Buddha teaching his first five disciples. Each year a ceremony celebrating the temple's founding attracts monks and laypeople from many lands.

The circular remains in the foreground are of a stupa or possibly a shrine; in the background is the foundation of a monastery, and behind it, a boundary wall. The modern Deer Park lies beyond this wall.

The extensive compound of Sārnāth is today an important religious center. Within its boundaries a new ten-acre park for deer has been established beside a lake. A Chinese temple, built in 1939, houses a marble image of the Buddha carved in Burma. Inside the compound a Jain temple marks the birthplace of Śreyanśanāth, the thirteenth Jain tīrthaṅkara. Outside the boundaries of the park are the Sārnāth Archaeological Museum and temples and educational centers recently established by monks of the Tibetan and Burmese Buddhist traditions, including the Mahābodhi Vidyālaya. The largest educational institution in Sārnāth is the Central Institute of Higher Tibetan Studies, which attracts students from all parts of the world.

Kuśinagara

"Lord, there are the six great cities of Śrāvastī, Sāketa, Campā, Vārāṇasī, Vaiśālī, and Rājagṛha, and others besides; why then has the Blessed One seen fit to reject these and to decide to die in this poor village, this sand-hole, this straggling village, this suburb, this semblance of a town?"

—Mūlasarvāstivādin Vinaya

In reply to his disciple's impassioned question, the Buddha explained to Ānanda the reason for his decision. Long ago, there was a king named Mahāsudarśana, who ruled with righteousness. Kuśinagara, then known as Keśavatī, was his capital city, thirty-six miles from east to west and twenty-seven miles from north to south. In memory of its former greatness, the Buddha would enter Parinirvāṇa in the environs of this city, capital of the Mallas, who greatly revered the Blessed One.

The Buddha began his last journey in Rājagṛha, capital city of the kingdom of Magadha (modern Bihār). Departing from the Vulture Peak, he traveled north through Magadha, crossed the Ganges, then stopped for a time near Vaiśālī.

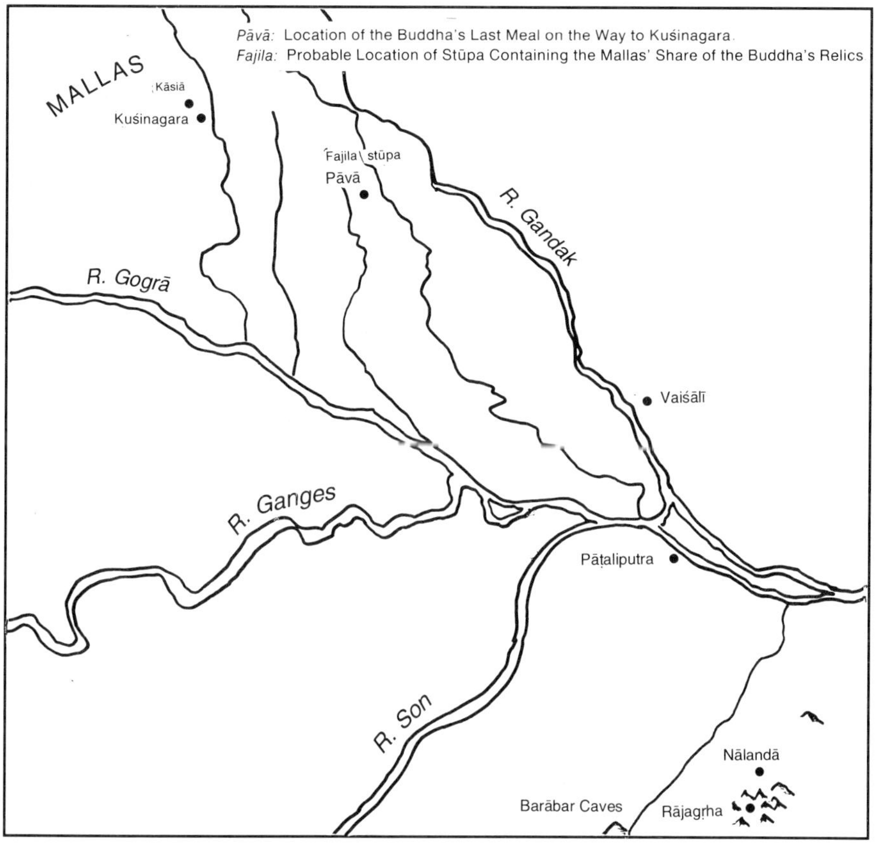

The approximate route of the Buddha's last journey

Continuing on, the Blessed One traveled the road that led through Bhandagrama and Hatthigrama. He took his last meal at the house of Cunda, in Pāvā (Papa, Padrauna) and set out on the last leg of his journey.

On the way to Kuśinagara, the Buddha became ill and stopped to rest several times. Then, in a grove of śala trees, he asked his faithful attendant Ānanda to prepare the place for his passing away. To the disciples gathered around him, the Enlightened One named the types of his teachings and summarized them in his last teaching, preserved in the Mahāparinirvāṇa-sūtra.

Three times the Buddha asked if there were questions in the mind of any disciple present; all remained silent. Then the

Blessed One gave his final teaching: "Bhikṣus, never forget. Decay is inherent to all composite things." With these words the breath completely left his body, and the Buddha entered Parinirvāṇa. Upon his passing, the earth shook, stars shot from the heavens, the sky burst into flames in the ten directions, and the air resounded with celestial music.

The disciple Aniruddha sent Ānanda into Kuśinagara to inform the Mallas that the Buddha had passed away. The Mallas honored the Buddha and watched over his body for seven days, then carried the body through the city of Kuśinagara and out through the eastern gate to the cremation ground. Throughout this procession flowers fell from the sky for miles around, covering the ground up to the knees. When the Mallas attempted to light the pyre, the flames would not take hold, allowing time for the arrival of the great disciple Mahākāśyapa, who had been in Rājagṛha when the Buddha entered Parinirvāṇa. After Mahākāśyapa paid homage to the Buddha's body, the pyre spontaneously burst into flame.

When the body of the Buddha was consumed, the Mallas extinguished the fire with milk, placed the relics in a golden vase, and brought the relics into Kuśinagara. From the eight kingdoms of the Madhyadeśa that reverenced the Buddha and his teachings, delegations gathered to claim a share of the Buddha's relics. The Brahmin Droṇa divided the relics into eight portions and gave a share to each group. Droṇa himself received the vase that held the relics, and the Brahmin Nyagrodha received the embers from the cremation fire. Each took the relics back to their own country and enshrined them in stūpas as the Buddha had requested.

Kuśinagara Becomes a Buddhist Center

Shortly after the Parinirvāṇa, the land of the Mallas was absorbed into the expanding Magadhan Empire. By the third century B.C.E., Kuśinagara was part of the vast empire ruled by Aśoka. When Aśoka visited Kuśinagara on his pilgrimage to the holy places, he built stūpas and erected pillars commemorating the final words and actions of the Buddha. Kuśinagara was a flourishing religious center in the fifth century, when the Chinese pilgrim Fa-hien passed through the area and described the stūpas and the monasteries built here. Soon after Fa-hien's visit, during the reign of Kumāragupta (415–456), a patron named Haribala (or Haribhadra) commissioned a large statue of the Buddha reclining in the Parinirvāṇa position to be placed in the vihāra at Kuśinagara and restored Kuśinagara's main stūpa.

Kuśinagara continued to thrive as an important Buddhist holy place at least until the end of the fifth century. In the seventh century, Hsüan-tsang found Kuśinagara's monuments greatly in need of restoration. The Aśokan stūpa, two hundred feet high, was in ruins. But nearby, in the place where the Buddha entered Parinirvāṇa, Hsüan-tsang saw the large brick vihāra; inside it was the statue of the Buddha lying on his right side, head to the north, in the position which he assumed before passing away.

Hsüan-tsang described other stūpas near the site of the Parinirvāṇa commemorating various important occurrences in the Buddha's lives. One stūpa marked the place where the Buddha, in a previous existence as a young quail, saved his companions; another stood where the Buddha as a courageous deer rescued many animals from fire. To the west of these stūpas was the stūpa of Subhadra, an old man who requested acceptance into the Sangha before the Parinirvāṇa and was the last monk the Buddha ordained. Stūpas also marked the site of the Buddha's cremation, the place where Mahākāśyapa paid homage to the Buddha for the last time, and the place where the Buddha's relics were divided.

Near the relic-dividing stūpa, Hsüan-tsang came to a village where, in the seventh century, a wealthy Brahmin had built a magnificent vihāra. Although King Śaśāṅka, who ruled

The restored Parinirvāṇa Stūpa in Kuśinagara

this part of India in the early seventh century, persecuted and dispersed the monks who lived near Kuśinagara, the Brahmin welcomed itinerant monks and pilgrims to his vihāra. Hsüan-tsang related that this Brahmin once hosted Rāhula, the Buddha's son, who stopped here in his travels. Rāhula, one of the Sixteen Great Arhats who vowed to protect the Dharma until the enlightenment of the future Buddha Maitreya, had not yet entered nirvāṇa.

Rediscovery of Kuśinagara

After the thirteenth century, Kuśinagara fell into obscurity. For nearly five hundred years, the site of the Buddha's Parinirvāṇa was honored in the Buddhist traditions but effectively lost to the world. In the nineteenth century, British officials noticed ruins near the village of Kasiā, thirty-five miles east of Gorakhpur, but they were unaware of the connection of these ruins with the Buddha until 1861, when the archaeologist Cunningham explored the area. Comparing the ruins he found with Hsüan-tsang's description of Kuśinagara, Cunningham located the ancient city of Kuśinagara next to the small village of Anirudhwa, about two miles from the larger village of Kasiā.

A large brick mound, excavated in 1876, was identified as the Parinirvāṇa Stūpa; this stūpa had once shared the same plinth (foundation platform) as a large temple. The plinth was found to be about seven feet thick; the temple that once rose from this foundation was probably erected between the eleventh and twelfth centuries over an earlier temple, presumably the original one. Evidence indicated that this site had been burned and looted, probably around the thirteenth century.

The size and location of the stūpa corresponded with Hsüan-tsang's description of the stūpa near the temple housing the statue of the Buddha. Within the mound, excavators found the great nirvāṇa image described by Hsüan-tsang, believed to have been sculpted at Mathurā. Although it was broken when discovered by the excavators in 1875, the statue has been restored. This ancient image, over eighteen feet in length, now lies in its original location, head to the north, on the place where the Buddha himself entered nirvāṇa.

Donations from Burma supported the restoration of the Parinirvāṇa Stūpa in 1927 and again in 1972. Clustered around this stūpa were remains of smaller stūpas, one of which may mark the place where Subhadra, the last disciple ordained by the Buddha, entered nirvāṇa.

Although the temple was restored to some extent in 1876, the restoration was not satisfactory. The ruins that served as a model for this restoration probably dated from the eleventh or twelfth century, when Buddhism underwent a revival here during the reign of the Kalachuri family. Evidence of an earlier temple could be seen at various places in the ruins. In 1956, in commemoration of the 2,500 Buddha Jayanti year,

The Nirvāṇa Temple, recently restored, rises from the plinth it shares with the restored Nirvāṇa Stūpa, built on the site of the Buddha's Parinirvāṇa.

the Nirvāṇa Temple was completely reconstructed. Today this graceful white building, lighted by large, arch-framed round windows facing the four directions, stands beside the renovated Parinirvāṇa Stūpa. Now, as in ages past, this structure protects the image of the Buddha upon his final resting place.

Around the Nirvāṇa Temple and Stūpa, excavations have uncovered the remains of the foundations of monasteries, rooms, and wells, testifying to the importance of Kuśinagara as a place of pilgrimage. The four monasteries that once faced

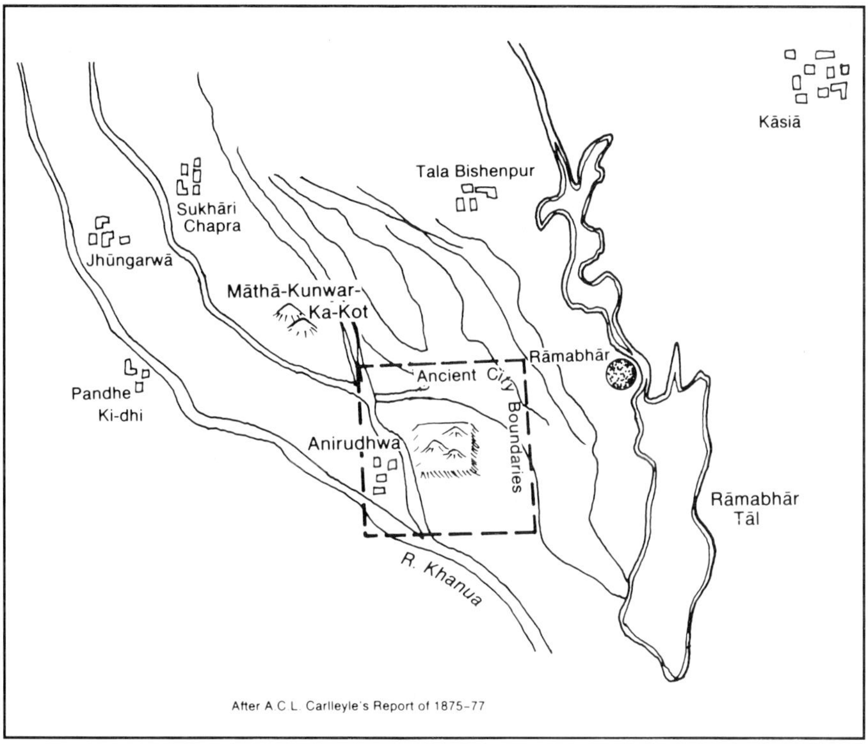

Sites at Kuśinagara associated with the Parinirvāṇa

this holy place were probably erected in the first century C.E. and destroyed in the early seventh century, before Hsüan-tsang visited the area. Remains of many small shrines and stūpas donated by Buddhists through the centuries abound in the area of these monuments.

The Cremation Stūpa

Less than a mile northwest from the site of the Parinirvāṇa Stūpa, a large brick mound rises forty-five feet above the surrounding plain. Known as Rāmābhār Tīla, the mound is the remains of a stūpa believed to mark the site where the Buddha's body was cremated. The Hiranyavatī River (now known as the Sonara) still flows to the east of this stūpa. Although treasure hunters have removed any relics that the stūpa may have contained, visitors can still navigate a narrow passage and view the burned earth at the bottom. Judging from its circumference, this stūpa is considered to have been twice the size of the Parinirvāṇa Stūpa. Smaller stūpas clustered around the large stūpa indicate that this site has long been considered an important place for offerings and prayer.

The Monastery of Māthā-kuarakot

An oblong mound standing nearly thirty feet high was discovered northeast of Rāmābhār Tīla. This mound, known as Māthā-kuarakot or Māthākuwar, was nearly six hundred feet long and between 180 and 270 feet wide. Excavation of the mound revealed a monastery surrounded by remains of a large number of smaller shrines and buildings.

At the monastery's center was a large stūpa enshrining a nine-foot-high statue of the Buddha touching the ground to call the earth to witness his lifetimes of meritorious actions. With this action the Buddha defeated Māra, Lord of Illusion, and entered the samādhi that culminated in complete, perfect enlightenment. The statue is carved out of blue stone from Bodh Gayā. Although it was broken when discovered, the statue has since been repaired and restored to its original place. An inscription on the statue dates it to the tenth or eleventh century, when the Kalachuri family ruled this region. Both the monastery and the central stūpa appear to have been constructed during this period.

Kuśinagara Today

Kuśinagara now attracts pilgrims and visitors from Asia, Europe, and America. Buddhists from Burma, China, Japan, and Tibet have now built temples, monasteries, and shrines around this ancient site. A museum near the Rāmabhār Stūpa houses sacred images found in the excavations. Home of the Candramaṇi school and a college that teaches Chinese, Burmese, and Tibetan, modern Kuśinagara is becoming a center for Buddhist education.

For those who wish to fully benefit from the pilgrimage experience, reading the Pāli Mahāparinibbana-sutta or the Mahāyāna Mahāparinirvāṇa-sūtra removes the obscurations of time, placing the reader in the Buddha's presence during his last hours. Then, circumambulating the peaceful grounds of the Nirvāṇa Temple and Stūpa or abiding in the stillness of meditation, pilgrims can reflect on the deep significance of impermanence and take comfort and inspiration from the Buddha's last teaching.

Śrāvastī

When the time came for the contest, the Buddha cast a mango seed on the ground; instantly the seed took root, and a great mango tree arose to shade the hall. After defeating the six philosophers and converting them to his teaching. the Enlightened One performed the Great Miracle of the Pairs.

Hearing that the Buddha had forbidden his disciples to display their powers before laymen, six non-Buddhist philosopher-magicians challenged the Buddha to a public exhibition of logic and supernormal powers in Śrāvastī, King Prasenajit's capital city. At that time the Buddha was residing in Rājagṛha, capital of the neighboring kingdom of Magadha. When Bimbisāra, king of Magadha, inquired of the Buddha how he would respond to the challenge, the Buddha replied, "If they perform miracles, I will do the same." "But have you not forbidden the performance of miracles?" said the king. "Great King," replied the Buddha, "I have not laid down such a precept for myself; the precept was intended only for my disciples." (Dhammapada-Aṭṭhakathā)

The Buddha announced that he would travel to Śrāvastī and defeat the challengers in the shade of a mango tree. While King Prasenajit erected a great hall for the debate, the six philosophers had all the mango trees in Śrāvastī cut down. When the time came for the contest, the Buddha cast a mango seed on the ground; instantly the seed took root and a great mango tree arose to shade the hall. The Buddha then defeated the six philosophers and converted them to his teaching, after which the Enlightened One performed the Miracle of the Pairs. The Mahāvastu describes this display:

"Then the Exalted One, standing in the air at the height of a palm tree, performed the Miracle of the Pairs. Flames engulfed the lower part of his body, and five hundred jets of water streamed from the upper part. Then flames leapt from the upper part of his body, and five hundred jets of water streamed from the lower part. Then, by his magic power, the Blessed One transformed himself into a bull with a quivering hump. Appearing in the east, the bull vanished and reappeared in the west. Vanishing in the west, it reappeared in the east. Vanishing in the north, it reappeared in the south. Vanishing in the south, it reappeared in the north. . . . Several thousand koṭis of beings, seeing this great miracle, became glad, joyful, and pleased."

After twenty-two variants of these 'pairs,' the Enlightened One seated himself on a lotus and multiplied Buddha-forms as far as the Akaniṣṭha Heaven. For this remarkable display of spiritual powers, Śrāvastī became known as the site of one of the eight great wonders.

Śrāvastī's claim as a holy place of the Dharma was already secure. Long the prosperous capital of Kosala, Śrāvastī was the setting of many of the Buddha's former lives as a Bodhisattva and the site of the greater number of his teachings as a fully awakened Buddha. Here the Buddha dwelled for most of the latter part of his life and shaped the Sangha, the community of those who followed the Buddha's way. Śrāvastī was also the center from which the Dharma spread westward during the time of the Buddha, nurturing the growth of the early Sangha as the Buddha's disciples carried the Dharma west and north across the subcontinent of South Asia.

Śrāvastī, Jewel of the Kosalan Kingdom

Śrāvastī's origins trace back long before the time of the Buddha to the epic period of Indian history, when the city is said to have been built by the Śrāvasti tribe. Although in ancient times Śrāvastī was more closely connected to Ayodhyā, legendary birthplace of Rāma, by the time of the Buddha it was the capital of Kosala, ruled by King Prasenajit, who figures prominently in the history of the Sangha.

In the fifth century B.C.E., Śrāvastī was situated at the juncture of three trade routes that connected the major towns of Kosala and greatly contributed to Śrāvastī's prosperity. One road led southwest, to Sāketa, Kauśāmbī, Vidiśā, Godhapura, Ujjayinī, and Paithana, on the upper reaches of the Godāvarī River. A second route led southeast from Śrāvastī, through Kapilavastu, Kuśinagara, Pāvā, and Vaiśālī to Rājagṛha, the capital of Bimbisāra, king of Magadha. A third route pointed northwest from Śrāvastī to Mathurā and continued west across the Rājputana Desert to Takṣaśilā and Gandhāra.

The city of Śrāvastī, surrounded by high walls topped with towers, was accessed through massive gates. These gates were large and high enough to accommodate magnificent royal processions. The Buddhist texts provide accounts of King Prasenajit's passage through the gates of Śrāvastī, riding in a chariot or mounted on the state elephant, accompanied by an impressive retinue of attendants.

The Buddha describes the region of Śrāvastī in several Sūtras. The Achiravatī River (modern Rapti) flowed through the wheat fields that surrounded the great city, the jewel of the ancient kingdom of Kosala; 57,000 families lived within its precincts. On its south was the spacious grove purchased from Prince Jeta and donated to the Sangha by the merchant Anāthapiṇḍada. This garden, the Jetavana, or Jeta's Grove, became an important center for the Sangha in the Buddha's time and for centuries thereafter. Here was the Gandhakuṭī, the Hall of Fragrance, where the Buddha taught the Dharma. Not far from the Jetavana was the Pūrvārāma and the Ekasalakatinduka Grove of Queen Māllikā, where wandering ascetics could find shelter.

The Pūrvārāma (Pāli, Pubbārāma Migārāmatupasada), the Eastern Monastery, was a two-storied building constructed of wood and stone, said to have had five hundred rooms on the ground floor and five hundred on the upper floor. This vihāra was donated by the lady Viśākhā, a foremost patroness of the early Sangha. According to the Dhammapada commentary, Viśākhā, daughter-in-law of a rich banker, sold a precious necklace of rare jewels to purchase the site for the Pūrvārāma and donated even more funds to build the vihāra. She also converted her father-in-law Mṛgara, who in turn provided support for large numbers of bhikṣus and bhikṣuṇīs. By this action, Viśākhā became the spiritual mother of her own father-in-law and was thereafter known as 'Mother Mṛgarā'. Śrāvastī was also the major residence of the Buddha's aunt and stepmother Mahāprajāpatī, head of a large congregation of bhikṣuṇīs.

Also near Śrāvastī was the Jālinī Forest, where on the road to the city the Buddha was attacked by Aṅgulimālīya, He Who Wears a Garland of Fingers. Aṅgulimālīya had made a vow to kill one thousand people and wore a finger of each of his victims around his neck to keep count. Knowing that Aṅgulimālīya had already killed 999 people, the Buddha transformed his appearance into that of Aṅgulimālīya's mother. So desperate was Aṅgulimālīya to fulfill his vow that he made great efforts to catch her, but she eluded his grasp. When Aṅgulimālīya was finally exhausted, the Buddha assumed his

Aṅgulimālīya's cave near Maheṭh, site of ancient Śrāvastī

true form and taught the murderer how to reflect on the consequences of his actions. Contemplating the suffering he had inflicted on so many people, Aṅgulimālīya repented and became a monk. Although his karma continued to afflict him, he did no further harm.

Śrāvastī of Fa-hien and Hsüan-tsang

After the death of Virūḍhaka, Prasenajit's son and destroyer of the Śākya clan, little is heard of Śrāvastī until the time of Vikramāditya (fourth or fifth century C.E, possibly Candragupta II), who is mentioned by Hsüan-tsang as a persecutor of Buddhism. The Jetavana was then an important center of the Sarvāstivādin school, which had established the Kosambakuṭī Vihāra. According to Paramārtha, who wrote a biography of Vasubandhu, during Vikramāditya's reign, the aged scholar Manorātha, author of the Vibhāṣa-śāstra and a teacher of Vasubandhu, was humiliated in a debate with non-Buddhist philosophers. The king then turned against the Buddhists, but Vasubandhu reopened the debate, restored the prestige of the Dharma, and converted the king to Buddhism. Śrāvastī began to decline shortly thereafter.

When Fa-hien visited Śrāvastī early in the fifth century, he found only two hundred inhabitants in this once great city. Although centuries had passed since the days of Śrāvastī's glory, everywhere the pilgrim found poignant reminders of the Buddha and the great Arhats. A stūpa stood on the site of Anāthapiṇḍada's house; another marked the location of the convent of Mahāprajāpatī, the Buddha's stepmother; and another stūpa stood on the place where the converted murderer Aṅgulimālīya was cremated. Still other stūpas nearby indicated additional sacred places. Fa-hien related that attempts by unbelievers to destroy these stūpas had been frustrated by great storms.

Fa-hien described the garden and grounds surrounding the Jetavana Vihāra (which Anāthapiṇḍada had purchased by covering it with gold coins). The garden had gates on the east and north. The Gandhakuṭī, the Hall of Fragrance, the place where the Buddha taught and resided, stood in the garden's center. Stūpas marked the site of special events that had taken place in this area. "The clear water of the ponds, the luxuriant groves, and numberless flowers of variegated hues combine to produce the picture of the Jetavana Vihāra." (HT xliv)

Fa-hien found new buildings on the site of the original seven-storied Jetavana Vihāra. According to Fa-hien, "In the old vihāra, lamps had shone in the Jetavana from evening to daylight with unfading splendor. A rat taking in his mouth the wick of a lamp set fire to one of the hanging canopies, and this resulted in a general conflagration and the entire destruction of the seven stories of the vihāra." (HT xlv)

Fa-hien also related the story of a sandalwood image of the Buddha, carved while the Buddha was residing in the

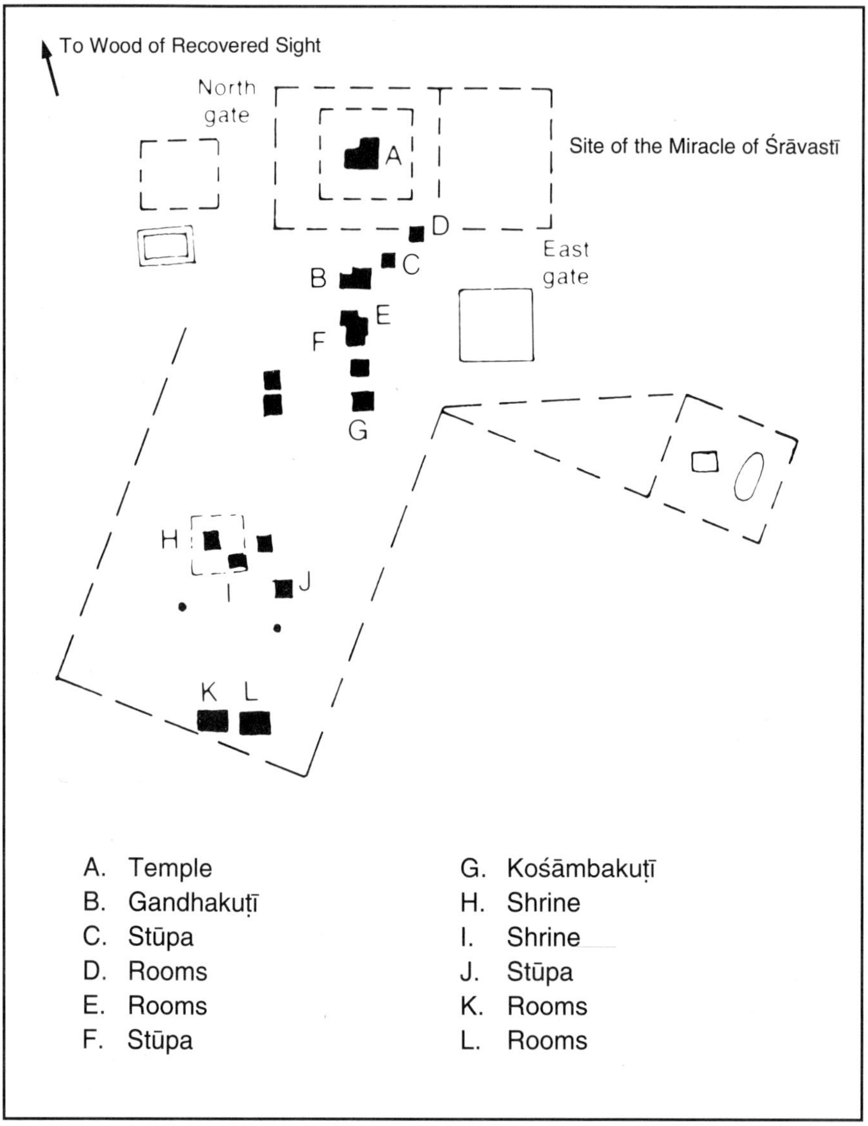

Jeta's Grove, where the Buddha shaped the growth of the Sangha.

Trāyastriṁśa Heaven. King Prasenajit, wishing to see the Buddha during the Enlightened One's absence, had the image carved and placed where the Buddha was accustomed to sit while teaching the Sangha. According to the tradition, when the Buddha returned and entered the vihāra, the statue went forward to meet him. The Buddha asked the statue to remain seated, saying: "After my nirvāṇa, you will be the model from which my followers shall carve my image." (HT xliv) (Hsüan-tsang attributed the carving of another early sandalwood Buddha-image to Udayana, king of Kauśāmbī, in a very similar account.)

Seventy paces north from the eastern gate, Fa-hien came to the site where the Buddha overcame the six non-Buddhist masters in a debate and performed the Miracle of Śrāvastī. (Depictions of the miracle of Śrāvastī were also carved in stone and depicted on wall-paintings at Bhārhut, Sāñcī, and Gandhāra.) In later times a chapel more than seventy feet high was built here and a seated figure of the Buddha was enshrined inside. Close by was the site where Devadatta, after attempting to poison the Buddha, dropped into the Avīci Hell, as had Chinchimanā, a nun who falsely accused the Buddha of improper conduct. For his destruction of Kapilavastu and the slaughter of the Śākyas, Virūḍhaka, king of Kosala, became the third to fall directly into the hells here together with his chief minister.

About a mile northwest of the vihāra was a wood called Recovered Sight, where five hundred men who were blinded by King Prasenajit for their misdeeds regained their vision after hearing the Buddha preach the Dharma. Overcome with joy, the men drove their staffs into the ground and prostrated themselves before the Buddha in gratitude. The staffs took root and became a thick grove of trees. In Fa-hien's time this grove was a favorite meditation place for monks who lived in the Jetavana.

About a mile from the Jetavana, Fa-hien saw the ruins of the Pūrvārāma built for the Buddha by the patroness Viśākhā. Southeast of Śrāvastī, a stūpa marked the place where the Buddha stood when King Virūḍhaka came with his army to destroy the country of the Śākyas, the Buddha's kinsmen.

West of the city the pilgrim Fa-hien found the stūpa of Kāśyapa, the Buddha immediately prior to Śākyamuni and the third Buddha of the Bhadrakalpa. According to Fa-hien, a great stūpa had been erected over the relics of Kāśyapa's entire body. Fa-hien also saw other places sacred to Kāśyapa: his place of birth, the place where he met his father after his enlightenment, and the place where he entered Parinirvāṇa. Further to the southeast, on the road to Kapilavastu, stūpas stood upon the sites of the same events in the lives of the Buddhas Krakucchanda and Kanakamuni, the first and second Buddhas of the Bhadrakalpa. Stūpas of these three Enlightened Ones were also seen by Hsüan-tsang who visited the site in the seventh century.

By the seventh century, the city of Śrāvastī was deserted and in ruins. The hundreds of monasteries were also mostly in ruin, though a few monks of the Saṁmatīya tradition still practiced here; Hsüan-tsang described them as devoted to the Dharma. But the buildings of the Jetavana had nearly vanished, and only foundations remained of the central seven-storied monastery.

In the midst of the ruins, Hsüan-tsang saw a small brick building that housed an image of the Buddha. On each side of Jetavana's eastern entryway, the pillars erected by Aśoka still stood seventy feet high. One of the pillars was topped by a Dharma wheel and the other by the figure of an ox. An ancient stūpa marked the well that once provided water to the Buddha. Hsüan-tsang could also still see the foundations of King Prasenajit's palace, stūpas marking the ruins of the hall Prasenajit built for the Buddha, and the ruins of Mahāprajāpatī's vihāra. Stūpas also stood where the Buddha converted Aṅgulimālīya to the Dharma and at the place where Anāthapiṇḍada had built his house.

Although little is known of Śrāvastī after Hsüan-tsang's visit, the families of the Gāhaḍavāla kings Madanapāla and Govindacandra who ruled this area in the twelfth century, supported Buddhism. Buddhist monks appear to have resided at the Jetavana Monastery until the mid-twelfth century.

Ruins of a monastery at Saheṭh, within the excavations of Jeta's Grove

Recovery of Śrāvastī

In 1863, when Cunningham began excavations, the location of Śrāvastī had been forgotten. Only a group of mounds indicated the presence of an archaeological site at the twin villages of Saheṭh-Maheṭh in Uttar Pradesh. At Saheṭh, excavators unearthed from one mound the head and shoulders of a Buddha statue and from another a statue of a standing Buddha more than seven feet tall. The style and the spotted sandstone used for the large statue indicated that the image was carved in Mathurā, an early center for Buddhist art. Since this statue was not mentioned by Fa-hien, it may have been covered over by the debris of the fire that destroyed the original seven-storied building.

Further excavation of this mound revealed the walls and floor of an ancient temple, the floor marked with the imprint of the Buddha's feet. An inscription near the footprints indicated that Saheṭh was truly the location of Jeta's Grove. The inscription described the statue as the gift of the Sarvāstivādin teachers of the Kośāmbakuṭī Vihāra. The presence of three deep lakes in the places where the Chinese pilgrims described Devadatta and others falling into the hell realms further

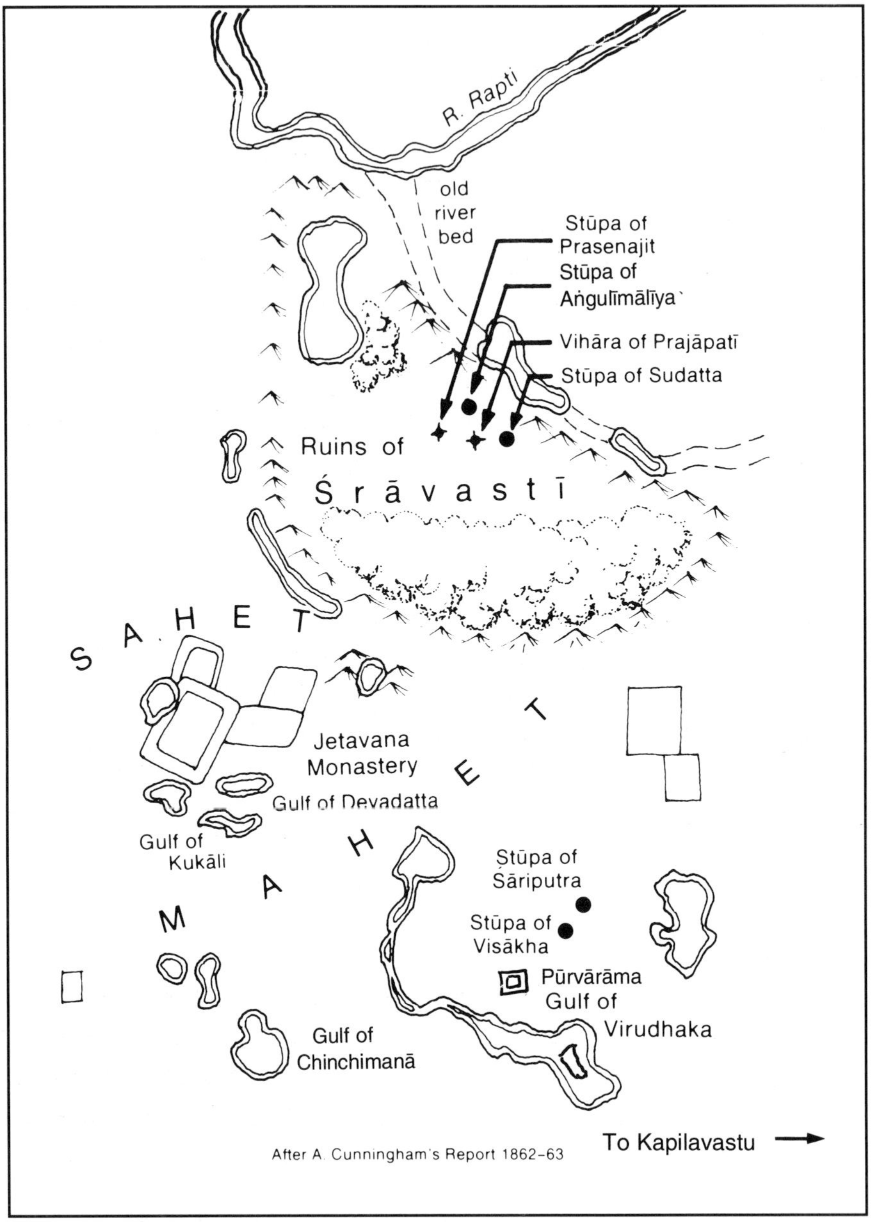

supported identification of this site as the Jetavana. Continuing excavations revealed sixteen distinct buildings at Saheṭh, mostly stūpas and shrines of relatively late date.

In the nineteenth century, the village of Rājgarh Gulāriya stood in the midst of the Grove of Recovered Sight. The trees were very ancient, although the legend of the blinded men had been forgotten. A large mound about one mile from the Jetavana appeared to be the site of the Pūrvārāma.

Maheṭh, a short distance from Saheṭh, proved to be the site of a larger, fortified town, now identified as the great city of Śrāvastī. The city's walls were exposed through excavations in 1908. Simultaneously, at Saheṭh, excavators unearthed more images of Buddhas and Bodhisattvas dating from the fifth to the twelfth centuries. Saheṭh's earliest statues, carved from red sandstone, appear to have come from Mathurā, whose artists supplied images to the monasteries and shrines of Sārnāth, Prayāga, and Śrāvastī. The later statues, dating to the ninth to twelfth centuries, are carved in the style of Magadha, indicating that Buddhism was active at Śrāvastī to a relatively late date. According to Fa-hien, there were ninety-eight monuments erected at Śrāvastī. Cunningham found the ruins of nine monasteries in the immediate neighborhood of the old city. He noted the foundations of at least ten temples and observed that there were probably as many more within two miles of the central area.

Śrāvastī Today

Although much has been lost, the ruins that remain at Saheṭh are well-preserved. Visitors to Saheṭh can see the excavated foundations of the Jetavana Monastery buildings, the most sacred of which is the Gandhakuṭī Vihāra, long a residence of the Buddha. The Jetavana Bodhi Tree, rooted from a sapling of the Bodhi Tree of Bodh Gayā, still stands on the grounds of the Jetavana.

Remnants of Śrāvastī's high walls still stand at Maheṭh, but little has been done to explore the site. Brush obscures much of the area, and there are no obvious remains of the palace or other residences. However, four original city gates remain, and other gates can be seen that were added over the centuries. The largest mounds near Maheṭh, the Pakkikūṭi and the Kacchikūṭi, are remains of stūpas, one of which is thought to be the Aṅgulimālīya Stūpa and the other the stūpa built to enshrine the remains of Anāthapiṇḍada, donor of the Jetavana and generous patron of the Sangha. The cave where Aṅgulimālīya lived, topped by a large brick structure, is accessible from the road leading through Maheṭh. But most of the ancient city of Śrāvastī still lies hidden beneath the ground. Further excavation may reveal much more of the original city, where the Buddha spent so many years of his life teaching people from all levels of society.

The Message of Śrāvastī

Śrāvastī is especially associated with teachings on the virtue of śīla, or moral perfection. In the Mahāyāna tradition, Śrāvastī is associated with the great Sangha of Bodhisattvas, especially in the Gaṇḍavyūha-sūtra. This eloquent teaching relates how the youth Sujata met the Buddha in Jeta's Grove and awakened the wish to become a Bodhisattva. Sujata then departed from Jeta's Grove on an extended pilgrimage to discover the way to accomplish his wish. Years later, having visited Bodhisattvas in all parts of India, Sujata returned to Śrāvastī feeling he had failed in his quest. To his amazement, he found Jeta's Grove transformed into a garden of magnificent jewels; in the midst of the garden rose the tower of Maitreya, where beings continually ascended and descended from the heavenly realms. When he saw the Buddha and his attendants, the great Bodhisattvas, resplendent in the beauty of awakened vision, Sujata realized that his journey had been one of transformation.

In recent years, Śrāvastī, as other pilgrimage sites, has been resettled by Buddhists from all traditions. Śrī Laṅkan, Burmese, Thai, and Chinese monks have built temples here; A Tibetan school has erected a stūpa on the grounds of the Śrī Laṅkan temple, and Japanese Buddhists have donated a magnificent bell for the Śrāvastī Park.

Sāṁkāśya

The Buddha descended to earth on a lapis lazuli ladder, accompanied by Brahmā on a golden ladder to his right and Indra and his host of devas on a crystal ladder to his left. The ladders sank into the earth, leaving only seven rungs above ground. Since that time, Sāṁkāśya has been honored as a site of one of the eight great wonders, the place where Buddhas of the past and present descended to earth from the Trāyastriṁśa Heaven.

Queen Māyā, the Buddha's mother, died seven days after the future Buddha's birth and was reborn in the heavenly realms. Since she had no opportunity to hear his teaching in this life, the Buddha manifested in the Heaven of the Thirty-three Gods to teach her the Abhidharma and ensure her progress on the path to enlightenment. After teaching his mother and large assemblies of devas for three months, the Buddha descended from the Heaven of the Thirty-three Gods on a celestial ladder. This sojourn in the heaven realms and the subsequent descent at Sāṁkāśya was one of the four great actions performed by all Buddhas.

Sāṁkāśya, modern Sankissa, is located on the upper Ganges River directly east of Mathurā in the Farrukhabad district

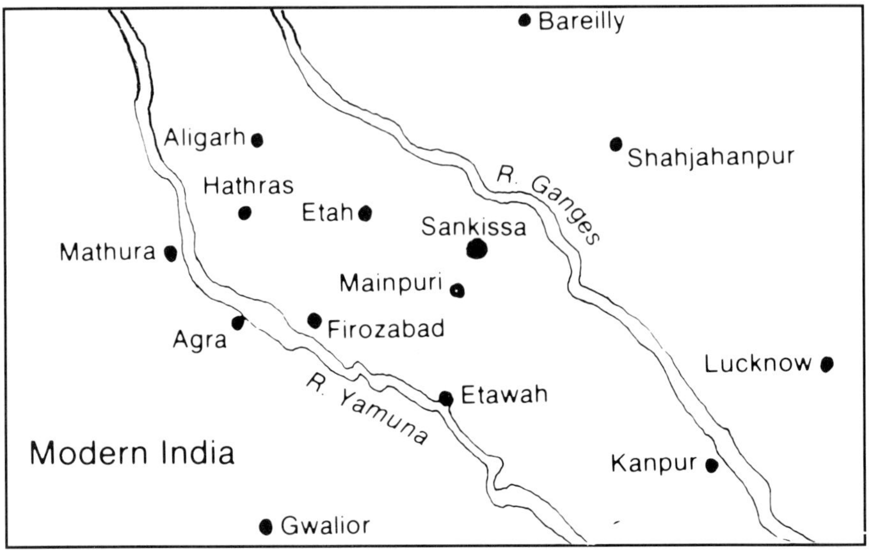

Sāṁkāśya is located in central India on the upper Ganges River.

of Uttar Pradesh. From ancient times, it has been known as the place where Śākyamuni Buddha, as have all Buddhas before him, descended bodily from the Heaven of the Thirty-three Gods.

During the third century B.C.E., the emperor Aśoka visited Sāṁkāśya and established the scene of the Buddha's return as a major place of pilgrimage. The site where the ladders entered the ground was excavated to the point where the diggers struck water; Aśoka then built a temple over the excavation and placed in it a statue of the Buddha descending the ladder. Behind the temple the king erected a pillar topped by an elephant capital.

Associated with miracles and a direct link to the heaven realms, Sāṁkāśya soon became a popular place of pilgrimage. In the fifth century, Fa-hien described the temples and stūpas that commemorated the wondrous events associated with Śrāvastī. About one thousand monks and nuns, followers of both Hīnayāna and Mahāyāna traditions, lived at the 'Dragon Vihāra', probably named for the nāga Kharewar said to have lived in a pool near the ladders. Another large monastery

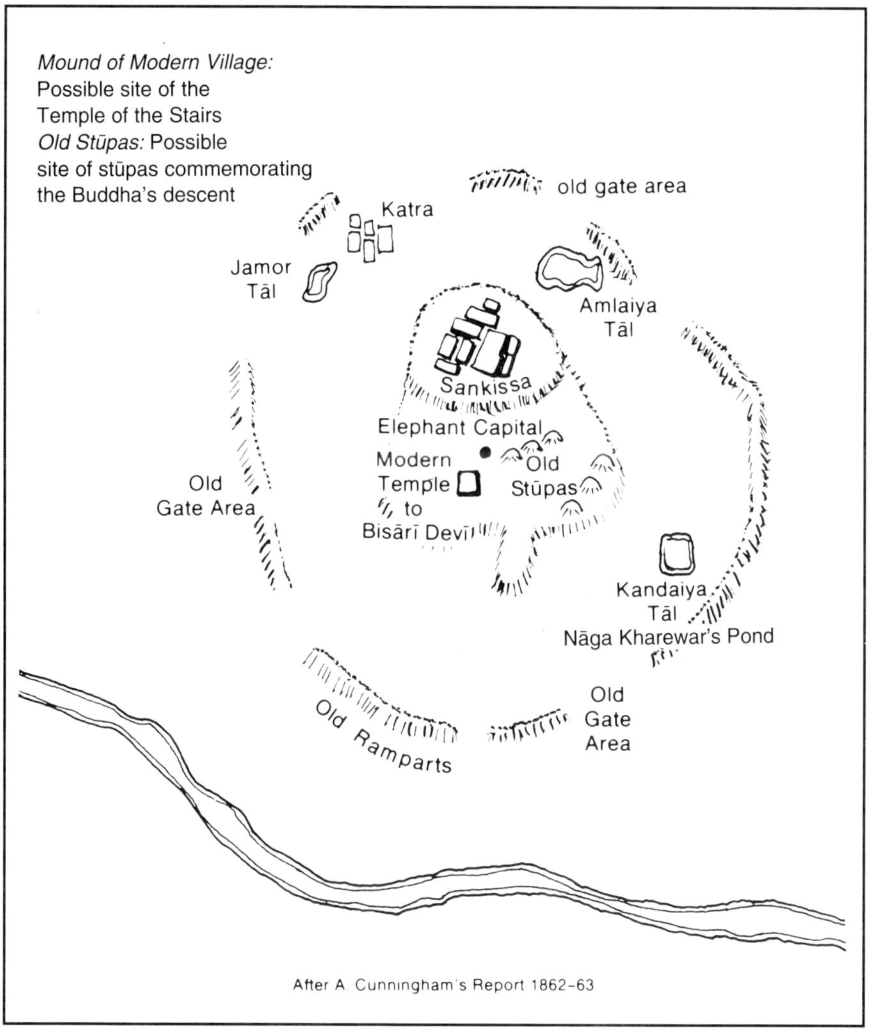

The site of Sāṁkāśya, with modern Sankissa on its central mound

housed between six and seven hundred bhikṣus. Fa-hien recorded that the country was very productive and the people rich beyond comparison.

The Dharma was still flourishing at Sāṁkāśya in the seventh century, when Hsüan-tsang observed four monasteries housing a total of about one thousand monks of the Sāṁmatīya tradition. About four miles east of the city was a temple built over the site of the three ladders "of beautiful construction, throughout which the artist has exhibited his greatest skill. The sacred image of the holy form [of the Buddha] is most wonderfully magnificent." (HT I:202) A hundred Saṁmatīya monks resided here, and a great many laymen lived nearby. Hsüan-tsang relates that some centuries ago the ladders had still existed in their original position, but by the time of his visit, they had sunk into the earth and disappeared. Neighboring rulers built new ladders where the old ladders had been and ornamented them with jewels. The new ladders were seventy feet high.

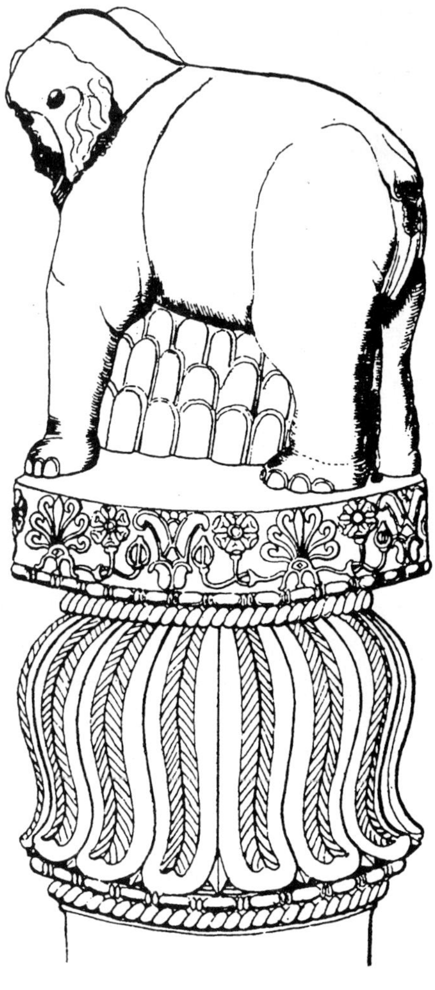

Aśoka's elephant capital, Saṁkāsya

Close beside the monastery could be seen a pillar seventy feet high built by Aśoka, purple in color, and shining as if wet. Hsüan-tsang described a lion capital atop its column rather than the elephant capital found later. He also noted stūpas commemorating the visits of the four Buddhas of the past and a stūpa on the location where the Tathāgata bathed after his descent from the heaven realms. A vihāra was built where the Buddha entered samādhi, and a foundation wall fifty paces in length marked the place where he walked.

Hsüan-tsang describes how the bhikṣuṇī Utpalavarṇā was transformed into a cakravartin monarch so as to be the first to behold the Buddha upon his return. He also wrote of the nāga pool to the southeast of the great stūpa, where the nāga Kharewar "protects the sacred traces with great care . . . Years may effect their destruction, but no human power can do so." (HT I:205)

After the seventh century, there was no further written account of Sāṁkāśya until the site was identified by Cunningham in 1842. The nāga pool could still be seen, and villagers still offered milk to the nāga Kharewar on Buddhist holy days and on days when rain was needed. There were mounds indicating where stūpas and monasteries had once stood, but all their bricks had been removed for use elsewhere.

Much of Sāṁkāśya, with its remnants of walls three and a half miles in circumference, awaits excavation; at present there is little to be seen. The Temple of the Stairs, now an active Śaivite shrine, cannot be excavated, but excavation at other points in the site might reveal more information about Sāṁkāśya and its history. A Nepalese Buddhist shrine was recently constructed at Sāṁkāśya, but only the elephant capital, its trunk and tail broken but otherwise intact, and the ruined Temple of the Stairs remain from the days when the Dharma flourished in India. The elephant capital, which fell from its pillar centuries ago, is now sheltered by a canopied shrine inside a fenced enclosure.

Of all the eight major places of pilgrimage, Sāṁkāśya is the most remote from centers of Buddhist activity and the least developed. Yet for many monks and laymen Sāṁkāśya remains a potent reminder of the acts of the Buddha, the place where, having fulfilled his responsibilities to his mother, he returned to earth from the heaven realms to continue his teachings among human beings.

Rājagṛha

"King Ajātaśatru possessed a very ferocious elephant. Devadatta, hearing that the Buddha was coming to Rājagṛha, arranged to have the elephant escape. As the Buddha came toward the city, Devadatta went to the palace terrace to see the Buddha killed, but when the elephant came rushing at the Buddha, the Enlightened One tamed the elephant with a few words, and the ferocious beast knelt at his feet."

—Mūlasarvāstivādin Vinaya

For this specific event, Rājagṛha, where the Buddha overcame several of Devadatta's attempts to do him bodily harm, became one of the Eight Great Wonders. Although the origins of Rājagṛha are not known, the ancient epics refer to it as Girivraja, the City Surrounded by Hills. The hills that enclose Rājagṛha are Vaibhāra-, Vipula-, Ṛṣi-, Udaya-, and Sona-giri (giri = hill). To the east are Chaṭhāgiri and Gṛdhrakūṭa, the famous Vulture Peak. The abode of the great Maṇi Nāga and long a site favored by sages and siddhas, the hills of Rājagṛha were noted for their hot springs and caves, which heightened their suitability for meditation.

The mountains' modern names are Baibharagiri, Vipulagiri, Ratnagiri, Sonagiri, Chattagiri, and Gṛdhrakūṭa. Udayagiri lies to the east of the southern approach to Rājagṛha, and Śailagiri rises to the northeast of Chattagiri.[1]

Rājagṛha was the capital of Magadha and the royal city of King Bimbisāra. The Lalitavistara-sūtra describes how the Bodhisattva Śākyamuni traveled to Rājagṛha after leaving his father's palace and dwelled for a time on Mt. Pāṇḍava, near the Vulture Peak Mountain. The mendicant prince first entered Rājagṛha through the eastern gate; King Bimbisāra observed him making his alms-round and had his servants ascertain where he was dwelling. The next morning, King Bimbisāra traveled to Mt. Pāṇḍava to welcome the Bodhisattva to his realm. The king was so impressed by Śākyamuni that he offered him half of his kingdom if he would remain in Rājagṛha. Although the mendicant's mind was set on enlightenment, he promised the king that he would return to Rājagṛha after he had attained his purpose.

About a year after his enlightenment, the Buddha returned to Rājagṛha as he had promised and rested just outside the city in a palm grove (Yaṣṭivana, Pāli Latthivana) near modern Jethian. As related in the texts and depicted in art, King Bimbisāra went to greet the Buddha and invited the Enlightened One and the thousand disciples accompanying him into the royal city. As a welcoming gesture of hospitality and appreciation, the king gave the Buddha his favorite pleasure garden, known as the Veṇuvana, the Bamboo Grove.

At Rājagṛha, the Buddha attracted many more outstanding disciples, including Śāriputra, foremost in knowledge of

1. Rājagṛha's famous hills are actually part of two parallel mountain ranges that stretch from Gayā on the west to Giryek, a site on the Pañcāna River, on the east. Fa-hien and Hsüan-tsang both followed a route that paralleled these mountain ranges when traveling from Bodh Gayā to Rājagṛha. The modern road follows this ancient route.

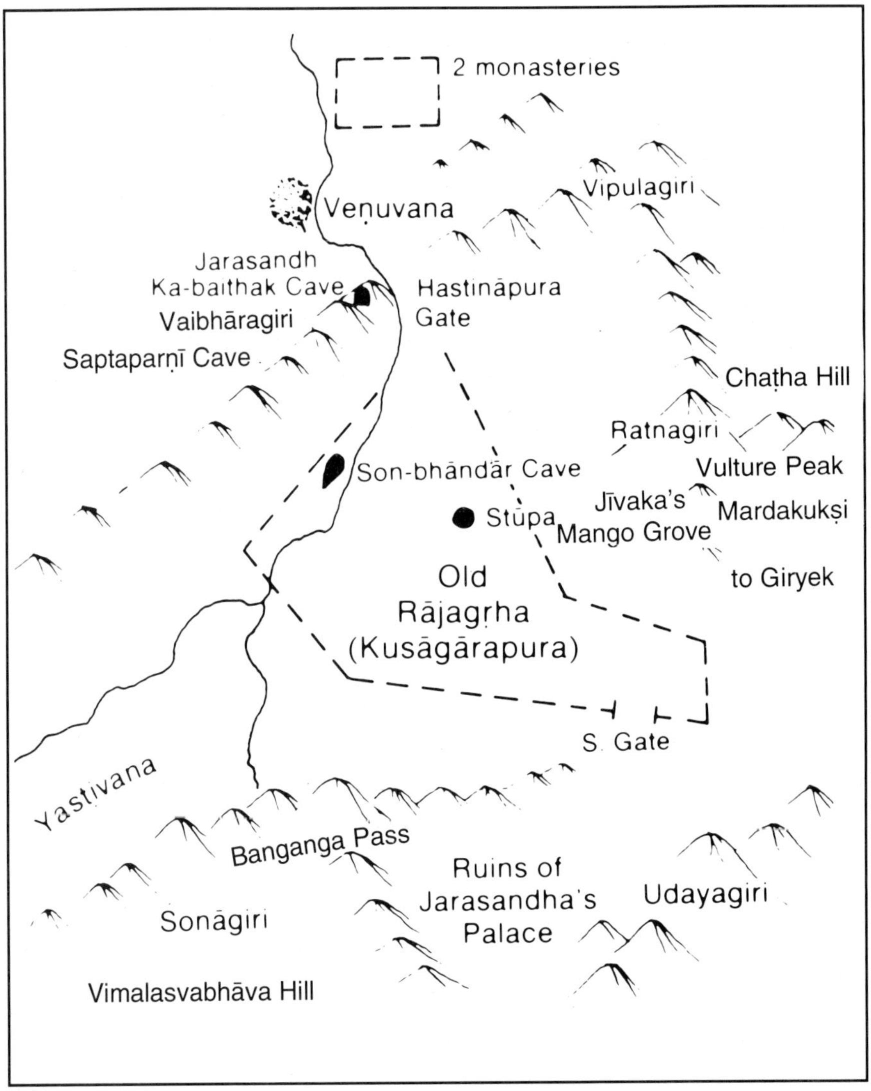

Rājagṛha (modern Rajgir) is rich in ancient sacred sites.

the Abhidharma, Maudgalyāyana, foremost in psychic powers, and Mahākāśyapa, the great ascetic and first patriarch of the Dharma. Here the Buddha and the Sangha spent at least five varṣakas, the annual three-month retreat held during the rainy season. Long before Rājagṛha was depicted in representations of the Eight Great Wonders, the city had earned an enduring place in Buddhist history as the first home for the Sangha and the site of many of the Buddha's teachings.

The Mahāpārinirvāṇa-sūtra relates that before departing Rājagṛha on his final journey to Kuśinagara, the Buddha blessed the city and named its serene and beautiful places:

> "Delightful is Rājagṛha; delightful is the Gṛdhrakūṭa [Vulture Peak]; delightful is the Gautama-nyagroda; delightful is Chaura-prapāta [the western precipice of the Vulture Peak]; delightful is the Saptaparṇī [the cave on the side of Vaibhāra Hill]; delightful is Kālaśilā [the Black Rock, a meditation site on the side of Ṛṣigiri, the Hill of the Sages]; delightful is Sarpaśuṇḍija-prāgbhāra [probably the slope of Mt. Vipula]; delightful is the Tapodārāma [the hot springs grove]; delightful is the Karaṇḍaka Lake [in Veṇuvana, the Bamboo Grove]; delightful is Jīvaka's Mango Grove; delightful is the Deer Park in Mardakukṣi."

Rājagṛha at the Time of the Buddha

At the time of the Buddha, Rājagṛha filled the round bowl of the valley formed by the surrounding five hills and was made nearly impregnable by massive and ancient stone walls. In the Buddha's lifetime, as the kingdom of Magadha expanded, the city outgrew the valley; Ajātaśatru, Bimbisāra's son and successor, constructed New Rājagṛha just outside the hills and extended the city walls to protect it.

After the Buddha's Parinirvāṇa, Ajātaśatru had a portion of the Buddha's relics brought to Rājagṛha and built a stūpa in which to enshrine them outside the western wall of 'New Rājagṛha.' Shortly thereafter, when five hundred Arhats met at Rājagṛha to recite the Buddha's teachings, Ajātaśatru furnished the Saptaparṇī Cave for their use. The Saptaparṇī Cave thus became the site of the First Council.

The Dharma centers of Rājagṛha remained vital through the reign of Ajātaśatru. The Buddha's disciple Ānanda maintained close relations with the king of Magadha as well as with the Mallas and other tribes of Vṛji, located north of

The Pippala House, also known as Jarāsandha-ka-baithak, an ancient stone structure on Mt. Vaibhāra that overlooks the northern pass into the city. The Buddha visited Mahākāśyapa here when the great disciple was ill.

Magadha on the northern side of the Ganges River. When the time came for Ānanda to enter nirvāṇa, Ānanda decided to pass away on an island in the Ganges, midway between Magadha and Vṛji, so that Magadha and Vṛji could both claim half of his relics. Ajātaśatru brought his share of Ānanda's relics to Rājagṛha and enshrined them within a stūpa built near the stūpa housing the relics of the Buddha.

During the reigns of Bimbisāra and Ajātaśatru, the kingdom of Magadha prospered; its borders expanded westward to include the ancient kingdom of Kāśī, Vārāṇasī, its capital city, and Sārnāth, site of the Buddha's first teaching. On the east, Bimbisāra annexed the kingdom of Aṅga (modern Bengal); his son Ajātaśatru crossed to the north bank of the

Ganges and conquered the lands of the Vṛjis and Mallas, bringing Kuśinagara and Vaiśālī under his rule. The hills of Rājagṛha, formerly viewed as protective, came to isolate the kings of Magadha from their growing empire, which now stretched across both sides of the Ganges River, India's major waterway. Kings after Ajātaśatru moved the capital north to Pāṭaliputra, strategically situated on the south bank of the Ganges. Although Rājagṛha retained its importance as a holy site, this once great city slipped into decline. Little is known of its subsequent history until the fifth century C.E.

Rājagṛha in the Fifth and Seventh Centuries

When the Chinese pilgrim Fa-hien visited Rājagṛha in the fifth century, he recorded that the old city was crumbling and no longer inhabited. The Vimalavatthu, a Pāli text, suggests that the city suffered from plague at some point in its history, which may have been a factor in its being abandoned. Jīvaka's Mango Grove northeast of the city was also in ruins. The Veṇuvana Vihāra north of the city still existed, however, and was being cared for by a congregation of monks. Fa-hien also was able to find the Śītavana, the Cemetery Grove, less than a mile north of the Veṇuvana.

Nearby, Fa-hien saw the Pippala Cave where the Buddha often meditated after the midday meal. Several miles west could be seen the stone cave known as the Saptaparṇīguha, where the Arhats convened after the Parinirvāṇa to recite the Buddha's teachings during the First Council of the Sangha. The Pāli chronicles state that this cave was in Mt. Webharo (= Mt. Vaibhāra), and a cave fitting that description has been identified on the northern side of the southwest spur of Mt. Vaibhāra. Many other stone cells that the Arhats used for meditation can also be seen today.

Fa-hien visited two sites in the area where the Dharma was recited simultaneously with the Arhats' convocation: the place where disciples who were not yet Arhats assembled lay west of the Saptaparṇī Cave, and Vimalasvabhāva Hill, where the Bodhisattvas compiled the Mahāyāna scriptures, was south of Rājagṛha. Here Avalokiteśvara recited the Sūtras, Maitreya the Vinaya, and Mañjuśrī the Abhidharma, with Vajrapāṇi assigned to protect the teachings until the time came for them to be fully revealed.

When Hsüan-tsang visited Rājagṛha, the foundation walls and decayed tree roots of Jīvaka's Mango Grove were still visible. Although the remains of Jīvaka's house and the hollow of an old well had also survived, Hsüan-tsang found only the stone foundation and brick walls of the Veṇuvana Vihāra. Nearby stood the stūpa built by Ajātaśatru over the Buddha's relics and the stūpa that enshrined half of Ānanda's relics. According to Hsüan-tsang, the relic stūpa constantly emitted miraculous light. King Aśoka, after worshipping at this stūpa, opened it to divide its relics among thousands of additional stūpas. Hsüan-tsang relates that Aśoka also erected a pillar with an elephant capital here, but no trace of such a pillar has been located in modern times.

Hsüan-tsang noted that one thousand Brahmin families as well as Jain and Buddhist practitioners were living in the area. Jain ascetics were engaged in the practice of austerities on Mt. Vaibhāra and solitary bhikṣus still meditated in a cave near the Pippala Grove, said to have been the abode of Asuras, fierce beings known as the 'jealous gods'. According to Hsüan-tsang, "Often people may see strange forms, as of nāgas, serpents, and lions, come forth from it. Those who see these things lose their reason and become dazed. Nevertheless, this excellent land is one in which holy saints dwell; occupying the spot consecrated by such sacred traces, they forget the calamities and evils that threaten them." (HT II:156–157)

Modern archaeological excavations have revealed the extent of Rājagṛha's walls and fortifications: The outer ramparts, thirteen feet thick in places, follow the crests of the

Rājagṛha's cyclopean walls follow the mountain ridges around the entire valley. These walls, built to protect the city, are thought to predate the time of the Buddha.

mountains surrounding the old city, with the inner ramparts enclosing the central part of the city. Although the outer walls of New Rājagṛha had already fallen into ruin by the seventh century, the remnants of the inner walls are still standing. Archaeologists have tentatively identified the Pippala Grove, a favorite retreat of Mahākāśyapa, where the Buddha also often stayed. But the location of the Śītavana, the Chilly Grove described as a home of the Sangha, still remains uncertain. Although Hsüan-tsang mentioned it was covered over by the construction of New Rājagṛha, the Pāli texts describe it as located on the side of a hill, which does not accord with the site of the new city.

Rājagṛha Today

The modern pilgrim to Rājagṛha can still see the sites blessed by the Buddha's presence: the Veṇuvana, or Bamboo Grove; Jīvaka's Mango Grove; the Gṛdhrakūṭa, the Vulture Peak, where the Buddha taught the Prajñāpāramitā; the Tapodārāma and the Tapodakandara, the hot water retreat and cavern; the Saptaparṇī Cave, site of the First Council of the Sangha; the royal garden at Āmbalaṭṭhika where the Buddha and his disciples rested on the way to Nālandā, and numerous other locations.

Today, as one enters Rājagṛha from the south, one travels through the Banganga Pass, where Rājagṛha's walls, India's most ancient structural remains, can clearly be seen stretching up the hills on either side of the road. Rising to a height of twelve feet and about seventeen feet thick, the walls here appear to be close to their original size. Proceeding northeast, the traveler comes to a stone enclosure to the right of the modern road, where the rock preserves the imprint of chariot wheels and inscriptions in an undeciphered 'shell' script.

Further along the road, to the right, is a large stone foundation said to be Bimbisāra's Jail. According to the commentary on the Sāmaññaphala-sutta, Ajātaśatru imprisoned his father, King Bimbisāra, in a storeroom or dungeon in the palace, from which the old king could see the Buddha teaching on the Vulture Peak. The large stone foundation at this site may be the foundation of the ancient palace.

A small square stone building on Mt. Vaibhāra rises from the west corner of the pass leading north from the old city.

Stairs descend to the shaded waters of Karaṇḍaka Lake in Veṇuvana Park, where the Buddha used to bathe. A statue of the Buddha overlooks this site. The Veṇuvana Vihāra appears to have been located a short distance to the south.

In its base are cave-like cells where it is thought that the Buddha visited Mahākāśyapa as the great disciple lay ill with a fever. Hsüan-tsang observed an 'Asura Cave' behind this structure; although the site of this cave has crumbled, in 1895 the remains of a long cavern could be discerned here. (Rajgir 16) This building, which offers a sweeping view of the approach to the old city of Rājagṛha, may be the remains of an ancient watchtower built long before the time of the Buddha. It is now known as Mahākāśyapa's House or the Pippala House, after the account relating that the Buddha visited Mahākāśyapa here when the disciple was ill. Further up the hill, to the west of Ādinātha, a modern Jain temple, a path leads along the crest of Mt. Vaibhāra to a series of caves identified as Saptaparṇī, site of the First Council.

A short distance outside the northern pass is a fenced park identified as the Veṇuvana, the Bamboo Grove, where a statue of the Buddha has been placed on the site thought to be the location of the original Veṇuvana Vihāra. Beside it is the Karaṇḍaka Lake, a large pool with steps leading down to the water. Outside the fence is the modern Veṇuvana Temple, also said to be on the site of the original Veṇuvana Vihāra. To the southeast, Chaṭhā Hill is crowned by the Viśvaśānti Stūpa erected in recent times by Japanese Buddhists. Statues on the stūpa represent the four great acts of the Buddha, and an adjoining temple contains images of the Buddha.

To the left of the road leading east to Chaṭhā Hill and the Vulture Peak is a fenced site with stone foundations said to be the site of Jīvaka's Mango Grove. Jīvaka, son of King Bimbisāra, was Ajātaśatru's half-brother and a skilled physician. His duties included the care of King Bimbisāra, the king's household, and the Buddha and the Buddha's disciples. Jīvaka lived in the palace, which was quite distant from the Bamboo Grove and the Vulture Peak, the places where the Buddha usually dwelled with his disciples. Since the physician had difficulty in visiting them twice a day, he built a vihāra for them in his Mango Grove.

Once the Buddha's cousin Devadatta, inflamed by envy, rolled a huge rock down the mountain toward the spot where the Buddha was walking outside his meditation cave on the Vulture Peak. A part of the rock struck the Buddha's foot, causing the Blessed One great pain. (This rock, which symbolizes Rājagṛha's claim as the site of one of the eight great wonders, can still be seen on the Vulture Peak today.) The disciples carried the Buddha to the Deer Park of Mardakukṣi near the foot of the Vulture Peak mountain and then to the Mango Grove, where he was attended by Jīvaka. From references in the Sūtras, Mardakukṣi appears to have been a favorite place of the Buddha. Eventually a monastery was built there.

The Vulture Peak overlooks the bowl-like valley of old Rājagṛha. In the distance Udayagiri and Sonagiri rise on the left and right of Rājagṛha's southern gate.

The Vulture Peak

"Once the Buddha was residing on the Vulture Peak at Rājagṛha. Through the virtue of the Tathāgata, this monarch of mountains was bounteous and majestic, radiating splendor and beauty. Its slopes were adorned with a vast array of flowers and fruit trees. By the power of the Buddha, yakṣas and tribes of savages lived peacefully here, as did birds and wild animals of every kind.

"The mountain's streams, lakes, and ponds were covered with lotuses, their banks fragrant with a vast variety of herbs. The rain clouds which crowned Vulture Peak were swept away by the mighty voices of the gods to reveal sparkling skies. High grasses the color of a peacock's throat covered the slopes, and the ground gave spring to the step. Lotuses the color of gold, crystal, and fire gave off incomparable fragrance in all directions.

Now, as in ancient times, pilgrims follow Bimbisāra's road that winds to the top of the Vulture Peak.

"Gods, men, and nāgas gave offerings of precious gems, incense, balsam, silks, and victory banners which formed clouds of brilliant color that ornamented the mountain. The essence of sandalwood floated in the breeze as gods, nāgas, and gandharvas offered gifts beyond imagining to honor the Tathāgata, who came forth from illusion, born from stainless action, free from defilements, manifesting the Dharma in all directions like a dream." —*Ratnakūṭa-sūtra*

Named both for its unusual shape and for the vultures that inhabited the region, Gṛdhrakūṭa, the Vulture Peak, is situated east of Rājagṛha's five periphery hills. It was on this

Pilgrims still visit the Vulture Peak Shrine to meditate and pray where the Buddha Śākyamuni taught the profound Prajñāpāramitā.

mountain that King Bimbisāra, "for the purpose of hearing the law," had a road built to the top of the peak. The paved stone path used by modern pilgrims is essentially this same road. The western face of the top of the Vulture Peak ends in a steep precipice; here, overlooking Rājagṛha, the Buddha gave the most profound of his teachings.

The fifth-century pilgrim Fa-hien described the mountain as picturesque and imposing. A short distance from the top was a cave where the Buddha used to sit in meditation. Another cave was found thirty paces to the northwest. Once, while the Buddha was meditating in the first cave and Ānanda in the second cave, Māra appeared to Ānanda in the form of a great vulture. Ānanda was terrified; but the Buddha made a cleft in the rock with his hand and reached through the rock to where Ānanda stood; stroking his shoulder, the Blessed One calmed Ānanda's fear. According to Fa-hien, this was how the mountain became known as the Vulture Peak.

The Buddha's meditation cave at the summit of Vulture Peak

Fa-hien ascended the mountain and offered flowers outside the cave that the Buddha had used for meditation. Holding back tears, the pilgrim said, "Here Buddha delivered the Śūraṅgama-sūtra. I, Fa-hien, was born when I could not meet with the Buddha; I only see the footprints which he has left, and nothing more." Fa-hien recited the Śūraṅgama-sūtra and stayed the night in the cave. (HT lx)

When Hsüan-tsang visited the Vulture Peak, a brick vihāra on the mountain top near the western precipice was still in existence. "It is high and wide and beautifully constructed; the door opens to the east. Here Tathāgata often stopped in ancient times and preached the law."(HT II:153) In Hsüan-tsang's time a life-sized figure of the Buddha teaching the Dharma stood near the vihāra. The statue of the Buddha and many terracotta seals found on the Vulture Peak are now in the museum at Nālandā, built to the north of the entrance to the great university. Hsüan-tsang describes a stūpa marking the place where the Buddha taught the Saddharmapuṇḍarīka, the White Lotus of the True Law, revealing to the assembly of Arhats the broad and deep vehicle of the Mahāyāna and the incomparable virtues of the Bodhisattva. Another stūpa rose from the mountain north of the Vulture Peak, where the Tathāgata had stood to view Rājagṛha and had taught the Dharma for seven days.

Modern visitors to the Vulture Peak follow in the footsteps of the Buddha and the Sangha as they ascend the heights of this ancient site to the place where the Buddha revealed the Prajñāpāramitā and other Mahāyāna Sūtras to the hosts of Bodhisattvas, Arhats, bhikṣus and bhikṣuṇīs, and beings from non-human realms. Only the brick foundations remain of the shrine Hsüan-tsang described on this cliff, which commands a view of the bowl-like valley that embraces the old city of Rājagṛha. Yet pilgrims from Asia, Europe, and America come here to stand on the very spot where the Buddha taught, to pay homage and meditate here, and to recite the Heart and the Diamond Sūtras, two of the shorter Prajñāpāramitā teachings memorized by many Dharma practitioners. The meditation caves used by the Buddha and the great Arhats, still maintained as shrines, are illuminated by the light of candles burning on the rock-altars within.

Giryek

About three miles northeast of the Vulture Peak, on the eastern end of the mountain range that stretches from Gayā to Giryek, a cylindrical brick tower twenty-eight feet in diameter and twenty-one feet high rises from a promontory overlooking the Pañcāna River. This monument, now known as Jarāsandha's Tower, stands on the place described by Fa-hien as the Hill of the Isolated Rock, where Indra questioned the Buddha on forty-two points of doctrine and, using his finger, wrote the Buddha's responses on the great stone. In the

Line drawing of the stūpa at Giryek (Jarāsandha's Tower), by A. Cunningham, from Reports 1862–1864, p. 19, plate xv. The stūpa's ornamentation is similar to the Mahābodhi Temple at Bodh Gayā; its original height was about fifty-five feet.

seventh century, Hsüan-tsang described the same event, but located it on the western peak of the Indraśaila Hill.

Hsüan-tsang mentioned a monastery built on the eastern peak of the Indraśaila Hill; in front of it was a stūpa known as the Haṁsa, or Goose Stūpa. According to Hsüan-tsang, a bhikṣu of one of the Hīnayāna schools noticed geese flying overhead, and called out in jest of the compassion emphasized by the Mahāyāna teachings, "Today the congregation of priests has not had sufficient food! O great beings! Now is your opportunity (for demonstrating the compassion of a Bodhisattva)!" (HT II:181) Immediately a goose fell dead at the bhikṣu's feet. Horrified, the bhikṣus of that monastery reconsidered their attitude toward the Mahāyāna teachings and decided to embrace the Bodhisattva path. To honor the goose, they built a stūpa over the goose's body.

In the nineteenth century, a pedestal with a figure of a large goose was found at Jarāsandha's Tower; from its location, the tower has been identified as the Goose Stūpa described by Hsüan-tsang. Since Fa-hien did not mention a stūpa here, it is assumed that the stūpa was built after his visit, perhaps around 500 C.E. In the nineteenth century, when General Cunningham excavated a mound next to its base, he found a square building with eighty-four small oval seals inscribed with the Ye Dharma mantra embedded in its mortar. Further archaeological excavations at Chandiman, a village near Giryek, unearthed a number of Buddhist images.

Kukkuṭapādagiri

Between Gayā and Rājagṛha, to the east of the Mahi River and great wild forest, rises the Kukkuṭapādagiri, the Cocksfoot Mountain, named for the shape of the three peaks that crowned its summit. Soon after the First Council following the Buddha's Parinirvāṇa, the great Arhat Mahākāśyapa went out through the southern gate of Rājagṛha, ascended this mountain, and wrapped himself in the robe given him by the Buddha. Then, seated in the depression in the center of the mountain's three peaks, the great Arhat entered samādhi. The mountain closed over him, sealing him inside, where he awaits the coming of the future Buddha Maitreya.

When King Ajātaśatru heard of Mahākāśyapa's departure, he immediately climbed the mountain accompanied by the Buddha's disciple and cousin Ānanda. Out of respect for the king's grief, yakṣas removed the concealing cover, allowing the king to view Mahākāśyapa seated in samādhi. To comfort the king, Ānanda described how, during the time of Maitreya, Mahākāśyapa's body would be brought forth and shown as the foremost among those who attain the twelve virtues of an ascetic. In honor of the great Arhat, King Ajātaśatru built a stūpa on this site.

Hsüan-tsang related that, "The sides of this mountain are high and rugged, the valleys and gorges are impenetrable. Tumultuous torrents rush down its sides, thick forests envelop the valleys, while tangled shrubs grow along its cavernous heights. Soaring upwards into the air are three sharp peaks; their tops are surrounded by the vapors of heaven, and their shapes lost in the clouds. Behind these hills the venerable Mahākāśyapa dwells wrapped in a condition of nirvāṇa. People do not dare to utter his name, and therefore they speak of the 'Gurupada', the venerable teacher." (HT II:142)

Hsüan-tsang described a stūpa built on the top of the mountain: "On quiet evenings those looking from a distance see sometimes a bright light as it were of a torch; but if they ascend the mountain there is nothing to be seen."(HT II:144)

In the nineteenth century, General Cunningham identified the Kukkuṭapādagiri with a hill near the modern village of Kurkihār, which has several mounds that have yielded statues and small votive stūpas (tsa-tsas) of dark blue stone. One of the mounds was the ruins of a stūpa; another was called

Sugatgarh, or House of Sugata. One statue represents the Buddha practicing hardships under the pipal tree with the Parinirvāṇa depicted above. Smaller statues depict the Buddha's birth and first teaching. Mahāyāna statues found in the vicinity include representations of the Bodhisattva Avalokiteśvara, Tārā, and the Buddha Akṣobhya, all dating from the ninth to twelfth centuries.

However, more recent examinations of the area point to two other hills, Gurpā and Sobhnāth, as more likely prospects for the site of Kukkuṭapādagiri. Of the two, Gurpā Hill most closely fits the physical description given by Hsüan-tsang and has on its summit the remains of an ancient stūpa. (JBRS 1956:246–249)

To the northeast of the Cocksfoot Mountain, closer to Rājagṛha, was Buddhavana, a mountainous site where the Buddha once stayed in a stone chamber. It is said that here Śakra, king of the devas, and Brahmā, lord of the formless realm, ground some sandalwood into incense with which to anoint the Buddha. Hsüan-tsang related that the sandalwood scent still remained on the rocks. He also mentioned that five hundred Arhats dwelled there "in a spiritual manner," and sometimes manifested to those who desired to meet them.

Archaeologists have long speculated about the modern site of Buddhavana. The most likely possibility to date appears to be Hānriā Hill, which has steep cliffs and a cave similar to the stone chamber described by Hsüan-tsang. The chamber is accessed by an ancient road leading up the hill to the mouth of the cave. The rocks near this cave extrude a glistening black substance with a distinctive musky odor; although the smell is quite different from sandalwood, there may be a connection between this substance and the ancient description. (JBRS 1956:251–267)

Vaiśālī

"The Licchavis of Vaiśālī heard of the arrival of the Blessed One, so they mounted their chariots and went to see him. Seeing them coming, the Buddha called the bhikṣus' attention to them: "Bhikṣus, you who have not been in the parks of the Trāyastriṁśa devas, these are like unto them for the glory of their appearance, their riches, and the beauty of their apparel."

—*Mūlasarvāstivādin Vinaya*

Vaiśālī, the Licchavis' capital, was the largest city of the Vṛjian confederacy, the world's oldest known republic. Before the time of the Buddha, the Licchavis, the Videhas, and the Mallas had formed this confederacy for mutual protection against their powerful neighbors, Kosala on their western border and Magadha to the south. The Mahānādī River formed the eastern boundary of Vṛji, and the Gandak River defined the western border. Beyond the Gandak was the large kingdom of Kosala, ruled by King Prasenajit during the time of the Buddha. The city of Vaiśālī itself was a place of great beauty, inhabited by people respected throughout northern India for their love of freedom, their peacefulness, and their prosperity.

On the Buddha's first visit to Vaiśālī after his enlightenment, he ended a great plague that was devastating the city and won the respect and love of the people. Another time when the Buddha visited Vaiśālī, a group of monkeys dug out a pool for the Buddha's use and offered him honey for refreshment. This event, which is depicted on bas-reliefs at Bhārhut, Sāñcī, and Gandhāra, was the great wonder that established Vaiśālī as a place of pilgrimage.

The Buddha often visited Vaiśālī in the course of his travels. The Bodhisattvacarya-nirdeśa-sūtra preserves an account of the marvels that attended one of the Buddha's entries into this garden city, which resembled an earthly paradise, so great was its prosperity and the elegance of its people. The Buddha remarked that the like of this city had never been seen, not even in the Heaven of the Thirty-three Gods.

Vaiśālī was the site of many of the Buddha's teachings, including the extensive Bhadrakalpika-sūtra. It was also the home of Vimalakīrti, the layman whose understanding of the Dharma amazed even the great Mahākāśyapa. The Vaiśālī courtesan Āmrapālī became a patroness of the Sangha and donated her garden, the Mango Grove, as a resting place for the Buddha and his disciples. It was in this garden that the Buddha, many years later, told his disciples, "In this place I have performed the last religious act of my earthly career," and announced he would soon enter Parinirvāṇa. Here the Buddha began the last part of his final journey. After his Parinirvāṇa, the Licchavis received a portion of the Buddha's relics and enshrined them in a stūpa in Vaiśālī. When Ānanda entered Parinirvāṇa, the Licchavis received half of his relics as well.

Some 110 years after the Buddha's Parinirvāṇa, Vaiśālī became the site of the Second Council of the Sangha. Seven hundred Arhats assembled here from Magadha and Mathurā to examine ten practices followed by the monks of Vaiśālī, for these practices were viewed by many as a relaxation of

Ruins of the Great Stūpa of Vaiśālī, one of the eight original stūpas built to enshrine the relics of the Buddha. From inner to outer, the layers reveal the first construction by the Licchavis, the enlargement made by Aśoka, and a second enlargment during the Kuṣāna period.

the Buddha's guidelines. Although all agreed to repudiate the ten practices and to adhere strictly to the original rules, differences persisted. In time, two distinct Buddhist traditions emerged: the Sthaviras, who adhered to more conservative views, and the Mahāsāṁghikas, who favored a more progressive approach. Vaiśālī, with its long tradition of independent thinkers, became a center of the Mahāsāṁghika tradition. When King Aśoka visited Vaiśālī on his pilgrimage to Buddhist holy places, he built a stūpa here and erected a high pillar topped with a stone lion.

In the fifth century, Fa-hien saw the chapel and stūpa of the Mahāvana, the Great Grove north of Vaiśālī, where the Buddha resided and taught the Dharma. The stūpa erected by the Licchavis over Ānanda's relics was located nearby. Fa-hien observed the ruins of a stūpa built by Āmrapālī. Another stūpa marked the site of the council of Vaiśālī.

In the seventh century, Hsüan-tsang described the country of Vṛji: "The soil is rich and fertile; flowers and fruits are produced in abundance. Mangos and bananas are very plentiful and much prized. The climate is agreeable and temperate." (HT II:66) Hsüan-tsang found Vaiśālī mostly in ruins, inhabited by only a few families. There was one active monastery housing a few bhikṣus of the Saṁmatīya tradition. Beside the monastery was a stūpa commemorating the teaching of the Vimalakīrti-nirdeśa-sūtra. A stūpa also marked the site of Vimalakīrti's house, and a stonepile nearby indicated where, as Vimalakīrti lay ill, he instructed the Bodhisattva Mañjuśrī. Other stūpas marked where Mahāprajāpatī, the Buddha's aunt, and other bhikṣuṇīs entered nirvāṇa.

Stūpas also stood where the Buddha stopped on the way to Kuśinagara, where the Enlightened One last gazed on Vaiśālī, and where he announced he would soon enter Parinirvāṇa—after revealing to Ānanda that he could, if he wished, extend his life to a kalpa. Ānanda, befuddled by Māra, Lord of Illusion, understood the significance of this statement too late to ask the Buddha to remain in the world.

Hsüan-tsang described the ancient stūpa built over the portion of the Buddha's relics given to the Licchavis of Vaiśālī. (This is one of the stūpas that Aśoka opened to obtain relics for erecting additional stūpas throughout his empire. When another king sought to do this at a later time, the earth trembled, and that king was too frightened to continue.) The stūpa that Aśoka built here was still evident in Hsüan-tsang's time, and beside it rose the lion-topped pillar. The Monkey Pool was clearly visible, as was the stūpa built where the monkeys had offered honey to the Buddha.

Northwest of the city Hsüan-tsang saw the stūpa where the Licchavis said their last farewell to the Buddha after following him out of the city and grieving at the news of his impending death. The stūpa that marked the site of the Second Council was also still standing. Further south, the pilgrim

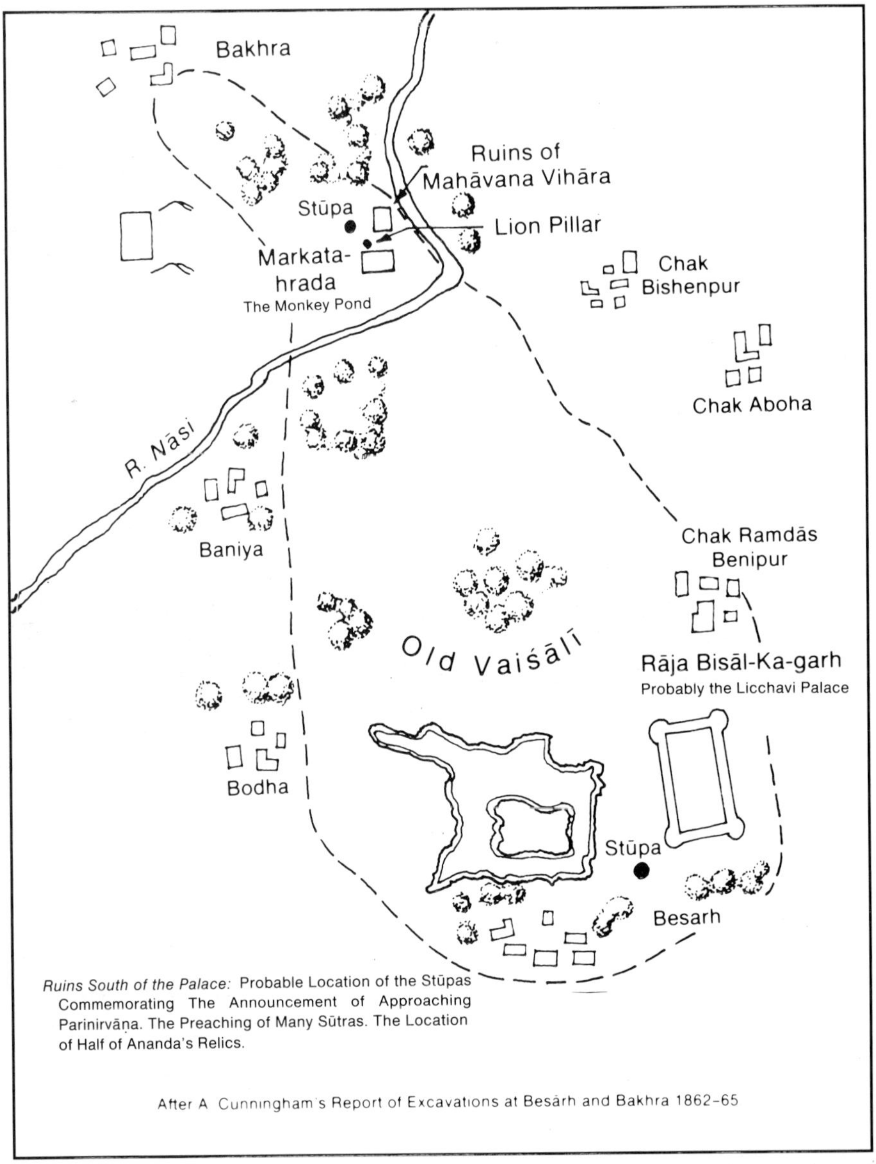

came to the monastery of Svetapura, which housed monks of the Mahāyāna tradition. The monastery, topped with massive towers, appears to have been thriving. Traces of the four past Buddhas of our aeon (Krakucchanda, Kanakamuni, Kāśyapa, and Śākyamuni) remained there, as well as an Aśokan stūpa. Southeast of this monastery, on the banks of the Ganges, Hsüan-tsang noted a stūpa marking the place where Ānanda divided his body between the peoples of Magadha and Vṛji.

Aśoka's lion still presides over the stūpa and Monkey Pond at Kohlua.

Hsüan-tsang eloquently communicated his sadness at seeing the condition of the Buddha's beautiful city. "Both within and without the city of Vaiśālī, and all round it, the sacred vestiges are so numerous that it would be difficult to recount them all. At every step commanding sites and old foundations are seen, which the succession of seasons and lapse of years have entirely destroyed. The forests are uprooted; the shallow lakes are dried up and stinking; nought but offensive remnants of decay can be recorded." (HT II:73)

In the nineteenth century, the village of Besarh, about twenty-seven miles northeast of Patna, was identified as ancient Vaiśālī. The site at Besarh consists of the remains of a large fort and the ruins of a brick stūpa. About a thousand feet from the fort is a mound of solid bricks more than twenty-three feet higher than the surrounding fields, but a Muslim graveyard now crowns the top of this mound, rendering excavation impossible. The stūpa erected by the Licchavis over their portion of the Buddha's relics has recently been excavated, but only the foundation and some low walls remain. Three concentric rings can clearly be seen in the foundation, revealing that the stūpa had been enlarged at least twice after its original construction.

A second concentration of Buddhist ruins exists at Kohlua, about two miles northwest of Besarh and one mile southeast of Bakhra (ancient Vaiśālī is believed to have encompassed both sites). The remains at Kohlua, grouped together beside a low mound, include the stone pillar with a lion capital described by Hsüan-tsang, a ruined stūpa of solid brick, the Monkey Pond dug for the Buddha, four sites of ancient buildings, and a perfectly preserved life-sized statue of the Buddha as an ascetic, discovered in the nineteenth century. These monuments are much as Hsüan-tsang described them more than thirteen centuries ago. Although the pillar bearing the lion is gradually sinking into the soft ground, it still stands over thirty-six feet high.

Modern pilgrims may share the sadness of Hsüan-tsang that so little remains of the beautiful city of Vaiśālī, the world's oldest known republic and a citadel of freedom in the ancient world. Although Aśoka's lion still guards the remains of a stūpa and a museum at Vaiśālī houses artifacts and images discovered here, it is difficult to imagine how Vaiśālī actually appeared when the Buddha taught the Dharma in its groves and gardens. Still, Vaiśālī, deeply loved by the Buddha and one of the strongest early Dharma centers, remains one of the eight major places of pilgrimage. Honor and respect for the remains of this sacred site can strengthen appreciation for the Sangha that keeps open the path to enlightenment. In lands new to the Dharma, appreciation for the blessings of the Sangha can inspire the study and practice of communities dedicated to the Buddhist teachings.

Part Two

The Madhyadeśa

Six Dharma Regions of India

From the earliest days of the Sangha, bhikṣus have traveled widely to propagate the teachings of liberation. One after the other, each region of India opened to the Buddha's teachings as the petals of a flower unfurl to greet the sun.

Shaped like a great vessel, India has for millenia accommodated wave after wave of diverse peoples and cultures. Whether bent on conquest or entering as peaceful settlers, eventually all became children of mother India and made their contribution to Indian civilization. In ancient times Indian culture flowed far to the northwest, touching the lives of Persians, Greeks, and Central Asians whose kingdoms bordered and sometimes crossed the Indus River. In turn, the influence of Indian culture has been felt deep in Afghanistan and Central Asia, where Buddhism and the values it carried fostered spiritual development, education, compassion, and peace. A similar current flowed south and southeast, to Śrī Laṅkā and the lands of Southeast Asia.

The growth of the Dharma throughout this vast region was influenced by the movements of culture, commerce, and struggles for empire. As early as the sixth or fifth centuries B.C.E., traveling bhikṣus encountered people of different traditions, from the strongly Brahmanic peoples of Kuru and Pañcāla in the north, to the independent republics of the east, where the Brahmanic traditions had penetrated only superficially. The Buddhist teachings note rivalries between ancient India's many kingdoms, which may have affected the growth of the Sangha in some regions. Later texts document the accomplishments of King Aśoka, who united nearly all of India and supported the growth of the Dharma throughout his empire around 250 B.C.E. From this time onward, if not before, bhikṣus began to travel the trade routes over land and ocean, accompanying the caravans of the rising merchant class throughout India and beyond. During the early centuries C.E., and possibly earlier, Buddhist monks reached most of Asia's major population centers.

This presentation of Buddhist sites begins with the Madhyadeśa and follows four major routes of travel and transmission leading out into greater India:

1. THE MIDDLE COUNTRY (MADHYADEŚA) The lower Ganges basin, bounded by the Himalayas on the north, the Vindhya Mountains on the south, and the Campā River on the east. During the Buddha's lifetime, the cities of Kauśāmbī, Sāketa, and Śrāvastī defined the Madhyadeśa's western border. This region, which corresponds to modern Bihār and the eastern part of Uttar Pradesh, was where the Buddha spent most of his life teaching the Dharma and establishing the Sangha.

2. THE CENTRAL VALLEYS The valleys of the upper Ganges and Yamunā rivers, the ancient lands of the Kurus, Pañcālas, and Śūrasenas, which were the center of Brahmanic culture and the focus of the Mahābhārata epic. This region corresponds with the greater part of modern Uttar Pradesh and extends north through Himachal Pradesh.

3. THE NORTHWEST refers to ancient Uttarāpatha, the route that led from the Central Valleys across the five rivers of the Punjab, through the Khyber Pass and into Afghanistan. Bounded by the Thar Desert of modern Rajasthan on the south and the Pamir Mountains and the arc of the upper Indus on the north, this region includes Kashmir, Takṣaśilā, Gandhāra, and Uḍḍiyāna, major Buddhist centers of the ancient world. Kashmir is now part of India, Takṣaśilā and Uḍḍiyāna are in Pakistan, and Gandhāra is in Afghanistan.

4. THE ROUTE WEST The region extending west from Sāñcī and Bhopal to the Arabian Sea, bounded on the west by the lower Indus River and on the south by the borders of modern Mahārāṣṭra. This region includes Sindh, the Thar Desert of Rājasthan, modern Gujarāt, and the famous cave temples of Mahārāṣṭra.

5. THE SOUTH The region along the ancient Dakṣiṇāpatha, the route south from Pratiṣṭhāna (Paithan) through the Āndhra country and southeast to the Buddhist centers along the Godāvarī and Kṛṣṇā rivers. This region includes the modern states of Āndhra Pradesh, Tamilnādu, Kerala, and Karṇaṭaka.

6. THE EAST (PRĀCYA) The lands east of the Madhyadeśa, including modern West Bengal, Bangladesh, Orissa, Assam, and Tripura.

General Pattern of the Sangha's Expansion

At the time of the Buddha, trade routes connected the cities of the Madhyadeśa to the rest of the ancient world. One led northwest, through Mathurā, the central valleys, and the plains of the Kurus to the river valleys of the Punjab, winding through mountainous passes east to Takṣāśilā, Uḍḍiyāna, Gandhāra, and the ancient lands that form modern Afghanistan. This was a well-traveled path, a ready-made route along which the Dharma could flow like a great river from the subcontinent of South Asia to the northwest, connecting with the Silk Road that encircled the Taklamakan Desert and provided a gateway to China. The route west followed the Ganges to Vārāṇasī and Kauśāmbī, through Vidiśa, Sāñcī, and Ujjayinī to the port of Bharukaccha, at the mouth of the Narmadā River. From Bharukaccha the route curved south to the area known as the Western Ghats, where the Sangha carved magnificent temples and residence halls out of the living rock.

Expansion to the south and east proceeded more slowly. To the south lay the Vindhya Mountains, a formidable barrier in ancient times, and populated by aboriginal tribes that even the kings of the day were reluctant to confront directly. Bhikṣus traveling southwest from the Madhyadeśa to Vidiśā found a route through passes and river valleys that led around the mountains and gave them access to India's southeastern coast. Another route led south from the western coast across the Deccan plateau to the Kṛṣṇa River, which bhikṣus followed east through the Āndhra country to the Indian Ocean.

To the east, bhikṣus following the tributaries of the Ganges River to the Bay of Bengal established monasteries in the ancient lands of Puṇḍravardhana and Vaṅga, which are now part of Bengal. From there bhikṣus continued eastward into Kāmarūpa, a kingdom in the valley of the great Brahmaputra River that corresponds to modern Assam. From Tāmralipti, a city on the southwestern tip of the Ganges delta, emissaries of the Dharma, tireless in communicating the teachings of liberation, traveled down the coastline into Kaliṅga then followed the river valleys inland, where they built temples and monasteries on Kaliṅga's lushly forested hills.

KASHMIR
PAKISTAN
TIBET
HIMACHAL PRADESH
PUNJAB
HARYĀNA
NEPAL
BHUTAN
RAJASTHAN
Śrāvastī
Kuśinagara
Vaiśālī
Pāṭaliputra
Kauśāmbī
Sārnāth
Vārāṇasī
Odantapurī
Nālandā
Rājagṛha
Vikramaśīla
Campā
Bodh Gayā
SINDH
GUJARAT
BANGLA DESH
WEST BENGAL
MADHYA PRADESH
ORISSA
MAHARASTRA
ANDHRA PRADESH
GOA
KARNATAKA
TAMIL NADU
KERALA
SRI LANKA

Madhyadeśa Heartland of the Dharma

The Madhyadeśa is the symbolic home of the Dharma, the place where through the ages there was practice, study, and reflection on the teachings of liberation. Nestled in the lower Ganges Basin between the Himalaya and Vindhya Mountains, the Madhyadeśa of the Buddha's time included the ancient kingdoms of Magadha and Kosala, the Vṛjian confederacy, and the republic of the Śākyas.

At the time of the Parinirvāṇa, the Dharma was known mostly in the Madhyadeśa, or Middle Country, which had been the central region of the historical Buddha's travels and teachings. Seven of the eight holy places of pilgrimage lie within this region, which encircles the basin of the lower Ganges River from Kauśambī on the west to Pāṭaliputra (Patna) on the east. The four most holy places—Lumbinī, in the north, the birthplace of the Buddha; Bodh Gayā in the south, the place of enlightenment; Sārnāth in the west, where the Enlightened One first turned the wheel of the Dharma; and

Kuśinagara in the east, the site of the Parinirvāṇa, define the area where the Dharma took root most strongly during the Buddha's lifetime. Within a circle formed by these sites lie Rājagṛha, Śrāvastī, and Vaiśālī, the three cities most often named in the Sūtras as places where the Buddha taught the Dharma.

Since Buddhism remained strong in the Madhyadeśa for about seventeen hundred years, there are many other sites important to the Buddha's life and the history of the Sangha in this area. So rich in vihāras (monasteries) was this region that a part of the Madhyadeśa became known as Bihār, a name derived from the Sanskrit word vihāra. Although most of these vihāras have long since disappeared, some locales are immortalized in Buddhist texts and the records of traveling pilgrims. Among these are Kapilavastu, where the Buddha grew to manhood; the villages around Kapilavastu; Pāṭaliputra, capital of the great Dharma king Aśoka and the center of many early Buddhist traditions; the region of Aṅga and its capital Campā, where the Buddha traveled and gave teachings; Kauśāmbī, one of the six principal cities of ancient India; Sāketa, an early home of the Buddhist Sangha; and the great Buddhist university of Nālandā.

Aṅga

Aṅga, once an independent kingdom, was absorbed into Magadha by King Bimbisāra shortly before the Buddha's enlightenment. Since that time Aṅga has been closely associated with Magadha and with it forms the modern state of Bihār. Ancient Aṅga roughly corresponds to the modern Bihāri districts of Bhagalpur and Monghyr.

In the Mahāparinirvāṇa-sūtra, the Buddha names Campā as one of India's six principal cities. Situated at the confluence of the Campā and Ganges rivers, Campā, Aṅga's ancient capital, was an important commercial port from which merchants traveled the seas to trade with Śri Laṅkā and Burma.

Campā was about one hundred miles east of Rājagṛha. The Buddhist texts record that Bimbisāra sent his son Ajātaśatru to Campā to govern the region.

The Buddha often visited Campā in the company of his disciples, frequently resting near the Gaggarā Pond, built by Queen Gaggarā in earlier days. Here wandering ascetics took shelter and exchanged philosophical views with each other or with those who gathered to question them. Vajjiyamāhita, a householder, approached the Buddha at Gaggarā and related what he had previously heard from such wandering ascetics, and how he had challenged their views. (AN V: 151-152) The Soṇadaṇḍa-sutta relates that at Gaggarā, the Blessed One converted the rich Brahmin Soṇadaṇḍa by teaching him that only one who has attained nirvāṇa is in fact a true Brahmin. It was also at Gaggarā that Śāriputra, empowered by the Buddha, gave the Dasuttara-sutta.

At another site near Campā, on the banks of the river, the Buddha engaged in a dialogue with Pessa the Elephant Tamer, who, greatly impressed with the presence and concentration of the Buddha's disciples, inquired how the Buddha had helped them tame their minds. The Buddha also traveled to Assapura, where he instructed the monks in conduct appropriate to the Sangha, advising them to live in solitude and abide in the four meditations. This teaching is known as the Assapura-sutta. Several other villages in Aṅga are also associated with visits of the Buddha and his disciples: Āpaṇa, where the Buddha taught the Potaliya-sutta for the benefit of the householder Potaliya, the Laṭukikopama-sutta for the Brahmin Udāyi, and the Seḷa-sutta; and Bhaddiyanāgara, birthplace of the patroness Viśākhā. While passing through northern Aṅga on his last journey to Kuśinagara, the Buddha gave his disciples a teaching at the village of Jambugrāma, located near Campā.

Fa-hien relates that Campā was rich in stūpas built on places where Śākyamuni, as well as the previous Buddhas of our present kalpa, had taught. He also mentions a group of Buddhist monks still living in the region. Hsüan-tsang, two centuries later, describes a score or more of monasteries near Campā. Although most were in ruins, a few monasteries were still active, housing about two hundred monks of the Śrāvaka tradition. Hsüan-tsang comments on the beauty of the area: "There are wonderful trees, (forming) flowering woods; the large rocks and dangerous precipices are the resort of men of wisdom and virtue; those who go there to see the place are reluctant to leave." It is possible that Campā is the Campāra often mentioned by Abhayadatta in his Lives of the Eighty-four Siddhas *(Buddha's Lions,* Berkeley, 1979). If so, the woods of Campā were once home to Pacari the pastry vendor, who was instructed by the Bodhisattva Avalokiteśvara, and to the siddha-king Kokalipa.

According to Hsüan-tsang, the city was well-fortified, with brick walls "several tens of feet high." The pilgrim observes that since Campā's reputation as a town of rich merchants would surely have attracted invaders, the foundations were set on a high embankment, providing a commanding view of the area and protection from attack.

Inscriptions recently found in the region of ancient Campā verify that Campā retained its prosperity and status as a royally favored city through the twelfth century., and excavations at Champānagar, near Bhagalpur, have clarified many details of Campā's history. (ACV 97) But Campā was located directly in the path of invasion, and its Buddhist sites were largely devastated at the end of the twelfth century.

The region of Campā served bhikṣus and pilgrims as a highway to the east for at least fourteen centuries. The great university Vikramaśīla, located on the Ganges River in the vicinity of Campā, attracted thousands of Buddhist scholars and practitioners. But few signs of Buddhist centers can be seen today on the overland route to Campā. In the nineteenth century Buddhist sites were discovered in the vicinity of the villages of Campāpur and Patharaghata. Carved reliefs of the Buddha and the Bodhisattva Avalokiteśvara, which appear to date to the eighth century C.E., have also been discovered on large rocks at Patharghata Hill, located eight miles northeast of Colgong, near the village of Antichak, a site now widely identified as the remains of the great university of Vikramaśīla. Three crowned images of the Buddha were recovered from this site; at least one is now housed in the museum of the Department of Ancient Indian History and Archaeology at Patna University. (ACV 53) A number of other Mahāyāna images have also been found at this site.

Dr. Ram Chandra Prasad describes an image of Ṣaḍakṣarī-Lokeśvara found at Colgong that dates to the twelfth century. Although the image was badly damaged, the refinements in ornamentation were clearly identifiable. (ACV 54–55) The island of Jahangira, situated in the Ganges River near Sultanganj, west of Bhagalpur, must have one time have been a shrine for Buddhists as it now is for Hindus; a bronze image of the Buddha was found there. Made during the reign of the Guptas, this statue is the earliest bronze image found to date in the Bhagalpur region.

Onshore, at Sultanganj, the ruins of the pillared halls of a monastery were discovered in 1864. In the ruins was a colossal seven-foot-high Buddha image made of copper. This finely molded statue, cast in the Gupta period around the fifth century C.E., is considered unique in the realm of Indian art and a monument to the sculptor's artistic genius. (ACP 65–66) In 1879 a brick stūpa constructed on an octagonal plinth was excavated from a mound at Sultanpur. Inside its base was a smaller stūpa containing a relic box that held the seven precious minerals (gold, silver, crystal, sapphire, ruby, emerald, and zircon) as well as a number of silver coins. From the coins, the construction of this stūpa can be dated to the time of Candragupta II, a powerful king of the Gupta Dynasty who ruled most of north India in the fourth century.

Pāṭaliputra

"The Tathāgata was traveling northward to Kuśinagara, when, turning round to the south and looking back at Magadha, he stood upon this stone and said to Ānanda, 'Now for the very last time I leave this foot-impression, being about to attain nirvāṇa and looking back at Magadha. A hundred years hence there shall be a King Aśoka; he shall build here his capital and establish his court; he shall protect the three religious treasures'." (HT II:90)

Pāṭaliputra (modern Patna) first entered history as Pāṭaligrama, the place where King Bimbisāra camped with his retinue to await the Buddha's return from Vaiśālī and where he showered flowers along the streets in the Blessed One's honor. Toward the end of his life, traveling north on his last journey, the Buddha noted that King Ajātaśatru was enlarging and fortifying the city in preparation for attacking the Vṛjis on the north side of the Ganges. At that time the Buddha predicted that Pāṭaliputra, strategically located on the juncture of the Ganges and the Son rivers, would become a great city, but in time it would suffer greatly from fire, water, and disputes amongst kinsmen.

When Ajātaśatru's son Udāyin became king, he (or possibly his successor) transferred the Magadhan capital from Rājagṛha to Pāṭaliputra and transformed the fortified city into a center of beauty and learning. In the early third century B.C.E., the conquests of Candragupta Maurya and his successor Bindusāra, Aśoka's father, made Pāṭaliputra the center of a great empire. The writings of Megasthenes, the Greek ambassador to Candragupta Maurya's court, leave no doubt as to Pāṭaliputra's beauty, culture, and sophistication. Megasthenes also described the extensive wooden ramparts that surrounded the city. Archaeologists have found the remains of such fortifications, which were much larger and more massive than modern historians had believed possible.

Pātaliputra's glory shone even brighter under the Dharma King Aśoka (c. 268-232 B.C.E.) the greatest of the Mauryan rulers. While there may have been a few Buddhist monasteries in Pāṭaliputra before Aśoka came to power, Aśoka's benevolent reign transformed Pāṭaliputra into a major Dharma center. Chief among the monasteries Aśoka built in Pāṭaliputra was the monastery in the Kukkuṭārāma, The Garden of the Rooster, which housed a thousand monks. Aśoka's own preceptor, the Arhat Yaśas, served as abbot. The Kukkuṭārāma Monastery was named after the garden, but it was linked so closely with Aśoka that it became known in the Pāli tradition as the Aśokārāma, Aśoka's Monastery.

In the second century B.C.E., the Kukkuṭārāma was destroyed by Puṣyamitra, the first of the Śiśunāga kings, in his fervor to reestablish the Brahmanic traditions and strengthen his claim to the Mauryan Empire. The rulers who succeeded Puṣyamitra were more supportive of the Dharma and allowed the monastery to be rebuilt. In the early centuries C.E., the Kukkuṭārāma became a center for Buddhist learning. At one time this monastery was associated with Aśvaghoṣa, the master who composed the Buddhacarita, an eloquent poetical account of the Buddha's life. King Kaniṣka, who directly ruled over Gandhāra and the Punjab and whose influence extended as far as Pāṭaliputra, is said to have pressured the ruler of Pāṭaliputra to send Aśvaghoṣa to his court, where Aśvaghoṣa was called upon to edit the śāstras produced during the Third Council of the Sangha.

Fa-hien arrived at Pāṭaliputra in the fifth century, having searched the monasteries of Central Asia, northwestern India, and traveled the length of the Ganges in search of the Vinaya texts, which contained the guidelines for the Sangha. Nowhere could he find the texts he wished to copy and take back to his homeland. All the Vinaya masters he met with relied on their prodigious memory and refrained from expressing the Vinaya in writing. Fa-hien finally located the works he sought in a Mahāyāna monastery at Pāṭaliputra. He was told that these Vinaya texts had been used by the Mahāsāṁghika assembly and contained the same set of precepts followed in the Jetavana Vihāra, the central monastery of Śrāvastī. Since the oral tradition was still strong, Fa-hien was able to obtain the Sarvāstivādin precepts through dictation. He observes that although the eighteen early Buddhist schools each had their own set of precepts, they differed only in minor details and agreed on the essentials.

In his writings, Fa-hien notes that Pāṭaliputra, then the capital of the vast Gupta Empire, was home to both Śrāvaka and Mahāyāna traditions: beside an Aśokan stūpa were two large monasteries at its side, one dedicated to the Mahāyāna and the other to the Śrāvaka tradition, which together housed about six to seven hundred monks. In all, this pilgrim-scholar spent three years in Pāṭaliputra, learning the language and copying such important texts as the Nirvāṇa-sūtra, Vaipulya-parinirvāṇa-sūtra, and the Mahāsāṁghika-abhidharma. His compatriot, To-ching, was so impressed by the Sangha at Pāṭaliputra and the knowledge available here that he refused to return to China.

The Hun invasion at the end of the fifth century seriously damaged Pāṭaliputra at a time when the Gupta fortunes were waning. In the seventh century, Śaśāṅka, king of Gauḍa (western Bengal) actively persecuted Buddhists in this area and demolished many temples and monasteries, It appears that Pāṭaliputra's overlord, King Harṣa, whose capital was far to the west in Kānyakubja, made no real effort to restore the city when he came to power.

When Hsüan-tsang arrived here in the seventh century, he found Pāṭaliputra "long deserted," with only the foundation walls remaining. "The saṅghārāmas, Deva (Hindu) temples, and stūpas which lie in ruins may be counted by hundreds. There are only two or three remaining (entire). To the north of the old palace, bordering on the Ganges River, there is a little town which contains about one thousand houses."

Hsüan-tsang mentions a ruined stūpa located to the south of the Garden of Hell. This garden was said to have been built by Aśoka in the early days of his reign for the purpose of enticing and slaying unwary travelers. This practice ended after the bhikṣu Samudra demonstrated the power of the Dharma in the garden and converted Aśoka to the Buddha's way. The stūpa was said to have been built by Aśoka in the middle of the royal compound after his conversion. Hsüan-tsang could clearly discern the stūpa's carved stone cupola and its surrounding balustrade. According to Hsüan-tsang, the stūpa emitted light from time to time and manifested signs of spiritual power.

A temple beside this stūpa contained an ancient shrine, said to have been built by Aśoka over a stone that bore the imprint of the Buddha's feet. When later kings sought to carry the stone away, they were unable to move it, although it was not large. Hsüan-tsang relates that when King Śaśāṅka broke this stone into pieces, it soon became whole again; when he threw it into the Ganges, it magically returned to its original place. Hsüan-tsang observes that the stone was still there and that the Buddha's footprints were clearly discernable.

Hsüan-tsang also saw a stūpa commemorating the visits of Buddhas of the past. A stone pillar nearby bore Aśoka's inscription recording that he donated his entire kingdom to the Sangha three times and bought it back with jewels and treasure. To the north of the remains of the palace was a stone house large as a mountain, which Aśoka had built for his half-brother. (Hsüan-tsang names him Mahendra, but the Avadānas refer to him as Vitāśoka, Sudatta, and Sugrātra, and the Mahāvaṁsa knows him as Tissakumāra) After Aśoka sentenced him to death for his arrogance, his brother understood the meaning of transience and awakened faith in the Dharma. Aśoka pardoned him, and he entered the Sangha at the Kukkuṭārāma, where he became an Arhat. When it became clear that the brother preferred to become a recluse rather than return to the world, Aśoka ordered that this house be built for him in Pāṭaliputra. (HT II:91–92)

Hsüan-tsang describes a great stūpa near the foundation walls of the Kukkuṭārāma, which lay to the southeast of the old city. This stūpa commemorated Aśoka's restoration to health after he offered the Sangha his last remaining possession. Nearby, another stūpa, known as Establishing the Sound of the Ghaṇṭa, was built to commemorate a great debate between Buddhists and tīrthikas (non-Buddhists) at Pāṭaliputra. When the great master Nāgārjuna was dwelling in Śrī Parvata, far to the south, tīrthikas challenged the masters at Pāṭaliputra to a debate. But the Buddhists refused the challenge, concerned that they had not developed the necessary skills and risked defeat, whereupon they would have to adopt the tīrthika's views. The king then forbade them to ring the ghaṇṭa, the bell that calls the learned ones to assemble.

For twelve years the ghaṇṭa was silent. Hearing of this, Nāgārjuna's disciple Āryadeva asked his master for permission to debate the heretics. The tīrthikas, aware of Āryadeva's skill, influenced the king to outlaw any assembly of Buddhist scholars and to prevent Āryadeva from entering the city. But Āryadeva traveled to Pāṭaliputra in disguise and made his way to the tower housing the bell. At early dawn he sounded the bell loudly. Seized and taken before the king, Āryadeva petitioned the king for an opportunity to debate the tīrthikas and demonstrate the validity of the Buddha's teaching. The king assented; Āryadeva won the debate in less than one hour, and the king built the stūpa to commemorate the restoration of the right of the Sangha to ring the ghaṇṭa.

About thirty miles southwest of the ruins of Pāṭaliputra, Hsüan-tsang came to the Tikadaka Monastery, whose four halls and high towers were connected by great double gates. This monastery, built by the last descendant of King Bimbisāra (probably Mahānandin), was a thriving Mahāyāna center housing one thousand monks. The traveler notes that scholars "flocking together in crowds" came from different cities and distant lands to live in this monastery.

The monastery's three temples, ornately carved, faced the middle gate: the middle temple held an image of Buddha about thirty feet high; an image of Tārā was enshrined in the left temple, and an image of the Bodhisattva Avalokiteśvara was in the right temple. All three images were shaped from stone. Not far from this monastery, in a mountainous declivity, nestled a monastery with about fifty Mahāyāna monks. It was here that the Buddhist master Guṇamati refuted the Saṁkhya views as propounded by Mādhava.

Although the Dharma revived in Pāṭaliputra when the Pālas rose to power in the eighth century, there is little specific information on Buddhist activities after that time. The Pāla kings lost control of Pāṭaliputra in the twelfth century, and in the thirteenth century Muslim invasions would have demolished whatever remained of Buddhism here. Today the modern city of Patna is built over many possible sites, rendering excavation nearly impossible. But considering that since the thirteenth century this site has been continually occupied by non-Buddhists, it is not likely that many remains of Buddhist activities could be found in this once flourishing center of the Dharma.

Kauśāmbī

The city of Kauśāmbī (Pāli, Kosāmbī, modern Kosām), was the capital of the ancient kingdom of Vatsa. Its location on the Yamunā River, close to the confluence of the Ganges, made it an important center of communication and trade between the eastern, northern, and western regions of India. Connected by routes leading north to the cities of Mathurā and Indraprasthā, east to Prayāga, Vārāṇasī, and Pāṭaliputra, and southwest to Ujjayinī, gateway to the western seaports, Kauśāmbī rose to prominence some centuries before the time of the Buddha. The Rāmāyana relates that Kauśāmbī was one of four cities (Kauśāmbī, Mahodaya, Dharmaranya, and Girivraja, ancient Rājagṛha) founded by the four sons of King Kuśa. The classical epics suggest that the city was laid out by its first ruler, Kuśamba, but according to the Paramāṭṭhajotika (a commentary on the Suttanipāta), Kauśāmbī was originally the dwelling place of the sage Kosamba. Other accounts relate the name to the Kosamba tree, said to have grown here in abundance.

At the Buddha's time Kauśāmbī was ruled by Udayana, who figures in several of the Buddha's teachings. Udayana and his kingdom appear to have served as a buffer between Magadha on the east and Avanti on the west; for a time the Avanti king Pradyota was on the verge of invading Magadha, ruled by Bimbisāra, but his conflicts with Udayana distracted him from this effort.

Udayana appears to have been a strong political force in his time. Buddhist accounts relate his abduction and escape from Pradyota, his elopement with Pradyota's daughter, and his sporadic skirmishes with Pradyota's army. A fiercely passionate man, Udayana was jealous of his wives' interest in the Dharma; he was rude to the Buddha's cousin Ānanda and attempted to have another disciple, Piṇḍola Bhāradvāja, killed by red ants. Finally, however, convinced of the benefits and power of the Dharma, Udayana permitted the Buddha's disciples to teach in his country.

Canonical accounts of the Parinirvāṇa mention Kauśāmbī as one of the six principal cities of northern India. According to the southern tradition, the Buddha spent two rainy seasons here. The fifth century scholar Buddhaghosa relates that three merchants of Kauśāmbī—Ghosita, Kukkuṭa, and Pāvārika—traveled by elephant to Śrāvastī. They met the Buddha in Jeta's Grove and invited him to Kauśāmbī, then returned home where each merchant built a place of retreat (arāma) for the Buddha and his disciples. These three retreats—the Ghositārāma, Kukkuṭārāma, and Pāvārikārāma—became important Dharma centers in the time of the Buddha; their influence increased when Kauśāmbī rose to prominence in the Aśokan Empire in the third century B.C.E.

The Ghositārāma in particular had a long and distinguished history; the Mahāvaṁsa mentions that thirty thousand bhikṣus from the Ghositārāma, headed by the Thera Urudhammarakkhita, came to Śrī Laṅkā in the first century B.C.E. during the reign of King Duṭṭhagāmini. The Kukkuṭārāma is remembered as the place where Vasubandhu composed the Vidyāmātratā-siddhi, and the Pāvārikārāma is where his older brother Asaṅga wrote the Yogācārabhūmi-śāstra. A fourth center, Badarikārāma, is mentioned in the Petavatthu, but its location is unknown.

In the third century, Aśoka issued the Edict of Kosām, in which he upheld the Dharma and discouraged individuals from provoking dissent in the community. (The pillar bearing this edict is now in Allahabad.) Fa-hien, writing in the fifth century, reports that monks of the Śrāvaka schools were dwelling in Kauśāmbī, but the Ghositārāma was in ruins.

When Hsüan-tsang visited the same area in the seventh century—after traveling southwest from Prayāga through "a forest infested by wild elephants and other fierce animals"—he found more than ten monasteries in the area, but all were in ruins. Only three hundred monks of the Śrāvaka tradition still resided in the area. Hsüan-tsang located the Ghositārāma outside the city on the southeast side next to an Aśokan stūpa that stood over two hundred feet high, revered for its healing power. (An inscription discovered at this site in recent times has confirmed this location.) Hsüan-tsang describes the Kukkuṭārāma, a two-storied building, as located to the southwest of the Ghositārāma, while Pāvārika's Mango Grove was to its east. The existence of the Pāvārikārāma, however, could only be inferred from the foundations of a building on the site.

Hsüan-tsang records that the country of Kauśāmbī was six thousand li (about one thousand miles) in circumference and the capital city itself was about thirty li (six miles). "The land is famous for its productivity. . . rice and sugarcane are plentiful. The climate is very hot, the manners of the people hard and rough. They cultivate learning and are very earnest in their religious life and in virtue." (HT I:235)

Hsüan-tsang also describes a temple housing a sandalwood statue of the seated Buddha. This statue, said to have been the first representation of the Buddha, was carved while the Buddha was dwelling in the Trāyastriṁśa Heaven teaching the Dharma to his mother. (A similar account describes this statue as having been carved in Śrāvastī.) In the seventh century the sandalwood statue stood in a vihāra sixty feet high, with a stone canopy raised above it; from time to time it emitted a divine light. Hsüan-tsang states that although princes of other countries had tried to carry the statue away, no one could move it. These rulers then had copies made of it in their kingdoms and maintained that these copies were actually the original.

According to the local tradition, King Udayana had asked Maudgalyāyana to transport an artist to heaven to observe the Buddha teaching so that the artist could carve his form. When the Buddha returned to earth, the statue rose to greet him, and the Buddha told the statue, "To teach and convert the unbelieving, to open the way for guiding future generations, that is your work." (Although this account is very similar to the description of the statue carved in Śrāvastī, the Vinaya mentions both statues.) About a hundred paces east of the temple of the sandalwood statue were traces of visits by earlier Buddhas of our aeon. There was also a well used by the Buddha and the ruins of the Buddha's bathing house.

Today Kauśāmbī is in ruins. The fortifications that remain on the flat ground of the site are still thirty feet high, and two small villages have grown up within the site's circumference. Although the overall scene is one of desolation, the sculpture and other art found in the region indicate that Kauśāmbī was long a major center of art and culture.

Sāketa

Sāketa, where the Buddha resided in the rainy seasons during the later part of his life, is identified by some scholars with the ancient city of Ayodhyā. The Rāmāyana, which uses the names Sāketa and Ayodhyā interchangeably, claims the city was founded by Manu, progenitor of all human beings. The Ayodhyā of Rāma is said to have been destroyed about 1426 B.C.E., and to have been deserted until the time of King Vikramāditya, who rebuilt the city as a memorial to Rāma. It is possible that this is the same Vikramāditya who was a powerful prince of Śrāvastī around 78 C.E.

The Dhammapada commentary, by contrast, relates that Sāketa was founded by Dhanañjaya, a wealthy merchant and father of the patroness Viśākhā. Both Buddhist and Brahmanic sources place Sāketa/Ayodhyā in the same region, on the bank of the Gomatī River in the ancient kingdom of Kosala, about midway between Śrāvastī and Kauśāmbī. In his report for the Archaeological Survey of India in 1862–63, Cunningham suggests that ruins at Sujankot, near Faizabad on the modern Ghāgra River, were the remains of Ayodhyā and Sāketa (the Sha-chi of Fa-hien and the Viśākha of Hsüan-tsang. Hsüan-tsang names another site 'O-yu-t'o, which probably refers to Ayodhyā.) The ruins at Sujankot are still largely unexplored; further research may clarify the relationship between Ayodhyā and Sāketa. In this discussion, Ayodhyā and Sāketa are described separately.

Viśākhā, a lay disciple of the Buddha, lived in Sāketa until her marriage to Pūrṇavardhana, son of Mṛgara, the wealthiest merchant in Śrāvastī. The Vinaya records her generosity to the Sangha, relating that she sold a necklace of great price to purchase land for the Pūrvārāma in Śrāvastī. The story of Viśākhā, the Sangha's foremost patroness, has survived the centuries as an example of devotion and selfless generosity. There was also a Pūrvārāma in Sāketa, which was said to have been built by the same Viśākhā. So connected is Viśākhā's name to this location that Hsüan-tsang refers to the entire city as Viśākhā. Coins found only at Sāketa bear inscriptions of Dhanadeva and Viśākhādatta, supporting this connection.

In the Buddha's time, the city of Sāketa had little political importance and appears to have been a rather small city. The Mahāvaṁsa mentions the existence of only two early monasteries there: the Pūrvārāma and the Kālakārāma. By the time of Hsüan-tsang, however, the city was thriving: "The country produces abundance of cereals, and is rich in flowers and fruits. The climate is mild and agreeable." (HT I:239) Hsüan-tsang describes the people of Saketa/Viśakha as being pure and honest, diligent in study and in the performance of meritorious actions. He counted twenty monasteries housing three thousand monks of the Saṁmatīya tradition, noting the presence of fifty Brahmanic temples and many adherents of the Brahmanic traditions.

South of the city was a large monastery. According to Hsüan-tsang, this was where the Arhat Devasarma wrote the Vijñānakāya-śāstra, "in which he defends the position that there is an 'I' as an individual. These doctrines excited much controversial discussion." (HT I:240) This was also the place where the Bodhisattva Dharmapāla successfully debated one hundred scholars of the Hīnayāna traditions. An Aśokan stūpa stood next to the monastery. Beside the stūpa there was a "wonderful tree" six or seven feet high, which always remained the same height. This is where the Buddha threw onto the ground a small twig he had used to brush his teeth; the twig took root and produced this tree. Despite efforts by heretics to cut the tree down, the tree soon grew back. Not far from the stūpa Hsüan-tsang found traces of visits by past Buddhas of our aeon; another stūpa nearby contained relics of the Buddha's hair and nail parings. "Sacred buildings here follow one another in succession; the woods, and lakes reflecting their shadows, are seen everywhere." (HT I:240)

In the 1860s, Cunningham, following Hsüan-tsang's description of the monasteries and the stūpa, identified a large mound south of Sāketa as the Aśokan stupa mentioned by Hsüan-tsang and another, more rectangular mound, as being one of the two early monasteries. A third mound appears to be the remains of the hair and nail stūpa described by Hsüan-tsang. To date, none of these sites has been fully researched.

'O-yu-t'o

'O-yu-t'o, located in the ancient kingdom of Kosala, on the Ganges at the western edge of the Madhyadeśa, was described by Hsüan-tsang as a thriving city-state: "The climate is temperate and agreeable, the manners of the people virtuous and amiable; they love the duties of religion and diligently devote themselves to learning." The pilgrim found in the area approximately one hundred monasteries and three thousand monks who studied the texts of both Śrāvaka and Mahāyāna traditions. He also visited the monastery where Vasubandhu spent several decades and composed śāstras systematizing the Abhidharma. Beside the monastery were the ruins of a teaching hall where the master Vasubandhu had explained the Dharma for the benefit of "kings of different countries, eminent men of the world, Śramaṇas and Brahmins." (HT I:225)

North of the city, on the banks of the Ganges, stood a large monastery adjacent to a large Aśokan stūpa. According to Hsüan-tsang, this was where the Buddha taught the Dharma for three months for the benefit of a congregation of devas. Beside this stūpa was another stūpa commemorating the place where the four Buddhas of the past once walked. About a mile west of the monastery was another stūpa that contained relics of the Tathāgata's hair and nails.

Ruins of the monastery of Śrīlabdha, who was a master of the Sautrāntika teachings, were located north of the hair and nail stūpa. About a mile southwest of the city was another monastery in a grove of mango trees; Hsüan-tsang states that this was the monastery where the great Mahāyāna master Asaṅga spent many years studying and teaching. Hsüan-tsang tells of how Asaṅga ascended from this monastery to the heavenly palace of Maitreya, obtained five important treatises from the great Bodhisattva, and taught them to his congregation here upon his return. (HT I:226) Hsüan-tsang also mentions Buddhasiṁha, disciple of Asaṅga, a man "of high talent and wide renown." (HT I:227) About eight miles northwest of Asaṅga's monastery stood a vihāra where Vasubandhu heard one of Asaṅga's disciples reciting the Daśabhūmika-sūtra and became aware of the significance of Mahāyāna teachings.

After extensive research, Cunningham identified Hsüan-tsang's 'O-yu-t'o with the town of Kākūpur, which in ancient times was a large city with a king of its own. In the nineteenth century, the ruins of the city consisted of many foundations made of large bricks, and a connected set of walls which was known locally as "the palace." There is some speculation that Kākūpur may be identified with the story of Sampaka, related in the Mūlasarvāstivādin Vinaya. (AR XX:88) Sampaka, a Śākya warrior, was exiled for drawing his bow on Virūḍhaka's army as it approached to attack Kapilavastu. (The Śākyas, following the Buddha's injunction not to take life, had forbidden the killing of their persecutors.) Sampaka made his way to the country of Bagud or Vagud, where he became king. If Bagud is indeed Kākūpur, the royal lineage of that kingdom descends from the Śākyas.

The University of Nālandā

The Madhyadeśa nurtured the rise of hundreds of monastic centers that supported concentrated study and practice of the Buddha's teachings. Some of these monasteries became famous throughout Asia for the excellence of their scholars, the quality of their educational programs, the elegance of their statuary and ornamentation, and their extensive collections of Buddhist texts. The earliest and most prestigious was the great university of Nālandā.

During the Buddha's lifetime, Nālandā was a small but prosperous Brahmin settlement seven miles north of Rājagṛha on the main route from King Bimbisāra's royal city to Vaiśālī, Śrāvastī, and the cities along the Ganges River. Through the years scholars have speculated on the origin of the name Nālandā, which has several possible derivations. Nāla means 'reed', and nālinī refers to a kind of lotus; Nālandā's many ponds were said to have been covered with lotuses, suggesting the name Nāḷandā for the entire village. I-tsing (seventh century C.E.,) wrote that Nālandā may have taken its name from the nāga king Nanda, considered to have inhabited a pool in that area. (A pond can still be seen just to the south of the ruins of Nālandā, exactly as Hsüan-tsang described it.)

According to a third line of reasoning, Nālandā means Charity without an End, or Sufficient to Provide for All. The town appears to have indeed been known for its charity and hospitality: the Sūtras portray Nālandā as a rich and flourishing village and describe the generosity of those who lived there, as in the account of the merchant Lepa, who once hosted the Buddha. Hsüan-tsang suggests another possibility for the origin of this name. In a past life as King Nālandā, the Buddha had established his capital here, which was named after the king. Nālandā is also known as Nālaka, Nālakagrama, and Nālendra.

The Mahāparinirvāṇa-sūtra relates that the Buddha visited Nālandā many times on his travels, often stopping at Pāvārika's Mango Grove to give teachings. On one such journey, the Buddha met his great disciple Mahākāśyapa, who immediately recognized the Buddha as the master he sought. The Brahmajāla-sūtra describes an example of how teachings unfolded as the Buddha traveled in company with the Sangha. As the Buddha was walking with his disciples from Rājagṛha to Nālandā, a vigorous dialogue arose between the Brahmin Suppiya and his student Brahmadatta, who were walking the road behind them. All the travelers stayed the night at the Mango Grove, where Suppiya and his disciple argued well into the evening. In the morning, the Buddha explained to his disciples the pitfalls of the two extremes of nihilism and eternalism. Caught up in the net of such views, beings are like Suppiya and his disciple: resolution and peace elude them and they can only struggle until they become exhausted.

According to Hsüan-tsang, five hundred merchants eventually bought the Mango Grove with its large central pond and donated it to the Buddha; the Buddha then taught the Dharma here for three months.

Nālandā's environs encompassed the villages of Kalapinaka and Killika, the birthplaces of Śāriputra and Maudgalyāyana respectively. These two great disciples entered nirvāṇa at Nālandā together with many thousands of their followers before the Buddha departed on his final journey. Shortly after that time, when the Enlightened One told Ānanda that he would pass away in Kuśinagara, Ānanda proposed Nālandā as a superior location. Ānanda argued that Nālandā was an even more auspicious site for departing the world than the ṛṣipatana at Sārnāth, the place where the ṛṣis entered nirvāṇa upon hearing that a Buddha was about to be born.

Eventually, stūpas were erected at Nālandā in honor of Śāriputra and Maudgalyāyana and their relics were placed inside them. Although Ajātaśatru supported the Sangha in all parts of his kingdom, there is no clear evidence that a permanent Buddhist settlement was established here in the early centuries after the Parinirvāṇa. When the capital of Magadha was moved to Pāṭaliputra, the Brahmins attached to the royal court may well have followed their king. Isolated from trade routes and no longer the seat of power, Rājagṛha declined and Nālandā sank into oblivion.

According to Tāranātha, who provides one of the few sources for Nālandā's early history, the village of Nālandā was in ruins at the time of Aśoka. Aśoka is said to have visited Nālandā on his pilgrimage; he gave offerings and erected a temple or shrine at the stūpa of Śāriputra.

About four hundred years after the Parinirvāṇa, when five hundred Mahāyāna bhaṭṭarakas (teachers) decided to build a center for the propagation of the Mahāyāna, Nālandā was chosen as the place from which the Mahāyāna would spread most widely. On the site where Aśoka had built Nālandā's first temple, the brothers Udbhaṭa and Śaṁkarapati, greatly learned in philosophy, built eight new temples for the five hundred Mahāyāna masters. Tāranātha mentions Avitarka as one of the original five hundred masters. The scholar Rāhulabhadra came to Nālandā in Avitarka's lifetime; he was ordained by the bhaṭṭāraka Rāhulaprabha or by the bhaṭṭāraka Kṛṣṇa. These masters laid the foundation for the new monastery that was to become a renowned center of learning.

The five hundred masters who established Nālandā brought with them the Mahāyāna Sūtras that had recently been committed to writing, and additional Sūtras were brought here as they came to light. The library of the monastery at Nālandā soon became the central repository of Mahāyāna texts. Also famous for its extensive Abhidharma collection, Nālandā's library supported the growth of a strong tradition of study, practice, and scholarship.

From the outset, the monastery of Nālandā produced a lineage of outstanding masters who set standards of excellence for those who followed in their footsteps. The most famous of these masters was Nāgārjuna, disciple of Rāhulabhadra, also known as the siddha Saraha. According to Buston, astrologers had told Nāgārjuna's parents that their son would live only seven years. Unable to bear their son's impending death, the parents sent the child away from their home in the care of a servant. Nāgārjuna came to Nālandā's gate, where he met the master Saraha. Following Saraha's instructions, Nāgārjuna overcame the prediction of an early death and entered the Sangha at Nālandā.

Centuries before Nālandā attracted the generosity of royal patrons, Nāgārjuna worked tirelessly to support its teachers and establish its educational standards. Mastering Rāhulabhadra's teachings, he penetrated the deep meanings of the Mahāyāna Sūtras and developed a skillful dialectic to convey the Madhyama, or Middle Way, that avoided the extremes of eternalism and nihilism. Challenging all doctrines of reality current in his day and demonstrating their fallacies, he extended the powers of reason to their limits, pointing beyond concepts to the immediate experience of reality.

The great master's work was continued by his disciple Āryadeva, who studied under Nāgārjuna in South India. Āryadeva came to Nālandā as a mature scholar; according to Tāranātha, he defeated the formidable tīrthika (non-Buddhist) philosopher Durdharṣakāla and converted him to the Buddhist doctrine. In the Tibetan tradition, Durdharṣakāla is also known as Mātṛceṭa or Aśvaghoṣa. Outside of Tibet, Mātṛceta and Aśvaghoṣa are often considered two different masters. Poetry of exquisite beauty is attributed to both names, but little is known of their lives or of their disciples. After Āryadeva, a succession of masters continued Nāgārjuna's lineage, which developed into the philosophical school known as Mādhyamika, those who follow the Middle Way.

According to Tāranātha, Asaṅga, renowned as the transcriber of the treatises of Maitreya and an outstanding explicator of the 'higher Abhidharma', lived at Nālandā for twelve years toward the end of his life. After his death, his brother Vasubandhu, author of the Abhidharmakoṣa and its commentary, became Nālandā's principal teacher. Vasubandhu is remembered in history as a master teacher; among the many disciples attributed to him were the great logician Dignāga, the philosopher Sthiramati, the Vinaya master Guṇabhadra, and Vimuktasena, learned explicator of Prajñāpāramitā.

By the end of the fourth or the early fifth century, Nālandā had become the major center for the lineages of Nāgārjuna and Asaṅga. From these lineages stemmed the two major Mahāyāna philosophical schools, Mādhyamika and Cittamātra. In the fifth century, Buddhapālita and Bhāvaviveka, philosophers who matured at Nālanda within Nāgārjuna's lineage, developed two major branches of Mādhyamika, while the followers of Asaṅga and Vasubandhu integrated the philosophy of Cittamātra into the practice system of Yogācāra. Sthiramati, who worked with Vasubandhu at Nālandā, developed the Abhidharma and extended Vasubandhu's teachings on consciousness through his commentaries.

Graduates of Nālandā returned to their home areas or traveled widely to extend the Dharma. Nāgārjuna and Āryadeva exemplified the selfless compassion of the Mahāyāna masters who traveled wherever their talents were most needed. Asaṅga and Vasubandhu, originally from Gandhāra in the far northwest, are said to have taught in many regions of India, Asaṅga in the west and Vasubandhu in Orissa. The South Indian masters Buddhapālita and Bhāvaviveka offered their knowledge and skills to their disciples in the south. Sthiramati went west to Valabhī, where he helped found or developed a monastery into a major center for Abhidharma and Vijñānavāda. Through the accomplishments of its outstanding masters, Nālandā became respected throughout India.

Rise of Nālandā University

As the excellence of Nālandā's scholarship became widely known, Buddhist scholars from all parts of India began traveling to Nālandā to study new methods of inquiry and engage in stimulating dialogues with Nālandā's paṇḍitas. After Durdharṣakāla, other non-Buddhist philosophers came to Nālandā to test their skills in debate. Many of Nālandā's great paṇḍitas rose to prominence by meeting such challenges with knowledge, vigor, and finely developed intellectual powers.

By the middle of the fifth century, the greatest intellects of the age, both Buddhist and non-Buddhist, were focusing their attention on complex epistemological views and doctrines. Here logic came to the fore, providing guidelines for the proofs of valid knowledge. Building on the philosophical systems developing in his time, the great logician Dignāga established the science of knowledge known as Pramāṇa.

According to Tāranātha, Dignāga, having completed his studies at Nālandā, was meditating in a cave in Kaliṅga when he heard that the tīrthika philosophers were challenging the paṇḍitas of Nālandā. Returning to Nālandā, Dignāga thoroughly addressed their doctrines, defeating the tīrthikas not once, but three times in succession. As a result, many of them converted to Buddhism and went on to work for the Dharma.

Such displays of intellectual accomplishments attracted the notice of the Gupta rulers, strong patrons of the arts who ruled northern India from 320 C.E. through the mid-sixth century. Although these kings were not Buddhists themselves, those who ruled in the fifth century supported Nālandā's expansion into a major university. According to Hsuan-tsang, Nālandā's main monastery was built by Śakrāditya, a king of the Gupta dynasty "who respected and esteemed the One Vehicle." (Śakrāditya, 'Sun of Power', is probably Kumāragupta I, who ruled between 415 and 455 C.E.)

An auspicious place was located for the foundation of the new monastery, but when the workers began digging, they wounded the body of a nāga. A distinguished soothsayer told the builders that the saṅghārāma they were building would become highly renowned; it would flourish a thousand years and become a model throughout greater India. But because the nāga was wounded here, the site would suffer disasters and much blood would be spilled.

The Gupta rulers continued to build at Nālandā throughout the fifth century. Purugupta, brother of Skandagupta, may also have been a patron of Nālandā. Coin evidence equates him with Śrī Vikrama; he (or his ancestor Candragupta II) may have been the same King Vikramāditya who allowed Vasubandhu to debate with the tīrthikas, an event which restored the prestige of the Dharma when it was at its ebb in northern India. Hsüan-tsang relates that "A long succession of kings continued the work of building Nālandā, using all the skill of the sculptor, till the whole is truly marvelous to behold." He adds that Buddhagupta built a monastery to the south of the great saṅghārāma. Tathāgatagupta built a monastery to the east, and Balāditya built a monastery to the northeast. Balāditya convened a great assembly to celebrate the completion of this monastery, inviting adherents of all religions as well as the common people. According to Hsüan-tsang, Balāditya later abdicated his throne and became a monk. After Balāditya, his son Vajra built a monastery on the west side of Nālandā.[1]

During the height of Gupta power, Nālandā rapidly expanded into an extensive complex of temples, shrines, and lecture and residential halls with a large and diverse population of faculty and students administered by an abbot. Construction on this scale required a large number of artisans; fortunately, this period of Nālandā's growth coincided with a major artistic renaissance throughout the Gupta Empire; Nālandā's prestige made it a worthy recipient of the sponsorship of kings and wealthy patrons alike, enabling Nālandā to benefit greatly from the work of India's finest artisans.

Nālandā at the Time of King Harṣa

In describing Nālandā at the time of King Harṣa, Hsüan-tsang writes of its wonders, limiting himself to only a few of the hundreds of buildings, shrines, images, and other monuments within the university complex. Thus we know that in the seventh century the pool of the nāga Nālandā was located south of the monastery; to its west was the vihāra where the Buddha taught the Dharma for three months. To the south a small stūpa marked the place where a bhikṣu from a distant land honored the Buddha and expressed a wish to become a cakravartin monarch. Also to the south stood a large figure of the Bodhisattva Avalokiteśvara and near it a stūpa with

1. Hsüan-tsang's Buddhagupta has been variously identified as the Gupta king Buddhagupta (477–500 C.E.) and as Skandagupta (456–467 C.E.) King Balāditya may be Narasiṁhagupta (470–473 C.E.), and Vajra may be Kumāragupta, who assumed the throne around 473 C.E. Seals found at Nālandā also associate Vajra with Viṣṇugupta.

Nālandā's Monastery 1, showing monastic cells surrounding central assembly halls

relics of the Buddha's hair and nails. A second image of Avalokiteśvara stood in the vihāra to the north. To the north the magnificent great hall built by Balādityarāja rose to a height of three hundred feet above the ground. Hsüan-tsang noted that this vihāra and the Buddha statue inside it resembled the great vihāra and its Buddha image at Bodh Gayā.

To the south of the great vihāra; another vihāra was being built under the sponsorship of Śīlādityarāja (King Harṣa). Hsüan-tsang described the vihāra as made of brass; if finished according to plan, it would be one hundred feet in length. There were also stūpas within the complex that marked places where Śākyamuni Buddha taught and where Buddhas of the past had sat in meditation. Hsüan-tsang saw several remarkable monuments outside Nālandā's perimeter wall. Among them was an eighty-foot-tall standing figure of the Buddha, made of copper, which Hsüan-tsang describes as having been donated by King Pūrṇavarma. North of this statue, enshrined in a brick vihāra, was a very tall figure of Tārā, a focal point

Stairs lead to the top of the main temple of Nālandā.

of festivals and ceremonies. On holy days, kings, ministers, and visiting dignitaries from neighboring states offered at this shrine "exquisite perfumes and flowers, holding gem-covered flags and canopies, while instruments of metal and stone resound in turns, mingled with the harmony of flutes and

Temples with niches for statuary stand on each corner; a stūpa is at the left.

harps. These religious assemblies last for seven days." (HT II:174–176) Hsüan-tsang goes on to tell how a king of Central India built a great monastery to the north of the main complex and surrounded the whole by a high wall constructed with only one gate. This 'king of central India' is most likely King

Harṣa (Harṣavardhana of Kanauj, reigned c. 606–647), who was ruling at the time of Hsüan-tsang's visit. Hsüan-tsang refers to Harṣa as a king who contributed significantly to Nālandā's development, including the donation of revenues from one hundred villages and two hundred households for the maintenance of its monasteries.

Nālandā's Legacy to the Dharma

As its reputation grew, Nālandā attracted scholars and students from all of India and eventually from the entire Buddhist world. Winning admission to the great university was an attainment in itself, and completion of its rigorous training ensured its graduates prestigious positions. Non-Buddhists and Buddhist laymen graduates went on to serve the royal courts or uphold various educational disciplines. Buddhist monks from Nālandā staffed the growing number of Mahāyāna monasteries and traveled to other lands to support Dharma transmission.

At Nālandā, Kamalabuddhi and Candrakīrti, heirs to the lineage of Buddhapālita, developed to perfection his dialectic device of prasaṅga, or 'necessary consequence' that defeats all statements concerning reality. In this they established the school known as Prāsaṅgika-Mādhyamika, while those who followed Bhāvaviveka's approach developed the Svātantrika-Mādhyamika school. In the late sixth or early seventh century, Nālandā witnessed perhaps the most prolonged and famous intellectual contest of its history, the great debate between Candrakīrti (then the upādhyāya, or head teacher of Nālandā) and the lay scholar Candragomin. Candrakīrti propounded the Mādhyamika as established by Nāgārjuna and Buddhapālita, and Candragomin championed the doctrine of vijñāna following the view of Asaṅga. According to Tāranātha, the debate continued for seven years and drew a large audience from the surrounding community. So equally matched were both masters, and so sound were both approaches to realization, that neither could refute the other. This debate stands as a classic in the annals of Buddhist history.

In the seventh century, Dharmapāla, native of Kāñcīpura and master teacher at Vajrāsana, became upādhyāya after Candrakīrti. Dharmapāla enhanced Nālandā's reputation by effectively refuting Saṁkhya and Vaiśeṣika views. He ordained the great logician Dharmakīrti (c. 600–660), whom I-tsing groups with Dharmapāla and Śīlabhadra as one of the famous men 'of late years'. Tāranātha records that the master Dharmapāla was upādhyāya for only a short time, and that he was succeeded by Jayadeva, teacher of Sāntideva, author of the Bodhicaryāvatāra, and the siddha Virūpa. Hsüan-tsang, however, places Dharmapāla immediately before his own mentor, Śīlabhadra.

According to Hsüan-tsang, Dharmapāla retired just before the Chinese pilgrim arrived at Nālandā in 635 C.E. Śīlabhadra, son of a king of Samataṭa (Bengal) and Dharmapāla's disciple, then became upādhyāya of Nālandā. During Hsüan-tsang's years at Nālandā, he studied with Śīlabhadra, engaged in debate with an accomplished non-Buddhist philosopher, and greatly impressed the Nālandā scholars with his mastery of Buddhist doctrine.

By Hsüan-tsang's time, Nālandā was an international center of learning. Pilgrims arrived at Nālandā not only from places throughout India, from Kashmir on the northwest to Kāñcīpura on the southeast, but also from China, Korea, and Tibet. Some, like Hsüan-tsang, traveled thousands of miles overland along the Silk Road, through Central Asia, Gandhāra, and the Khyber Pass, then southeast to Mathurā and Kauśāmbī, and along the Ganges to Nālandā. Others, like I-tsing, traveled the precarious sea route along the islands of Java, Sumatra, the Malacca Straits, up the coast of Burma, past Arakan, to Tāmralipti at the mouth of the Ganges. I-tsing, who arrived at Tāmralipti in 673 C.E. and traveled inland to

Detail of a corner temple, a shrine, and a stūpa of Nālandā's central monument.

Nālandā, met fifty-seven pilgrims from China and Korea during his ten years' sojourn at the great university.

During I-tsing's time, Nālandā had six colleges with a total student body of between three and five thousand students, housed in eight multistoried vihāras. Three buildings, the Ratnasāgara, Ratnodadhi (where the Prajñāpāramitā Sūtras and numerous Tantras were stored), and the Ratnāgañjaka, housed the university's library, famed for its collection of Abhidharma and Mahāyāna texts. I-tsing described Nālandā's central temple: "The building is four square, like a city. There are four large gateways of three stories each. Each story is some ten feet in height. The whole is covered with tiles." (Beal, JRAS (n.s.) 13:571) Concerning Nālandā's masters, he relates that "All these men are equally renowned for their brilliant character, equal to the ancients and anxious to follow in the steps of the sages. When they have understood the arguments of logic, they aspire to be like Jina (Dignāga); while testing the doctrine of Yogācāra, they zealously search into the theory of Asaṅga. When they discourse on 'non-existence,', they imitate Nāgārjuna, while when treating of 'existence', they thoroughly fathom the teaching of Saṁghabhadra."

Nālandā During the Pāla Dynasty

The Pāla kings ruled an area including Bihār and Bengal from the eighth to the tenth centuries and governed a smaller area in eastern India during the eleventh and early twelfth centuries. Most of the Pāla kings were Buddhists and generous supporters of the Dharma; they built new monasteries, provided artisans for beautifying the monasteries and universities that flourished during their reign, and sponsored the needs of masters and students. During the reigns of Gopāla, Dharmapāla, and Devapāla, who ruled in the eighth and ninth centuries, Nālandā reached the height of its splendor.

In the eighth century, Nālandā's head teacher was the great scholar Śāntarakṣita, holder of the Vinaya lineage transmitted through the Buddha's son Rāhula and the lineages of all streams of Mahāyāna philosophy and logic. (Śāntarakṣita may have also been associated with the university of Vikramaśīla, which was built by Dharmapāla in the eighth century.) After Śāntarakṣita went to Tibet at the invitation of King Khri-srong-lde-btsan, his disciple Haribhadra continued his lineage in India. A second disciple, Kamalaśīla, continued Śāntarakṣita's work in Tibet.

Nālandā's renown continued to inspire admiration. In the ninth century, during Devapāla's reign, Bālaputradeva, king of Suvarṇadvīpa (the 'Golden Island', Sumatra), had a new monastery constructed here. A ninth-century copper plate inscription found at Nālandā records that the monastery built by Bālaputradeva was white with lofty stuccoed dwellings, intended to house monks of good qualities. (EI XIV:327) This inscription relates that Nālandā was a center where venerable

This twelve-armed representation of the Bodhisattva Avalokiteśvara is among the treasures of the Nālandā Museum.

bhikṣus assembled from the four quarters; it was a place where resided Bodhisattvas well-versed in Tantras, a store-house for jewels of the Dharma (rare manuscripts) that attracted many learned paṇḍitas, and an emporium which supplied medicine to the sick, alms to the beggar, garments to the naked, and shelter to the homeless. (JBRS 30:205)

Little is known of Nālandā's later history. The Chinese Buddhist schools were disrupted in the ninth century and Tibet also went through a period of disruption and political turmoil. Although Tibetans traveled to India from the tenth century on, the focus of their studies appears to have shifted from Nālandā to the newer universities built nearby, most notably to Vikramaśīla. From the eighth century on, both universities appear to have shared the same upādhyāya. Although the Pālas who reigned in the tenth century had lost the western part of their empire, they continued to support Nālandā and provide for its statuary and ornamentation. It is likely that as Muslim incursions disrupted religion and culture in western and northwestern India, Nālandā provided a refuge for scholars from those lands. In eastern Magadha and Bengal, the Dharma and the traditional arts continued to flourish through the tenth and eleventh centuries.

The last Pāla patron was King Govindapāladeva, who died in 1197. But years before, around 1144, the Senas had taken nearly all that remained of the Pāla Empire. The Senas, who ruled eastern India after 1144, neither supported nor protected Buddhism. (There is some speculation that the Senas fortified Nālandā, which had high walls protected by gates, and used part of it as a garrison. It is clear from the writings of contemporary Arab historians that the invading Turks perceived Nālandā to be a fort.)

Soon, however, with the invasion of the Muslim Ghūrids, a Turkish tribe (Tāranātha's Turuṣkas), the Sena kings retreated into the easternmost regions of Bengal while Muhammad Bhakhtyār Khaljī (1197–1206) and his army systematically destroyed the great Buddhist centers of Magadha and Aṅga. Nālandā, Vikramaśīla, Odantapurī, Somapurī, and probably even more Buddhist centers fell victim to Muhammad Khaljī's wave of destruction. His army was finally stopped by border tribes in the foothills between Assam and Tibet, where the Brahmaputra River descends from the Tibetan plateau.

Tāranātha relates that a portion of the Turuṣka army encamped nearby and for some years thereafter mounted raid after raid on Nālandā and other monasteries in Bihār. Although monks appear to have reoccupied the site, invaders continued their policy of destruction. In 1235 the Tibetan monk Dharmasvāmin traveled to Nālandā, where he found the temples and vihāras badly damaged and sparsely inhabited. While he was there, three hundred Turuṣkas descended upon Nālandā, killing all present save for Dharmasvāmin and an aged abbot, who concealed themselves inside one of the two temples spared. While some religious activity may have persisted in the ruins, the university of Nālandā effectively ceased to exist in the thirteenth century.

According to Tāranātha, the destruction by the Turuṣkas was the third time that Nālandā had suffered great losses through fire. The first occurred when the Huns swept through this area and attacked Pāṭaliputra around 500 C.E.; the second was inflicted by tīrthikas bent on avenging an insult, which happened shortly after the earlier damage was repaired; and the last was the final destruction at the hands of the Turks. Thousands of manuscripts, including Nālandā's extensive collection of Abhidharma texts, were lost in these calamities. Bu-ston gives a list of texts known to have been partially or completely lost, but the actual loss may be far greater.

Recovery of Nālandā

For centuries, even the name of Nālandā was forgotten in India. The site became known locally as Baragaon, a corrupt

A large shrine at Nālandā surrounded by small votive stūpas

form of Vihāragrāma, or village of the monastery. In the 1860s, when this site was identified as Nālandā, the remains of the great university consisted of numerous masses of brick ruins; a row of high conical mounds represented the ruins of gigantic temples attached to the main monastery of Nālandā, and countless smaller mounds in the landscape covered the remains of many additional stūpas and buildings. However, the pool of the nāga Nālandā could be seen to the south of the monastery; the central monastery's foundations, readily discernable, measured 1600 by 400 feet. Systematic excavations began in 1915–1916, and continued through 1982–1983.

Modern archaeological research and excavations have located nearly all the sites Hsüan-tsang described. According to Cunningham, the archaeologist who worked here in the 1860s, the ruins of Nālandā were so extensive that the first people to examine the site thought this must have been a king's palace, and some residents of this area considered it the palace of

Bimbisāra and his ancestors. Cunningham's identification of this site as Nālandā was confirmed by the discovery of seals bearing the name Nālandā Mahāvihāra.

Nālandā has now been extensively excavated, revealing a gigantic complex of monasteries, stūpas, temples, and roads. Most of the ruins belong to the Pāla period, dating from the eighth to the twelfth centuries, with only a very few finds predating the Pāla Dynasty. As of this writing, the excavated area of Nālandā is surrounded by grass lawns and gardens; an occasional rise in the land indicates foundations of buildings erected outside Nālandā's main wall, which have yet to be excavated. When one considers that the long path to the main gate passes through a park once filled with stūpas, shrines, and people engaged in the daily activities of a university town, then a fuller picture of Nālandā's size emerges from what is now a spacious park.

Within the main monastery, today's visitors can clearly discern three levels of construction: the highest dates from the Pāla Dynasty, the middle level dates from the time of King Harṣa, and the lowest level dates to the early Gupta Dynasty. As one descends these layers, exposed through excavation, it becomes clear that Nālandā's main monastery was indeed rebuilt twice using the previous level as a foundation. On the top level, individual cells with built-in sleeping niches branch off from the central halls. On the second level, the outlines of arches of windows from the first level below can be seen rising above the level of the floor.

Stairs constructed during this century to give access to the second and first levels pass by a large storeroom which still held jars of rice when excavators opened it in the nineteenth century. The stairs lead to a great hall, which one can readily imagine filled with students attentive to the words of the great masters. Descending to the first and oldest levels, visitors pass through ancient hallways that link rows of monastic cells and

Monastic cells on the third and most recent level of Nālandā's main monastery, showing the sleeping platforms used by the monks.

view empty shrine niches that once held magnificent images of the Buddhas and Bodhisattvas.

Cunningham remarked that this site possessed finer and more numerous specimens of sculpture than any other place he had studied. The sculptures unearthed were made of different kinds of stone brought from other regions of Bihār and Bengal; a few sculptures were carved from dark gray andalusite from the Choganagpur plateau, from chlorite muscovite schist, or from slate. Many statues were sculpted from a dark gray graphite-type stone that gives a metallic lustre when polished. A large statue discovered at the foot of one of the mounds was originally enshrined in one of the temples.

The art of Nālandā, originally inspired by the sculptures of Sārnāth, developed its own distinctive style. The long coexistence of Hīnayāna and Mahāyāna traditions contributed to this artistic expression, which further benefited from the

Bodhisattva Avalokiteśvara

flowering of the arts during the Gupta Dynasty. Another wave of artistic development gave rise to the highly detailed iconography of the Tantras, which flourished here during the reign of the Pāla kings. The beauty and power of Nālandā's rich artistic heritage inspired visitors and students attracted to Nālandā from throughout the Buddhist world. As a result, Nālandā's sculptures had a tremendous influence on the artistic development of other Buddhist lands, especially the art of Nepal, Tibet, and Indonesia.

About fifteen years ago, the Central Advisory Board of Museums decided to remove the bronzes from the Nālandā archaeological site and disperse them among the major Indian museums. Fortunately, this plan was never implemented, and Nālandā was allowed to keep what little remained of its rich heritage. The Nālandā Museum was constructed a short distance from the ruins to house a collection of images and other artifacts from Nālandā's years of glory. Although many have been lost, the bronze statues found at Nālandā, reverenced in centuries past by thousands of Nālandā's masters and students, provide a glimpse of the beauty and quality of its artistic and spiritual traditions.

Odantapurī

During the eighth century, large monastic centers inspired by Nālandā were built by the kings of the Pāla Dynasty. Two of the most famous were in the Madhyadeśa: Odantapurī, whose origins are rooted in legend, and Vikramaśīla, center for study of the Prajñāpāramitā.

All that is known of Odantapurī's history is gleaned from Tibetan records, which provide only fragmentary information concerning this large monastic center, said to have had as many as twelve thousand students. (BA II:1031) According to Tāranātha, Odantapurī was founded in the eighth century during the reign of King Gopāla or Devapāla. Its origins trace to an interaction between a tīrthika yogi named Narada and a lay follower of the Dharma known as Uḍya-upāsaka. Uḍya-upāsaka, having obtained his teacher's permission, helped Narada perform a sādhana which yielded them a magical sword and a substantial amount of gold. Narada then told him that the gold would replenish itself continuously if he took care to spend it only on meritorious works. With this gold the layman built the vihāra of Odantapurī, said to have been an elegant structure modeled on the pattern of the cosmos, with a lofty shrine representing Mt. Meru at the center and buildings representing a continent in each of the four directions.

As it was built by a wealthy layman, Odantapurī was not dependent on the generosity of patrons for its maintenance. Replenished unceasingly by meritorious actions, the supply of gold paid for the temple and all of its statues and ornamentations, and supported five hundred bhikṣus and five laymen for many years. Before he died, Uḍya-upāsaka buried the gold, with the prayer that it prove useful to beings in the future. He then entrusted the care of Odantapurī to King Devapāla.

The Tibetan scholar Bu-ston cites another tradition. When King Dharmapāla was a youth, he developed a strong desire to build a temple more magnificent than all the others. The royal soothsayers advised him to prepare a special lamp, place it before his tutelary deity, and make his request. Then Dharmapāla's servant was to throw the lamp away and the temple would have to be built wherever the lamp landed.

When Dharmapāla performed this ritual, however, a raven picked up the lamp and dropped it into a lake. The youth was dismayed, for it appeared that his request was rejected. That night a nāga appeared to Dharmapāla, saying if Dharmapāla performed sacrifices for seven weeks, he would cause this lake to dry up. When Dharmapāla agreed, the nāga dried up the lake. On the fresh new field that emerged, Dharmapāla built the magnificent monastery of Odantapurī.

Since bSam-yas, the first Tibetan monastery, was constructed around 749 on the model of Odantapurī, Odantapurī must have been built by the middle of the eighth century. The monastery appears to have had a strong connection with the Prajñāpāramitā teachings. In the late eighth or early ninth century, the scholar Haribhadra, who propitiated Maitreya for assistance in understanding the Prajñāpāramitā, had a vision of Odantapurī; from the clouds above its central temple emerged the form of Maitreya, who clarified Haribhadra's understanding and instructed him on the method of preparing commentaries on the Prajñāpāramitā teachings.

The Pāla kings became Odantapurī's most generous sponsors. Tāranātha relates that King Mahāpāla, who ruled for forty-one years, supported Odantapurī's Sangha of Saindhava-śrāvakas and Sinhalese bhikṣus, and built the Uruvasa Vihāra to be their residence. Although Vikramaśīla continued to flourish, Mahāpāla made Odantapurī his primary center of veneration; he also supported centers for Buddhist studies at Nālandā and at Somapurī in eastern Bengal.

The *Blue Annals* records that Atīśa Dīpaṁkaraśrījñāna studied at Odantapurī for two years under the Śrāvaka master Dharmarakṣita before he became abbot of Vikramaśīla in the early eleventh century. But Odantapurī may have even then been declining; Nag-tsho, Atīśa's biographer, mentions that Odantapurī had only fifty-three monks when Atīśa was here.

Odantapurī fell to the Turuṣka invaders around 1198; a Muslim chronicler recorded its destruction, naming Ikhtiyar-ud-din Muhammad bin Bhakhtyār Khaljī as the leader of the invading army. ". . . he invaded Bihār, took its capital Udantapura, put to death the Buddhist monks dwelling in its great monastery, and returned with his plunder, which included the library of the monastery, to make obeisance to Aibek, now established at Delhi. . . " (CHI II:42)

Minhaz, a thirteenth-century Persian historian, recorded an eye-witness account of Odantapurī's destruction in the Tabaquāt-i-Nāsīrī: "Muhammad Bhakhtyār with great vigor and audacity rushed in at the gate of the fort and gained possession of the place. Great plunder fell into the hands of the victors. Most of the inhabitants were Brahmins with shaven heads. They were put to death. Large numbers of books were found there, and when the Muhammadans saw them, they called for some person to explain their contents. But all the men had been killed." (Elliot II:306). When Dharmasvāmin visited the area in 1234, he noted that the town of Odantapura was a Muslim encampment, from which the Turuṣkas were still mounting raids against Nālandā.

The name of Odantapurī vanished from the historical record after its conversion to a Muslim stronghold. When Cunningham researched the area in the nineteenth century, Nālandā had just been identified; Tāranātha's *History* had not yet been translated from Tibetan, and Odantapurī's existence was unknown to western scholars. Noting the name of Bihār as a memory of a vihāra that may have been located here, Cunningham searched for signs of Buddhist activity, but could find only votive stūpas and fragments of figures, one of which bore an inscription dating it to 900 C.E.

Cunningham described the Muslim village and noted the 'cyclopean walls' of an old fort nearby, but paid them no further attention. Northwest of the town he noticed a long, isolated hill with a steep cliff on its north face and an easy slope on the south. On the top of the hill was a brick platform that appeared to be the foundation of a stūpa. Although this hill was recognized as a probable Buddhist site, the large number of Muslim graves on the hill precluded the possibility of excavation.

Only recently has the site of the university been sought and identified with the town of Bihārsharif, about seven miles northeast from Nālandā. Although fragments of images have been found in a large tank here, Bihārsharif sits directly upon the site, and it has not been possible to search further for Odantapurī's remains.

Vikramaśīla

Kāmpāla, master of Mahāmudrā, noticed the singular shape of a hillock on the bank of the Ganges and predicted that a great monastery would be built here under royal auspices. Reborn as Dharmapāla, heir to the Pāla Empire, he fulfilled this prophecy by constructing Vikramaśīla.

—*Tāranātha*

Next to Nālandā, the university of Vikramaśīla is probably the most widely known of India's great Buddhist centers of learning. Our knowledge of the university and its scholars derives primarily from translations preserved in Tibet, from accounts by Tibetans who studied with Vikramaśīla's masters, or from the Tibetan historian Tāranātha. During the Pāla and Sena dynasties, Tibetans maintained a close connection with eastern India, particularly with Vikramaśīla, and the paṇḍitas of Vikramaśīla figure prominently in the second transmission of the Dharma to Tibet.

According to Tāranātha, Vikramaśīla was located in Magadha, at the top of a hill overlooking the Ganges. Its central temple is said to have been encircled by fifty-three smaller temples dedicated to the Guhya Tantra and fifty-four ordinary temples, forming a complex of 108 temples surrounded by a boundary wall. Upon its completion, King Dharmapāla provided for a staff of 108 paṇḍitas and six administrators. Each paṇḍita was responsible for teaching a special aspect of doctrine, and the head of the monastery was charged with watching over Nālandā as well.

The inspiration for Vikramaśīla's creation is attributed to the paṇḍita Haribhadra, disciple of the outstanding eighth-century scholar Śāntarakṣita. As a young scholar, Haribhadra attracted the attention of King Dharmapāla who invited him to teach in eastern India. While living at Trikaṭuka monastery, Haribhadra taught the Prajñāpāramitā to thousands and began to explicate these profound teachings in a series of masterful commentaries. In time, Haribhadra became Dharmapāla's spiritual preceptor and his guide for building Vikramaśīla.

Unlike Nālandā, which developed over a period of centuries, Vikramaśīla was from the outset a fully formed university which attracted scholars and students from India, Kashmir, and Tibet. Nālandā initially supplied Vikramaśīla with most of its scholars; within a few decades of its founding, Vikramaśīla became, next to Nālandā, the greatest center of learning in all of India. Tāranātha relates that the abbot of Vikramaśīla also took responsibility for Nālandā. All three of Magadha's universities—Nālandā, Vikramaśīla, and Odantapurī—were within easy traveling distance, and it is possible that prominent paṇḍitas taught at all of them.

Masters of Vikramaśīla

Study of the Mantrayāna flourished at Vikramaśīla under the leadership of Haribhadra's principal disciple Buddhajñāna, the first of Vikramaśīla's twelve great Mantrayāna masters. Holder of lineages transmitted by the Uḍḍiyāna siddha Līlavajra and the yoginī Guṇeru, Buddhajñāna established the teaching of Guhyasamāja at Vikramaśīla, for which this university became widely known. The lineages of Kriyā, Caryā, and Yoga were continued by Buddhajñāna's disciple Buddhaguhya, who transmitted all these lineages to his Tibetan disciples.

According to Tāranātha, twelve great Mantrayāna masters served as head teachers at Vikramaśīla during the early years of its existence. After Buddhajñānapāda came Dīpaṁkarabhadra, master of the Kriyā Tantras and author of forty-two works preserved in the bsTan-'gyur. After him was the master Laṅkājayabhadra, or Jayabhadra of Laṅkā, who became a bhikṣu in Śrī Laṅkā, studied the Mahāyāna at Nālandā, and became a Mantrayāna adept at Vikramaśīla, where he had a vision of Cakrasaṁvara. Tāranātha writes that he taught the Cakrasaṁvara Tantra in South India before he returned to Vikramaśīla and served as Vajrācārya (tantric master).

Śrīdhara, known for teaching the Mahāmāyā Tantra in South India, was Vikramaśīla's fourth Vajrācārya. According to Tāranātha, Śrīdhara held the Yamāri lineage of Jñānapāda and in later life benefited from the instruction of the siddha Kṛṣṇācārya. He composed at least thirty-two texts, mostly on the Raktayamāri and Kṛṣṇayamāri teachings. Following him was the master Bhavabhadra, learned in Vijñānavāda philosophy as well as the teachings of fifty Tantras; Bhavyakīrti, scholar of the Tantras; Līlavajra, a siddha and master of the Yamāri Tantra; Durjayacandra; Kṛṣṇasamayavajra, in the lineage of Buddhajñānapāda; and Tathāgatarakṣita, who attained realization through Yamāri and Saṁvara practices. The eleventh Vajrācārya was Bodhibhadra, an upāsika or lay scholar proficient in the practice of the Guhya mantras, and the twelfth was the bhikṣu Kamalarakṣita, scholar of the Prajñāpāramitā, Guhyasamāja, and Yamāri teachings.

This succession of twelve Vajrācāryas were followed in the tenth century by eight masters in charge of Vikramaśīla's six principal areas of study. These masters, known as the Six

Gatekeepers, were Ratnākaraśānti, keeper of the eastern gate, Mantrayāna master and scholar of Prajñāpāramitā, Mādhyamika, logic, and grammar; Vāgīśvarakīrti, keeper of the western gate, philosopher and Mantrayāna adept; Prajñākaramati, keeper of the southern gate, renowned for his knowledge of Madhyamaka and Prajñāpāramitā; and Nāropa, followed by Bodhibhadra, keepers of the northern gate. Nāropa was a scholar and accomplished siddha; Bodhibhadra was primarily concerned with sambhāra, the vows and conduct that guide the Bodhisattvas and Mantrayāna practitioner. Ratnavajra of Kashmīr and Jñānaśrīmitra of Bengal were known as the central pillars. Both were distinguished logicians and masterful Mantrayāna teachers.

A series of Mantrayāna adepts followed them as Vajrācārya of Vikramaśīla up until the time of Atīśa Dīpaṁkaraśrījñāna (982–1054 C.E.), who took leave from Vikramaśīla to assist Dharma transmission in Tibet and remained in Tibet for the remainder of his life to support study and translation. Tāranātha names nine principal teachers after Atīśa, ending with the master logician Śākyaśrī (1127–1225 C.E.). Śākyaśrī and other panditas fled Vikramaśīla just in time to escape the Turuṣka army. He eventually traveled to Tibet, where he transmitted his lineages and taught for ten years before returning to his homeland in Kashmīr.

Discovery of Vikramaśīla

Today, after years of conjecture over Vikramaśīla's site, the most probable location is the hill at Patharghata, about twenty-four miles east of Bhagalpur, a city on the Ganges about 150 miles east of Nālandā. The distinct topography—a steep promontory facing the eastward flow, where the river flows north instead of east—accords with traditional descriptions, and a partial inscription found at the site indicates that this is indeed the great vihāra of Vikramaśīla. Excavations at

Ruins of Vikramaśīla Mahāvihāra at Patharghata Hill, Bhagalpur District

the small village of Antichak, begun in 1960, have gradually unearthed a monastery built around a cruciform temple, similar to the description of Odantapurī and to the ruins of Somapurī, described on page 419.

The first monument uncovered was the ruins of a multi-storied stūpa complex forty-eight feet in height and seventy-six feet wide, surrounded by two layers of circumambulation paths connected by stairs. A twelfth-century inscription found on the base of a pillar describes how Sāhura, a ruler of Campā, turned back an attack by the rulers of Vaṅga, a kingdom to the southeast, providing some evidence that the monastery was threatened by Indian aggressors as well as by Muslim invasions, and that the local chieftain was strong enough at that time to protect it.

More recent excavations have unearthed the monastic cells surrounding the central monument on four sides, revealing the full extent of the walled area as 1083 feet on each side. This 'rim structure' contained at least 208 cells with large round tower-like projections on the corners and smaller round and rectangular projections on the sides, spaced about seventy five feet apart. A second structure, found about a hundred feet south and east of the monastery, was engineered to allow for ventillation and cooling from air passing over a reservoir. It is thought to have been a library constructed in this special manner to preserve palm-leaf manuscripts. (ACV 85–88)

Outside the monastery's rim structure, excavators discovered remains of smaller and cruder structures made of bricks apparently salvaged from the monastery after its destruction. While some of these later buildings, such as votive stūpas, may represent efforts by Buddhists to rebuild, it is clear that many of these shrines were built by people who were hostile to Buddhism. Prasad describes this scene as "probably the first instance of great vandalism in the history of India." (ACV 88) Vikramaśīla, Nālandā, and Odantapurī, their masters, and their spiritual and artistic treasures can never be replaced, and their loss was a great tragedy. But even in ruins, Nālandā's remains are an eloquent memorial to generations of enlightened masters dedicated to the transmission of knowledge that illuminates the beauty and value of a human existence.

Part Three

The Central Valleys

Gilgit
KASHMIR
Śrīnagar
Jālandhara
PAKISTAN
TIBET
Śrughna
Indraprasthā
Ahicchatra
NEPAL
Mathurā
Sāṁkāśya
RAJASTHAN
Vairāṭa
Kānyakubja
BHUTAN
Sāketa
SINDH
Prayāga
Vārāṇasī
BIHAR
BANGLA DESH
GUJARAT
WEST BENGAL
MADHYA PRADESH
MAHARASTRA
ORISSA
ANDHRA PRADESH
GOA
KARNATAKA
TAMIL NADU
KERALA
SRI LANKA

The Central Valleys

Visits by the Buddha and his disciples set the wheel of the Dharma in motion in the Central Valleys of the Yamunā and Ganges rivers, but it was in the reign of Aśoka that Buddhism began to flourish, led by the Sarvāstivādins of Mathurā and supported by a strong artistic tradition.

At the time of the events extolled in the Mahābhārata, the plains and valleys watered by the upper Ganges and the Yamunā and Sarasvatī rivers were the center of Brahmanic culture and the Vedic religion from which it arose. This region, home to the Pañcālas, Kurus, Śūrasenas, and Matsyas, was the Āryavarta, the Venerable Land; today it is divided into the modern states of Haryāna, Himachal Pradesh, eastern Rājasthan, and the western half of Uttar Pradesh.

Through the centuries, as Brahmanic culture penetrated all of India, the plains and valleys of the ancient Āryavarta retained their place as the central homeland of Indian culture. After the once-mighty Sarasvatī River dwindled in size and importance, the Sutlej (Śutudrī) River became this region's natural northwestern boundary. Northwest of the Sutlej lay the Punjab and Kashmīr, bounded by the Indus River, India's traditional border. Beyond the Indus lay the outposts of a shifting kaleidoscope of cultures and empires, from the Persians and Greeks of the sixth to first centuries B.C.E. to the Muslim Turks of the tenth to thirteenth centuries C.E.

Even in ancient times the valleys of the Yamunā and Upper Ganges were easily-traversed channels linking the northwestern passes and the lower Ganges basin. With the increase in trade and the rise of the merchant class, towns established as protective fortresses burgeoned into centers of commerce. Along the banks of the upper Ganges arose the cities of Kānyakubja, Sāṁkāśya, and Hastināpura. In the valley of the Yamunā, another major route connecting the northwest with central India, Mathurā and Indraprasthā (modern Delhi) developed into major cities.

At the time of the Buddha, Vedic culture had spread from the Āryavarta throughout northern India, encompassing the kingdoms of Kosala and Magadha, the early home of the Buddhist Sangha. Even so, there were deep spiritual and cultural differences between the peoples of the Āryavarta, the Brahmanic homeland, and the Madhyadeśa that nurtured the growth of the Buddhist Sangha. The peoples of the Āryavarta adhered strongly to Vedic rituals and traditions, which included veneration of Brahmins, strict observance of class distinctions, and animal sacrifice. Historical information in the Buddhist texts indicates that these traditions were not yet well established in the Madhyadeśa.

In contrast to the Madhyadeśa, Buddhism was slow to develop a popular base in the Central Valleys. The only site in this region to become one of the eight major places of pilgrimage was Sāṁkāśya, a city on the upper Ganges, where the Buddha descended to earth after teaching the Abhidharma to his mother in the Heaven of the Thirty-three Gods. Although it is clear that the Buddha did not spend much time in the Central Valleys, at least once the Enlightened One traveled with five hundred disciples north along the Yamunā River to Mathurā and further west to Virāṭa (Bairāta, Pāli Verañjā, modern Jaipur), where he spent a rainy season retreat. The region was then experiencing a famine; the stay must have been uncomfortable, for the Buddha mentions, along with Mathurā's problems of uneven ground, thickness of dust, vicious dogs, and many yakṣas (nature spirits), that alms were difficult to obtain. (AN III:256)

The Aśokāvadāna, a history of King Aśoka preserved in the Sarvāstivādin tradition, relates that the Buddha visited Kashmīr, Gandhāra, and Mathurā, where he made predictions concerning the introduction of the Dharma in these lands. Stūpas described by Fa-hien and Hsüan-tsang commemorated places where the Buddha taught the Dharma in Mathurā, Kānyakubja, Ayodhyā, Hayamukha, Śrughna, Goviśana, Vīraśāna, and Ahicchatra.

Avantipura, king of the Śūrasenas, welcomed the Buddha's disciple Mahākātyāyana, who came to Virāṭa and resided for a time at the Gundāvana Monastery. This would indicate that there were bhikṣus already living here. Early on, itinerant bhikṣus began to travel through central India following the long-established routes northwest toward the Punjab and Kashmīr; some may have remained in the Central Valleys. The Mūlasarvāstivādin Vinaya relates that one hundred years after the Parinirvāṇa, thirty mendicant monks from Mathurā came to the council of Vaiśālī. However, from the accounts of the patriarchs Śāṇavāsa and Upagupta, the Buddha's teachings took root slowly in this region. It was not until Aśoka's time that Upagupta established the first permanent center in Mathurā and converted a large number of its inhabitants.

The growth of Buddhism in the Central Valleys was disrupted around 183 B.C.E. when Puṣyamitra Śuṅga rose to power, ending the Mauryan Dynasty established by Aśoka's grandfather. A strong supporter of the Brahmanic traditions, Puṣyamitra reinstated the horse sacrifice and other elaborate

Vedic rituals which had fallen into disuse during Aśoka's time. According to Tāranātha, Puṣyamitra destroyed Aśoka's monastery at Pāṭaliputra and vigorously persecuted the Buddhists in the Central Valleys from Kānyakubja to Jālandhara.

The second century B.C.E. also saw the rise of new Brahmanic cults centered on Viṣṇu as a personal deity, a one god and the focus of devotion. New temples were built to Viṣṇu and his avatars (manifestations), the most popular of which was Kṛṣṇa. Since the Viṣṇu cults were strongest in the Central Valleys and the legends of Kṛṣṇa center on Mathurā, it is likely that the devotional appeal of this movement with Mathurā as its major holy place slowed the growth of Buddhism here.

While the kings who succeeded Puṣyamitra were favorably inclined toward Buddhism, the empire once ruled by Aśoka was disintegrating. The Bactrian Greeks occupied the Northwest from their capital at Sākala, located south of the Chenāb River, and invaded India as far as Pāṭaliputra at the beginning of Puṣyamitra's reign. Although they soon withdrew from central India, they settled into the western provinces of Aparānta and Sindh, and at least once clashed with Puṣyamitra's forces near Jālandhara. The principalities that arose in the Central Valleys were governed by Kṣatriya families who ruled more or less independently, depending on the strength of the Śuṅga kings. From Kauśāmbī to the eastern Punjab, these principalities formed buffer zones between the Śuṅgas and the invaders that pushed into India from the northwest.

The Śakas, a Central Asian tribe, displaced the Greeks in the west and northwest and moved into the Central Valleys in the first century B.C.E.; they were closely followed by the Parthians, who migrated southeast from the region of the Caspian Sea, and by the Kuṣāṇas, another Central Asian tribe. Toward the end of the first century C.E., the Kuṣāṇas ruled the northwestern provinces and all of central India. At the height of their power, the Kuṣāṇas enjoyed a wide sphere of influence extending from Pāṭaliputra to the Central Asian kingdom of Khotan. Although the Kuṣāṇas supplanted the Śakas, the Śakas retained some measure of prominence, often serving the Kuṣāṇas as local governors and administrators.

The Śakas and Kuṣāṇa rulers supported Buddhism, and some were generous donors to the Sangha. Sudāśa, a Śaka governor of Mathurā, built the Guha Vihāra for the Sangha, and the Kuṣāṇa King Huviṣka built the Huviṣka Vihāra near the city of Mathurā at Jamalpur. Although the vihāra was later destroyed, the ruins, rich in beautiful carvings, indicate that it was a thriving center. The most famous of all Kuṣāṇa kings was Kaniṣka, who ruled the Central Valleys from his capital at Peshawar, in Gandhāra, probably around the end of the first century C.E. Interested in Buddhism and desiring to clarify the nature of the diverse Buddhist traditions, King Kaniṣka convened an important council of the Sangha. This gathering, known as the Third Council in the northern traditions, probably took place at Jālandhara, just south of the Sutlej River, although some sources locate it in Kashmīr.

Under Kuṣāṇa rule, Mathurā became the cultural center for all of northern India and the Buddhist schools centered here flourished strongly. From the first through the third century C.E., Buddhist monasteries and temples arose all along the route from Mathurā to Jālandhara, providing the impetus for a major artistic tradition centered at Mathurā. The artistic tradition of Mathurā, noted for its precisely proportioned images of the Buddha, appears to have developed before or during Kuṣāṇa rule. Whereas the Śuṅga art of the second century B.C.E. had preferred to represent the Buddha symbolically, Mathuran art focused on sculpting the Buddha's physical form. By the second century C.E., representations of the Buddha carved in the distinctive white-spotted red sandstone of Mathuran quarries were being carried to monasteries throughout northern India.

As emphasized by the art historian John Huntington, the appearance of developed iconographic images sculpted in stone indicate a long period of experimentation in less expensive materials such as wood. Thus the Mathuran stone figures were almost certainly preceded by several centuries of artistic development, which would place the formation of Buddha images much earlier than Western scholars have generally accepted. As early as the second century C.E., Mathuran artisans were sculpting stone figures not only of Śākyamuni Buddha, but also of Amitābha Buddha and the Bodhisattvas Avalokiteśvara, Vajrapāṇi and Padmapāṇi. (Math 85–92) A well-preserved statue of the Buddha attended by Vajrapāṇi and Padmapāṇi was found at a site in Ahicchatra; dated to the early second century (Kuṣāṇa period), this statue is now housed in the National Museum of New Delhi. (Math pl.9.III)

The Mathuran style strongly influenced the art of the Gupta period. Although the Gupta aesthetic predominated after the third century C.E., Mathuran sculptors continued to supply art for Buddhist monuments through the reign of King Harṣa (mid-seventh century). Fine images produced in Mathurā have been discovered throughout the Madhyadeśa.

The Visits of Fa-hien and Hsüan-tsang

When Fa-hien traveled through central India in the fifth century, he passed temples "one after another, with some myriad of priests in them" on the way to Mathurā. During the reign of King Harṣa, a strong supporter of Buddhism, Hsüan-tsang also traveled this region. He found the Dharma flourishing in the area of Harṣa's greatest influence, particularly in Mathurā, Ayodhyā, and Kānyakubja, Harṣa's capital city; fifteen thousand monks lived in monasteries near these three cities. The regions of Śrughna, Ahicchatra, Sāṁkāśya, and Hayamukha each had monasteries housing one thousand monks, and Sthāneśvara and Matipura housed a total of fifteen hundred monks.

Hsüan-tsang names the major Buddhist communities active at the time of his travels in central India. Three communities often mentioned—Mahāsāṁghikas, Saṁmatīyas, and Sarvāstivādins—were branches of the Śrāvaka (listener) tradition. There were also many monks of the Mahāyāna tradition, followers of the greater vehicle. Hsüan-tsang notes that the Saṁmatīyas had centers in Ahicchatra and Sāṁkāśya, with one thousand monks in each city; the Sarvāstivādins had a monastery housing eight hundred monks in Matipura, while followers of unspecified traditions lived in Mathurā, Sthāneśwara, Śrughna, Goviśana, and Kānyakubja. The Mahāyāna traditions were well-established in Mathurā, Vīraśāna, and Kānyakubja. But the Mahāsāṁghikas, populous in other regions, appear to have vanished from central India.

Waning of Buddhism in the Central Valleys

After the death of King Harṣa in 647 or 648 C.E., central India again fragmented into smaller kingdoms, each struggling for power and territory. Although little is known of the Dharma centers in this region after the death of King Harṣa, archaeological evidence reveals that in many instances the Buddhist temples were demolished and Hindu temples built on their foundations.

Vying for pieces of Harṣa's empire, the warrior kings of the Central Valleys had little time or wealth to expend in supporting religion and the arts that did not directly enhance their position. Brahmanic rituals were revived and impressive forts were constructed, but the building of new cultural monuments declined. Unstable political conditions made travel dangerous, which tended to isolate the Dharma communities of central India. As Hsüan-tsang notes, there were rival factions in Harṣa's empire jealous of Buddhism and probably eager to assert themselves after the Dharma's powerful protector had passed away.

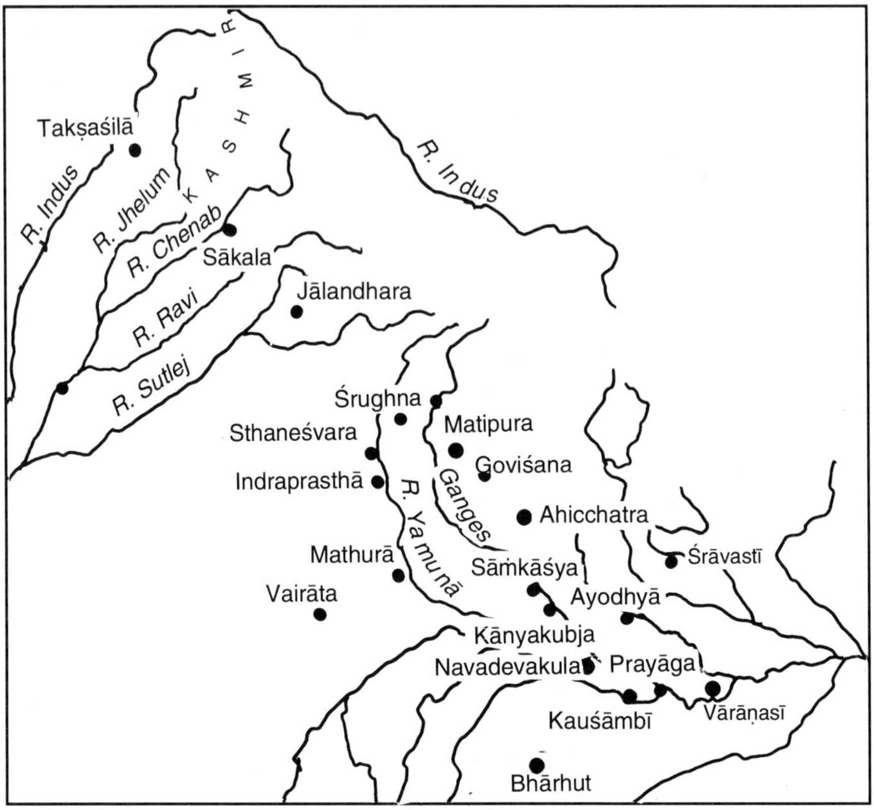

Seventh-century cities of the Yamunā and Upper Ganges valleys

In the ninth and tenth centuries, the Gurjara-Pratīhāra kings came to power in Kānyakubja. Although their leadership relieved tension between the rival factions, peace was short-lived: The Rāṣṭrakūṭas invaded from the south and were driven from Kānyakubja with difficulty. Weakened by centuries of internal strife, the princes of India were unable to defend themselves against the Muslim Turks who descended upon central India in great waves in the eleventh century. Led by Mahmūd of Ghaznī, the invaders captured and pillaged Kānyakubja and Mathurā between 1001 and 1027. The Central Valleys enjoyed a brief respite between 1027 and 1191, but the Turkish armies returned to stay at the end of the twelfth century. In Delhi (ancient Indraprasthā), in the heart of Brahmanic culture, the invaders established their center of operations.

Indian resistance, while vigorous, arose too late to be effective. With the establishment of the Sultanate of Delhi in 1206, central India came completely under Muslim control. Although Muslim factions arose and fought amongst themselves for decades thereafter, aggravating social upheavals and destruction in central India, the government of central India was firmly in Muslim hands.

Just as Buddhist monuments of the Central Valleys had provided the foundations for Hindu temples, the Hindu temples, in turn, were now pulled down to became the foundations of Muslim mosques. However, the Brahmanic tradition, always strong in central India, survived the years of disruption and regained much of its strength in this region. But the Buddhadharma had greater difficulties. Long before the Turkish occupation the influence of the Dharma had been seriously weakened, and most of the Buddhist monks and scholars from this region had sought refuge in the monastic centers of eastern India. Whatever remnants of Buddhism were not destroyed or supplanted by the end of the tenth century had been demolished in wave after wave of Muslim incursions. Today there is little to be seen of Buddhism in the Central Valleys outside of the images preserved in museums at Delhi and Mathurā.

In 1959, the mountains of Himachal Pradesh became the refuge of Buddhists from Tibet. The Dalai Lama established his center at Dharamsala, and monks and lamas of the four major Tibetan Buddhist traditions built monasteries and educational institutes in this northern region of central India. The study and practice of Buddhism now thrives in Himachal Pradesh, and Buddhist centers here attract a continual stream of Western visitors.

Mathurā

While visiting Mathurā, the Buddha predicted the founding of the Naṭabhāṭiya Vihāra on the slopes of Mt. Urumuṇḍa. A hundred years after the Blessed One's Parinirvāṇa, a son named Upagupta would be born to a merchant of Mathurā. Śāṇavāsa, third patriarch of the Dharma, would ordain Upagupta, who would reside in the Naṭabhāṭiya Monastery and convert many thousands to the teachings of liberation.

As the Buddha had predicted, about a hundred years after the Parinirvana, the brothers Naṭa and Bhaṇṭa built a place of retreat on Mt. Urumuṇḍa. This center became known as the Naṭabhāṭiya Vihāra, a combination of the brothers' names. The disciple Ānanda conveyed the Buddha's prophecy to Śāṇavāsa. After Upagupta was born into the family of an incense merchant in Mathurā, Śāṇavāsa, third patriarch of the Dharma, watched over him as he grew up and ordained him into the Sangha. In time Upagupta attained the state of an Arhat and took up residence in the Naṭabhāṭiya Vihāra on Mt. Urumuṇḍa. Before passing into nirvāṇa, Śāṇavāsa entrusted the Dharma to his care.

Upagupta's teaching, offered freely to everyone, attracted a large following. Accounts in the Vinaya texts record that Māra, Lord of Illusion, feared that Upagupta's teaching would weaken his power over the minds of living beings. One day, while the townspeople were assembled on Mt. Urumuṇḍa, Māra showered rice on Mathurā, enticing some to return to the city. The next day, Māra caused fine clothing to fall on the city, which lured even more people away. The third day Māra created a shower of silver, on the fourth day, gold, and on the fifth day, precious jewels, until only a few townspeople remained with Upagupta. Even those few were drawn away when Māra transformed his family into celestial dancers and musicians, who led the townspeople back to the city.

Upagupta followed Māra's troupe to the city, where he congratulated them upon their performance and flung garlands about their necks. Immediately Māra and his demon family were revealed as hideous beings with putrifying corpses of humans and dogs dangling from their necks. Covering their noses in disgust, the townspeople fled. Māra pleaded with Upagupta to release his family; obtaining Māra's promise that he would obey Upagupta, the Arhat released the demons.

Upagupta then asked Māra the shape-changer to assume the form of the Buddha, whom Upagupta had been born too late to meet in person. Māra then appeared in the Buddha's form. So splendid was his manifestation as the Buddha that Upagupta was completely overcome with feeling. Forgetting who it was that actually stood in front of him, he threw himself at Māra's feet. Upagupta served the Dharma for thirty-one years; as the Buddha Śākyamuni had predicted, Upagupta became renowned for the great power of his compassion. During his lifetime many attained the state of an Arhat at the monastery on Mt. Urumuṇḍa. So accomplished was Upagupta that he has been honored as a 'Buddha without the marks,' referring to the thirty-two major and eighty-four marks on the body of a great being.

This account of Upagupta appears in the Mūlasarvāstivādin Vinaya; other accounts are given in the Aśokāvadāna and Divyāvadāna, also preserved in the Sarvāstivādin tradition. According to the Aśokāvadāna, the Arhat Upagupta, knowing of Aśoka's intense desire to support the Dharma, traveled by raft to Pāṭaliputra, where Aśoka came to meet and honor the great Arhat. Upagupta took Aśoka on pilgrimage to the places consecrated by the Buddha's presence and explained the significance of each site. In the Pāli tradition, it was Moggaliputta Tissa who lived near Mathurā on the Ahogaṅga hill and who came on a raft to Pāṭaliputra.

During Aśoka's benevolent rule, Mathurā became the most prominent center of Buddhism in the Central Valleys, supporting the flow of bhikṣus traveling to Takṣaśilā and Kashmīr, which were part of Aśoka's empire. Among the earliest of the Buddhist schools to move northwest were the Sarvāstivādins of Pāṭaliputra, capital of the Mauryan Empire. The Sarvāstivādins, who developed a strong Dhyāna (meditation) tradition, soon became the largest and most influential of the Buddhist schools at Mathurā. They adopted Sanskrit as the language of their sacred texts, a tradition that served them well in dialogues with the Brahmanic philosophers of the Central Valleys. The Dharmaguptakas, Mahāsāṁghikas, and Saṁmatīyas also founded monasteries here which served as centers for further expansion to the northwest. Mahāyāna images found in the Central Valleys indicates that Mahāyāna traditions were active here before the early second century C.E., and that some Buddhists in the region of Mathurā engaged in devotional practices focused on Amitābha Buddha.

Mathurā at the Time of King Harṣa

When Fa-hien arrived in Mathurā early in the fifth century, he counted twenty monasteries housing a total of three thousand monks. During his month-long stay in this region, the monks held a great assembly to engage in discourses upon the Dharma. After this meeting, the monks all walked to the stūpa of Śāriputra, where they offered incense and kept lamps burning through the night.

Hsüan-tsang, who arrived in Mathurā in 634 C.E., describes its area as approximately eighty-five miles in circumference, with the city itself having a circumference of about three miles. The king and his ministers were Buddhists, and there were twenty Buddhist monasteries in the region, housing a total of two thousand resident monks who studied the texts of both the Hīnayāna and Mahāyāna traditions. Hsüan-tsang describes three Aśokan stūpas and signs of the visits of past Buddhas evident near the city. He notes at least six stūpas containing relics of the Buddha's principal disciples (Śāriputra, Maudgalyāyana, Pūrṇa, Upāli, Ānanda, and Rāhula) and stūpas of Mañjuśrī and other great Bodhisattvas.

Hsüan-tsang describes how large numbers of people gathered at these stūpas to make offerings on important religious holidays. Three long fasts were observed in the first, fifth, and ninth months of the lunar calendar, and six fast days were observed in the remaining months. On fast days, the monks honored the stūpa of the Buddha's disciple who best exemplified their practice: Those who studied the Abhidharma honored the stūpa of Śāriputra; those who practiced meditation honored the stūpa of Maudgalyāyana; those who recited the Sūtras paid respects to the stūpa of Pūrṇa; and those who studied the Vinaya paid homage to the stūpa of Upāli. All the bhikṣuṇīs worshipped at the stūpa of Ānanda and all the śrāmaṇeras (novices) at the stūpa of Rāhula, while the followers of the Mahāyāna paid homage to the stūpas of the great Bodhisattvas.

According to Hsüan-tsang, "On these days they honor the stūpas with offerings. They spread out their jeweled banners and create a network of parasols; smoke from incense rises in clouds; flowers are scattered in every direction like rain; the sun and the moon are concealed by the clouds which hang over the moist valleys. The king of the country and the great ministers apply themselves to these religious duties with zeal." (HT I:181)

When Hsüan-tsang visited the monastery of Upagupta, he observed that the monastery was entered through a valley "as by gates," and that cells for the monks were carved from the hillsides. North of the monastery was a room constructed of stone about twenty feet high and thirty feet wide, filled with wooden tokens four inches long. Here the venerable Upagupta taught the Dharma; whenever he converted a man and his wife, so that both attained the state of an Arhat, he would place one token in this house.

About four miles southeast of the stone room stood a stūpa built next to a great dry marsh. This was where a monkey had offered a pot of honey to the Buddha. The Buddha accepted the gift and asked the monkey to distribute the honey to the monks. Leaping with joy, the monkey fell into a deep hole and died. For his meritorious offering to the Buddha, he was reborn as a man. Nearby were stūpas commemorating places where Śāriputra, Maudgalyāyana, and other disciples had practiced meditation. Places where the Buddha taught were marked with inscriptions on trees or posts.

Modern Discoveries at Mathurā

In the nineteenth century, the archaeologist Alexander Cunningham, following Hsüan-tsang's directions, located the probable site of Upagupta's monastery west of the old fort of Mathurā. He found many Buddhist artifacts at this site, including a golden casket enclosing seven precious jewels. More artifacts and inscriptions were found nearby, in the place where the monkey is said to have made his offering of honey.

At the Katra, or marketplace outside Mathurā, there was evidence of successive Buddhist, Hindu, and Muslim occupation. Archaeological explorations of the site revealed that a mosque dating from the seventeenth century had been built over the foundation of a Hindu temple. Buddhist artifacts were found below the temple, including a pillar with a Gupta period inscription and fragments of Buddhist gateways and railings. A well yielded a perfectly preserved statue of the Buddha, three and a half feet in height, dated Saṁvat 281, or 359 C.E. The inscription on the statue's pedestal identified this monastery as the Yaśa Vihāra, the Splendid Monastery. Fragments of other statues, including the hand and arm of a very large statue, were also found in the well. Considering that the mosque on the top layer was deteriorating and was no longer used, Cunningham concluded that this site would be an excellent prospect for excavation.

Inscriptions identified a mound outside the city as the site of at least two monasteries: the Huviṣka Vihāra built by the Śaka king Huviṣka in the first century C.E. and the Kuṇḍa-Suka Vihāra. The bases of thirty pillars discovered at the site of the Huviṣka Vihāra give the names of the donors who presented these columns to the monastery. The inscriptions also indicate that at one time there had been at least seventy pillars here. The hand of a stone statue found at this site, with a palm twelve inches across, indicates that the whole image must have been at least twenty feet high. The Kuṇḍa-Suka Vihāra has been tentatively identified as the place mentioned above where the monkey fell into the pool. Many high mounds near Mathurā are covered with fragments of stone and brick. Although their history has been forgotten, a group of seven mounds to the south of the city might be the seven 'disciple' stūpas mentioned by Hsüan-tsang.

Excavations at these mounds have uncovered a wide variety of statues, bas-reliefs, pillars, railings, votive stūpas, and other forms of Buddhist art. While some appear to date from the period of Śaka rule (around the first century B.C.E.), the great majority of artistic remains are from the Kuṣāṇa period (around the first to second centuries C.E.). Most of the statues discovered by 1864 were either standing or sitting representations of the Buddha in different attitudes of teaching. This accords with Hsüan-tsang's description of the monuments marking the places where the Buddha taught the Dharma. One sculpture, identified as carved during the Śaka period, depicts the Buddha seated on Mt. Meru, the center of the world in Buddhist cosmology. The Mathurā Museum houses most of the Buddhist art discovered here.

East of Mathurā is the region of ancient Matsya, a hot semi-desert country located in modern Rājasthan. Matsya was the home of warriors known for their ferocity; its capital was Virāṭa, or Bairāṭ, where the Buddha once spent a rainy season retreat with five hundred of his disciples. After Aśoka visited Virāṭa, he erected a pillar here and had an exhortation to virtuous action carved into a large rock. This rock inscription is known as the Bhabru Edict.

The Huns descended on the Central Valleys in the early sixth century, devastating everything in their path. In the mid-seventh century Hsüan-tsang found only eight monasteries here, mostly in ruin. In modern times, archaeologists have discovered at Virāṭa the remains of a Buddhist temple made of brick; its walls were inscribed with sacred texts written in the Brāhmi script of Aśoka's time and a stūpa had been built inside it. This temple, which appears to date to Aśoka's time, is considered one of the earliest surviving Buddhist temples in India. It is likely that this type of construction served as a model for the artisans who later excavated the cave temples of western and eastern India. (BCAI 36)

The Northwestern Cities of Central India

Northwest of Mathurā, in cities strongly influenced by Brahmanical traditions, traces of Buddhism are few and difficult to locate. The journals of Chinese pilgrims provide our only guides to the monasteries and stūpas that supported the study and practice of Buddhism here. In recent times, archaeologists have examined some of the sites they described, but only a few have been excavated.

At the northwestern corner of the Indian Punjab, near modern Amritsar, Hsüan-tsang came to the country of Chīnapati, the winter residence of Chinese hostages once held by King Kaniṣka as an assurance of peaceful relations with China. The hostages, who had introduced peaches to the region, were still remembered with great respect.

To the southeast of the Chīnapati capital, probably close to modern Sūltanpur, was the Tāmasavana, the Monastery of the Dark Forest, where three hundred monks studied the doctrines of the Sarvāstivādin school. Here, three hundred years after the Buddha's Parinirvāṇa, the Sarvāstivādin master Kātyāyana composed the Jñānaprasthāna, one of the seven basic Abhidharma texts. According to some Buddhist sources, the council convened by Kaniṣka was held here, but other traditions cite Kashmīr or Jālandhara as the site of the great convocation. Near the monastery stood an Aśokan stūpa two hundred feet high, commemorating the site visited by the four Buddhas of the Bhadrakalpa, our present aeon. A great number of small stūpas and large stone houses filled the neighboring area, where innumerable Arhats had entered nirvāṇa.

At the Nagaradhana Monastery near Jālandhara, a city northeast of Chīnapati, Hsüan-tsang met Candravarma, an accomplished Tripiṭaka master, and studied the Prakaraṇapāda-vibhāṣa-śāstra with him for four months. (Hwui 76–77) In this land of thick forests and abundant fruits and flowers, Buddhism was the dominant religion. Hsüan-tsang counted fifty monasteries with about two thousand monks of both the Śrāvaka and Mahāyāna traditions and only three Śaivite temples with some five hundred devotees.

From Jālandhara, Hsüan-tsang traveled northeast along a precarious route that led over high mountain passes, through deep valleys, and over high ravines. Udita, ruler of Jālandhara, accompanied Hsüan-tsang for a time on his journey. Arriving in Kulūta, a remote mountainous kingdom in the Himalayan foothills, rich in medicinal herbs, Hsüan-tsang counted about twenty monasteries housing nearly a thousand Mahāyāna monks and another few monasteries of the Śrāvaka traditions. An Aśokan stūpa marked a site once visited by the Buddha and his disciples.

Southeast of Jālandhara was the land of Śatadru, named for the Śatadru (Śutudrī, or Sutlej), the River that Flows in a Hundred Branches. Although Hsüan-tsang found all the people here were Buddhists, he counted only ten monasteries, all in ruins, and only a few monks.

Sthāneśwara

Sthāneśwara (Thāneśwar) is one of the oldest historical sites in India. It was built in the center of a great plain known as Kurukṣetra, Field of the Kurus, or as Dharmakṣetra, Field of Virtue, in honor of the warriors who fell here during the Mahābhārata wars in the ninth or tenth centuries B.C.E. Little is known of the history of the Dharma in this stronghold of Brahmanic culture. However, in the seventh century C.E., Hsüan-tsang discovered three monasteries here that housed about seven hundred monks, all followers of the Śrāvaka traditions. Hsüan-tsang observes: "The climate is genial, though hot. The manners of the people are cold and insincere. The families are rich and given to excessive luxury. They are much addicted to the use of magical arts . . . . Most of the people follow after worldly gain; a few give themselves to agricultural pursuits." Northwest of the city there was a single Aśokan stūpa about three hundred feet high, built of yellowish red bricks, "very bright and shining." The stūpa held relics of the Buddha and frequently emitted a brilliant light. (HT I:186)

About seventeen miles south of the city, Hsüan-tsang came to a monastery named Gokaṇṭha, where the monks were "well-mannered and possessed of quiet dignity." Around the monastery were a succession of stūpas encircled by circumambulation paths.

Śrughna

Hsüan-tsang describes the kingdom of Śrughna as sixty-six miles northeast of Sthaneśvara, bounded on the Ganges on the east and by high mountains on the north. What had been the capital city was built on the west bank of the Yamunā River, which ran through the kingdom. Hsüan-tsang found the city deserted and beginning to go to ruin. Although most people of the region belonged to Brahmanic sects, "They greatly esteem the pursuit of learning, principally of the wisdom that brings happiness." (HT I:187) In the seventh century there were five monasteries in Śrughna, housing about one thousand monks, most of whom adhered to the Śrāvaka traditions. In contrast, there were a hundred Deva (Śaivite) temples belonging to the non-Buddhist traditions.

West of the Yamunā River stood an Aśokan stūpa commemorating the place where the Buddha had taught the Dharma. Beside it were stūpas containing hair and nail relics of the Buddha and stūpas enshrining hair and nail relics of Śāriputra, Maudgalyāyana, and other Arhats. According to Hsüan-tsang, "After the Tathāgata had entered nirvāṇa, this country was the seat of heretical teaching. The faithful were perverted to false doctrine and forsook the orthodox views. Now there are but five saṅghārāmas, all in places where Buddhist masters debated with the heretics and Brahmins and prevailed; they (the monasteries) were erected on this account." Hsüan-tsang resided at one of these five monasteries for about four months, where he engaged the monks in lengthy discussions of difficult points of doctrine.

The modern site of Śrughna may be Paota, a place about fifty miles northeast of the Gokaṇṭha Monastery. However, following Hsüan-tsang's estimates of distance, the more likely location would be the nearby site of Khalsi, where an Aśokan rock edict was found on a large quartz boulder. This rock is ten feet high by ten feet long and about eight feet thick at its base. An elephant figure is inscribed on the northern face of the rock and the edict on its southern face.

Matipura

According to Hsüan-tsang, the people of the country of Matipura, located southeast of Śrughna and east of the Ganges, greatly respected learning and were deeply versed in the use of charms and magic. The king observed the Brahmanic tradition, but about half of his people followed the Dharma.

Hsüan-tsang counted some twenty monasteries housing approximately eight hundred monks, mostly adherents of the Sarvāstivādin school. South of the capital city stood a small monastery housing about fifty monks. Hsüan-tsang considered this monastery the place where Guṇaprabha, disciple of Vasubandhu, composed nearly a hundred treatises. (Other accounts say that Guṇaprabha lived in the Agrapura Monastery in Mathurā.)

To the north lay another monastery where Saṁghabhadra, the great Kashmīri Sarvāstivādin master, is said to have died. According to Hsüan-tsang, Saṁghabhadra came here to debate the Abhidharma with Vasubandhu but passed away shortly after he arrived. Saṁghabhadra was cremated, and his remains were enshrined in a stūpa erected in a grove of mango trees. Nearby stood another stūpa holding the relics of another Kashmīri Sarvāstivādin master, Vimalamitra, who had died nearby.

In modern times Matipura has been identified with Madawar (also spelled Mundore or Mundawar) in the district of Rohilkhand. The ruins of the old town of Matipura form a mound about ten feet above the surrounding area. By the nineteenth century there was no trace of the monasteries or stūpas described by Hsüan-tsang, but their sites could be located using the pilgrim's descriptions. Guṇaprabha's monastery is now the site of a Muslim shrine, built with bricks probably salvaged from the monastery. Another shrine in the middle of a mango grove appears to be on the spot where Saṁghabhadra's stūpa once stood. The stūpa of Vimalamitra would have been on the boundary of this same mango grove.

Hsüan-tsang describes a town named Kiu-pi-shwong-na (Goviśana) about seventy miles southeast of Matipura. He considered that the townspeople were mostly interested in worldly pursuits, but he found two monasteries that housed a hundred Śrāvaka monks. Next to an old monastery outside the town, an Aśokan stūpa two hundred feet high marked the place where the Buddha had taught the essential points of the Dharma. In the nineteenth century, a solid brick mound twenty feet tall was found near the small village of Khargpur, near Kasipur. It is thought that mound may be the remains of the stūpa Hsüan-tsang described.

Ahicchatra

The city of Ahicchatra, which means Serpent-Canopy, traces its name to an ancient tale of a king found sleeping, guarded by a cobra. When Hsüan-tsang visited Ahicchatra, the capital of North Pañcāla, he found it to be a stronghold of Brahmanic culture. He commented that: "This country is naturally protected, being flanked by mountain crags. It produces wheat, and there are many woods and fountains. The climate is soft and agreeable, and the people sincere and truthful. They love religion and apply themselves to learning." (HT I: 200)

Hsüan-tsang noted ten Buddhist monasteries in the area, which altogether housed a thousand monks, all adherents of the Saṁmatīya tradition. Outside the main town Hsüan-tsang saw a stūpa built by King Aśoka next to a pool inhabited by a nāga (serpentine being). Here, for seven days, the Buddha taught the Dharma for the benefit of a nāga king. Beside the stūpa were four smaller stūpas commemorating the visits of the four Buddhas of our aeon.

In the nineteenth century, three Buddhist sites were excavated at Ahicchatra. The first site was that of a large brick stūpa, locally known as the Chatra, meaning cobra's hood or canopy, which was identified as the large stūpa described by Hsüan-tsang. The Chatra Stūpa's original height was estimated to have been fifty-seven feet; it was later enlarged to a height of seventy-seven feet, with a diameter of seventy-five feet. In the nineteenth century, the ruins still rose forty feet from the surrounding fields. Around this large stūpa were the ruins of four smaller stūpas and three temples; another mound proved to be another type of building. Although the 'serpent-pond' could not be clearly identified, in all other respects the site agreed exactly with Hsüan-tsang's description.

The second site, known as Katari Khera, was located just east of the village of Nasratganj and north of an ancient fort. Although much of the original brickwork had been removed for reuse in modern constructions, excavation revealed the remains of a small temple. A portion of a Buddha image, thought to be the temple's original central statue, was found at the site, together with an inscribed pillar recording the gift of Mahādari, disciple of the teacher Indranandi, to the temple of Parvamati. (ASI I:263)

The third site, only partially excavated, appears to have been a very large monastery, with a central temple eighty to one hundred feet tall. Further excavation may reveal more about this site, which has not yet been identified.

Pi-lo-shan-na

Half-way between Ahicchatra and Sāṁkāśya, Hsüan-tsang passed through the country of Pi-lo-shan-na, which Cunningham suggests is the same as Atranji-khera. In this territory, populated by people "violent and headstrong," Hsüan-tsang found two Mahāyāna monasteries housing some three hundred monks. An old monastery stood in the center of the capital city; next to it was the ruins of a stūpa built by Aśoka, which was still more than a hundred feet high.

If the identification of Pi-lo-shan-na with Atranji is accurate, the forty-five-foot high stūpa mound found at Atranji in the nineteenth century may be the Aśokan stūpa Hsüan-tsang described. Two small mounds on its east side may be the monasteries that stood near it. The stūpa mound has been extensively mined for bricks, and excavation would be necessary to verify how much of the foundations remain.

Kānyakubja (Kanauj)

Further south, and more centrally located on the Ganges River, stood the city of Kānyakubja. Fa-hien, visiting there in the fifth century, noted the existence of only two monasteries belonging to the Śrāvakayāna traditions and a stūpa where the Buddha had given teachings on impermanence and suffering. By the time Hsüan-tsang visited Kānyakubja two hundred years later, Kānyakubja was King Harṣa's capital city—a flourishing center of culture and commerce built on the banks of the Ganges and protected by strong walls and deep moats. Hsüan-tsang describes Kānyakubja's many "flowers and trees, lakes and ponds, bright and pure and shining like mirrors," seen on every side. "Valuable merchandise is collected here in great quantities. The people are well-off and contented, the houses are rich and well-built." (HT I:206)

Hsüan-tsang states that about half the people of the city were followers of the Buddhadharma, and the other half followed various other traditions. Under King Harṣa's protection and patronage, the Dharma was flourishing: there were some one hundred monasteries housing about ten thousand monks who studied both the Śrāvakayāna and Mahāyāna teachings. Hsüan-tsang describes a magnificent monastery built by King Harṣa, which was set on fire by adherents of non-Buddhist traditions jealous of the king's attention to the Dharma. The king banished the five hundred instigators of this crime, who had also plotted against the king's life.

The stūpa described by Fa-hien was still standing; Hsüan-tsang estimates that the great stūpa, located over a mile southeast of the city, was two hundred feet high. Nearby was a small stūpa with relics of the Buddha's hair and nails, renowned for its healing powers.

To the northwest of Kānyakubja, Hsüan-tsang discovered another Aśokan stūpa built on the place where the Buddha had taught the Dharma for seven days. Nearby were signs of the visits of Buddhas of the past. South of the stūpa, on the banks of the Ganges, were three monasteries enclosed within the same walls, each having separate gates. All three of them housed finely ornamented statues of the Buddha. Among one temple's treasures was a tooth relic of the Buddha, which King Harṣa had obtained from the king of Kashmīr. On holidays this relic was displayed on a high throne, and thousands of people burned incense and placed flowers before it.

A hundred-foot high temple stood to the right and left side of the monastery; each temple had stone foundations and brick walls. Statues of the Buddha, one made of gold and silver and the other of copper, were located in the center of the temples. A small building was located in front of each of the temples. To the southeast, Hsüan-tsang found a very large monastery two hundred feet high, which also had a stone foundation and brick walls. Inside, Hsüan-tsang saw a statue of the Buddha thirty feet tall, made of copper and decorated with precious gems. The walls of the temple were ornamented with bas-reliefs of scenes from the Buddha's previous lives as a Bodhisattva.

In 1016, when Mahmūd of Ghaznī approached Kānyakubja at the head of his army, his chronicler recorded that, "He saw a city which raised its head to the skies, and which in strength and structure might justly boast to have no equal." (ASI I:279) During Mahmūd's invasion and the ensuing centuries of Muslim occupation, nearly all traces of Buddhist and Hindu monuments and culture vanished. Of all the places Hsüan-tsang describes, none could be positively identified in the nineteenth century. The Ganges River had changed its course since the seventh century, which complicated the search for these Buddhist sites. One large mound covered with broken bricks, located southeast of modern Kanauj, is considered a probable site for the three monasteries and the temple of the tooth relic. To the south about eight hundred feet is another large mound which may be the site of the great vihāra that housed the large Buddha statue. Neither of these sites has been excavated.

At Navadevakula,situated on the Ganges River about seventeen miles southeast of Kānyakubja, Hsüan-tsang counted five hundred Sarvāstivādin monks living in a complex of three monasteries. Directly in front of the monastery stood an Aśokan stūpa on the place where the Buddha taught the Dharma for seven days; although its foundations had sunk into the ground, it was still one hundred feet high. Less than a mile to the north stood another Aśokan stūpa two hundred feet high, commemorating the site where five hundred yakṣas heard the Buddha teach the Dharma. Comprehending the significance of the teaching, the yakṣas were freed from their present forms and reborn in the heaven realms. (HT I:224) No trace of this site could be found in the nineteenth century. Since the Ganges had changed its course here and had leveled everything in its path, any remains of Navadevakula were probably swept away by the river.

Hayamukha

At Hayamukha, about fifty miles down the Ganges River from Ayodhyā, Hsüan-tsang counted five monasteries housing about a thousand monks of the Saṁmatīya tradition. Southeast of the city stood a stūpa built by Aśoka, about two hundred feet high, commemorating a place where the Buddha had taught the Dharma for three months. Nearby Hsüan-tsang saw a second stone stūpa that contained relics of the Buddha's hair and nails. Next to this stūpa was a monastery that housed about two hundred monks. According to Hsüan-tsang, this was the place where Buddhadasa composed the Sarvāstivādin Mahāvibhāṣa-śāstra: "There is here a richly adorned statue of Buddha, as grave and dignified as if really alive. The towers and balconies of the monastery are wonderfully carved and constructed, and rise up imposingly above the building." (HT I:230)

In the nineteenth century, Cunningham tentatively identified Hayamukha as the town of Daundiakhera, once a capital of Rājput rulers, where there are ruins of an old fort. Since no remains that accord with Hsüan-tsang's description have been found, this identification remains speculative.

Prayāga

Prayāga, modern Allahabad, is located at the confluence of the Ganges and Yamunā rivers. There Hsüan-tsang found only two monasteries, each housing only a few monks of the Śrāvaka tradition: "This country is about five thousand *li* in circuit, and the capital, which lies between two branches of the river, is about twenty *li* round (six *li* = about a mile). The grain products are very abundant, and fruit-trees grown in great luxuriance. The climate is warm and agreeable; the people are gentle and compliant in their disposition. They love learning but are very much given to heresy." (HT I:230)

To the southwest of Prayāga stood an Aśokan stūpa, commemorating the place where the Buddha had refuted the tīrthikas. Beside this stūpa stood another stūpa containing hair and nail relics and traces of the four Buddhas of the past. According to Hsüan-tsang, the old monastery next to this stūpa was where Āryadeva wrote the Śataśāstra, refuted the principles of the Śrāvaka schools, and silenced the tīrthika philosophers.

Hsüan-tsang describes a custom observed in Prayāga for centuries: Every five years the king would celebrate a great charity offering at a place known as the Enclosure of Charity. On this occasion he would give away all the wealth accumulated over the past five years. Hsüan-tsang had personally observed King Harṣa celebrate this ceremony. The king first honored a statue of the Buddha with offerings. He then made gifts to the monks, to distinguished individuals of his realm, to his subjects, and to the widows, orphans, and mendicants who gathered here to receive the king's munificence. After he had given away everything, including his diadem and jeweled necklaces, the lesser kings of his realm presented him with their jewels and robes, replenishing King Harṣa's treasury.

According to Hsüan-tsang, the Brahmanic and other non-Buddhist traditions were especially strong in Prayāga. Beliefs involving the merit of religious suicide, promulgated by some ascetic schools of tīrthikas, were widely held and acted upon. The Akṣayavata, the undecaying banyan tree, was a popular site of such sacrifices.

Although the people of modern Allahabad still worship this tree, there are no traces of the stūpas and monasteries described by Hsüan-tsang. The old city of Prayāga was abandoned when the Yamunā River changed its course and has now completely disappeared. A stone pillar considered to be from Prayāga, erected by King Aśoka and containing one of his edicts on Buddhism, was moved to Allahabad by the Mughal emperor Jahangir sometime after 1605. The place where this pillar originally stood is not known. The pillar, pulled down a second time in the early nineteenth century to make way for a construction project, was repositioned in 1838, when the Asiatic Society made efforts to restore it.

Buddhism in Kashmīr

The Buddha regarded Kashmīr as the best place for meditation that one could wish for, and history confirmed the truth of his vision. Well-established by the time of the Dharma king Aśoka, Buddhism flourished in Kashmīr for nearly sixteen hundred years, supported by a strong tradition of meditation, the development of Abhidharma, and the transmission of the Mahāyāna philosophical traditions.

Kashmīr forms the northernmost state of modern India, bounded by the Karakoram mountains on the north-east, Himachal Pradesh on the south, and Pakistan on the West. Its northern boundary arches above the northernmost reach of the Indus River to the base of the Little Pamir range. Through Kashmīr flow two main rivers, the Indus and the Vitastā (modern Jhelum). The third of the 'five waters' of the Punjab, the Chandrabhāga River (modern Chenab) flows through the south of Kashmīr where the land descends to the plains of northern India.

The Consecration of Kashmīr

In ancient times, the name Kashmīr generally referred to the Vale of Kashmīr, the oval-shaped valley watered by the Vitastā River, which is dotted by spectacularly beautiful lakes. The Vinaya relates that at the time of the Buddha, Kashmīr was covered by a great lake which was home to the nāgas, powerful serpentine beings that live in the watery realms. The Buddha regarded Kashmīr as an excellent place for meditation and an ideal environment for leading the religious life. The Enlightened One predicted that after his Parinirvāṇa, a bhikṣu named Madhyāntika would conquer the nāga Hulunta and introduce the Dharma here.

Madhyāntika, having received this prophecy from Ānanda, the Buddha's disciple and second patriarch of the Dharma, went to Kashmīr in the fiftieth year after the Buddha's Parinirvāṇa. He sat down in meditation on a high mountain crag, knowing that his presence would attract the nāgas' attention. As his mind focused in concentration, the earth trembled, and the nāgas drew upon their powers to distract him.

When the nāgas caused rain to fall in great torrents and sought to do him physical harm, Madhyāntika concentrated on mercy, and the nāgas could not move even a part of his garment. Then the nāgas caused arrows to fall from the sky upon him, but the arrows turned to a shower of fragrant flowers. Thunderbolts, huge arrows, and swords and axes followed, but all these fell around Madhyāntika as blue lotus blossoms. Astonished, the nāgas approached the Arhat and asked what he wished from them. Madhyāntika told them of the Buddha's prediction, that the land of Kashmīr, so suited for meditation, would be a fertile ground for the Dharma; therefore the nāgas should grant him the land, and he would establish here the Buddha's teaching.

The nāgas agreed to give Madhyāntika all the land he could cover when seated in vajrāsana (the cross-legged meditation posture). Through the power of his meditation, Madhyāntika was able to cover an area encompassing nine valleys. The nāgas then asked Madhyāntika how many disciples he would bring to Kashmīr; when the sage told them five hundred Arhats would come, the nāgas agreed to cede this large expanse of land if Madhyāntika could guarantee the presence of so many Arhats. Madhyāntika requested permission to bring householders also to live on the land, for they would be needed to farm the land and support the Sangha. The nāgas agreed, on the condition that when the Dharma was exhausted, they would take back the land and restore the great lake that once covered it.

So provinces were laid out, villages built, and householders brought to settle the land. Madhyāntika established five hundred monasteries, one for each of the five hundred Arhats. To give the householders a basis for prosperity, Madhyāntika took them to the Gandhamādana mountain and asked them to gather saffron plants to cultivate in their fields. This action greatly upset the nāgas who lived there, but Madhyāntika soothed their fears. The nāgas agreed that as long as the Buddhadharma endured, Madhyāntika could take saffron plants from the mountain. The householders then planted the saffron in their fields; Madhyāntika blessed the plants, and the saffron flourished abundantly.

Madhyāntika worked for the Dharma in Kashmīr until the end of his days. When he entered nirvana, his body was cremated and his relics enshrined in the stūpa built to receive them. But the Dharma appears to have experienced difficulties in the centuries that followed. Hsüan-tsang adds that after the death of Madhyāntika, the Kritīyas, the people he had brought to settle the land, became arrogant and began to view themselves as Kashmīr's rightful rulers. As related by the Chinese pilgrim, whenever the Kritīyas came to power in Kashmīr they obstructed the growth of the Dharma.

Early History of Kashmīr

Bordered by Central Asia, Tibet, and the outpost satrapy states of Persia and Greece, Kaṣhmīr is enclosed by very high mountains and difficult to access. To the southwest, invaders and merchant caravans continually streamed through the Khyber Pass that gave entrance to the heartland of India, but narrow passes and mountainous terrain protected Kashmīr from all but the most determined conquerors. The flow of cultural influence was primarily from India; Candragupta Maurya, Aśoka's grandfather, brought Kashmīr into his empire in the fourth century B.C.E., and his grandson Aśoka maintained it within his empire also.

According to tradition, Aśoka founded the capital city south of the present Śrīnagar. The Aśokan capital was variously known as Śrīnagara (venerable city) or as Adhiṣṭhāna (chief town), and its site is known today as Pāndrethān (Sanskrit Purāṇādhiṣṭhāna, 'old chief town') (AAI 254; HT I:158n). Pāndrethān obviously became a major Buddhist center early in its history; in recent times, remains of stūpas, a monastery courtyard, and a Bodhisattva image have been unearthed from this site. (The present Śrīnagar, capital of Kashmīr, was built a short distance north of Pāndrethān.) Hsüan-tsang mentions that Aśoka pacified the Kritīyas who were obstructing the Dharma, and the Dharma prospered during his reign. He is said to have dedicated the whole country to five hundred Sarvāstivādin Arhats who had taken refuge in Kashmīr and to have built five hundred monasteries.

In establishing Kashmīr's early history, the Rājataraṅgiṇī (River of Kings), the central chronicle of Kashmīr by the twelfth century poet Kalhaṇa, relates that Aśoka built vihāras and stūpas at Vitastātra (modern Vethavutur), a place considered in ancient times to be the source of the Vitastā River. He erected more stūpas and founded monasteries at Śuṣkaletra (modern Hukhalitar, eighteen miles from Śrīnagar) (RT I:102; BCAI 157). Kalhaṇa also refers to a Buddhist king named

Surendra, who sponsored two monasteries in Kashmīr before Aśoka's time: the Narendra Vihāra, in Sauraka (modern Suru, near Dardistan, far to the north) and the Saurasa Vihāra (modern Sowur, also north of Śrīnagar). His descendant King Jalauka, who reigned after Aśoka, is described as a persecutor of Buddhism until Krtyā, a Buddhist laywoman, persuaded him to abstain from his destructive actions. The king is said to have built the Jolora Vihāra on a site known today as Zalor. (RT I:93, 118; BCAI 157). To date, no remains of these three monasteries has been found.

Jalauka, or possibly Krtyā, supported construction of the Kṛtyāśrama Vihāra, a large monastery which flourished until the eleventh century. Its ruins have been located in the village of Kitshom near Baramulla; nearby, in the village of Bodhamul, have been found the remains of a temple. The name Bodhamul, derived from Buddhamūla, meaning Source of Enlightenment, preserves the village's ancient association with a Buddhist center.

The Sarvāstivādins prospered during the reign of the Kuṣāṇa kings who held sovereignty over Kashmīr from the first century B.C.E. to the middle of the second century C.E. The Rājataraṅginī mentions that the Kuṣāṇa kings Huṣka, Juṣka, and Kaṇiṣka all built monasteries and temples at the Śuṣkaletra Vihāra and at other sites as well. The Kuṣāṇa king most closely associated with Buddhism was King Kaniṣka, who took an active interest in the teachings and convened a council of the Sangha in either Kashmīr or Jālandhara, a city south of Kashmīr proper between the Beas and the Sutlej Rivers. Bu-ston states that the council was held in the Kuvana Vihāra, specially built in Kashmīr for this purpose. (BU II:97)

When the Kuṣāṇas founded the cities of Kaniṣkapura (modern Kanispur) and Huviṣkapura (modern Uskur), they supported the construction of monasteries and stūpas nearby. Huviṣkapura in particular became an important Buddhist center in Kuṣāṇa times. Its monasteries underwent major renovations in the fourth and eighth centuries, and sustained the Sangha for at least seven hundred years.

The Kuṣāṇas, known to the Chinese as Yüeh-chih, were a Central Asian tribe that forged a vast empire extending north past Khotan, west through Afghanistan to the borders of Iran, and east as far as Vārāṇasī. Their rule protected access to the Silk Road, the caravan route that encircled the Taklamakan Basin of Central Asia and linked China with the Middle East. Following the trade routes, Sarvāstivādin bhikṣus and Mahāyāna masters alike established monasteries in the oasis states of Central Asia—Kashgar, Khotan, Kuchā, and Niya. In the fourth century, a major translation center was established at Tun-huang, where the Silk Road met China's western boundary. Kashmīri bhikṣus may well have been among the masters who worked for the Dharma at Tun-huang.

After the Kuṣāṇas, Kashmīr enjoyed relative autonomy; located outside the Gupta and Harṣa empires of the fourth through seventh centuries, Kashmīr was ruled mostly by local kings. The Rājataraṅginī records that the great master Nāgārjuna lived for a time at a vihāra in the Ṣaḍarhadvana (modern Hārwan), and that his knowledge enhanced Kashmīr's reputation as a center of learning. But when Abhimanyu became king, the monasteries lost royal patronage and could not sustain their educational programs. Nāgārjuna moved to South India, where he eventually passed away on Śrī Parvata. The Ṣaḍarhadvana, the Grove of Six Arhats, is thought to commemorate Vasumitra, Pārśva, Aśvaghoṣa, and other leaders of the Arhats associated with the Buddhist council convened by King Kaniṣka. (BCAI 159)

According to Hsüan-tsang, six hundred years after the Parinirvāṇa, the king of Himatala of the country of Tukhara, a descendant from the Śākyas expelled from Kapilavastu during the Buddha's lifetime, heard that the Kritīyas were again obstructing the Dharma. Disguising his warriors as merchants, he led them into Kashmīr and took possession of the kingdom by force. He brought the monks back to Kashmīr and built a monastery for them, then returned to his own country after rededicating Kashmīr to the Dharma. But the Kritīyas remained hostile to Buddhism; eventually they returned to power and restored the temples of their religion. (HT I:149–151)

Although such accounts indicate that there were periods of opposition to Buddhism, the Sarvāstivādins who lived in Kashmīr persevered and developed their monasteries into distinguished centers of learning. The isolated valley of central Kashmīr nurtured the development of the Sarvāstivādin Abhidharma, the systematic analyses of experience that provided the foundation of Buddhist philosophy. The Kashmīri scholars became widely respected; among them were the Sarvāstivādin masters Kātyāyaniputra and Vasumitra, the Vaibhāṣika teacher Dharmatrāta, the Sautrāntika masters Sthavira and Śrīlabdha (Śrīlāṭa), and the Vaibhāṣika teacher Saṁghabhadra, whose most famous student was the great scholar Vasubandhu.

Outstanding masters trained in Kashmīr were instrumental in translating the Dharma into the languages of Central Asia and China. One of the most famous of these translators was Kumārajīva, son of a Brahmin and a Khotanese princess. As a youth, Kumārajīva (344–413 C.E.) traveled to Kashmīr with his mother and studied the Āgamas with the master Bandhudatta. Then he returned to Central Asia and met the Kashmīri paṇḍita Vimalakṣa in Kuchā. Kumārajīva continued his studies with Vimalakṣa until the Chinese conquest around the turn of the century, when both master and disciple were taken into China. Thereafter Kumārajīva directed the translation center set up in Ch'ang-an, capital of the Chinese Empire. Much of what is known about Kashmīri Buddhism of this time derives from the comments of this great translator.

Kumārajīva's contemporary Buddhabhadra, who with Fa-hien translated the Mahāparinirvāṇa-sūtra into Chinese, completed his education in Kashmīr under the guidance of Buddhasena, a master known for his expertise in dhyāna, a form of yogic meditation. At the end of the fourth century, interest in dhyāna was growing in China, and teachers such as Buddhasena and the fifth-century master Dharmabhikṣu began to attract Chinese as well as Central Asian students.

The Rājataraṅgiṇī relates that King Meghavahana, whose rule began in 438 C.E., supported the Dharma and his wives built monasteries close to Śrīnagar: Yukadevī built the Nadavana Vihāra at Nadavana (modern Narvor); Indradevī sponsored the Indradevī Vihāra; Khādanā built the Khādanā Vihāra at Khadaniyar; Bimbā sponsored the Bimbā Vihāra, and Sammā built the Sammā Vihāra, Queen Amṛtaprabhā, a native of Ladakh, built the Amṛtabhavana Monastery near Vicharnag, about three miles north of Śrīnagar, and dedicated it to the Buddha Amitāyus, indicating that this was a Mahāyāna monastery. This monastery, located and excavated by M.A. Stein, had a solid stūpa and probably a peripheral wall.

In the sixth century, Buddhism in Kashmīr suffered greatly from the invasion of the Hephthalite, or White Huns. According to Hsüan-tsang, Mihirakula sought refuge in Kashmīr after losing ground to his rivals in the northwest. He then assassinated the Kashmīri king and used Kashmīr as a base to conquer Gandhāra, completely destroying all the Buddhist monasteries. Mihirakula appears to have attacked religious monuments indiscriminately, both Buddhist and Brahmanic, although according to the Rājataraṅgiṇī, Mihirakula later supported the Brahmins generously.

Some historians question whether Mihirakula really entered Kashmīr; however, the Huns' hostility to the Dharma and persecution of monks was well-remembered through the centuries. As Hsüan-tsang witnessed just a century later, the Huns' destruction of Buddhist monuments and temples had been quite thorough.

After the death of Mihirakula, his son Baka (known to Tāranātha as Mahāsammata, to the Mañjuśrīmūlakalpa as Buddhapakṣa, and to Bu-ston as Bhadanta) is said to have rebuilt many monasteries and temples destroyed by his father. During the reign of King Pravarasena (sixth century), the king's uncle Jayendra sponsored the building of a large Buddhist monastery, the Jayendra Vihāra, near the capital and enshrined in it a colossal metal Buddha image. (A later ruler, King Kṣemagupta, burned down this monastery, melted down the statue, and erected a Hindu shrine on its foundation.) Pravarasena's minister Moraka sponsored the building of the Morakabhavana Vihāra, which according to the Rājataraṅgiṇī became widely known. (RT III:356). Skanda, the minister of Pravarasena's successor Yudhiṣṭhira, sponsored the Skandabhavana Vihāra, a site now known as Khandabhavan, near Śrīnagar. The wife of King Raṇāditya, Yudhiṣṭhira's successor, donated a Buddha image to this vihāra.

The Visit of Hsüan-tsang

Traveling from Central Asia, Hsüan-tsang entered India along the Swat Valley, following the difficult route over mountains, along precipices, and over chain bridges strung across gorges. Arriving in Kashmīr around 630 C.E., Hsüan-tsang describes the kingdom as very extensive and enclosed by high mountains on all sides. "The neighboring states that have attacked it have never succeeded in subduing it." The capital city was bordered by a great river, which corresponds to the modern city of Śrīnagar located on the Vitastā. Hsüan-tsang mentions the old capital to the south and a great mountain known today as Takht-i-Sulimān. "The soil is fit for producing cereals and abounds with fruits and flowers. Here also are dragon-horses and the fragrant tumeric, fo-chu, and medicinal plants. The climate is cold and stern. There is much snow but little wind. The people wear leather doublets and clothes of white linen. . . The people are handsome in appearance, but they are given to cunning. They love learning and are well instructed." (HT I:148) Upon his arrival, Hsüan-tsang resided at the Huviṣkapura Vihāra.

The king of Kashmīr (not named by Hsüan-tsang but probably Durlabhavardhana) welcomed the Chinese traveler and provided him with twenty scribes to help him copy manuscripts. Hsüan-tsang remained in Kashmīr about two years to collect manuscripts and visit the sacred sites. His chief residence was the Jayendra Monastery, where he received instruction from an aged Kashmīri master.

The Kashmīri master of Jayendra was: "a man of high moral character. He observed with the greatest strictness the religious rules and ordinances. He was possessed of the highest intelligence and acquainted with all the points of a true disciple. His talents were eminent, his spiritual powers exalted, and his disposition affectionate." (Hwui 70) When the Chinese pilgrim questioned him on the doctrines of his tradition, the master was so impressed by his Chinese guest that even though he was enfeebled by age, he gave full response; their dialogues attracted all the scholars in the kingdom. Hwui-li relates Hsüan-tsang's high regard for Kashmīri scholars: "This country from remote times was distinguished for learning. These priests were all of high religious merit and conspicuous virtue; they possessed noticeable talent and the power to clearly explain doctrine." (Hwui 71)

Hsüan-tsang counted a total of about one hundred monasteries and five thousand monks in the central region of Kashmīr. Each of the four Aśokan-style stūpas he found contained relics of the Buddha. Hsüan-tsang visited the monastery at the foot of Takht-i-Sulimān that held the Buddha's tooth relic, the monastery where the master Skandhila wrote the Vibhāṣa-prakaraṇa-śāstra, and the ruins of the monastery where the Sarvāstivādin master Saṁghabhadra worked for the Dharma and taught his famous pupil Vasubandhu. Stūpas enshrining the relics of great Arhats stood on each side of

Buddhist sites in Kashmīr

Saṁghabhadra's monastery and about thirty Mahāyāna monks were living nearby: "The wild beasts and mountain apes gather flowers to offer as religious oblations. Throughout the year they continue these offerings without interruption, as if it were a traditional service. Many miraculous circumstances occur on this mountain." (HT I:160)

About two and a half miles south of the tooth relic monastery was a small monastery that enshrined a miraculous statue of Avalokiteśvara. Hsüan-tsang describes a specific devotional practice offered here: Those who wished to see the true form of the Bodhisattva took a vow before this statue to fast to death if necessary. At some point Avalokiteśvara would emerge from the statue, revealing to the devotee his marvelously colored form. This practice was still being transmitted in the tenth century by the Kashmīri nun Lakṣmī; it entered Tibet in the twelfth century (ND 189).

Some miles from the capital city was the monastery of the Abhidharma master Pūrṇa, who composed a commentary on the Vibhāṣa-śāstra. There was also in this vicinity one Mahāsāṁghika monastery with about a hundred monks, where, according to Hsüan-tsang, the master Bodhila composed the Tattvasañcaya-śāstra. Hsüan-tsang's biographer and contemporary Hwui Li names Kashmīri masters active at that time: the Sarvāstivādins Sugatamitra and Vasumitra; the Mahāsāṁghikas Sūryadeva and Jinatrāta; and the Mahāyānists Viśuddhasiṁha and Jinabandhu.

Hsüan-tsang described other countries along the upper Indus river that were then centrally ruled from Kashmīr: Siṁhapura and Urasa to the north of Kashmīr proper, and Punach and Rājapurī to the south. He observed that the people of these lands were fierce and courageous, but somewhat given to deceit, except in Punach, which was a predominantly Buddhist region. In mountainous Siṁhapura there were three monasteries. One was in ruins, and the other two housed three hundred Mahāyāna monks. Near the city there was a great park with ten reflecting pools and a two-hundred-foot high Aśokan-style stūpa. This region was also a holy place for the Jains, who had a temple in the area. In the mountain-encircled valley of Urasa there was one stūpa built by Aśoka and a monastery with but a few Mahāyāna monks. To the south, Rājapurī and Punach together had fifteen monasteries, mostly deserted.

At Mulbek, on the route between Śrīnagar and Leh, capital of Ladakh, travelers today can see a nearly thirty-foot-high statue of the Bodhisattva Maitreya, hewn from the face of a pinnacle of rock. Hsüan-tsang does not describe this figure, which may date from the eighth or ninth centuries.

The Kārkoṭa Kings

In 602 or 626, Durlabhavardhana, the first king of the Kārkoṭa Dynasty, came to power. His reign signalled a renaissance of prosperity for Kashmīr and a revitalization of its Dharma traditions supported by members of the royal family. His queen Anaṅgalekhā built the Anaṅgabhavana Vihāra at Candragrāma (modern Chandragom), and his daughter-in-law Prakāśadevī sponsored the construction of a monastery near the capital. (RT IV:3, 79) The Kārkoṭas ruled Kashmīr until 1003; they were followed by the first and second Lohara dynasties (1003–1101, 1101–1171), then by a succession of later Hindu kings (1171–1320).

While Hsüan-tsang's description of Buddhism in Kashmīr reflects his sadness over what had been lost, even as he was writing the Dharma was entering a period of recovery. By the eighth century, Kashmīr was well known in Tibet as a center of Buddhist learning. Bu-ston records that Srong-btsan-sgam-po, seventh-century king of Tibet, sent his minister Thon-mi Sambhoṭa to Kashmīr to study systems of writing as a basis for developing a Tibetan script. In the eighth century, Khri-srong-lde-btsan invited Kashmīri bhikṣus and scholars to establish the Sangha in Tibet and to participate in translating Buddhist texts from Sanskrit into Tibetan.

At this critical juncture, Muktāpīḍa-Lalitāditya (700–737) became king. Although Muslim forces were expanding into Central Asia and pushing into Afghanistan and Sindh in the eighth century, the combination of Kashmīr's remote location and Lalitāditya's strong leadership inhibited an invasion of Kashmīr. In 751, with the help of the Qarloq Turks, the Arabs defeated the Chinese in a decisive battle near the Talas River. After that battle, only the Uighurs of the Taklamakan Basin maintained the Dharma in Central Asia.

Kashmīr became an island of calm for the Buddhists of Central Asia, who were driven from their homes by the Muslim conquests. The refugee Buddhists helped strengthen the Dharma in Kashmīr and contributed to the flowering of Kashmīr's art and culture. Among them was Caṅkuṇa, a devout Central Asian Buddhist who became Lalitāditya's minister. So brilliant was he that the Rājataraṅgiṇī records that Caṅkuṇa was an alchemist who "filled the king's coffers with gold." Between Caṅkuṇa's skills and the king's military prowess, Kashmīr prospered during this time, and the Dharma flourished under royal patronage.

Lalitāditya founded the Rāja Vihāra and a temple in Parihāsapura, his new capital fourteen miles west of Śrīnagar on the Jhelum River. He had made for the temple a great copper statue of the Buddha, described in the Rājataraṅgiṇī as reaching the skies. He also had a large vihāra and stūpa built at Huṣkapura. The minister Caṅkuṇa established a temple at Śrīnagar and a temple and great stūpa at Parihāsapura, and his son-in-law Īśānacandra also built a temple in the area.

The temple and the stūpa of Parihāsapura were well-known throughout the region; although there is little left of these great monuments, their likeness is believed to be preserved on the murals of Alchi, a cave temple in Western Tibet. From the extent of the remains, the height of the temple has been estimated at between ninety and 120 feet, and the colossal Buddha image enshrined in it may have been ninety feet high. A number of sculptures have been found at this site.

According to the Rājataraṅgiṇī, Kāvya, the king of Lāṭa, built "the sacred Kāvya Vihāra, a veritable marvel," during that time. The paṇḍita Sarvajñāmitra, one of the twelve Kashmīri masters who helped establish the Sangha in Tibet, resided here before traveling to the land of snow. (RT IV:210) Some of Lalitāditya's successors also actively supported the Dharma. His grandson Jayāpīḍa (752-783) sponsored one temple and three images of the Buddha at Jayapura (modern Anderkot). His queen Jayādevī and his minister also built vihāras here. (RT IV:506ff)

The Chinese traveler Ou-k'ong reported that Buddhism was flourishing in Kashmīr at the time of his visit (759–763). Three hundred monasteries were active, and the Sarvāstivādins were still the predominant school. He describes the Amṛtabhavana monastery built in the fifth century by Queen Amṛtaprabhā as a place for foreign monks; ruins of this monastery have been located at Antbhavan Vicharnag, three miles north of Śrīnagar (BK 45–47). Ou-k'ong also mentions some monasteries founded by Turks. These Turks were obviously Buddhist, most likely refugees from lands taken over by Muslims, but their origin is unclear. It is possible that the term refers also to Tokharians, an Indo-European-speaking people of Central Asia.

During the eighth and ninth centuries, twelve Sarvāstivādin monks from Kashmīr helped to establish the Dharma in Tibet. Among them were Sarvajñāmitra, Vidyākaraprabha, Dharmākara, and Jinamitra who translated the Vinaya texts, and Dānaśīla, Munivarman, and Śīlendrabodhi, who with Jinamitra and a number of Tibetan lo-tsā-bas translated the Sūtras. In the ninth century, at the request of King Ral-pa-can, Jinamitra, Dānaśīla, Śīlendrabodhi, Surendrabodhi, and Bodhimitra worked with Ye-shes-sde, sKa-ba dPal-brtsegs, and other skilled Tibetan lo-tsā-bas in editing translations, regularizing vocabulary, and compiling the Mahāvyutpatti, a massive lexicon of Sanskrit Buddhist terms and their Tibetan equivalents.

The flow of Kashmīris to Tibet ended when Ral-pa-can died and his successor Glang Dar-ma actively persecuted the Dharma in Tibet. Glang Dar-ma's rule was short; a period of chaos followed upon his death, but order was eventually restored. Beginning in the tenth century, Rin-chen-bzang-po, Blo-ldan-shes-rab, and other Tibetans traveled to Kashmīr to study the Prajñāpāramitā, Mādhyamika, and logic with outstanding Kashmīri masters. Many Kashmīri monks accompanied Rin-chen-bzang-po on his return to Tibet and many others settled in the Kashmīri/Tibetan borderlands, where they taught Tibetan disciples and supported the second transmission of the Dharma to Tibet.

Logic and Prajñāpāramitā

The growth of Kashmīri interest in logic dates from the time of the Sarvāstivādin monk Saṁghabhadra (c. fourth century), the teacher of Vasubandhu. According to Hsüan-tsang, Saṁghabhadra wrote the Nyāyānusaraśāstra, a treatise on logic, while residing in a mountain retreat near the capital city. But the school of logic that flourished in Kashmīr from the eighth century on developed from a fresh tradition introduced from India. This tradition was begun by Dignāga, a disciple of Vasubandhu, and continued by Dharmakīrti, who developed Dignāga's writings on Pramāṇa ('necessary consequence') in a masterful series of treatises. The writings of these two great masters established a strong tradition of logical analysis in India, Kashmīr, and Tibet.

Tāranātha relates that the lineage of Dignāga and Dharmakīrti was introduced into Kashmīr by three Kashmīris who had studied at Nālandā: Vidyākarasiṁha, Devasiṁha, and Devavidyākara. However, little more is heard of these masters. It was the eighth-century Indian masters Vinītadeva and Dharmottara who clearly established the study of pramāṇa in Kashmīr. Vinītadeva adhered to the literal interpretation of Dharmakīrti's works, while Dharmottara leaned toward a broader view. Together, Vinītadeva and Dharmottara were singularly well-qualified to transmit all facets of Dharmakīrti's thought to Kashmīr.

Kashmīr, like Tibet, appears to have experienced economic and political difficulties in the mid-ninth century, when the Kārkoṭa rulers were supplanted by the Utpala kings. Political instability continued through the tenth century; at least one monastery, the Jayendra Vihāra, was destroyed at this time during a civil insurrection. Although these conditions cloud the history of Buddhism in Kashmīr during the ninth and tenth centuries, toward the end of this period, the study of logic was flourishing in both India and Kashmīr. The resurgence of interest in logic was led by Prajñākaragupta, Yamāri, and Śankarānanda, all masters of the late ninth or early tenth centuries; Śankarānanda was definitely from Kashmīr, as was the eleventh-century logician Jñānaśrīmitra. It is possible that two other prominent logicians, Yamāri and Prajñākaragupta's disciple Ravigupta, were also Kashmīri. All these masters were important in the second period of Dharma transmission to Tibet.

Transmitted through Haribhadra and his disciple Buddhajñāna, the Prajñāpāramitā teachings took strong hold in Kashmīr. A family of lay masters beginning with Ratnavajra developed this tradition in Śrīnagar. Ratnavajra, a Kashmīri scholar, occupied the prestigious position of Central Pillar of Vikramaśīla before returning to his homeland. Holder of both Prajñāpāramitā and Mantrayāna lineages, Ratnavajra went to Tibet, where he translated Mantrayāna texts with Rin-chen-bzang-po at mTho-lding Monastery in Western Tibet and supervised the reconstruction of the terrace of bSam-yas Monastery in Central Tibet (BA 378).

Ratnavajra's son was Mahājana, a teacher of Atīśa and a collaborator of Marpa, the famous teacher of Milarepa. Mahājana's son was Sajjana, Kashmīr's brightest luminary of the Prajñāpāramitā teachings. Sajjana is also credited with reviving the study of Cittamātra, based on texts rediscovered in India by Maitri-pa and brought to Kashmīr by Ānandakīrti. Sajjana's son Sukṣmajana was the last of this illustrious family, but Sajjana's disciple Jñānaśrī went to Tibet, where he transmitted the teachings of Maitreya and the Pramāṇa tradition of Dignāga and Dharmakīrti. Through Jñānaśrī and other disciples of this Kashmīri school, Tibet received the full benefits of these important traditions.

Kashmīri Masters in Tibet

During the tenth to twelfth centuries, Kashmīri paṇḍitas vigorously supported the second transmission of the Dharma to Tibet. In a mutually beneficial association, they transmitted their knowledge and realization to their Tibetan students in India and Kashmīr, and many of them traveled to Tibet to help with translating the sacred texts. The siddha-scholar Nāropa, teacher of Marpa, Milarepa's teacher, is said to have studied in Kashmīr, and at least one modern scholar argues that Nāropa's hermitage, Puṣpahari, was located in Kashmīr. (ND 178). The Kashmīri master Bodhibhadra, who may have been Nāropa's disciple, was instrumental in introducing the Kālacakra teachings to Tibet.

The Tibetan Rin-chen-bzang-po went to Kashmīr three times, where he mastered the philosophical traditions under as many as seventy-five paṇḍitas, including Ratnavajra. He invited a large number of Kashmīri paṇḍitas to his monastery of mTho-lding, where he collaborated with them on translation. Blo-ldan-shes-rab went to Kashmīr in 1077 to study logic with the monk Parahitabhadra and the Prajñāpāramitā with Sajjana; returning to Tibet after seventeen years, he transmitted these traditions to many thousands of disciples. His countryman Pa-tshab Nyi-ma-grags, like many other Tibetans, also came to Kashmīr where he studied for twenty-three years before returning to Tibet. In Tibet, Pa-tshab collaborated on translations with the Kashmīri paṇḍitas Kanakavarman and Muditaśrī.

The long list of Kashmīri masters who served the Dharma in Tibet includes Subhūtiśrīśānti, famous teacher and translator of Prajñāpāramitā, who revitalized its study at mTho-lding Monastery; and Somanātha, master of the Kālacakra teachings, who worked with the Tibetan translator 'Bro Shes-rab-grags in translating the root text of the Kālacakra system and its major commentary, the Vimalaprabhā. Subhūtiśrīśānti's contributions included translations of the Eight Thousand-line Prajñāpāramitā and an important commentary, the Abhisamayālamkārāloka. Working with dGe-ba'i-blo-gros, he translated major commentaries on Dharmakīrti's Pramāṇa-vārttika, and with Ting-nge-'dzin-bzang-po and other Tibetans, he translated a number of Kālacakra teachings. In eleventh-century Tibet he was known as Kha-che Paṇ-chen, 'the great Kashmīri Paṇḍita'.

At the beginning of the thirteenth century, Śākyaśrī, the last of the great Kashmīri scholars, led a group of paṇḍitas to Tibet after Vikramaśīla was destroyed. An outstanding teacher, Śākyaśrī was also honored with the name Kha-che Paṇ-chen. His most famous disciple was Sakya Paṇḍita, one of the great masters of the Sa-skya tradition.

Decline of the Dharma in Kashmīr

During the twelfth century, Kashmīr was rent by civil unrest when the power of the king was challenged by regional rulers and the countryside fell into anarchy. Centers where Kashmīris and Tibetans worked together were endangered and some monasteries were burned. Although Jayasiṁha, who ruled c. 1128 to 1154, restored order, Kashmīris were probably well aware that the Muslim armies to the south were ravaging India and incursions into Kashmīr were immanent. It is likely that these conditions contributed to the increasing flow of paṇḍitas to Tibet, where the Dharma was flourishing and the conditions for contributing to scholarship and translation efforts were far more favorable.

When the paṇḍita Śākyaśri returned to Kashmīr from Tibet in 1222, he found that the Dharma had declined during his long absence and there were few monks remaining. According to the Blue Annals, he reestablished the Kashmīri king in the Dharma and spent the final three years of his life restoring the monasteries and statues. (BA 710) However, the momentum of political change in Kashmīr cut short the effects of his labor.

The Rājataraṅgiṇī, the main resource for Kashmīri history, ends in 1250, and later chronicles are not very detailed. From what can be gleaned of events thereafter, it appears that the tension between the king and powerful landholders continued, erupting periodically into serious struggles for power. The Muslim Turks became involved: Having infiltrated the capital, they assassinated the king in 1286 and forced the division of Kashmīr into two kingdoms. Although Hindu supremacy was reasserted over the whole valley early in the fourteenth century, Kashmīr's troubles continued. An army, either Muslim or Mongol, plundered Kashmīr, and a Tibetan adventurer became governor. Shortly after his death, the first Muslim ruler of the whole of Kashmīr came to power (ND 252–255).

For a time the government appears to have tolerated all Kashmīr's religions, but later governments repressed them. By the fifteenth century Buddhist activity had nearly ceased. The entire country was fully absorbed into the Mughal empire after the seventeenth century, and it is likely that many of Kashmīr's surviving Buddhists resettled on the route leading to Tibet. To the east, in the valleys nestled between Kashmīr and Tibet, Buddhist communities in Ladakh, Lahoul, Spiti, and Guge have flourished to the present day.

Archaeological Remains

In light of the number of vihāras, shrines, and monuments mentioned in the Rājataraṅginī, the remains uncovered to date provide a fragmentary but important record of Buddhist activities in Kashmīr and insight into the distinctive quality of Kashmīri art, which blends Indian, Gandhāran, Persian, and Central Asian art forms into a rich and elegant style. Excavation of the Ṣaḍarhadvana Monastery at Hārwan, lo-

Ruins of the Ṣaḍarhadvana Vihāra at Harwān, once an important center of learning

cated in 1925 two miles from Śrīnagar's famous Shalimar Gardens, has yielded remains of a large temple and a monastery with a stūpa in the paved central courtyard, and a section of wall. The clay tiles of the courtyard's original floor are stamped with Kharoṣṭhī script in a style associated with the later Kuṣāṇas (fourth century C.E.). Similar tiles were unearthed at Ahan in 1962, together with remains of monastery walls and a stūpa.

Within the ruins of Lalitāditya's capital city Parihāsapura, near modern Paraspor, archaeologists have located several important Buddhist monuments, including the Rāja Vihāra of Lalitāditya, which was obviously a major focus of Buddhist activity; ruins of other vihāras and large shrines are clustered in the immediate area. One of these temples probably held the great Buddha image brought from Magadha and donated by King Lalitāditya. To the north of the

Rāja Vihāra are the remains of the monastery built by the minister Caṅkuṇa, excavated from a mound four hundred feet square, which also appears to have housed a large image. Ruins found at Huṣkapura have been identified as the Mukta Vihāra. Pāndrethān, site of Aśoka's capital Śrīnagara, has also been proven an important Buddhist site.

Gilgit

Gilgit, the Bru-zha of the Tibetans, is located in greater Kashmīr, above the central valley of the Vitastā (Jhelum) River. From ancient times Gilgit was an important link with Central Asia. A pass north of the Gilgit Valley connected Gilgit with the Buddhist centers of Central Asia, and for centuries the main routes bhikṣus followed to Central Asia led through Gilgit, Chitral, and the Swat Valley. During the eighth century, the Chinese army and Turkish Muslim invaders engaged in a series of struggles for Gilgit. These hostilities drove Buddhists in Gilgit to take refuge closer to the Kashmīri capital of Parihāsapura. However, during a period of persecution in the mid-tenth century, Kashmīri Buddhists took refuge in Gilgit, where they enjoyed the protection of the Sahi rulers.

In 1931 an important find of more than two hundred Sanskrit Buddhist manuscripts was unearthed from a ruined stūpa in Gilgit. These texts, known as the Gilgit manuscripts, date to the fifth or sixth century C.E. Most of them are the only extant copies in Sanskrit of such important Mahāyāna texts as the 25,000-Line Prajñāpāramitā, the Samādhirāja, Saddharmapuṇḍarīka, and Bhaiṣajyaguru Sūtras, and the Mūlasarvāstivādin Vinaya. Their discovery stimulated the study of Buddhist texts in the West and resulted in the translation into English of essential Mahāyāna texts. Today the Gilgit manuscripts are housed in the National Archives of India in New Delhi. That so valuable a collection of texts was found in Gilgit indicates that in ancient times Gilgit was very likely an important Mahāyāna center.

Part Four

Dharma Centers on the Route West

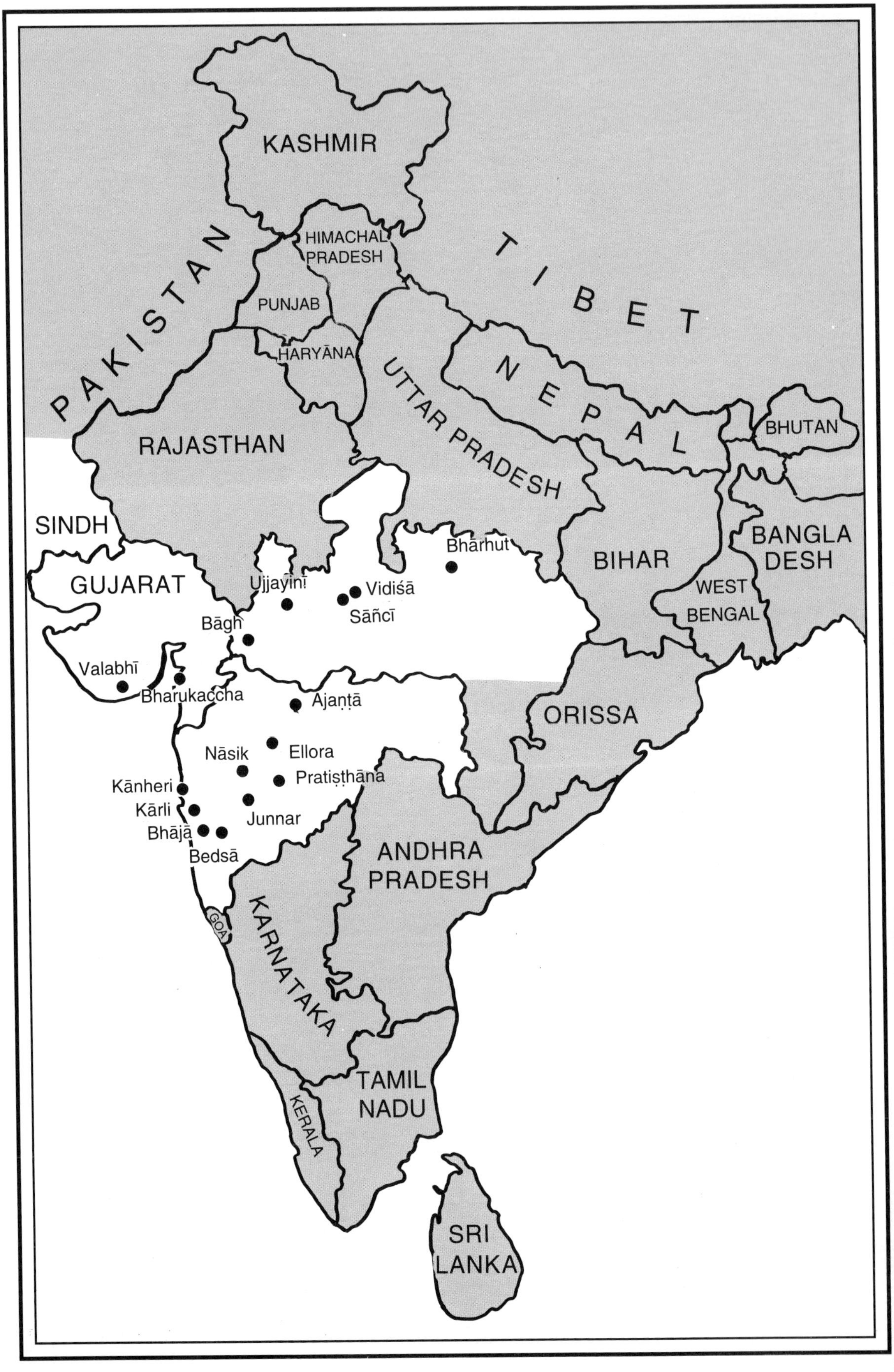

KASHMIR
HIMACHAL PRADESH
PUNJAB
HARYĀNA
PAKISTAN
TIBET
NEPAL
BHUTAN
UTTAR PRADESH
RAJASTHAN
SINDH
GUJARAT
BIHAR
BANGLA DESH
WEST BENGAL
ORISSA
ANDHRA PRADESH
KARNATAKA
GOA
TAMIL NADU
KERALA
SRI LANKA
Bharhut
Ujjayinī
Vidiśā
Sāñcī
Bāgh
Valabhī
Bharukaccha
Ajaṇṭā
Nāsik
Ellora
Pratiṣṭhāna
Kānheri
Kārli
Junnar
Bhājā
Bedsā

Monuments of Ancient Avanti

The Great Stūpa of Sāñcī and the Bhīlsa Topes testify to the longevity and strength of Buddhism in ancient Avanti, the prosperous kingdom west of the Madhyadeśa.

From the time of the Buddha, the great trade route connecting the Madhyadeśa (Middle Country) with the rich seaport cities of India's western coast provided a conduit for the transmission of the Dharma. Early in the history of the Sangha, Arhats and Mahātheras established major Dharma centers in Bhārhut, Vidiśā, Sāñcī, and Ujjayinī, cities which defined the route west from Kauśāmbī to Bharukaccha. From east to west, the section of India discussed here encompasses the ancient kingdoms of Avanti, Aparānta, Surāṣṭra, Kaccha, and Sindh. These lands are bounded on the north and east by the Yamunā River and on the south by the Satpura mountains—an area encompassing the modern Indian states of Gujarāt, Rājasthān, and the northern part of Madhya Pradesh as well as the Pakistani province of Sindh.

The early history of Buddhism in the modern state of Mahārāṣṭra is closely connected with the Sātavāhana kings who ruled the Deccan between the first century B.C.E. and the third century C.E. After that time, however, Buddhism in Mahārāṣṭra was more closely linked to the north. For that reason, the extraordinary cave temples of Mahārāṣṭra are described at the end of this section.

Avanti at the Time of the Buddha

At the time of the Buddha, the four most prominent kingdoms of India were Magadha, Kosala, Vatsa, and Avanti. Avanti, the westernmost of these four kingdoms, shared a common border with Magadha, ruled by King Bimbisāra. To the northeast was the kingdom of Vatsa, where King Udayana ruled from his capital at Kauśāmbī, and beyond Vatsa lay the kingdom of Kosala, ruled by Prasenajit, a king who requested teachings from the Buddha and supported the Sangha in his realm. Ancient Avanti corresponds to the central and western part of modern Madhya Pradesh, or the region encompassing the cities of Vidiśā on the east and Ujjain on the west.

King Pradyota ruled Avanti from his capital at Ujjayinī (Pāli Ujjeni, modern Ujjain), on the Sipra River. Located at the convergence of three major trade routes, this ancient city was from its earliest days a prosperous center of commerce. The route west led to the seaports of the western coast, the route east led to the major eastern cities of the Ganges Basin, and the route south and southeast led to cities engaged in the rich sea trade with Śrī Laṅkā and Southeast Asia. The southern route also connected Ujjayinī directly with Māhiṣmatī and Pratiṣṭhāna (Paithan) on the upper Godāvarī, the gateway to the Dakṣiṇāpatha, the route to South India. This was the route taken by the disciples of Bavari, sent from the south by their master to question the Buddha. From their home on the upper Godāvarī River, they traveled though Ujjayinī and the new settlement of Vidiśā in eastern Avanti. From there they traveled to Kauśāmbī and followed the Ganges River east to the Madhyadeśa.

During the Buddha's lifetime, Avanti became an outpost of the Dharma that was entrusted to the supervision of the Arhat Mahākātyāyana, a native of Ujjayinī. While still a youth, Mahākātyāyana, son of one of King Pradyota's councilors, had been sent by the king to Śrāvastī to invite the Buddha to Ujjayinī. Upon hearing the Buddha teach, Mahākātyāyana and his seven companions all became Arhats and joined the Sangha. The Buddha then asked the young Brahmin and his companions to bring the Dharma to Ujjayinī in his place. Mahākātyāyana and his companions returned to Ujjayinī, where Pradyota welcomed them and gave them one of his parks as a home for the Dharma.

Mahākātyāyana appears to have been the first to spread the Dharma in the regions of Ujjayinī and Mathurā. According to the Dīpavaṁsa, Mahākātyāyana was known for his skill in explaining the Buddha's teachings in detail. He composed a work explicating the Āgamas, which was still in use in southern India centuries later. Works attributed to Mahākātyāyana (the Petakopadesa and Nettippakarana, as well as the Kaccayanavyākārana or Kaccayanagandha, a grammatical work) were also known to Buddhaghosa, the famous South Indian scholar who edited the ancient Sinhalese commentaries in the fifth century.

As Mahākātyāyana's disciples continued the tradition he established, Avanti became an early center of learning that combined study of the scriptures with awareness of the value of clear expression. The major trade route linking the Ganges with the western coast led through Avanti, and merchants traveled freely through Avanti to the cities of Śrāvastī and Vārāṇasī. Many of these merchants had the opportunity to hear the Buddha teach at Śrāvastī, and they returned to the west with some understanding of the Dharma. Among them was the Arhat Pūrṇa of Sopāraka (a town on the western coast), who dedicated his life to transmitting the Buddha's teaching in his homeland. The Theragāthā, a Pāli canonical text, records the conversion of the caravan leader Soṇakuṭikaṇṇa (Sanskrit, Śroṇakoṭikarṇa). Isidaṭṭa, the son of another caravan leader, became a disciple of Mahākātyāyana before meeting the Buddha in the Madhyadeśa. Both Soṇakuṭikaṇṇa and Isidaṭṭa propagated the Dharma in Avanti. Through the efforts of Mahākātyāyana, Pūrṇa, and other great Arhats, the Dharma was transmitted in the west during the lifetime of the Buddha.

However, political and cultural conditions in Avanti appear to have hindered the early growth of the Sangha. King Pradyota was known as 'The Cruel'; he was aggressive and warlike, particularly toward King Udayana of Vatsa and occasionally even toward Bimbisāra, king of Magadha. The Vinaya accounts record that during the Dharma's early years in Avanti it was difficult to assemble even the ten monks needed for ordination, and some of the Vinaya rules imposed undue hardships on the monks in light of cultural and climatic conditions in Avanti. When Soṇakuṭikaṇṇa traveled to Śrāvastī to visit the Buddha, Mahākātyāyana asked him to explain the hardships in Avanti to the Buddha and request easements in some minor rules. The Buddha granted this request; he authorized five monks to be present for ordinations if the ten normally required could not be located and gave permission for the monks of Avanti to wear thick-soled shoes, take frequent baths, and use hide coverlets for bedding.

Avanti's political power diminished after King Pradyota's death. Around 400 B.C.E., the Magadhan king Śiśunāga annexed the land of Avanti, opening the way for the growth of permanent Buddhist centers in Avanti and the Dharma's westward expansion. Nurtured by the rise of the merchant class and prosperity from the flow of trade, Ujjayinī and Vidiśa, Avanti's two major cities, supported the growth of the Sangha in western and eastern Avanti. Accounts of the Vaiśālī convocation note that eighty-eight Arhats from Avanti attended the Second Council, which was held one hundred years after the Buddha's Parinirvāṇa.

The Śuṅga kings, who came to power in the last half of the second century B.C.E., supported an unprecedented wave of construction, renovation, and ornamentation of Buddhist monasteries and stūpas in Avanti. Much of this work was funded by wealthy donors, primarily merchants and townspeople appreciative of the Buddhist teachings. The building of Bhārhut, Sāñcī, and other Buddhist centers near the prosperous city of Vidiśā contributed greatly to the growth of the Śuṅga artistic school, India's first coherent artistic tradition. With the monuments and sculptures of the Śuṅga period, art became a major vehicle for communicating the Buddhist teachings to the lay Sangha and a strong support for devotional practices.

When the Sātavāhana kings of the Deccan extended their influence into Avanti in the early centuries C.E., Śuṅga art became known further south; the effects of its style can be seen in the early cave temples to the southwest and in the artistic tradition of southeastern centers from Jaggayyapeta to Amarāvatī, located on the Kṛṣṇa River. Under the Gupta kings, who came to power early in the fourth century C.E., artistic representations of Buddhist images created an even greater harmony of aesthetic and spiritual beauty.

In the fifth century, during the reign of the Gupta emperor Skandagupta, the Huns, a Central Asian tribe, conquered Gandhāra (modern Afghanistan) and ravaged Buddhist monasteries throughout the northwest. Although Skandagupta defeated them decisively, they soon regrouped in the northwest and from there mounted fresh incursions into the heart of India. From their leader's family, these Huns were known as Ye-tha, Hephthalites, or Ephthalites, or simply as White Huns. Under the leadership of Toramāṇa, they invaded western India as far as Eran, a city north of Sāñcī. Although it is likely that the Huns did not occupy western India for any prolonged amount of time, they caused extensive damage. Their destructiveness increased when Mihirakula, the son of Toramāṇa, assumed power in 515 C.E. Mihirakula ravaged monasteries in a wide swath between northwestern India and Magadha. It was not until 560 C.E. that he and his forces were completely expelled from India. In 567 C.E., the Turks and Persians joined forces to crush the central Hun Empire on the Oxus River, ending the Huns as a threat to India. It was about this time that the Gupta Empire began to disintegrate and ties between the Gupta capital at Pāṭaliputra and the western regions weakened.

Avanti's main Buddhist centers appear to have survived these events and to have flourished here through the seventh-century reign of King Harṣa. Hsüan-tsang relates that sixty years before his visit to India, a king named Śīlāditya, Son of Virtue, ruled Avanti for fifty years with great compassion and wisdom. He built a vihāra next to his palace in Ujjayinī, Avanti's capital, had images of the Buddhas placed there, and supported a congregation of monks. "He was humane, affectionate, generous, and sweetly attached to his people. He was, from the first, supremely reverent to the doctrine of the three precious ones; and from the time he became king to his death, no improper word had proceeded from his mouth, nor had his face ever flushed with passion. . . . He impressed on the chief people of his kingdom to avoid taking life, and hence the beasts of the desert became attached to men and the wolves ceased to be injurious." (Hwui 148) Each year King Śīlāditya sponsored an assembly of the Sangha, convening monks from the four directions. At this time he offered the monks the 'four essentials' as well as religious robes and precious substances for ceremonies. Hsüan-tsang adds that this meritorious custom was still observed in his time.

Although Harṣa may not have ruled all of Avanti, the accounts of Hsüan-tsang clearly indicate that he exerted great influence in Avanti and also in the western states of Aparānta and Gujarāt. With Harṣa's death, his empire fragmented into autonomous principalities that vied for power amongst themselves. The times favored the Kṣatriya warrior ethic, which encouraged the revival of Brahmanic rituals and revitalized the Hindu traditions. While these factors hindered the growth of Buddhism in Avanti, the Buddhist centers of Sāñcī and Bhārhut appear to have survived until the Muslim invasions in the eleventh century.

Vidiśā

According to the Mahāvaṁsa, Vidiśā was founded by a group of Śākyas who had escaped from the massacre at Kapilavastu and settled in eastern Avanti. Its location at the conjunction of major trade routes from the west and south ensured its rapid growth and prosperity. Vidiśā's success powered Avanti's rise to prominence in the centuries after the Buddha's Parinirvāṇa, when Vidiśā became the capital of eastern Avanti.

In the third century B.C.E., when King Bindusāra appointed his son Aśoka viceroy of Avanti, Aśoka made his home in Vidiśā. Here he married Devī, who bore him two children: Mahinda and Sanghamittā, the brother and sister who later established the Dharma in Śrī Laṅkā. When Aśoka moved to Pāṭaliputra to claim the throne after his father's death, Devī maintained her home in Vidiśā. After her children were ordained by Moggaliputta Tissa in Pāṭaliputra, Devī commemorated this event by building the Vidiśāgiri Vihāra on the Cetiya Hill. Her son Mahinda visited the Vidiśāgiri Vihāra just before departing to bring the Dharma to Śrī Laṅkā. This monastery, which appears to have been the earliest permanent residence for monks in Avanti, became an important center of the Sthavira tradition. Patronized by prosperous merchants, the Sthavira community of bhikṣus flourished in this region. During the reign of the Śuṅga kings, who ruled

c. 187–175 B.C.E., the city of Vidiśā developed into a thriving center of trade, able to support the building of exceptionally fine monuments. In modern times sites of more than sixty stūpas, known as the Bhīlsa Topes, have been located near Vidiśā (modern Bhīlsa), about twenty-six miles northeast of Bhopal. The Bhīlsa Topes consist of five major clusters of stūpas, at Sāñcī, Senari, Satdhara, Bhojpur, and Andher. The largest and best preserved monuments are at Sāñcī, located south of Vidiśā on the summit of a forested hill.

Sāñcī

Inscriptions in the ancient Brāhmī script refer to Sāñcī as Kākanāva or Kākanāya, while epigraphs composed in the Gupta period refer to Sāñcī as Kākanādaboṭa. Sāñcī has also been known as Boṭa-Śrīparvata, which may refer to Cetiyagiri, the Sanctuary Mountain, or to the Mt. Vedisa mentioned in the Sinhalese chronicles. Famous for its magnificent stūpa with four imposingly high stone gates, Sāñcī is considered one of the most beautiful and perfect monuments of ancient India. The great stūpa is still in excellent condition; together with the extensive ruins of monasteries and other monuments, it bears eloquent witness to the vitality and longevity of the Dharma in this region.

The history of Sāñcī spans thirteen centuries, from the time of Aśoka to around the eleventh century. In the third century B.C.E., Aśoka erected a pillar inscribed with an edict here as well as the great stūpa and various other monuments. The original Mahāstūpa was later largely destroyed, probably by Puṣyamitra, the first king of the Śuṅga Dynasty. Shortly after Puṣyamitra's demise, another Śuṅga king, either Agnimitra or his successor, restored the Mahāstūpa. He had a stone sheathing built around the stūpa and filled in the intervening space with heavy rubble, which expanded the stūpa to

Left: The Eastern Gate of the Great Stūpa of Sāñcī

The pillars of Sāñcī's main temple still stand close to the Mahāstūpa.

twice its original size. The whole hill was paved in stone about this time. The exquisitely carved gates and railings were added when the Sātavāhanas of Āndhra ruled most of Avanti during the first century B.C.E. The carvings depict scenes from the Buddha's life and illustrations of the Vessantara, Sāma, and other Jātaka stories, together with the figures of protective deities.

The scope and grandeur of Sāñcī, like Bhārhut, indicate that the monasteries here were supported by prosperous lay communities. Inscriptions on the gateways record the names of donors and their native cities. Although most of the donors were from the surrounding region of Mālwā, some were from such distant lands as Kāmboja and Gandhāra, which lay far to the northwest beyond the Indus River. Acknowledgments of lay donors name their occupations, which range from queen to dressmaker and weaver, from governor and mer-

Remains of a monastery near the great stūpa at Sāñcī

chant to craftsman and scribe. Associations and guilds were also listed as donors of Sāñcī's elaborate sculptures.

Several inscriptions carved at Sāñcī during the Śuṅga period name the Sutaṁtikas, or Sautrāntikas, although this term may not refer to the Buddhist philosophical school that flourished somewhat later in the northwest. Other inscriptions confirm that the Haimavatas, a branch of the Sthaviravādins, had a long-standing association with Sāñcī.

In the eleventh century, Muslim invaders took control of the northwest and mounted raids in central and western India. Although the area surrounding Sāñcī was devastated several times, Sāñcī's monuments were somehow untouched. They appear to have remained undisturbed for centuries until Cunningham identified Sāñcī as a Buddhist site in the nineteenth century. At that time the stūpa's dome was intact and some of the balustrades on the top of the dome were still in place. Three of the four gateways of the great stūpa were standing, and the southern gate was lying where it had fallen. Two other large stūpas were also well-preserved, and remains of eight smaller stūpas and other buildings stood nearby.

Today, the great stūpa stands about fifty-four feet at the highest point of its hemispherical dome. To its northeast is a subsidiary stūpa, approached through a gate similar, but smaller than, the gates of the main stūpa. On the southeast there is a high stone plinth with rows of pillars and steps leading to its surface; this plinth, which may date to Aśoka's time, appears to have supported a wooden building, most likely a temple. To the southwest there is another empty plinth, and a little lower on the hill is another stūpa with sculptured railings.

The great stūpa is one of twenty stūpas that may still be seen at Sāñcī, all of which are in fairly good condition. However, excavations show that more than fifty Buddhist monuments once existed at the site, including stūpas, temples, monasteries, and commemorative pillars that date from the time of Aśoka to the eleventh century C.E. More than nine hundred inscriptions have been found in this complex. Inscriptions on five urns unearthed from one of the stūpas connect the relics preserved in the urns with Majjhima and with a sage of the Kāśyapa family, both emissaries to the Himalayan region during the time of Aśoka. Another urn may contain the remains of the Arhat Moggaliputta Tissa, also associated with Aśoka.

None of the inscriptions name any particular Buddhist school; however, this region was known to have been the main Sthavira center from the time of Aśoka. Aśoka's son Mahinda resided at Vidiśā before bringing the Dharma to Śrī Laṅkā, and there is a strong possibility that Pāli, the language of the Southern Canon, is very close if not identical to the Prākrit, or spoken language, of ancient Vidiśā.

Now as in ages past, Sāñcī is an excellent site for reflection and meditation.

Remains of eight stūpas were discovered at Sonari, six miles southwest of Sāñcī. Inscriptions on a relic casket found at the site name the Arhats Majjhima, Kassapagotta, and Dundubhissara of the Haimavata tradition. To the west, on Mt. Satdhāra, are seven stūpas, one of which was over ninety feet in diameter. In a smaller stūpa at this site were found two empty caskets bearing the names of Śāriputra and Mahāmaudgalyāyana, two of the Buddha's principal disciples.

At Bhojpur, seven miles southwest of Sāñcī, are the remains of thirty-three stūpas; three small but well-preserved stūpas were found nearby at Andher. Inscriptions found on reliquaries in the Andher stūpas name the Haimavata Arhats Majjhima and Kassapagotta, and urns at the Bhojpur site name additional masters. To the south, on the Narmadā River near the ancient city of Māhiṣmatī, is a site known today only as Itbardi, the Brick Mountain. Remains of eleven stūpas made of brick were found here and tentatively dated in the second century B.C.E. Inscriptions and coins found at the site link this complex of eleven stūpas with the great stūpa at Bhārhut to the northeast.

Bhārhut

The great stūpa of Bhārhut, located on the major trade route from Bharukaccha to Kauśāmbī in the region of Mālwā, appears to have been built during the Śuṅga Dynasty, around the middle of the second century B.C.E. Constructed of bricks, the stūpa in modern times attracted the attention of local villagers, who mined it for building materials until the British archaeologist Cunningham discovered it in 1873. Subsequent excavations revealed portions of a gateway and carved railings that once circled the stūpa; these were removed and preserved in the Indian Museum at Calcutta.

The stūpa of Bhārhut appears to have been similar to the great stūpa at Sāñcī; the eastern gateway, which stood about twenty-two feet high, was covered with sculptured reliefs of scenes from the Jātakas, accounts of the Buddha's previous lives. Nearly all surfaces were ornamented with sculpted panels and round medallion-like carvings.

Inscriptions verify that these scenes illustrate places and events described in the Sūtras, such as the Nāga Jātaka, Queen Māyā's dream, a king's royal procession to visit the Buddha, the shrines and trees of Jeta's Grove at Śrāvastī, and the merchant Anāthapiṇḍada covering Jeta's Grove with coins to purchase it for the Sangha. Some of the figures appear to capture contemporary details; one figure is readily recognizable as a Greek warrior, with his sword, distinctly styled hair, clothing, and boots.

Perhaps the most studied relief found at Bhārhut is the depiction of the Bodhi Tree shrine at Bodh Gayā. Carved during the Śuṅga period, this relief provides the earliest record of a monument erected at the site of the Buddha's enlightenment. Another well-known relief, carved as a circular medallion, depicts the Mahākapi Jātaka, as retold in *The King and the Mangoes* (Berkeley: Dharma Publishing, 1976). In a previous life the Bodhisattva was a monkey king who created a bridge over a chasm by stretching his body between two trees, one on each side. This way the monkeys escaped from the king who wanted to destroy them so that he could have all the fruit from their mango tree. The monkey king's back was broken in this effort and he fell to the ground. Filled with admiration, the human king queried the reasons for his actions and received a teaching on the responsibility of leadership and the duties of a wise king.

Bhārhut, like Sāñcī, was well supported and received the attention of generations of skilled artisans. Inscriptions at Bhārhut record the names of 126 donors from twenty-eight different places, from Pāṭaliputra in the east to Nāsik in Mahārāṣṭra. Most of the donors were laymen and laywomen, but princes and princesses, bhikṣus and bhikṣuṇīs are also named as contributors.

Ujjayinī

The Dakṣiṇagiri Monastery near Ujjayinī, where Aśoka's son Mahinda spent six months preparing for his travels to Śrī Lāṅkā, also became an important Sthavira center that supported the growth of the Sangha in the west. The Mahāvaṁsa records that in the first century B.C.E., Urusamgharakkhita of Dakṣiṇagiri (Pāli, Dakkhinagiri) brought forty thousand bhikṣus to Śrī Laṅkā to attend the consecration of the Mahāthūpa, the Great Stūpa of Anurādhapura.

In his description of Ujjayinī as it appeared in the seventh century, Hsüan-tsang notes that the city and its environs were prosperous; however, the present king was a devout Brahman and not well-disposed toward the Dharma. Although there were thirty or more monasteries near Ujjayinī, they were mostly in ruins. The three or so that were still in use housed three hundred monks who studied both the Śrāvakayāna and Mahāyāna teachings.

Hsüan-tsang's account of Ujjayinī contrasts with his general description of Mālava, which appears to refer to western Avanti. According to Hsüan-tsang, Mālava was one of the two regions (the second was Magadha) in India most renowned for the great learning of their people. "The disposition of the men is virtuous and docile, and they are in general of remarkable intelligence. Their language is elegant and clear, and their learning is wide and profound." Mālava's two hundred monasteries housed about two thousand monks, mostly of the Saṁmatīya tradition; the followers of the Śaivite tradition were also numerous in this region. The king of Mālava also ruled Ānandapura, to the north, and Kaccha, to the west.

Ānandapura, a prosperous region, supported about ten monasteries with less than one thousand monks of the Saṁmatīya tradition. Hsüan-tsang describes Kaccha as an appendage of Mālava, with both countries very similar with respect to the land, climate, and nature of their people. He counted ten monasteries in Kaccha housing about one thousand monks of both Mahāyāna and Śrāvakayāna traditions.

In the seventh century, King Harṣa of Kanauj brought the western regions of Avanti, Valabhī, Kaccha, and Mālwā into his empire, but Sindh and the great desert region (Rājpuṭana, modern Rājasthan), ruled by the Gurjaras, remained outside his influence. Hsüan-tsang's account of the region of Vidiśā and Ujjayinī indicate that the Dharma had not significantly recovered there by the seventh century. Little is known of the Buddhist activities here after his time.

Aparānta
The Western Coast

Enriched by access to the trade routes of land and sea, the countries of Aparānta prospered during the the Buddha's lifetime and for centuries after his Parinirvāṇa. Bhikṣus established Buddhism here at an early date, and the western Sanghas developed strong traditions of meditation and scholarship. The caves of Mahārāṣṭra have survived the centuries, revealing the significance of Buddhist art to the Indian cultural heritage.

Aparānta, the coastal region between the Narmadā River and the uppermost reaches of the Godāvarī, included the entire Kāthiāwar peninsula (Surāṣṭra) and the seaports of Bharukaccha and Sopāraka—western India's links to the sea trade, Śrī Laṅkā, and the cities of Southeast Asia.

The first to actively propagate the Dharma in the coastal region of Aparānta was the Arhat Pūrṇa, a direct disciple of the Buddha. Pūrṇa was a rich merchant from Sopāraka (Pāli, Supāraka, modern Sopāra), capital of Aparānta at the time of the Buddha. Upon hearing the Buddha teach in Śrāvastī, he requested ordination and entered the Sangha. After becoming an Arhat, Pūrṇa resolved to bring the Dharma to his homeland. When he returned to Sopāraka, he built the Candanamala Prasada Monastery and invited the Buddha to teach there. Accompanied by five hundred disciples, the Buddha flew to Sopāraka and stayed at the monastery for one night. Leaving his footprint on the bank of the Narmadā, the Buddha returned to Śrāvastī the next day.

In the late fourth century B.C.E., Candragupta Maurya brought Aparānta into the Mauryan Empire together with Surāṣṭra and Sindh. During the reign of his grandson Aśoka, the Arhat Moggaliputta Tissa sent emissaries throughout India and beyond to propagate the Buddha's teachings in distant regions. Emissaries led by the bhikkhu Yonaka Dhammarakkhita (Dhammarakkhita the Greek) taught the Dharma in Aparānta. An Aśokan edict has been found in Sopāraka, and relic caskets of stone, silver, and gold have been unearthed from the remains of an old stūpa near the city.

After a period of persecution instigated in the second century B.C.E. by Puṣyamitra, the first of the Śuṅga kings, Buddhism flourished along the western coast. Around 110 B.C.E., the Śakas, a Central Asian tribe that had migrated into northern Persia, entered the province of Sindh. After establishing themselves in Sindh, they pushed east into Aparānta. In their wake came the Parthians and the Kuṣāṇas. The Śakas of Sindh and Aparānta served the Kuṣāṇas as provincial governors (satraps), exercising more or less autonomy as Kuṣāṇa power in the region waned or waxed.

When the Kuṣāṇa Empire disintegrated early in the third century C.E., Śaka satraps continued to rule the western provinces until the early fifth century, when Candragupta II, son of Samudragupta, the powerful Gupta king, brought the regions of Aparānta and Surāṣṭra (the Kāthiāwar Peninsula, modern Gujarāt) into the Gupta Empire. The warrior kings of the Maitraka clan protected Surāṣṭra during the Hun incursions of the late fifth and early sixth century. Their efforts spared Valabhī and the coast of Aparānta the destruction suffered by the provinces of central India.

When Hsüan-tsang visited Aparānta during the seventh century, he noted that King Harṣa of Kanauj, a powerful protector of the Dharma, exerted a strong influence in this western region. Nearly all kings and governors of the western provinces accommodated Buddhism, and some actively supported the Dharma traditions.

Bharukaccha

The seaport of Bharukaccha, modern Broach, figures in the Jātakas as the home of merchants and the place where adventurers embarked in search of fabulous treasure. In this thriving city located at the mouth of the Narmadā River, Hsüan-tsang found ten monasteries housing three hundred monks who followed the Sthavira and Mahāyāna traditions. The people of Bharukaccha earned their living from the sea; concerning them, Hsüan-tsang writes, "they do not cultivate study, and are wedded to error and true doctrine alike." (HT II:259–60)

Valabhī

Valabhī, located on the Kāthiāwar Peninsula, lay on the overland route linking Bharukaccha with cities further west in Surāṣṭra. Although Buddhism was present in the region of Valabhī from early times, Valabhī rose to prominence as a Buddhist center toward the end of the fifth century, when the Maitraka kings came to power in this far western land. Under the rule of the Maitrakas, who supported Buddhism, Valabhī became a center of learning known throughout all of India. According to a copper plate inscription, the princess Duḍḍā, a niece of King Dhruvasena I (reigned c. 525–545), sponsored the construction of Valabhī's first monastery. This structure was so large that it was known as a 'mandala of monasteries', indicating that it encompassed other monasteries within its perimeter. At least one monastery in the compound was dedicated as the residence of bhikṣuṇīs (nuns), and inscriptions indicate that Duḍḍā herself may have joined the order of bhikṣuṇīs. In the sixth century, Mimmā, another woman of the royal family, also sponsored a monastery and became a bhikṣuṇī.

Inscriptions record that at least thirteen additional monasteries were built to house Buddhists attracted to the monasteries of Valabhī from all parts of India. Bhikṣus of the eighteen Śrāvaka schools lived and studied here together with bhikṣus of the Mahāyāna tradition. The monasteries supported devotional practices and their libraries had large collections of Buddhist texts.

In the seventh century, Hsüan-tsang found the region of Valabhī densely populated, with rich establishments supported by about a hundred wealthy families. These families probably prospered from the lucrative sea trade, for "The rare and valuable products of distant regions are here stored in great quantities." (HT II:266) The people of Valabhī supported some hundred monasteries with about six thousand monks, mostly adherents of the Saṁmitīya tradition. Near Valabhī was the Śrī Bappapāda Monastery, where Vasubandhu's disciples Guṇamati and Sthiramati once resided and wrote their treatises. According to a grant of Dharasena I, Sthiramati was the founder of the Śrī Bappapāda monastery. Sthiramati developed Vasubandhu's Vijñānavāda teachings and Guṇamati focused on Vinaya and Abhidharma. Guṇamati's disciple Vasumitra continued the Abhidharma lineage and composed commentaries on the Abhidharmakoṣa, one of Vasubandhu's major works.

Paramārtha, a monk from Ujjayinī and also a disciple of Guṇamati, is well-known for his biography of Vasubandhu, which survives today only in Chinese translation. After completing his studies, Paramārtha made his way to China, where he translated more than thirty texts, including treatises by Guṇamati and Vasumitra.

In Hsüan-tsang's time, Valabhī was a major center for Śrāvakayāna and Vijñānavāda studies, second only to Nālandā as India's major university. I-tsing mentions that Nālandā and Valabhī were the two places in India where scholars came to complete their education. (I-tsing 177) Dhruvapaṭa, Valabhī's king, was the nephew of King Śīlāditya of Mālava and the son-in-law of Śīlāditya, king of Kānyakubja (Harṣavardana of Kanauj). Hsüan-tsang relates that "He [Dhruvapaṭa] is of a lively and hasty disposition; his wisdom and statecraft are shallow. Quite recently he has attached himself sincerely to faith in the three Precious Ones (The Three Jewels—Buddha, Dharma, and Sangha). Yearly he summons a great assembly and for seven days gives away most valuable gems, exquisite meats, and on the priests he bestows in charity the three garments and medicaments, or their equivalent in value, and precious articles made of rare and costly gems of the seven sorts. Having given these in charity, he redeems them at twice their price. He esteems virtue and honors the good; he reverences those who are noted for their wisdom. The great priests who come from distant regions he particularly honors and respects." (HT II:267) King Dhruvapaṭa's power extended throughout the rich peninsula of Surāṣṭra. According to epigraphic evidence, he was also known as Dharmāditya, Sun of the Dharma. (HCIP 4:63)

West of Valabhī, in densely populated Surāṣṭra, there were about fifty monasteries housing three thousand monks, most of whom belonged to 'the Sthavira school of the Great Vehicle'. (By this term, Hsüan-tsang refers to the school known in Śrī Laṅkā as Abhayagirivāsins, who were later absorbed into the Mahāvihāra school.) Hsüan-tsang describes a monastery carved out of solid rock on the top of the densely forested Mt. Ujjanta. "Here saints and sages roam and rest, and Rishis endowed with spiritual faculties congregate and stay." (HT II:269)

In Gurjara, north of Surāṣṭra and Kaccha, Hsüan-tsang found Buddhism in decline; in this desert region, there was but one monastery housing about a hundred Sarvāstivādin monks. The temples of the Brahmanic sects and their devotees outnumbered the Buddhists ten to one. Hsüan-tsang highly regarded Gurjara's young king as a wise leader devoted to the Dharma.

Sindh

According to Hsüan-tsang, Buddhism was flourishing in seventh-century Sindh, a land abounding in gold, silver, and copper and ruled by a Śūdra king who revered the Dharma. Several tens of Aśokan stūpas commemorated the Buddha's visit to this land. Hsüan-tsang relates that the great patriarch Upagupta, Aśoka's contemporary, came here often to explain the Dharma and guide those wishing to follow the teachings. He notes that temples and stūpas had been built in places visited by Upagupta. In all, the Chinese pilgrim counted several hundred monasteries housing ten thousand monks, all of the Saṁmitīya tradition. So many shrines, monasteries, and stūpas were in Sindh that Hsüan-tsang remarked, "These buildings are seen everywhere. We can only speak of them briefly." (HT II:273) But Hsüan-tsang adds that the monks living in the monasteries were lax in following the Vinaya; those who were earnest about practice lived alone in desert places or in mountains and forest retreats.

The city of P'i-shen-p'o-pu-lo (Viśavapura, Vasmapura, Balmapura, Minagara), the capital of Sindh, may have been close to the site of Mohenjo Daro, a great prehistoric city abandoned around 1500 B.C.E. During Kuṣāṇa times (first century B.C.E.–second century C.E.), a large Buddhist stūpa and a monastery were built on the high ridge of the Mohenjo Daro ruins. When the site was excavated between 1922–1923, the monastery was described as a spacious quadrangle open to the sky, with a lofty stūpa in the middle and rows of monastic buildings enclosing the central courtyard on four sides. The stūpa's plinth, or foundation platform, was twenty feet high; the drum had deteriorated to a height of eight feet by the twentieth century, but its diameter was over thirty-three feet and its center appeared to have been hollow. According to Marshall, who had excavated a large number of Kuṣāṇa ruins, the drum of the stūpa was embellished with columns and probably rose three stories from its plinth.

Small votive stūpas and additional quarters for monks surrounded the central stūpa. The buildings around the courtyard were probably two stories high, with a veranda facing the courtyard. A large quantity of ashes found at the site indicated that wood had been used for construction and that the monastery had been destroyed by fire. The whole monastery showed clear indications of having been repaired or rebuilt many times on an increasingly higher level for a period of three to four centuries of continuous occupation.

Coins found at the site suggest that this monastery was inhabited between 150–500 C.E., or from the time of the Kuṣāṇa king Vasudeva I to the end of the Gupta Empire. Before excavation, the site stood seventy-two feet above the surrounding countryside. If this monastery and stūpa were destroyed around 500 C.E., Hsüan-tsang may have seen them on his travels in Sindh, but he made no special mention of these monuments.

In the marshlands along the Indus River, Hsüan-tsang came upon a large community of people who shaved their heads and dressed like bhikṣus, but in all other respects lived worldly lives. It was said that in centuries past an Arhat had visited this region; noting the violent temperament of the people, he stayed with them a while and influenced them to adopt more gentle ways. When they became capable of understanding the teachings, they abandoned their old ways, refrained from taking life, and took the vows of bhikṣus. Although in the seventh century they maintained the outer appearance of religious practitioners, they no longer observed the Vinaya. Conducting themselves as laypeople, they held to Hīnayāna views and disparaged the Mahāyāna.

At the mouth of the Indus River, on the Arabian Sea, was the kingdom Hsüan-tsang referred to as 'O-tien-p'o-chi-lo; it is possible that Khie-tsi-shi-fa-lo, the capital city, may be ancient Daibal (modern Karachi). Here, as elsewhere in the kingdoms of Sindh, the people greatly esteemed Buddhism. About eighty monasteries in the region housed five thousand monks of the Saṁmatīya tradition, and Aśokan stūpas marked traces of the Buddha's visits. In the 1920s, Buddhist offertory tablets were found at Tharro Hill near Gujo, a village about fifty miles north of the mouth of the Indus.

Further west, along the northern coast of the Arabian Sea, lay the kingdom of Laṅgala. Hsüan-tsang noted around a hundred monasteries housing six thousand monks who studied the teachings of both Śrāvaka and Mahāyāna traditions. In the seventh century, this region was ruled by Persia, although the language and script used here were very similar to Indian forms. While Hsüan-tsang did not travel into Persia itself, he heard that there were two or three monasteries in Persia housing several hundred Sarvāstivādin monks, and that one of them then housed the Buddha's almsbowl.

Both Fa-hien and Hsūan-tsang knew of a tradition that the Buddha's almsbowl would be preserved for a period of time in lands that had received the Dharma. Fa-hien was told in the fifth century that the almsbowl, originally preserved in Vaiśālī, was in Gandhāra. After a time it would go to Central Asia, to the country ruled by the Yüeh-chih, to Khotan, and to Kuchā; from there it would be taken to China, then to Śrī Laṅkā and to the Madhyadeśa. From there it would be taken to the Tuṣita Heaven, where it would divide itself into four bowls that would pass into the hands of the four world guardians. After the enlightenment of the Buddha Maitreya, the four world guardians would come to the Vajrāsana and offer the bowls to Maitreya, as they had offered them to Śākyamuni Buddha. Maitreya also would place the bowls one inside the other and press them into a single bowl. In this way, the almsbowl would pass in turn to each of the thousand Buddhas of our aeon. (HT lxxviii)

North of Laṅgala, about two hundred miles north of the Arabian Sea and west of the Indus River, was the kingdom of Pītaśilā, a region dependent on Sindh. Here Hsüan-tsang found some fifty monasteries housing about three thousand monks of the Saṁmatīya tradition. A short distance north of the main settlement stood an Aśokan stūpa several hundred feet high, commemorating the place where the Buddha, in a previous existence as a great sage, patiently endured the king's cruelty. To the east was an old monastery, said to have been built by the great Arhat Kātyāyana, and a stūpa marking traces of visits by previous Buddhas.

Hsüan-tsang describes 'O-fan-ch'a (Avanda?) as a kingdom dependent on Sindh located northeast of Pītaśilā. While the people were rough and their language simple, many had sincere faith in the Three Jewels. The twenty monasteries here housed two thousand monks, mostly of the Saṁmatīya tradition, and Aśokan stūpas northeast of the city marked sites visited by Śākyamuni and other Buddhas of past times.

In Mūlasthānapura (Multan), a prosperous settlement located north of Sindh in the Punjab's fertile valleys, Hsüan-tsang found about ten monasteries, mostly in ruins, with only a few monks. A large temple to Āditya, the sun, was the most prominent religious monument in this area. "Men from all countries come here to offer up their prayers; there are always some thousands doing so." (HT II:274–275)

Eclipse of the Dharma in Western India

While the history of Buddhism in these western regions is scanty, the information available indicates that Buddhism grew steadily in lands west of the Madhyadeśa from the time of the Buddha until the early eighth century. After King Harṣa's death, local rulers engaged in prolonged struggles for portions of his empire; these embroilments disrupted and weakened Buddhist centers throughout the western region. Internal disputes continued even when a clear and present danger arose on India's western border.

Shifts of power within Islam had sparked Arab expansion eastward. An early naval attempt between 636 and 637 to raid Thana, near Bombay, failed, but western Sindh proved more vulnerable. Arab raids on its western border and coastal region began in 644, but a strong effort to occupy Sindh was not made until the early eighth century, when the Arab capture of Baluchistān, the region directly north of Sindh, opened a route for invasion. In 712, after several early attempts failed, Mohammad-bin-Qasim, at eighteen years of age, was charged with conquering Sindh. He gathered a large army as he headed east and conquered the port city of Daibal (modern Karachi) with an army of fifteen thousand men. Accounts of this invasion, recorded by contemporaries who were part of the army, note that inhabitants of Daibal were given the opportunity to convert to Islam; those who refused were killed. Seven hundred women who were "under the protection of Buddha," either nuns or refugees from the fighting, were captured and sent back to Hajjaj, the Arab capital. Both Hindu and Buddhist temples were torn down and mosques built on their foundations.

Dahir, king of Sindh, paid little attention to the Arab presence in his kingdom and did not fight until Qasim's army marched on his stronghold. After capturing Dahir and his sons, Qasim continued unopposed north to Multan (Mūlasthāna), the principal city of the middle Indus. His army plundered the city and obtained such a large quantity of gold that Multan became known as the City of Gold. Soon after, Qasim was recalled to the capital and executed on the order of the Caliphate. The Arab military expansion ceased, and the Arabs settled in to occupy the province of Sindh.

The purpose of occupying Sindh was both strategic and economic; the people were taxed heavily and the Arabs obtained much gold. But Sindh was essentially a poor province; when the flow of treasure ceased, the Caliphs lost interest in protecting their eastern holdings. The Arabs of Sindh became increasingly independent; their rule was fragmented into several smaller units, and rapid dynastic changes weakened their hold on Sindh.

At this critical time, the militarily strong states of western India could have banded together and driven the weakened Arab forces from their border. But Sindh had long been a geographically isolated province, and the princes of western India, distracted by their own internal disputes, largely ignored the Arab presence here.

Valabhī, the region's strongest Buddhist center, eventually became a victim of these disputes. In the eighth century, besieged by Arab raids and caught up in power struggles with its Indian neighbors, the kingdom of Valabhī disintegrated. When the monasteries of Valabhī were destroyed, their scholars and bhikṣus sought refuge in the great Buddhist centers of the Madhyadeśa, which were rapidly expanding under the benevolent rule of the Pāla kings.

Cave Temples of Western India

Excavated out of the living rock, the cave temples of Mahārāṣṭra rank among the world's great wonders. For centuries communities of bhikṣus lived and meditated here, surrounded by sculpted columns, images, stūpas, shrines, and eloquently expressive paintings.

The monks and nuns of the earliest Sangha were mendicants, essentially homeless wanderers who came together once a year to observe the three-month rainy season retreat (varṣaka). These observances took place in caves or in temporary dwellings erected in groves dedicated for the Sangha's use. Meditation was practiced in caves or in the open air, and shrines or small temples served as places for offering and devotion. In time, temporary dwellings gave way to more permanent buildings, and settled communities of bhikṣus and bhikṣuṇīs began to form. The elements of an established Buddhist center—temple, shrine, stūpa, and dwellings for monks and nuns—developed gradually over a period of several centuries.

Nothing remains of the temples and dwellings of the earliest permanent centers, which were probably made of wood. Toward the end of the second century B.C.E., the early wood sanctuaries began to serve as prototypes for temples carved out of solid rock. While caves had long been used by mendicants of all religious traditions, the early Buddhist Sanghas excavated caves capable of housing whole communities and developed them into architectural masterpieces. The earliest caves were relatively simple rock-hewn caverns, and the caves that served as temples were carved to emulate the appearance of above-ground wooden temples, like the temple caves of Bhājā. The tendency to recreate the familiar wooden architecture in stone persisted, but as the art of stone carving developed, artisans gradually developed a distinctive cave architecture, rich in sculpture and ornamentation. To date, around twelve hundred excavated caves have been located in India, and about three quarters of these caves were created by Buddhist communities. (HBIS 237)

The cave complexes that housed Buddhist communities included temples (caityas), stūpas, assembly halls, and monastic dwellings. The vihāras, or monks' residences, usually consisted of a central courtyard surrounded by the monks' rooms, which were sometimes layered three stories high. A separate excavation was usually made for the temple, which consisted of a long rectangular hall, rounded at the back to accommodate a stūpa or a Buddha statue at the far end. Pillars supporting a barrel-vaulted roof defined aisles at each side of the temple and curved around the stūpa or statue at the back of the room. The temples traditionally had three doors, one central door opening to the main hall and two smaller side doors opening onto the side aisles.

Cave Temples of Mahārāṣṭra

On the west coast of India, the western Deccan plateau falls to the coast in steep gorges and cliffs in the region known as the Western Ghats. The region is largely rocky mountains, with little wood for building materials. But in many places the rock is soft and relatively easy to carve, making this region a natural location for the excavation of caves. Great clusters of cave temples, monasteries, and cells for meditation were discovered in the northern part of this range of hills, located in the modern state of Mahārāṣṭra. Among them are the famous cave complexes of Ajaṇṭā, Ellora, Nāsik, Kānheri, Kārli, and Bhājā.

Most of these sites developed into major Buddhist centers between 100 B.C.E. and 200 C.E., although some of the cave complexes were established somewhat earlier or later. During these centuries, western Mahārāṣṭra was alternatively ruled by the Sātavāhana kings of the Deccan or by Śaka satraps, Central Asians who had moved into India from the northwest in the closing years B.C.E. The Śakas generally supported Buddhism, and their names often appear as donors in inscriptions found at Buddhist sites.

The Sātavāhanas shaped an empire in the Deccan about the same time that the Śakas entered India, and they maintained it for nearly three hundred years. At first the Narmadā River formed a natural boundary between the Śakas on the north and the Sātavāhanas of the south. But this boundary shifted when the Śakas invaded the northwest Deccan early in the first century C.E. Around 125 C.E., the Sātavāhana king Gautamīputra Sātakarṇi drove the Śakas from the modern Mahārāṣṭra and Gujarāt regions, bringing these provinces, rich in cave temples, firmly into the Sātavāhana Empire.

From their capital at Pratiṣṭhāna (Paithan) on the upper Godāvarī River, the Sātavāhanas, at their greatest extent, directly ruled the whole region bounded by Mālwā and Saurāṣṭra in the north and by the Kṛṣṇā River in the south. This kingdom linked the Buddhist communities of the Western Ghats with the communities of South India for several critical centuries of growth. Although the early Sātavāhana kings appear to have followed Brahmanic traditions, the Dharma flourished under their rule. However, early in the third century C.E., the Sātavāhana Empire began to disintegrate, and the Vākāṭakas began their rise to power in the Deccan. From that time, southern India was fragmented into several kingdoms, and conflicts between them may have hindered travel between the eastern and western coasts.

Aside from the evidence of the long-time use of the cave temples and the grandeur of the art found at these sites, little is known of Buddhism in Mahārāṣṭra. In nearly all cases inscriptions in the caves themselves provide the only records available of the Buddhist communities here, which appear to have persisted in this region up to the eighth century and perhaps even longer. However, these inscriptions indicate that royal support for the Buddhist communities became less reliable after the end of the Sātavāhana Empire. Only some of the early Vākāṭaka kings provided for the Buddhist communities, whereas the later Vākāṭakas and the Traikuṭakas who succeeded them near the end of the fifth century were more vigorous sponsors of cave temples and sculptures.

Buddhist cave sites in Mahārāṣṭra may have been excavated as late as the eighth century. One isolated cave of this era was discovered at Tagara, modern Ter, in the Sholapur district, and others have been discovered around Bombay, near the villages of Jogeswari and Kondwite and on the island of Gharapurī in the Bombay harbor. The Gharapurī site is also known as Elephanta, named by the Portuguese for the giant stone elephant that stands guard at the mouth of one of the caves. While most of the Elephanta caves are Hindu, one appears to be a Buddhist temple.

The strongly Hindu Rāṣṭrakūṭas came to power in the eighth century. Valabhī, the last major center of Buddhist learning, was destroyed about the same time. Isolated and deprived of patronage, Buddhist communities in Mahārāṣṭra weakened. After Buddhism waned in the western regions, some of the sites were used by Hindu and Jain communities, who either converted Buddhist caves to their own use or excavated new ones. However, most of the cave temples—even those of Ajaṇṭā—were abandoned and forgotten.

Mahārāṣṭra

Hsüan-tsang, in the seventh century, describes the region of Mahārāṣṭra as rich and fertile, a productive land with a hot climate. "The disposition of the people is honest and simple; they are tall of stature and of a stern, vindictive character. To their benefactors they are grateful; to their enemies relentless." (HT II:256) The Kṣatriya, or warrior ethic, was very strong in this region, which maintained its independence even from the powerful King Harṣa of Central India.

Here, in this land "fond of learning," Hsüan-tsang found about one hundred monasteries housing approximately five thousand monks who practiced both the Śrāvakayāna and Mahāyāna teachings. He saw five Aśokan stūpas on sites visited by the four previous Buddhas of our aeon as well as many other stūpas of brick and stone too numerous to count. Near the capital city (as yet unidentified, but possibly Pratiṣṭhāna), Hsüan-tsang found a monastery with a stone image of the Bodhisattva Avalokiteśvara, which he described as possessing great spiritual power. While there was significant Buddhist activity, it is clear that the Brahmanic religions were growing rapidly here in the seventh century.

Ajaṇṭā

When Hsüan-tsang traveled through this region, he described a monastery built into a great mountain with towering crags and a precipice to the east, which corresponds to the caves of Ajaṇṭā. Ajaṇṭā is located in the Indhyadri hills of eastern Mahārāṣṭra along an elbow of the Waghora River: "Its lofty halls and deep side-aisles stretch through the face of the rocks. Story above story they are backed by the crag and face the valley." (HT II:257) Hsüan-tsang mentions that this monastery was built by the Arhat Ācāra from western India, which agrees with an inscription in one of Ajaṇṭā's caves stating that the monastery was built by the Sthavira ascetic Acala in honor of his mother, who became an Arhat in her next birth. According to other inscriptions, one of the early caves was donated by King Pulumayi's relatives and another by merchants.

Considered one of the world's artistic marvels, Ajaṇṭā would have been an active Buddhist center in the seventh century. Hsüan-tsang describes a monastery here as one hundred feet high; in the middle was a seventy-foot-high stone figure of the Buddha, surmounted by a seven-stage stone canopy. Scenes of the Buddha's previous lives as a Bodhisattva, intricately carved and inlaid with precious stones, ornamented the walls. Two stone elephants, one on each side, guarded the gates. Hsüan-tsang mentions a tradition that 'Jina Bodhisattva' often stayed in this holy place.

Ajaṇṭā has a long history. Adherents of the Śrāvakayāna schools created five of its twenty-eight caves, but abandoned the area around 250 C.E. Inscriptions at Ajaṇṭā indicate that the Vākāṭaka kings of the fourth century supported Buddhism and sponsored the creation of some of the most exquisitely ornamented caves. Around 450 C.E., Mahāyāna monks resettled this complex and during the late Gupta period began to create the other twenty-three caves, working outward on both sides from the original caves. Excavation and renovation was carried out most vigorously during the fifth and early sixth centuries when Buddhism was receiving generous patronage from merchant families and individuals associated with the royal court of the Vākāṭaka king Hariṣeṇa (c. 500 C.E.). Two of the later caves were donated by a minister and another official of King Hariṣeṇa. Inscriptions found in the caves indicate that the Vākāṭaka kings declined sometime before the last half of the

Overleaf: The cave temples of Ajaṇṭā are carved out of the living rock.

sixth century, when the Cālukya and Rāṣṭrakūṭa kings came to power in the northern Deccan. The Cālukyas flourished in the last half of the sixth and through the seventh century. The Rāṣṭrakūṭas became strong in the eighth and ninth centuries, and the Cālukyas regained power in the eleventh and twelfth centuries.

Although most of Ajaṇṭā's cave building took place in the fifth century, work on the caves continued well into the seventh century, somewhat later than the other cave complexes. Some of the caves (caves 3, 5, 8, 14, 18, 20, 22, 24, 25) were left undeveloped or unfinished; cave 24 in particular shows promise of having been conceived as the largest of the Ajaṇṭā temple caves.

Historians generally believe that work stopped at Ajaṇṭā during the chaos following the defeat of Pulakesin II by Narasiṁhavarman Pallava in 642 C.E. It is thought that the builders of Ajaṇṭā continued their work at Ellora, to the southwest. Once abandoned, the Ajaṇṭā caves were forgotten after Buddhism declined in this region. Undisturbed for centuries, the paintings retained much of their beauty.

In one of history's momentous accidents, a hunting party of British officers happened upon the caves in 1819. This finding was heralded as one of the greatest artistic discoveries of all time. Scholars and art historians have now brought the beauty and unique significance of Ajaṇṭā to the world's attention. Today the caves of Ajaṇṭā are widely known and attract visitors from all parts of the world.

Of all India's cave temples, Ajaṇṭā preserves the widest range of artistic beauty, housing masterpieces of both sculpture and wall-painting. The caves themselves, carved out of solid rock to represent the interior of wooden temples, are sculptural marvels that preserve in stone a unique architectural heritage. But Ajaṇṭā is best known for its exquisite and expressive paintings. Preserved from the ravages of time and

Entrance to a monastery cave at Ajaṇṭā

cataclysmic events, these paintings have recently suffered damage from weathering arising from greater use of the caves and from ill-advised restoration attempts earlier this century. Yet they rarely fail to elicit admiration and wonder from those who make the effort to view them.

In the caves carved or renovated by Mahāyāna residents, even the monk's residences were transformed from simple cells into well-adorned halls and sleeping rooms. One of the inscriptions in a monastery cave (number 16) relates that the sponsor, Varāhadeva, King Hariṣeṇa's minister, intended this monk's residence to have elegant paintings, statues of nymphs, beautiful pillars and stairs, and a temple with a Buddha image for worship, to the extent that it would resemble the palaces of the lord of gods. (AAI 253–254)

The later caves are famous for their wall-paintings that replicate scenes from the Sūtras. There are elaborate friezes in the temple halls and beautiful frescoes in many of the larger caves. Nearly all available space in the cave temples of later date is filled with elegantly carved images and the pillars are ornately ornamented. On the ceilings, the naturalistic sculptural forms on the lower part of the temple give way to geometric and figurative designs.

The modern pilgrim to Ajaṇṭā can enter most of the caves. A circular path accessed by stairs connects the caves, beginning with cave 1 and progressing to cave 27; caves 28 and 29 open further up on the cliff and access is much more difficult. Caves 9, 10, 19, and 20 are caitya, or temple caves; the rest of the finished caves are vihāras, or monks' residences and assembly halls. The following caves hold the most significant artistic treasures:

Cave 1, considered to have been excavated in the first half of the seventh century, was among the last vihāra caves carved; its spacious central hall is rich in painting and sculpture, including the famous paintings known as the 'Black Princess' and the 'Dying Princess'. A depiction of Padmapāṇi holding a blue lotus still radiates sublime compassion. This cave also has a painting of the Bodhisattva Vajrapāṇi, and a scene from the Mahājanaka Jātaka depicts Prince Janaka enjoying the delights of his palace before renouncing his princely heritage.

Right: The Bodhisattva Padmapāṇi holding a blue lotus, one of the famous paintings from the wall of the assembly hall of cave 1, Ajaṇṭā.

Cave 2, a vihāra cave probably excavated in the fifth century, consists of a spacious central hall surrounded on three sides with small rooms for monks. An outer room separates the entrance from the central hall, and a shrine room with a seated image of the Buddha opens off the central hall's far wall. The entire cave, including the columns and walls, is richly carved and painted; the ceiling is painted in gridlike designs using mandalic representations in the center of the hall and animal and plant motifs around the sides. Painted scenes related to the Jātakas and the birth of the Buddha adorn the walls, and sculptures of the yakṣinī Hāritī and her consort Pāñcika preside over the Hāritī shrine.

Cave 4, Ajaṇṭā's largest vihāra cave, was left unfinished. Among the finely-carved sculptures found here is a representation of people running to the compassionate Bodhisattva Avalokiteśvara for protection from the eight great dangers. This and other representations of Bodhisattvas indicate that this cave was related to the Mahāyāna traditions.

Cave 6 is a vihāra cave; the shrine room houses a Buddha image. Its large central hall is surrounded on three sides by two stories of monks' rooms, the only cave of this type at Ajaṇṭā. The lower story has partially collapsed, obstructing the entrance. Paintings can still be seen on the doors to the monks' rooms upstairs.

Cave 7 is also a vihāra cave, but has a unique interior design. Cave 8, one of the earlier caves, is used today to house the modern generator that provides electricity for lighting some of the caves.

Caves 9 and 10 are the oldest caitya caves at Ajaṇṭā; both date from the earliest period of construction and served as temples for Śrāvaka schools. While both caves are similar in

Right: Facade of Ajaṇṭā's cave 19, a temple cave carved during the Vākāṭaka period, c. fifth century C.E.

design, cave 9 is by far the smaller cave. A rounded arched window rises above the entry door; columns line the sides of the cave, which has a stūpa at its far end. This cave was later renovated and occupied by Mahāyāna practitioners; the two Buddha statues standing at the entrance probably date from this later period of renovation. The wall paintings here are badly deteriorated.

Cave 10 is considered the earliest of all the Ajaṇṭā caves; it is also the largest of the temple caves and the first to have been seen by the British officers from the top of the cliffs. The deep wide hall has a Jātaka fresco dating from the first century B.C.E., which appears to have been made by Āndhra artists. From its elegant use of light and shade, and the delineation of facial expressions, art historians regard this fresco as more advanced in style than other art of its time. The art of this temple is badly deteriorated, partially because its facade has collapsed, allowing light into the interior, and partially due to vandalism in the early years following its discovery.

Caves 11 and 12 are also early caves of the Śrāvaka tradition, while cave 13 appears to have been one of the first Mahāyāna caves excavated at Ajaṇṭā.

Cave 16, a vihāra cave, is famous for its wall painting depicting the death of Sundarī, wife of Nanda, the Buddha's half-brother. Although Nanda felt drawn to the religious life, he could not bear to part from his beautiful wife until the Buddha showed him the delights of the heavenly realms. When he renounced worldly life and left home to become a monk, Sundarī died of grief.

Cave 17 was a Mahāyāna vihāra similar to cave 2, but smaller and simpler in ornamentation. Its central hall, entered through an outer room separate from the main hall, is

Right: Detail of the right corner of Ajaṇṭā's cave 19, with sculptures of the Buddha offering enlightened knowledge and teaching the Dharma.

surrounded on three sides with small rooms for monks. At the end of the central hall is a shrine room with an image of the Buddha Śākyamuni teaching the Dharma. The murals of cave 17 are beautifully composed and the best preserved of Ajaṇṭā's wall-paintings. Cave 17 has representations of the Buddha's homecoming and the story of Siṁhāla, who conquered the demon rulers of Śrī Laṅkā and established the first human settlement. Paintings of Buddhas illuminate the ceiling, and a wall painting depicts the future Buddha Maitreya surrounded by his assembly. Outside the temple, on the entryway, is a gracefully-carved scene from the Viśvāntara Jātaka depicting Prince Maṇicūḍa and his wife. As in the other caves, color was used on all surfaces, creating a more striking effect than the weathered stone one sees today.

Cave 19, a temple cave probably carved during the fifth century, has a grid-like facade deeply carved into the face of a cliff. A protruding roof covers its comparatively small entrance door and forms a small balcony above it. The entryway and its balcony are surmounted by a great arching window; figures of the Buddha, either delineated by columns or set into them, cover most of the rest of the cave's facade, which is set into the face of the cliff. A lifesize figure of the Buddha with his son Rāhula as a child stands to the right of the entrance, and another figure of the Buddha is carved to the left of the doorway. Celestial beings hold a crown above the head of each of these Buddhas, both shown in the gift-bestowing gesture, offering the blessings of enlightenment for those who practice within.

Massive columns line the interior of the cave; Buddhas in the meditation mudrā appear in their wide capitals, and above them larger Buddha figures shown teaching and bestowing the gift of enlightenment encircle the temple's interior. A tall stūpa, mounted on a platform, stands at the end of the hall; the body of the stūpa is ringed in columns and on its front is a standing image of the Buddha. The arch of its dome is

The interior of cave 26, one of Ajaṇṭā's temple caves, showing the pillars around the stūpa at the far end of the hall, the ribbed and vaulted ceiling, and the detailed carvings on the capitals and the walls above.

surmounted by a high three-tiered harmikā which stretches nearly the full height of the vaulted ceiling.

Cave 26, a temple cave, has a facade closely resembling the entrance to cave 19, although the facade of cave 26 has been damaged. Although both temples are carved about the same distance into the cliff, the anteroom of cave 26 is much shorter than that of cave 19 and the curved interior of the central temple is much wider and longer. The walls of cave 26 are lined with elaborately carved columns topped by wide, elegant capitals. Above the capitals, massive stone friezes with carved columns framing images of the Buddha encircle the temples' interior. As in the other temple caves, the columns form an aisle between them and the wall which served as a path for circumambulation. Along this path are important scenes from the Buddha's life: the conquest of Māra at Bodh Gayā and the Parinirvāṇa at Kuśinagara, represented by a reclining figure of the Buddha more than twenty feet long. Intended to awaken understanding of the significance of these events, this art is breathtakingly powerful in its subject, composition, and scope.

The temple's roof is a high arch with deep ribs carved to resemble rafters. Near the end of the cave is a high stone stūpa with a lifesize figure of the Buddha teaching the Dharma seated facing the entryway. The stūpa itself is richly carved; tall columns frame the central Buddha image, and two rows of smaller columns form niches for standing images of the Buddha. The entire interior was once painted in rich colors.

At Pitalkhorā, southwest of Ajaṇṭā, there is a smaller complex of caves consisting of a temple and dwelling places for monks. Inscriptions found on the cave's pillars indicate that the caves date to the late Mauryan or Śuṅga times.

Bāgh

At Bāgh, in Madhya Pradesh, about 150 miles northwest of Ajaṇṭā, there are nine caves that appear to have been excavated between the fifth and seventh centuries C.E. and inhabited by Mahāyāna Sanghas. There are indications that the elegant paintings within, though now badly deteriorated, would have rivaled those of Ajaṇṭā, and an inscription in Cave 2 even refers to the monastery as Kalāyana, Abode of Art. However, the soft rock has not held up well through time;

Facade of a vihāra cave at Ellora

water has seeped through the cave walls and damaged all its ornamentation. Reproductions of the wall paintings in the cave known as the Rang Mahal (Painted Hall), made when the paintings were in better condition, can be seen in the Archaeological Museum in Gwalior.

Ellora

Ellora, about nineteen miles north of Auraṅgabad and about sixty miles from Ajaṇṭā, is the site of thirty-four cave temples, constructed between the seventh and the tenth centuries. Scholars believe that the builders of the Ajaṇṭā caves

A vista of images of enlightenment appears to emanate directly from the face of the cliffs at Ellora. The view is taken from inside the opposite bank of caves.

stopped construction for some reason and came to Ellora to continue their work. The caves extend north and south for approximately a mile on the face of a low ridge of hills overlooking a vast plain. Of this complex of caves, seventeen were made by Hindus and the most recent five by Jains. The twelve Buddhist caves are the oldest, dating from six hundred to eight hundred C.E.

Only one of the Buddhist caves is a temple; eleven are vihāras. Two of the large vihāra caves are three stories high. The temple cave, known as the Viśvakarma, or Carpenter's Cave, takes its name from the ribs on the ceiling, which were carved to look like wooden beams. Inside the temple, a large Buddha statue stands before a nearly thirty-foot-high stūpa. Light enters the temple through an ornately-carved window placed in the temple's entryway. The entryways of most of the

Facade of the richly ornamented cave 3 at Nāsik

temples, carved into the sloping hillsides, are framed in imposing facades, one of which is fifty feet high. Ellora's caves are famous for their elegant Buddhist sculptures, which include representations of the five Dhyāni Buddhas and Bodhisattvas accompanied by graceful figures of gandharvas and other symbolic representations.

Nāsik

At Nāsik, about a hundred miles inland from the Bay of Bombay, stands the Trimbak mountain range which in ancient times was known as the Triraśmi or Tiraṇu. Thirty-three caves known as the Pāṇḍu Leṇa were carved into the eastern side of these mountains, about three hundred feet above the level of the road. The caves are all finely ornamented in a style both rich and variegated, emulating carved wood. An inscription in one cave indicates that it was commissioned by an official of Nāsik during the reign of King Kāṅha, identified as

Kṛṣṇā, brother of Sīmuka, founder of the Sātavāhana Dynasty. This places the temple as having been built in the first half of the second century B.C.E.

During the first or second century C.E., Nāsik became part of a Śaka satrapy. Inscriptions at the site record that the Śaka governor Nahapāna, who ruled this region around 119–125 C.E., donated land and maintenance to the Sangha and sponsored the building or ornamentation of one of the caves. Although Nāsik was later recaptured by the Sātavāhanas, there was no interruption of Dharma activities in the area. Gotamīputra Śrī Sātakarṇi and members of his family donated land and caves, and a cave excavated earlier by the ascetic Bopaki was enlarged by Vāsu, wife of a general who served King Yajñaśrī Sātakarṇi, probably around 174–203 C.E.

Some caves at Nāsik were donated to the Bhadrāyaṇīyas, one of the eighteen Śrāvaka traditions, and others to mendicant monks belonging to the 'Sangha of the Four Directions', referring to traveling bhikṣus unaffiliated with any specific school. A large Mahāyāna image of the Buddha found enshrined in one of the caves indicates that Mahāyāna bhikṣus also lived and practiced here.

Kānheri

Kānheri, located on Salsette Island a short distance north of Bombay, is the site of 109 cave temples. Most are small rooms for living quarters and meditation that open onto a veranda, with a view of forested hills and streams. Although exact dating is difficult, they appear to have been excavated and used between the second and ninth centuries C.E.

Inscriptions associate the Kānheri caves with the Sangha of Bhikṣus, the Sangha of the Four Directions, and the Śrāvaka traditions known as Bhadrāyaṇīyas and Aparaśailas. The caves were sponsored by patrons from such distant places as Dhānyakāṭaka in Āndhra and Kalyāṇa in Kārṇaṭaka, as well as by local donors. A record of donations indicates that the local laity also sponsored buildings near the city of Pratiṣṭhāna, at the Āmbālikā Vihāra in Kalyāṇa, and elsewhere.

The largest of these 109 caves is known as the Great Caitya (Temple) Cave. Rich in sculpture and ornamentation, this cave temple is more than eighty feet long, nearly forty feet wide, and about thirty-four feet high. Inscriptions indicate that it was donated by the merchants Gajasena and Gajamita to the Bhadrāyaṇīya school during the reign of King Yajñaśrī Sātakarṇi, near the end of the second century C.E. The style of the sculptures and the depictions of Bodhisattvas indicate that Kānheri was also a center for Mahāyāna practices.

Kānheri appears to have experienced a revival of artistic efforts during the late fifth and sixth centuries, when older caves were renovated and new ones excavated. An inscription at the site indicates that this revival may have been prompted by the patronage of the Traikuṭaka kings, who assumed power in this area after the decline of the Vākāṭakas.

Sculptures belonging to the period of the Traikuṭaka kings abound in these caves; distinctly Mahāyāna, the representations include maṇḍalas and depictions of the Dhyāni Buddhas and Bodhisattvas. One cave has preserved a statue of the eleven-headed form of Avalokiteśvara dating from about the fifth or sixth century C.E., the only one of its kind known to exist in India outside of the late Pāla statues.

Kārli

Cave temples known as the Valūraka Leṇa are located near Kārli in the Borghata Hills on the road between the modern cities of Bombay and Poona. The great temple hall, the largest cave in all of India, is considered one of India's finest artistic monuments. Inscriptions in the temple document that its excavation was sponsored by the merchant Bhūtapāla of Vaijayantī, a site in Āndhra associated with Nāgārjunakoṇḍa.

A rock-cut portico fifteen feet deep and fifty-two feet wide frames the front of the main hall. The rectangular hall, spacious and deep, measures 124 × 45 feet, with a vaulted roof forty-six feet high. Three doorways open onto the main hall, one leading directly into the center and the others opening to the aisles on each side. Thirty-seven pillars placed in a horseshoe shape define the side aisles and curve around the stūpa at the far end of the hall; fifteen of these pillars are exquisitely carved and the others have plain octagonal shapes. The walls of the entryway are richly sculpted and the flat portions were once painted with scenes from the Buddha's life.

The great temple cave is believed to have been created in the early centuries C.E. Inscriptions found in the cave indicate that the temple was the gift of a guild, and names of individual donors were carved on eleven pillars within the cave. One pillar was given by an adherent of the Dharmottarīya tradition; from their names, the sponsors of nine pillars appear to have been Greeks.

Contributions for construction and maintenance of the temples here came from a variety of sources. Usabhadata, a Śaka governor, donated the village of Karajika (modern Karjat) "for the support of all those in the universal order who had gone forth from their homes and were staying at the cave-temple." (HIBS 239) Karajika's connection with the temple continued even after the Sātavāhanas drove the Śakas out of Mahārāṣṭra in the second century C.E. Inscriptions indicate that during this later period, the temple was being cared for by Mahāsāṁghika monks. North of Kārlī, at Ambivale near modern Karjat, is a single cave that appears to have been separate from the Kārli caves. A short inscription in Pāli was found on one of its four pillars. Caves have also been found at Kondane, seven miles from the Karjat station. Inscriptions here indicate that the temple caves were built earlier than the monastery caves, perhaps about the same time as the oldest caves at Bhājā.

Bhājā

The eighteen caves found at Bhājā (west of Kārli, in the Western Ghats, not far from Poona), are older and smaller than those at Kārli, with the oldest caves dating from the second century B.C.E. In the main temple, the oldest temple cave of the Deccan, twenty-seven octagonal pillars about eleven feet tall are carved along the main hall and around the shrine, dividing the hall into a central nave with two side aisles. The barrel-vaulted roof is carved to simulate a framework of curved ribs, emulating construction in wood. Historians consider the early caves an effort to reproduce the earliest temples, which were probably formed of arched ribs joined at the top and covered with thatch. The central nave is cut deep into the rock; a small stūpa carved from the rock is at its far end. The large rock-cut sculptured reliefs convey a sense of expansive vitality.

The exterior of the cave suggests the entrance to a palace or possibly a celestial city. The entrance is framed with a high arch surmounted with carvings of buildings and smaller arches, resembling a city skyline; flanking the entryway are two stories of windows. This cave is considered one of the earliest of its type in India. Eight inscriptions were found here; four record names of donors, but none give the name of any particular school. A smaller cave with five cells for monks' quarters opens next to the temple cave.

A complex of caves excavated somewhat later was found at Bedsā, located a short distance south of Bhājā. The main temple at Bedsā is constructed similarly to that of Kārli. Still more Buddhist sites have been found a little further south at Mahad, on the bank of the Savitrī River, and at Kuda, about forty-five miles from Bombay. Buddhist caves were also excavated at Karhad and at Śelarwadi, both located near Mahad. The complex of sixty caves in the Agaśiva Hills near Karhad is the largest of the two sites.

Junnar

Junnar, located forty-six miles north of Poona, appears to have been an early and very large Buddhist center. Five sets of cave temples, a total of 150 caves, appear to have been excavated and carved here between the first century B.C.E. and the second century C.E. About thirty inscriptions found in the caves record donations of stūpas, temples, water tanks, mango trees, and land. In addition to Indian patrons, the donors include at least three Greeks and one Śaka. One inscription records a donation of a cave and water tank to nuns of the Dharmottarīya sect.

Waning of Buddhism in Mahārāṣṭra

Little is known of specific Buddhist activity in western Mahārāṣṭra after the time of Hsüan-tsang. Although some of Mahārāṣṭra's caves appear to have been occupied during the eighth century, there is no evidence that Buddhism persisted in this region to any significant degree after the destruction of Valabhī around the end of the seventh century. The history of western India from the eighth century to the wars preceding the Muslim occupation reveals the rise of numerous states embroiled in nearly continuous conflicts. It is possible that these conditions interfered with the flow of patronage from wealthy merchants and royal families, or that the revitalization of Hinduism attracted the middle classes which were Buddhism's strongest supporters. It is also possible that the destruction of Valabhī weakened and isolated the Buddhists of Mahārāṣṭra. Without a clear historical record, the search for specific reasons for the decline of Buddhism in Mahārāṣṭra ends in the misty realm of speculation.

Part Five

Buddhism in the Northwest

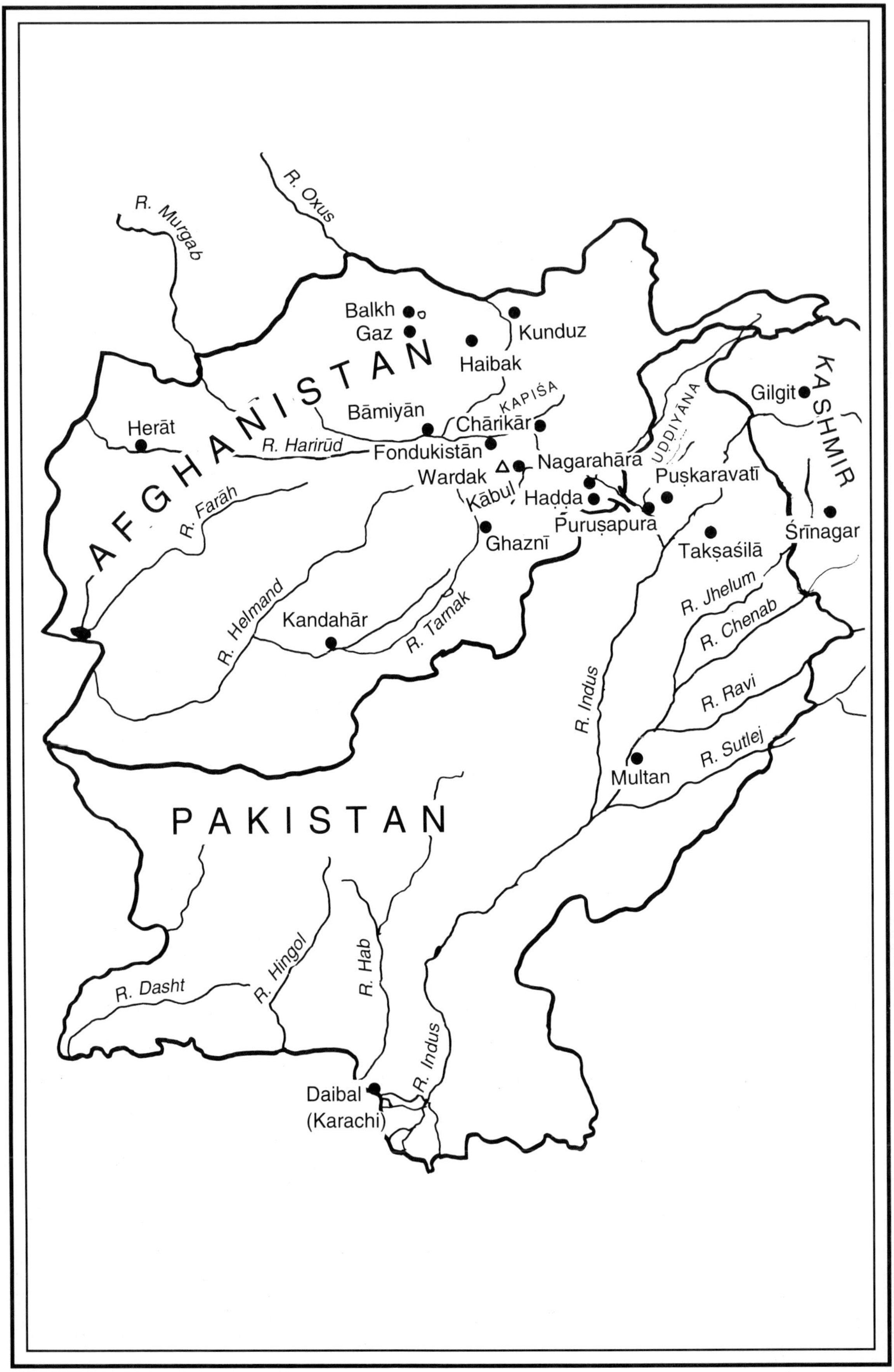

R. Oxus
R. Murgab
Balkh
Gaz
Kunduz
AFGHANISTAN
Haibak
KAPIŚA
Bāmiyān
Chārikār
Herāt
R. Harirūd
Fondukistān
Nagarahāra
UDDIYĀNA
Gilgit
KASHMIR
Wardak
Kābul
Haḍḍa
Puṣkaravatī
R. Farāh
Puruṣapura
Ghaznī
Takṣaśilā
Śrīnagar
R. Helmand
R. Jhelum
Kandahār
R. Tarnak
R. Chenab
R. Indus
R. Ravi
R. Sutlej
Multan
PAKISTAN
R. Hab
R. Hingol
R. Dasht
R. Indus
Daibal
(Karachi)

Uttarāpatha
The Far Northwest

To an extent almost unimaginable today, Buddhism thrived along the Uttarāpatha, the route leading from the cities of the Punjab through the Khyber Pass to Balkh, Samarkhand, and the oasis states of Central Asia. For centuries, sites blessed by the Buddha's presence attracted pilgrims to the far northwest.

Bounded on the north by the Oxus River and the mountains of the Hindu Kush range, the countries of the far Northwest served India as buffer zones, separating the heartland of Indian culture from the Persian and Greek empire builders and the restless tribes of Central Asia. At the time of the Buddha, trade routes connected the cities of the Ganges Basin with Jālandhara and Sākala in the Punjab and with Takṣaśilā and Peshāwar in Gandhāra, before winding west through the Khyber Pass to Kābul and continuing west to Herāt, the gateway to the Persian Empire.

Since trade routes could easily become avenues for invasion, the Northwest was a strategically critical area. Along the route northwest lay many small principalities often consisting of a walled city and its surrounding sphere of influence. The size and influence of these cities tended to wax or wane according to the fortunes of the larger empires which periodically engulfed the northwest.

The region stretching from the northern provinces of Central India to the Khyber Pass has traditionally been known as Uttarāpatha. Although the lands north and west of the Khyber Pass have never been part of India, they were linked to India during the time of the Śaka and Kuṣāṇa kings, from the first century B.C.E. to the third century C.E. Thereafter, this region maintained contact with Indian culture largely through the travels and activities of Buddhist monks, who continued to live in the far northwest (modern Pakistan and Afghanistan) until the eighth or ninth century.

From the sixth to the fourth centuries B.C.E., the countries of the Northwest were successively governed by the Persian Achaemenid Empire (559–336 B.C.E.) and by the Macedonians under Alexander thc Great (336–306 B.C.E.). Candragupta Maurya brought the eastern part of the area into the Indian cultural sphere in 306 B.C.E., and his grandson Aśoka continued the process of securing it. Both Aśoka and later his son Kuṇāla served as viceroys from Takṣaśilā, the northwestern capital of the Mauryan Empire, before they ascended the imperial throne at Pāṭaliputra.

Early Associations with Buddhism

According to the northern Buddhist traditions, the Dharma was brought to the northwest by the merchants Trapuṣa and Bhallika, who had met the Buddha in Bodh Gayā shortly after his enlightenment and become his first lay disciples. The merchants were from Utkala (Pāli, Ukkala, which the Lalitavistara-sūtra and the Mahāvastu, a Vinaya text, located in the Northwest. The Pāli tradition places Ukkala east of Magadha, in northern Orissa.) The Buddha gave the merchants cuttings of his hair and nails, which they took back with them to the city of Asitāñjana and enshrined in stūpas. Hsüan-tsang describes stūpas built by Trapuṣa and Bhallika in Balkh.

The Dharma began to take firm root in this region soon after the division of the Sangha into two main branches: the Sthaviras, or Elders, and the Mahāsāṁghika, the Great Assembly. By the third century C.E., these branches gave rise to additional schools, and bhikṣus of many of these traditions settled in the lands northwest of India. Among the earliest were the Mahāsāṁghikas and Sarvāstivādins, who moved northwest from their centers in Mathurā.

During the reign of Aśoka, the great patron of the Dharma (c. 269–232 B.C.E.), Buddhism flowered in the Uttarāpatha. Aśoka had at least fourteen edicts in the Kharoṣṭhī script carved on boulders in Shāhbāzgaṛhī and Mansehra and an edict in the Aramaic script carved at Lampaka. Aśokan inscriptions have been discovered as far west as Kandahār, as well as in Gandhāra and Takṣaśilā. A fragment of an Aśokan edict has also been found at Dauranta near Jalalabad.

During Aśoka's reign, Mogalliputta Tissa sent nine teams of bhikṣus from Pāṭaliputra to propagate the Dharma widely. The Mahāvaṁsa relates that Majjhāntika was sent to Kashmir and Gandhāra, and Mahārakkhita to the Yona country. Although we lack specific information as to where Mahārakkhita traveled, the land of the Yonas (Sanskrit, Yavanas or Greeks) in Aśoka's time would most likely have been the lands west of the Indus, in the northern part of modern Afghanistan, where remnants of Alexander the Great's army had settled in the fourth century B.C.E. Bhikṣus from many of the eighteen early schools followed the Arhats to the Northwest and established centers in Takṣaśilā, Kapiśa (modern Begram), in Urasa, in Bāmiyān, and in Ghaznī.

Buddhism under Indo-Greek Rule

The Greeks appear to have been tolerant and in some cases actively supportive of the Buddhist communities developing in their lands. In the second century B.C., as Aśoka's successors weakened their hold on the empire, the Greeks began to push eastward. As they moved into the Punjab and down India's western coast, they increasingly came into contact with Buddhist teachings.

The Greek king best known to Buddhist history is King Menander (Pāli, Milinda), who came to power between 163 and 115 B.C.E. His kingdom stretched west beyond the Indus through the lands of Gandhāra, Uḍḍiyāna, and Sindh, and southeast through Kaccha and Surāṣṭra. Some authorities include Kandahār in his kingdom, which he ruled from his capital city of Sākala (modern Siālkot), situated near the Chenāb River in eastern Pakistan.

King Menander's interest and support of the Dharma can be seen in the Milindapañha, a contemporary text preserved in Chinese and Pāli. The Milindapañha records Menander's dialogue with Nāgasena, a monk from the Vattaniya Monastery. Menander's previous interviews with the Buddhist master Ayupāla had stimulated the king's interest, and he had sent for Nāgasena to answer specific questions.

Buddhism flourished in the northwestern countries under Greek rule. By the opening of the first century B.C.E., major Buddhist centers existed far west of India's traditional borders, from Takṣaśilā and Peshāwar in Gandhāra to Uḍḍiyāna on the north, and west to Kapiśa, Wardak, and Bāmiyān, all regions of modern Afghanistan. The Mahāsāṁghika schools (Lokottaravādin, Ekyavyavahārika, and Bahuśrutīya) were most numerous in Kandahār, Balkh, and Bāmiyān, with the Sthavira and Sarvāstivādin centers emerging most strongly in Kashmīr and Gandhāra to the east. The Mahāvāṁsa records that Yona Mahādhammarakkhita brought thirty thousand bhikṣus to the consecration of the Mahāthūpa in Śrī Laṅkā and mentions that Mahādeva visited Śrī Laṅkā from Pallavabhogga (land of the Parthians) with 46,000 bhikṣus. The visits of delegations of bhikṣus from such a great distance indicates that Buddhism was well-established in the Northwest in the first century B.C.E. Although Tāranātha describes extensive damage to Buddhism at the hands of the Śuṅga king Puṣyamitra, who supplanted the Mauryan rulers in India, the Northwest was spared this destruction. The Dharma continued to flourish through the reigns of the Śaka, Parthian, and Kuṣāṇa kings who succeeded the Greeks in the first century B.C.E. The discovery of a Mahāyāna reliquary in a stūpa at Bīmarān indicates that Mahāyāna monks may have also settled here even before Kaniṣka came to power. According to Hsüan-tsang, the Mahāyāna was thriving in Uḍḍiyana, Kapiśa, and Tsao-ku-f'a in the seventh century.

A Tradition of Pilgrimage

The Northwest became widely known as a place where Śākyamuni and Buddhas before him practiced the virtues of a Bodhisattva for countless lifetimes. The sites of many of the Jātakas (stories of the past lives of the Buddha) and Avadānas (accounts of the Buddha and his disciples) could be located in the lands of the Northwest. Takṣaśilā was the site of the Candraprabhā Jataka; Gandhāra was where, as Prince Vessantara, the Bodhisattva demonstrated the perfection of generosity and where, as King Śībi, he gave his body for the benefit of others. The Buddhists of the Northwest preserved extensive collections of Jātakas and Avadānas. The Mahāvastu, a Lokottaravādin text, contains a large compilation of Avadānas, and still more appear in the Sarvāstvādin compilations, the Divyāvadāna and Avadānakalpalatā.

The presence in the Northwest of sacred sites blessed by the Buddha's presence—in his life as Śākyamuni, in past lives, or by corporeal relics and artifacts—attracted the devotion of generations of pilgrims. Balkh, a northern province of modern Afghanistan, was even known as "Little Rājagṛha," presumably because it corresponded in some manner to King Bimbisāra's city so important in the life of the Buddha. In light of the efforts Chinese pilgrims made to reach the northwestern cities, the entire region may have been viewed as a counterpart to the holy land of the Madhyadeśa.

Throughout the Northwest, monasteries along the trade routes accommodated pilgrims to the holy places as well as monks who traveled the trade routes north and east to Central Asia and China and west toward Iran and the Mediterranean Sea. These Dharma centers were usually located close to the cities where caravans rested and renewed their supplies.

The visits of the Chinese pilgrims Fa-hien, Sung-yun, and Hsüan-tsang span more than two centuries. As they visited many of the same regions and described monuments, monasteries, customs, and Buddhist activities, their records are valuable historical resources. They also provide insight into the courage, devotion, and determination necessary to follow the pilgrim's path. The journey was arduous beyond belief, yet the pilgrims' complaints were few. Crossing the Snowy Mountains of the Hindu Kush, Fa-hien remarks that here there is snow in both winter and summer. "Moreover, there are poison-dragons (nāgas), who when evil-purposed spit poison, winds, rain, snow, drifting sand, and gravel-stones; not one of ten thousand meeting these calamities escapes." (HT xxix) In entering India from Afghanistan, Fa-hien lost two of his companions, the second of whom died in his arms in deep cold on the snowy mountains. There was only a moment for grieving before the survivors were forced to move on. As the pilgrim said in his sorrow, to be among the fortunate was not the purpose of their journey. (HT xxxvi)

Gandhāra

Buddhism lived long and flourished in the warm land of Gandhāra, meeting ground of Persian, Greek, Central Asian, and Indian cultures, and the home of people who loved art and literature. Here the great masters of Abhidharma lived and wrote their treatises, and sages and saints circumambulated some of the largest stūpas ever raised to recall humanity to its enlightened heritage.

The kingdom of Gandhāra was situated in the lower Kābul Valley, along the Kābul River between the Kunar and Indus rivers. From the sixth century B.C.E. to the early fifth century C.E., this region experienced successive waves of Persian, Greek, Indian, Śaka, Parthian, and Kuṣāṇa rule. The merging of Iranian, Central Asian, and Indian peoples created a unique culture known for its interest in art, religion, and education. In ancient times, Gandhāra's capital was Puṣkarāvatī, said to have been founded by Puṣkara, named in the Purānas as the son of Bharata and the nephew of Rāma. When the Greeks of Bactria expanded their domains to the east, they moved their capital to Takṣaśilā. In the early centuries C.E., the Kuṣāṇas, a Central Asian tribe, changed the capital once more, moving it west to Puruṣapura, a short distance south of Puṣkarāvatī.

Fa-hien, describing fifth-century Gandhāra, mentions that many Gandhārans belonged to the Śrāvaka schools. In the sixth century, the pilgrim Sung-yun remarked that although the people "once had respect for the Dharma," the present king was "strongly opposed to the Dharma, and preferred to worship demons." (HT c) This king, a leader of the Huns, guarded the frontier with seven hundred war elephants. At the time of Sung-yun's travels, the Huns were about to ravage Dharma centers from the Punjab to Pāṭaliputra. At the time of Hsüan-tsang's visit in the seventh century, Gandhāra was governed by deputies from Kapiśa, and many of Gandhāra's towns and villages were deserted.

Hsüan-tsang writes, "The country is rich in cereals, and produces a variety of flowers and fruits; it abounds also in sugarcane, from the juice of which they prepare solid sugar. The climate is warm and soft; they love literature; a few believe in the true law (Buddhism)." (HT 98) By the seventh century only remnants of the Dharma remained in this land; Hsüan-tsang observed about one thousand monasteries deserted and in ruins, covered with shrubs, and "solitary to the last degree." The stūpas were mostly in ruins, yet the hundred or so Hindu temples were flourishing. Most of the inhabitants belonged to non-Buddhist religions; Hsüan-tsang found only a few followers of the Dharma.

Puruṣapura

Puruṣapura (modern Peshāwar), the capital of the Kuṣāṇa Empire, has a long association with Buddhism. Tradition relates that all the Buddhas of our aeon, past, present, and future, have or will visit this site and consecrate it to the Dharma. Among Puruṣapura's many monuments described by pilgrims was a huge pipala tree about a hundred feet high shading statues of the four previous Buddhas of our aeon. These statues commemorated places where these Buddhas had rested and where the thousand Buddhas yet to come will also visit in their time. Hsüan-tsang writes that it was here that Śākyamuni Buddha told Ānanda that four hundred years after the Parinirvāṇa, King Kaniṣka would rule this land; he would build a stūpa and place inside it some of the Buddha Śākyamuni's relics.

The prophecy came to fruition; after Kaniṣka became king, he came upon four children building a stūpa here out of cow's dung. This and other events convinced the king that this was a holy place, and he decided to build a larger stūpa over the children's small one. But however high the king built his stūpa, the small stūpa grew even higher. When finished, the king's stūpa stood on a base of five stages (150 feet); the body of carved wood rose thirteen stories (four hundred feet) from this base, and the body of the stūpa was crowned with an iron pillar eighty-eight feet high, bringing its height to 638 feet.

Hsüan-tsang describes a number of Buddha statues and a hundred little stūpas that rose like a forest on each side of the great stūpa, which was considered to have healing properties. Sages and saints were often seen walking among the stūpas; the fragrance of incense and musical sounds emanated from this area whenever they were present.

Sung-yun writes that Puruṣapura's great stūpa was made from carved wood, with stairs leading to the top, and covered by a roof carved from many different varieties of wood. The stūpa was capped by a gilded iron pillar encircled by fifteen copper discs, said to have been set in place after much difficulty by the four heavenly kings (the lokapālas, or world guardians). Sung-yun saw this stūpa as being by far the greatest in size and importance of all the pagodas of the lands west of China. Fa-hien describes the stūpa as incomparably beautiful, the highest stūpa in Jambudvīpa (the rose-apple continent, usually identified as India). To the southeast of

Kaniṣka's stūpa stood a colossal marble image of the Buddha, eighteen feet in height.

According to the early Chinese pilgrims, the Buddha had predicted that after this stūpa had been destroyed by fire and rebuilt seven times, his teachings would disappear from the world. Sung-yun mentions that the stūpa had already been destroyed three times by lightning. Hsüan-tsang relates that when he arrived in the seventh century, the stūpa had just been destroyed for the fourth time and was then undergoing its fifth reconstruction.

In modern times archaeologists located the site of this stūpa at Shāh-ji-ki-ḍherī and revealed its base through excavation. The foundation, which is all that remains, measures 286 feet in diameter, indicating that this was easily the largest stūpa of its kind. (HCIP 3:492) The reliquary was recovered from the ruins of this great stūpa and placed in the Peshāwar Museum. Known as the 'Kaniṣka reliquary', it is inscribed with Kaniṣka's name and topped with a seated statue of a Buddha, with two standing figures on either side. Its inscription identifies the reliquary with the Sarvāstivādin school. The excavated ruins of the stūpa's foundation have been covered over; today little remains to be seen.

The Sarvāstivādin tradition flourished here during the time of King Kaniṣka and for many centuries thereafter. This city was the birthplace of the great fourth to fifth-century scholars Asaṅga and Vasubandhu, and its monasteries were closely associated with the analysis and practices that developed the Abhidharma. Among them was the Kaniṣka Vihāra, where Vasubandhu wrote the Abhidharmakoṣa and where his mentor Manorātha composed the Vibhāṣa-śāstra. The Chinese travelers describe this vihāra as a beautifully constructed old monastery built by Kaniṣka west of his great stūpa and cared for by Śrāvaka monks. In the seventh century, however, there were only a few monks living here. Nearby was the monastery of the Brahmin Pārśvika, who became a monk at the age of eighty and attained realization in three years.

Sung-yun describes a perfectly round, twenty-seven foot-high tower in Puruṣapura renowned for its predictive abilities. If one was lucky, the bells of the tower would ring when the tower walls were touched; but if unlucky, the bells would not ring no matter how hard one pushed at the tower's sides. Sung-yun's companion, desiring to know if they would return safely home, touched the tower and was gratified to hear the bells ring loudly.

Around nine miles to the northeast, on the other side of the Kābul River, was the old capital of Puṣkāravatī. At the time of Hsüan-tsang's visit Puṣkāravatī still had a large population. Outside the city was an Aśokan stūpa marking a site where the four former Buddhas had taught the Dharma. Teachers from India had also taught here: This was where the scholar Vasumitra, named as one of the five hundred Arhats who attended the council convened by Aśoka, wrote his treatise known as the Abhidharma-prakaraṇa. About a mile north of the town was a monastery with a few monks of the Śrāvaka tradition. Here Vasumitra's uncle Dharmatrāta had written the Samyuktābhidharma-śāstra. (HT110)

Close by was a large stūpa several hundred feet high, faced with carved wood and veined stone, built where the Buddha, in one thousand past lives as a king of this land, had given his eyes for the benefit of others. About nine miles northwest another large stūpa marked where the Buddha had converted the demoness Harītī, who in grief for the loss of her child had been ravaging the countryside, and obtained her promise to refrain from harming people. From that time Harītī has been propitiated by women seeking to have children. Another nine miles north was a third stūpa where the Bodhisattva Śyāma, mistakenly wounded by a poisoned arrow, was healed by the strength of his faith and medications given by Śakra, lord of the gods. The site of the Harītī Stūpa has been identified as

Saramakh-ḍherī and the place of Śyāma's healing has been equated with Penano-ḍherī.

Some distance to the southeast, at the town Po-lu-sha, were sites related to the life of the generous Prince Sudāna (Vessantara), who was exiled upon giving his father's elephant to a greedy Brahman. Followed by his family, the prince traveled the countryside, giving all he possessed to whomever asked for it. Tested by Śakra, lord of the gods, he demonstrated the level of selfless generosity perfected by the great Bodhisattvas in giving away his children, his wife, and his own eyes.

Two monasteries, one housing fifty Śrāvaka monks and the other fifty Mahāyāna monks, still stood at the time of Hsüan-tsang's visit. The walls of one monastery had an eloquent depiction of the famous account of Prince Sudāna, which the master philosopher and poet Candragomin shaped into a Buddhist drama *(Joy for the World,* Dharma Publishing, 1986). Four stūpas also marked sacred sites in this vicinity, which was known in India as Varṣapura. In the nineteenth century, Cunningham identified the site of the Vessantara Jātaka as Paloḍherī.

Gandhāran Art

When the Parthians, an Iranian tribe, wrested Gandhāra from the Śakas in the first century B.C.E., they brought with them skilled Hellenic artisans. Accustomed to working in stone, these artisans were more familiar with secular ornamental art than they were to using art as religious expression; they knew nothing of Buddhist iconography and were unacquainted with the views expressed through Buddhist imagery. In Gandhāra they had ample opportunities to work on sculptures and ornamentations of Buddhist monuments as well as the design of the royal palaces and other secular buildings. As they became more familiar with the spiritual qualities of

Buddhism, Greek motifs gave way to religious images and symbols carved with elegance and grace, but now endowed with deeper understanding of their purpose and value.

When the Kuṣāṇas came to power in Gandhāra, the demand on the artisans began to increase. Art historians have noted that the finest spiritual expressions of Gandhāran art lasted only about fifty years. After this period, so many new monasteries were being built that artisans had to concentrate on standard forms to satisfy the demand for sculpture and ornamentation, at the expense of inventiveness and creativity.

The Gandhāran style does not appear to have influenced the course of Buddhist art in the heartland of India. This may well be because the region east of the Indus and Jhelum rivers did not produce stone that was amenable to carving, so the Gandhāran forms could not be reproduced in the neighboring regions. Since high-quality art was available in Mathurā, there would have been no reason to take extraordinary measures to import Gandhāran figures. Also, the art of Mathurā, which represented the ideal proportions and form of the Buddha, adheres more closely to the descriptions in the Buddhist texts and has long been considered more iconographically precise than the Gandhāran style. But in terms of endowing the naturalistic human form with ethereal beauty, Gandhāran art set high standards for any time or place.

The production of Gandhāran art waned after the death of the last Kuṣāṇa king, Vasudeva (c. 230 C.E.). But so efficient were the artisans and so great the quantity of art produced that many masterpieces survived centuries of destruction. Among these was a magnificent statue of the Bodhisattva Maitreya, over six feet tall, that was recovered from the site of Takht-i-Bāhi, a large monastic complex built during the reign of the Kuṣāṇa kings. It is now housed in the Lahore Museum, along with the famous statue of the Fasting Buddha found at Sikri. The same site yielded a Gandhāran sculpture of the Prince Gautama taking leave of his charioteer Chandaka

Ruins of a monastery at Takht-i-Bāhi

and his favorite horse Kaṇṭhaka after departing from his father's palace, as well as a sculpted scene of the Bodhisattva inside the palace reflecting on the sufferings of existence.

The art of Gandhāra was revived in the fourth and early fifth centuries, when Kuṣāṇas from Bactria, led by Kidara, took over Takṣaśilā and other regions in the Northwest. The artisans of this period used clay and stucco rather than stone, which gave them much greater freedom of expression. Although little is known of the political developments of this period, examples of this art indicate that the later Kuṣāṇas continued to patronize Buddhism and that they were able to preserve enough of Gandhāra's culture to maintain a high standard of sacred art.

Takṣaśilā

"East of the ancient cities, almost every hilltop and terrace was occupied by a Buddhist settlement, while those in the cool glens between the hills or crowning low knolls in the open valleys were just as numerous, and in the cities there were many more."
—John Marshall, in *Guide to Taxila*

The Sanskrit word Takṣaśilā could mean "cut stone," or even "cut-off head," for it was here that the Bodhisattva, perfecting generosity in a previous existence, made a gift of his head. Takṣaśilā is also known as Taxila, the Greek form of its name. For much of its early history, Takṣaśilā, like the other lands on India's northwest border, was an independent capital city surrounded by lands it governed. A settlement nestled in a bowl-like valley created by mountains and rivers, Takṣaṣilā's proximity to the Khyber Pass made it a natural gateway linking India and the great trade routes to the west.

Archaeological evidence suggests that the earliest foundations of Takṣaśilā date to the sixth century B.C.E., when the Persian army of Cyrus the Great, ruler of the Achaemenid Empire, occupied the region of Gandhāra. The Persians appear to have maintained control of Gandhāra at least through the reign of Cyrus' successor Darius I, a contemporary of King Bimbisāra. In the second century C.E., the Bactrian Greeks extended their influence deep into Aśoka's former empire. They expanded Gandhāra's borders and made Takṣaśilā the principal city of Gandhāra.

According to the Pāli commentaries, Pukkusāti was king of Takṣaśilā at the time of Śākyamuni Buddha and maintained friendly relations with King Bimbisāra. Caravans routinely traveled the route between Takṣaśilā and Magadha and carried messages and gifts the kings sent to one another. In return for one such gift, King Bimbisāra sent Pukkusāti gold plates engraved with descriptions of the Buddha, Dharma, and Sangha and several Dharma teachings. After reading the plates, Pukkusāti renounced the world and traveled to the Madhyadeśa to meet the Buddha. The Buddha came upon Pukkusāti in Rājagṛha; noting his pleasing demeanor, the Buddha taught the Dhātuvibhaṅga-sutta, the Discourse on the Analysis of the Elements, for his benefit.

Takṣaśilā first became part of India during the reign of Candragupta Maurya (c. 324–300 B.C.E.), Aśoka's grandfather, who linked the city by road to Pāṭaliputra and connected it to routes traversing the Indus to Kapiśa, Bactria, and further west. During Aśoka's reign, Takṣaśilā became a center of Buddhist activity. When Aśoka came to power, he strongly supported Buddhism's growth in the northwest. At Takṣaśilā he built the great Dharmarājika Stūpa with an adjoining monastery and erected a large stone pillar beside it. The stūpa commemorating the end of his son Kuṇāla's blindness may also have been built during Aśoka's reign.

In Aśoka's time, Takṣaśilā was already a respected center of learning, a place where the sons of ministers and kings were sent to complete their education in the Vedas, grammar, medicine, and the arts. Buddhist centers established in Takṣaśilā continued this tradition; monasteries at Takṣaśilā and elsewhere in the northwest became renowned as centers of logic and analysis. As the Dharma flowed through the northwest into Central Asia and circled the oasis states of Central Asia's Taklamakan Basin, the monasteries of Takṣaśilā attracted monks from Bactria, Sogdia, and Central Asia.

In the early second century B.C.E., Puṣyamitra seized the throne of the Mauryan Empire and came to power in its capital, Paṭaliputra. Reinstituting Brahmanic practices that had fallen into disuse, he persecuted Buddhists and fought with the Greeks on his northwestern border. Although some Buddhist monuments were heavily damaged during his reign, Buddhism in the northwest was not seriously effected and soon recovered its momentum. After Puṣyamitra, Takṣaśilā came once again under foreign domination. But the procession of Greek, Śaka, Parthian, and Kuṣāṇa kings who ruled between the second century B.C.E. and the third century C.E. generally supported the Dharma, which flourished throughout their kingdoms and beyond.

With the opening of the Silk Road in 112 B.C.E., merchants of Takṣaśilā gained access to the major trade routes linking China with Mesopotamia, through a branch of the route that ran south and east from Takṣaśilā to Kapiśa. As Takṣaśilā became a thriving mercantile center, its economic and political importance increased. Bhikṣus accompanying the caravans traveled to Central Asia, China, and possibly into the Middle East.

For Central Asian and Parthian monks, Takṣaśilā was their connection with the heartland of the Dharma; at Takṣaśilā they could refine translation skills and master the Tripiṭaka with accomplished teachers. From Takṣaśilā, many Parthian and Central Asian monks went to China, where they served as translators and teachers. According to Hsüan-tsang, Takṣaśilā's neighbors, Gandhāra and Uḍḍiyāna, had at least one thousand monasteries each. Takṣaśilā, in its prime the foremost center of learning for India and Central Asia, almost certainly surpassed these lands in the number and magnitude of its monuments to the Dharma.

Visits of the Chinese Pilgrims

When Fa-hien passed through Takṣaśilā in the early fifth century, Buddhism was flourishing in Gandhāra and in its neighboring states. But in the latter part of the fifth century, the whole region was ravaged by the Hephthalite Huns. The date of the Hephthalite invasion was fixed by the Chinese pilgrim Sung Yun, who recorded in 520 C.E. that Gandhāra had been devastated by the Ye-tha (Hephthalites) two generations before, or around 480 C.E. Coins found in burned monasteries in Takṣaśilā confirm this date. The destruction wrought by the Hephthalites was thorough, and tales of their savagery and violence lingered long in the memories of people throughout India. Although they inhabited the area less than a hundred years, Takṣaśilā was not able to recover its autonomy or its cultural, religious, and political prominence.

When Hsüan-tsang arrived in Takṣaśilā around 630 C.E., he found the region under the rule of Kashmir, although he noted that it had formerly been governed from Kapiśa. "The land is renowned for its fertility and produces rich harvests. It is very full of streams and fountains. Flowers and fruits are abundant. The climate is agreeably temperate. The people are lively and courageous, and they honor the three gems. Although there are many monasteries, most are ruinous and deserted, and there are very few priests; those that there are study the Great Vehicle." (HT I:137)

Fa-hien and Hsüan-tsang both describe three great stūpas built by Aśoka in Takṣaśilā. The Treasure of Maitreya Stūpa, one hundred feet high, commemorated the place where the Buddha Śākyamuni predicted that a treasure of gems would spontaneously appear upon the coming of the next Buddha, Maitreya. Whenever an earthquake occurred in this region, the vicinity of this stūpa remained perfectly still. Another stūpa commemorates the Gift of the Head, the place where in a previous life as a Bodhisattva, Śākyamuni cut off his own head for the sake of another. Nearby was the monastery where the Sautrāntika master Kumāralabdha composed his treatises. Although the monastery was in decline, a few monks still lived there in the seventh century. This may have been the place where the eighth-century master Haribhadra, disciple of Śāntarakṣita and preceptor of King Dharmapāla, met his disciple Buddhajñāna.

Outside Takṣaśilā stood the hundred-foot-high stūpa of Kuṇāla, son of Aśoka and former governor of Takṣaśilā. This stūpa marked the place where Kuṇāla was blinded at his stepmother's instigation without the knowledge of Aśoka; his sight was later restored at Pāṭaliputra through an act of truth. Hsüan-tsang described this stūpa as a place where the blind come to pray for the restoration of their sight.

About eleven miles north of the city was the pool of the nāga king Elāpatra, where lotus flowers of various colors reflected multihued rays of light. At the time of the Buddha Kāśyapa, this nāga was a bhikṣu who destroyed an Elāpatra tree beloved by nāgas, and for this was reborn as a nāga. In Hsüan-tsang's time people came to this pool to propitiate the nāga for the blessings of rain or fair weather.

Archaeology of Takṣaśilā

The ruins of Takṣaśilā, discovered in modern times about twenty-two miles from Rāwalpiṇḍi, within the boundaries of modern Pakistan, still evoke wonder. As John Marshall writes in *Guide to Takṣaśilā,* "East of the ancient cities, almost every hill-top and terrace was occupied by a Buddhist settlement, while those in the cool glens between the hills or crowning low knolls in the open valleys were just as numerous; and in the cities themselves there were many more. The great majority of these monuments date from the first five centuries of the Christian era, and none of those now visible are as early as the Mauryan kings; but if the strength and vitality of a religion can be gauged from its monumental remains, no one seeing this vast galaxy of ruins can doubt the overwhelming success which ultimately rewarded Aśoka's efforts in this part of his empire." (GT 17)

When archaeologists began to research this site, their work was complicated by the discovery that Takṣaśilā had been relocated several times in its long history. Three distinct locations have now been identified. The oldest foundations were found in the Bhir Mound, the remains of buildings inhabited in the fifth or sixth century B.C.E., when the area was ruled by the Persian Achaemenid Dynasty. The second oldest location was the site at Sirkap, built by the Indo-Greeks of the second century C.E., and the third and most recent site was at Sirsukh, founded by the Kuṣāṇa rulers. Since Buddhist monuments were normally built in the outlying regions of a city, these relocations probably did not disrupt the development of Buddhist centers here.

Mounds indicating the location of Buddhist monuments stretch along the valleys and on the hills surrounding Takṣaśilā, creating a "galaxy of monuments" that once gleamed with white plastered walls and domes. The most prominent remains are those of the Dharmarājika Stūpa built by Aśoka, which still stands forty-five feet high at the foot of the south side of the Hathial spur, on a plateau above the Tamranala River. The stūpa, named after the Dharmarāja (Dharma king) Aśoka, was probably reconstructed by Kaniṣka in the first or second century C.E. The deep band of ornamental stonework on the stūpa is later in style and was probably added by the Kidara Kuṣāṇas in the fourth century.

The main stūpa, 150 feet at its largest diameter, was built to endure the ages; its body is supported by a core of concentric rings of stone walls. It is still encircled by smaller stūpas, which appear to have been damaged around 25–30 C.E. when an earthquake devastated Takṣaśilā. After this disaster, most buildings and stūpas were strengthened with durable stone facing. A whole complex of gateways and shrines was later built around the central stūpa. Relics found here during modern excavations were given to Śrī Laṅkā to be enshrined at the Temple of the Tooth Relic in Kandy.

Additional ruins of monasteries, and stūpas have been found south of the Dharmarājika Stūpa at the sites of Khader Mohra and Akhaure. Another large complex, second only to the Dharmarājika site, is Candraśīla, located at Kalwan on the Margala spur a little more than a mile south of the Dharmarājika Stūpa. Here monasteries, stūpas, and shrines were built on three terraces formed of rock ledges projecting from a hill. The ruins on the middle terrace measured 450 × 270 feet and consisted of a courtyard with a stūpa and three large groups of monastic cells. The lower and upper terraces supported smaller sites that appear to have been constructed at different times, between Kaniṣka's time and the fifth century C.E. A number of broken Buddha images and a relic casket were found here. (Taxila II:322)

Remains of Buddhist buildings were found at Pippala, Jaulian, and Mohra Moradu, all located between two and three miles distant from the Kuṇāla Stūpa. From the Pippala Mound were unearthed ruins of Takṣaśīla's most ancient monastery. Considered to predate the Kuṣāṇa period, this monastery displays a floor plan and style of construction found in later monasteries throughout northern India. It is thought to be the most ancient Buddhist monastery discovered in India to date. At Jaulian, ruins of another monastery were discovered on top of a hill three hundred feet high. Near the monastery, thought to date between the second and fifth centuries C.E., are the ruins of two large stūpas; the presence of many smaller stūpas and shrines around them emphasize the site's importance in ancient times.

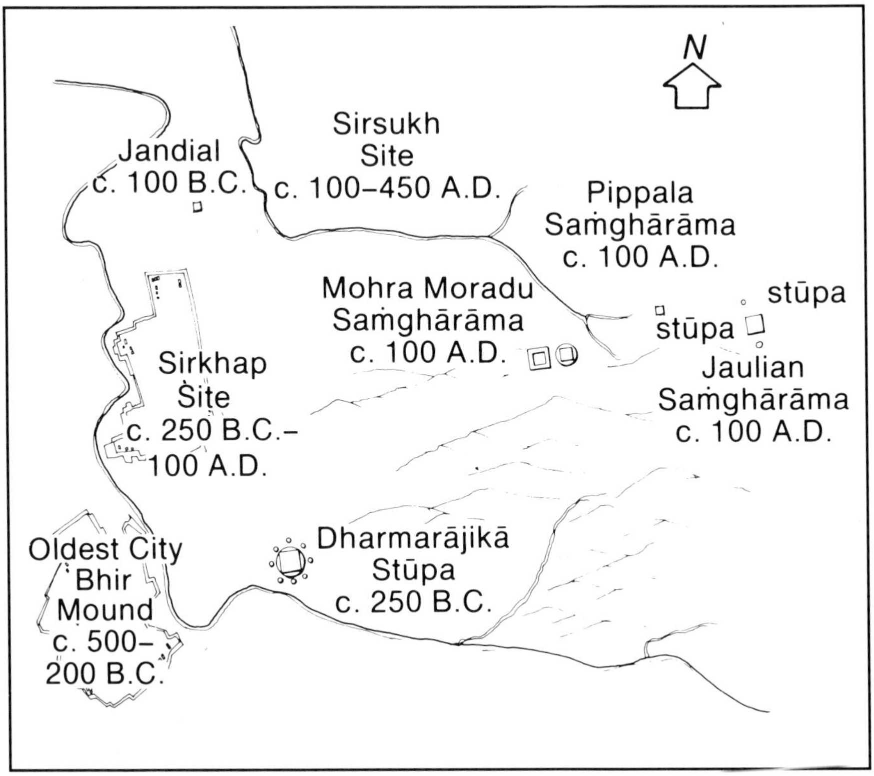

Major sites at Takṣaśilā

Hsüan-tsang's Takṣaśilā was the site now known as Sirsukh, and the four Buddhist monuments he described have been located nearby. The monument with the pool of the nāga Elāpatra is the modern Panja Sahib at Hasan Abdal, and the Treasure of Maitreya Stūpa is now a ruin on the ridge above Boati Pind. Following the description given by Hsüan-tsang, the Gift of the Head Stūpa has been identified as the Bhallar Stūpa on the western outcropping of the Sarda Hill, and the Stūpa of Kuṇāla is most likely the one found on the northern side of the Hathial Hill.

The Bhallar Stūpa, located on the top of the Sarda Hill to the north of Takṣaśilā, still rises to an imposing height. Protected from the elements by its stone facing, the distinctive rounded body of the stūpa consists of six or seven tiers. Excavations near the stūpa have revealed the ruins of a large monastery, identified as the one Hsüan-tsang associated with the Sautrāntika master Kumāralabdha.

The ruins thought to be the foundation of the Kuṇāla Stūpa would support a stūpa of the size Hsüan-tsang described; the three steps of its base are still intact. A much smaller stūpa, nearly ten feet high and made of rough limestone blocks, was found intact in the core of this stūpa. The smaller stūpa appears to have been built when the Śakas ruled this area, and the larger one constructed over it sometime between the third and fourth centuries C.E. A monastery, with rooms opening to a central courtyard, used to stand to the west of the stūpa; in places the remains of its walls are still up to fourteen feet high. Four mounds excavated at Lalchak, also near Sirsukh, yielded remains of a monastery and two stūpas which appear to have been built between the third and fourth centuries C.E.

A plinth eighty feet square and twenty inches high has been found at Bhadalpur, located near the village of Bhera. To the east of this platform, which could have supported a massive stūpa, were found ruins of a large monastery. Some of the stūpas and monasteries built in more remote sites near Takṣaśilā have been found better preserved, with quantities of art in relatively good condition. For the historian, Takṣaśilā is a veritable museum of artifacts, invaluable for reconstructing the complex movements of people and empire. For the Buddhist, Takṣaśilā even in ruins testifies to the Dharma's vitality in the distant past and reminds us of the impermanence of all conditioned things.

Uḍḍiyāna

Although Uḍḍiyāna is increasingly associated with the Swat Valley just east of the upper Indus River, it remains the mystic land of Indrabhūti and the Great Guru Padmasambhava. Ruins of Buddhist monuments fill the land, yet little is really known is really known of how Buddhism evolved here.

In ancient times, the region known as Uḍḍiyāna stretched west through the Khyber Pass into modern Afghanistan as well as northeast, occupying the entire valley between the Swat and Kunar rivers. But at some point the kingdom was split in two. Hsüan-tsang informs us that the land west of the Khyber Pass became known as Nagarahāra, and only the Swat Valley on the eastern side of the pass retained the name Uḍḍiyāna. The Swat Valley now lies in the northern part of modern Pakistan.

Inhabited since paleolithic times, the Swat Valley was settled by Indo-Iranian peoples before the fourth century B.C.E. Alexander the Great entered the valley around 327 B.C.E. and advanced at least as far as Udegram. The date when Buddhism entered Uḍḍiyāna is more difficult to ascertain.

According to traditional accounts, the royal lineage of Uḍḍiyāna was descended from a prince of the Śākyas, who made his way to Uḍḍiyāna after the destruction of Kapilavastu, married a Nāga princess, and became king of that land. His son Uttarasena succeeded him as king. After Śākyamuni Buddha entered Parinirvāṇa, King Uttarasena came to Kuśinagara, obtained a portion of the Buddha's relics, and brought them to Uḍḍiyāna, where he enshrined the relics in a stūpa. The elephant that had carried the relics died and was transformed into stone.

The Dharma has a long association with the mystic land of Uḍḍiyāna, home of King Indrabhūti and birthplace of the Great Guru Padmasambhava. According to the Nyingma, or original tradition of Tibetan Buddhism, it was at Uḍḍiyāna that knowledge of the Mahā, Anu, and Atiyoga—the Inner Tantras preserved in Tibet within the Nyingma tradition—first entered the human plane. Although a detailed examination of the time and place for the development of these important lineages is beyond the scope of this book, a brief summary may invite a more thorough investigation into the history of Uḍḍiyāna and its connection with ruins found in the Swat Valley.

King Indrabhūti (rGyal-po rDza) received the transmission of the Mahāyoga Tantras twenty-eight years after the Buddha's Parinirvāṇa. From rGyal-po rDza the lineage passed successively to the siddhas Kukkurarāja, Indrabhūti, Siṁharāja, and Uparāja, who taught the Princess Gomadevī; then from Gomadevī to the siddha Līlavajra, who transmitted the lineage to Buddhaguhya, Vimalamitra, and Padmasambhava. Through these three great masters, the Mahāyoga lineage passed directly into Tibet.

The Anuyoga lineage progressed similarly. Revealed in Uḍḍiyāna to King Indrabhūti in seven visions, the lineage passed to Uparāja, Indrabhūti the Younger, and Kukkurarāja, who transmitted it to dGa'-rab-rdo-rje. dGa'-rab-rdo-rje transmitted it to his two disciples, Vajrahasya and Prabhahasti, King of Zahor. Prabhahasti instructed Śākyaprabha and Śākyasiṁha, a manifestation of Padmasambhava. Śākyasiṁha bestowed the teachings on Dhanarakṣita at Vajrāsana, site of the Buddha's enlightenment; Dhanarakṣita transmitted them to the siddha Hūṁkara in the Diamond Cavern of Uḍḍiyāna. Meditating in the Asura Cavern between India and Persia, Hūṁkara attained realization. These teachings were disseminated through Hūṁkara's disciples. By the eighth century, when Tibetan masters sought the Anuyoga teachings, the Anuyoga lineage was established in Bru-zha, the region encompassing Gilgit, northwest of the vale of Kashmir.

The Atiyoga, the Teachings of the Great Perfection, were transmitted directly to dGa'-rab-rdo-rje, grandson of King Uparāja of Uḍḍiyāna. dGa'-rab-rdo-rje transmitted the Atiyoga in a charnel ground near Vajrāsana, where it was successively practiced by Manjuśrīmitra and Śrī Siṁha, who transmitted the lineage to his disciples: Padmasambhava, Jñānasūtra, and Vimalamitra. Vimalamitra brought the Atiyoga texts to Uḍḍiyāna in the eighth century, where he taught until invited to transmit his lineage in Tibet.

According to the gSar-ma, or new tradition of Tibetan Buddhism, the Tantras were transmitted to King Indrabhūti, who transcribed and taught them to the people of Uḍḍiyāna. As a result of these teachings, all inhabitants of the land, even the insects, attained enlightenment and vanished, leaving no bodily remains. The nāgas, seeing the land of Uḍḍiyana empty of living beings, transformed it into a lake.

In time, Vajrapāṇi revealed the Tantras to the nāgas living in this lake; as their consciousness developed, they became human beings and lived in villages on the lake's shore. As they continued to practice the subtle teachings, their realization increased, and their sons and daughters became ḍākas and ḍākinīs. The lake and the region around it then became known as Uḍḍiyāna, the Land of the Ḍākinīs. In time the lake dried up; in its center appeared a temple containing all the Tantras. Over the centuries, accomplished masters have retrieved most of these Tantras and disseminated them widely: King Vasukalpa obtained the Guhyasamāja Tantra, Nāgārjuna the Hevajra Tantra, and Kukkuripa the Mahāmāyā and Bhairava Tantras. (DR 441–442) In Tibet, these two traditions concerning Uḍḍiyāna have come down within the rNying-ma and gSar-ma schools.

Buddhism in the Swat Valley

It is likely that the Śrāvaka schools of Buddhism entered the valley near the end of the Mauryan period, between 250 and 187 B.C.E., about the same time as elsewhere in the northwest. The Swat Valley rose to prominence under the Yavanas, the Indo-Greeks who ruled this region from the mid-third century to approximately 85 B.C.E. As in other northwestern lands, Buddhism flourished here during the Kuṣāṇa period (first to third centuries C.E.,) when it exerted great influence on the art and culture of the entire northwest. As reflected in its art, Swat was a diverse culture embracing Greek, Iranian, Central Asian, and Indian elements.

In the fifth century, when Fa-hien visited the area, Uḍḍiyāna was India's northernmost province. To the north beyond Uḍḍiyāna rose the mountains of the Hindu Kush that separated Uḍḍiyāna from Central Asia. Fa-hien notes that the people used the language of middle India, and the Dharma was flourishing. There were more than five hundred monasteries of the Śrāvakayāna tradition in the area, all of which extended hospitality to traveling monks. The Buddha's almsbowl was enshrined in one of these monasteries, where seven hundred monks regularly assembled to honor it, as did many of the local people.

In the sixth century, Sung-yen also noted many thriving monasteries in the area. He mentions that the king was devoted to the Dharma, and that ancient legends preserved accounts of the Buddha's activities here. Sung-yun saw the place where the Buddha dried his robe after a violent storm brought about by a nāga, the trace of the Buddha's footprint, and other holy places described by Fa-hien and Hsüan-tsang.

Between the sixth and seventh centuries, however, the monasteries and holy places of Uḍḍiyāna suffered devastations by flood, earthquake, and landslides. These disasters affected not only Buddhist centers, but also the valley's entire population. When Hsüan-tsang visited the valley in the seventh century, he found the ruins of approximately fourteen hundred monasteries on both sides of the river. Once these monasteries had housed up to eighteen thousand monks, but few were left. Hsüan-tsang attributes this decline to persecution by Mihirakula, leader of the Huns.

The Śrāvaka schools did not continue here as distinct traditions after the seventh century. Hsüan-tsang observed that most of the monks in Uḍḍiyāna followed the Mahāyāna. Five Śrāvaka schools—Sarvāstivādin, Dharmagupta, Mahīśāsaka, Kāśyapīya, and Mahāsāṁghika—must have been active here in the past, but in Hsüan-tsang's time, only their Vinayas survived as living traditions. These Vinaya lineages continued to form the basis of all monastic training and discipline in Uḍḍiyāna.

Hsüan-tsang recounts Uḍḍiyāna's many wonders and describes how in every direction stūpas rose over sites sacred to the Sangha. To the east of Mungali (Maṅgalapura), the capital city, was a stūpa commemorating where the Buddha, in a previous birth as a sage, practiced the perfection of patience. The Buddha's footprint could be seen impressed in a rock in the place where he stood while describing some of his former births. An Aśokan stūpa commemorated the occasion when, as King Śibi, the Bodhisattva gave his flesh to a hawk to save the life of a dove. In another place marked by a stūpa, the Buddha, as Lord Śakra, changed his form into a great serpent and offered his body as medicine to an entire valley of people suffering from a severe pestilence.

To the north was a stūpa indicating where the Buddha, as a peacock king, struck a rock with his beak and produced water for his followers who were dying of thirst. According to Hsüan-tsang, this site was still renowned for its healing powers. To the southwest of the town of Mungali, beside a great river, stood the stūpa built by King Uttarasena to enshrine the relics of the Buddha. Beside the stūpa, Hsüan-tsang observed the rock shaped like an elephant, where the elephant that had carried the relics from Kuśinagara had been transformed into stone. A little over five miles away was a statue of Avalokiteśvara, famed for its miraculous powers.

Traveling further, Hsüan-tsang came to the valley Ta-li-lo (the modern Daril Valley); there, next to a monastery, he saw a hundred-foot-high statue of the Buddha Maitreya (eighty feet high per Fa-hien) said to have been created by the Arhat Madhyāntika. Tradition holds that the Arhat used his powers to send a sculptor to the Tuṣita Heaven, there to observe Maitreya in order to replicate his likeness in this colossal statue. According to Fa-hien, kings of surrounding countries still vied with each other in making the most appropriate offerings to the statue. There was a local tradition that it was only after the creation of this image (which Fa-hien places three hundred years after the Parinirvāṇa), that the śramaṇas from India were able to carry the Dharma beyond this river.

The journey from Uḍḍiyāna into the country of Bolor led Hsüan-tsang over precipices and valleys, over suspension bridges and wood footways across the great gorges of the Sin-tu (Indus) River. There Hsüan-tsang counted about a hundred monasteries housing about a thousand monks, but he observed that these monks had "no great zeal for learning" and were careless in their Vinaya observations. Again Hsüan-tsang braved the dangerous river crossing: "The river is about three or four li (roughly a half mile) in width, and flows southwest. Its waters are pure and clear as a mirror as they roll along with impetuous flow. Poisonous nāgas and hurtful beasts occupy the caverns and clefts along its sides. If a man tries to cross the river carrying with him valuable gems or rare kinds of flowers or fruits, or especially relics of Buddha, the boat is frequently engulfed by the waves." (HT I:136)

Archaeology of Uḍḍiyāna

In the early eleventh century, Uḍḍiyāna was conquered by Mahmūd of Ghaznī, leader of the Muslim Ghaznavids. Although little is known of its subsequent history, it appears to have been relatively autonomous until modern times. Uḍḍiyāna now lies within the borders of Pakistan, where it forms the modern state of Swat, and the city of Mingora, near the conjunction of the Swat and Jambil rivers, is its largest commercial center.

Although there were preliminary excavations made earlier in this century, it was not until 1956 that a cooperative effort between an Italian archaeological team and the Pakistani government led to a systematic archaeological investigation. The leader of the expedition, D. Faccenna, remarked that from the town of Barikot, close to the entrance of the Swat Valley, wherever one looked one could see important ruins half hidden among the valleys that radiated outward from this central point. (GES 13)

Research focused on sites around Udegram and Butkara. Above the village of Udegram, itself an important site, rises the remains of a large complex of buildings built on a spur of the mountain range. A large staircase, constructed and added to over a period of many years, leads to the central part of the complex. The site covers more than two acres of ground. About one third of the site had been excavated as of 1964, revealing at least twenty periods of construction. Finds of coins date the lowest levels of current excavation to the second century C.E., but still lower levels exist that could date to the time of Alexander the Great. These lower levels appear to have been abandoned around the end of the fifth century C.E. The upper portion has been dated between the seventh and tenth centuries. This grand structure, termed "The Castle" by its excavators, was conquered by Mahmūd of Ghaznī in the eleventh century C.E. After a period of Muslim rule, a Buddhist community may have inhabited the site for a time between the thirteenth and fourteenth centuries. (GES 20–22)

Buddhist sites were excavated in the Jambil Valley southeast of Mingora, near the towns of Butkara and Panr. The entire Jambil Valley is rich in sites that reveal the Swat culture's stability and its long and uninterrupted association with Buddhism. As Faccenna records, "Everywhere along the terraces or at the foot of the smaller valleys one finds mounds, stelae, rock-cut reliefs with the figures of Buddhas and Bodhisattvas, the remains of inhabited sites and gravestones." (GES 25)

The great stūpa at Butkara stands in the center of 215 other religious structures, mostly smaller stūpas and monastic dwellings. Stones were stripped from this stūpa in recent times to furnish building materials for Mingora. Excavation revealed layer upon layer of construction. Coins of King Menander were found in the oldest part of the stūpa, indicating that building began during the time of the Indo-Greeks. Finds of coins in the later parts of the stūpa indicate that construction continued through the sixth century.

The Butkara Stūpa complex was probably at the height of its beauty when the pilgrim Sung Yun visited Uḍḍiyāna in the sixth century. By the time of Hsüan-tsang's visit in the seventh century it had been either abandoned or ruined. The entire structure, along with all other monuments in the area, collapsed in the seventh century in what appears to have been a sudden natural disaster. Another great stūpa was erected around the late seventh century or early eighth century, but

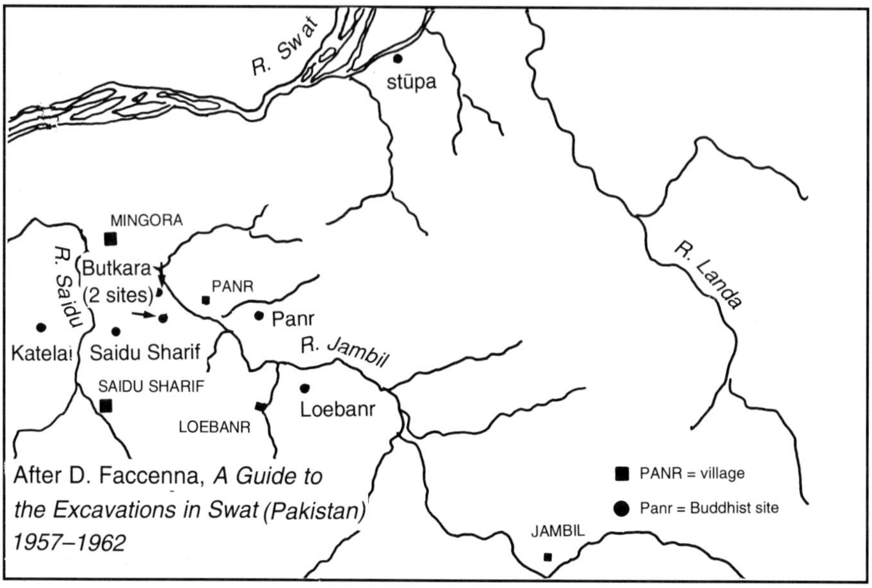

After D. Faccenna, *A Guide to the Excavations in Swat (Pakistan) 1957–1962*

the entire site was sealed before the invasion of Mahmūd of Ghaznī and was not occupied after that time.

The Buddhist remains at Panr consist of stūpas and dwellings arranged on a hillside, constructed on two main terraces connected by stairs. As at Butkara, the buildings were erected over a period of many years and present a rich tapestry of architectural designs. The oldest remains may date to the first century C.E., when stūpa designs changed throughout the Swat Valley and soapstone began to be used for construction. Although the buildings here were heavily damaged, their sculptures and ornamental carvings have been well enough preserved to reveal a highly developed artistic tradition. It was clear that artists and craftsmen enhanced their work with paints and gilding. In addition to the sites of Butkara and Panr, remains of stūpas have been located at Shararai, Loebanr, and Gerjulai on one side of the Jambil River, and at Barama, Shingharai, and Garasa on the other side. Additional sites stretch nearly continuously throughout the valley. The art and other artifacts found at the sites excavated in Swat are now in the Swat Museum at Saidu Sharif, a short distance south of Mingora.

Buddhism in Afghanistan

"These people are remarkable, among all their neighbors, for a love of religion; from the highest form of worship accorded the Three Jewels down to the worship of the hundred spirits, there is not the least absence of earnestness and the utmost devotion of heart."

—Hsüan-tsang

West of the Khyber Pass, in what is now Afghanistan, Fa-hien found the Dharma flourishing in the early fifth century C.E. There were both Mahāyāna and Hīnayāna centers, and the monks of both traditions received Fa-hien with great hospitality. Traveling southeast toward Mathurā, Fa-hien passed temples "one after the other," each well-inhabited and thriving. In the mid-seventh century, Hsüan-tsang also observed thriving Buddhist communities here.

Today, the soaring remains of a stūpa in remote Guldara, Afghanistan testify to the vigor of Buddhism and the richness of its artistic heritage in Afghanistan's ancient culture. Its empty niches, framed with Grecian-style columns, were capable of accommodating unusually large sculptures. This stūpa and the ruins of a monastery nearby appear to have been built in the second century C.E. Remains of stūpas have also been found at Bīmarān; an inscription on a reliquary urn from one stūpa notes that the patron Śivarakṣita built this stūpa to enshrine relics of the Buddha during the time of the Śaka rulers. At Wardak, west of Kābul, an inscription relates that relics of the Buddha had been given to monks of the Mahāsāṁghika school and enshrined within the Vagramariga Monastery. A prayer for King Huviṣka's good fortune was also found at Wardak.

Aśoka erected edicts inscribed in the Kharoṣṭhī script on rocks in Shāhbāzgaṛhī and Mansehra and one in Aramaic script at Lampaka. Three edicts in Greek and Aramaic have been found as far west as Kandahār, in the heart of modern Afghanistan.

Nagarahāra

The northwestern city of Nagarahāra is famed as the place where Śākyamuni, in aeons past, bought flowers from a young girl to present to the Buddha Dīpaṁkara. As a result of this offering and the merit accumulated through past actions, Śākyamuni received from Dīpaṁkara the prediction of his enlightenment in a future aeon. Although it is clear that Nagarahāra was located at the junction of the Surkhar and Kābul rivers, a natural gateway into the far northwestern reaches of the Indian subcontinent, Nagarahāra's exact location remains unverified.

It is also difficult to ascertain exactly when Nagarahāra became a major center of Buddhism. The earliest reference to Buddhism at Nagarahāra is found on an inscription on the lion capital at Mathurā. This inscription, made at the time of Śoḍāsa, who governed Mathurā between 10 B.C.E. and 5 C.E., notes that the center of the Sarvāstivādins was located in

Nagarahāra. The Chinese accounts verify that both Śrāvakayāna and Mahāyāna Buddhist traditions were flourishing here in the fifth century, and that the Dharma formed an important part of the cultural and religious life of the people at that time. The presence of many monasteries, or vihāras, may well have given the region of Nagarahāra its name. Nagarahāra may have originally been Nagaravihāra, meaning 'monastery which is like a city' or 'monastery of the city'.

Fa-hien, approaching Nagarahāra from the northeast, relates the difficulty of traveling in that mountainous region: "The mountain-side is simply a stone wall standing up 10,000 feet. Looking down, the sight is confused, and on going forward there is no sure foothold." Hsüan-tsang described the area as surrounded on four sides by overhanging precipices and other natural barriers.

Although the city and its surrounding region enjoyed periods of autonomy, in the seventh century Nagarahāra was ruled by the king of Kapiśa, whom Hsüan-tsang describes as a strong supporter of Mahāyāna Buddhism. Hsüan-tsang also mentions a stūpa three hundred feet high built by Aśoka, "wonderfully constructed of stone beautifully adorned and carved," that marked the place where Śākyamuni received his prediction of enlightenment. Nearby stood another stūpa that commemorated the buying of the flowers. According to Hsüan-tsang, flowers still rained from the sky on holy days in memory of this auspicious event, and people responded with offerings. To the west was a monastery which housed a few monks, and to the south, away from the road, was another small stūpa.

The ruins of an ancient great stūpa could be seen in the town itself; tradition related that this stūpa was once very large and magnificent and housed a tooth relic of the Buddha. By Hsüan-tsang's time only the foundations remained, although in the fifth century the stūpa seems to have been intact. Fa-hien describes the Dauranta, or Tooth Relic Stūpa and notes that offerings were made there. Another stūpa about thirty feet high stood by the ruins; no one could recall who erected this monument, and local people claimed that it fell from the sky and placed itself on that spot.

Fa-hien describes a monastery at Hi-lo (Hiḍḍa or Haḍḍa) on the borders of Nagarahāra that preserved a relic of the Buddha's skullbone. The relic, gilded and adorned with the seven precious substances, was displayed and put away daily in a precise and respectful ritual: "Every night the relic is put away in a small tower five feet high, which opens and shuts to receive it. . . . Many people gather there to make offerings, and the king has assigned guards to protect the precious relic." (HT xxxiv) Hsüan-tsang, in the seventh century, describes the skullbone as preserved in a two-storied tower ornamented with painted beams and red columns. He saw the relic enshrined in a small stūpa on the top floor, together with other relics of the Buddha, including the Tathāgata's staff and robe. The king of Kapiśa had assigned five Brahmins to attend these precious relics with continual offerings of incense and flowers. Two centuries earlier, in Fa-hien's time, the Buddha's staff and robe were housed in separate vihāras.

South of Nagarahāra, next to a great waterfall, Fa-hien found the cavern of the nāga Gopāla, where the Buddha left his shadow to help the nāga overcome his evil karma and adhere to the path of virtue. In the fifth century, Fa-hien observed that the shadow, visible from a distance of ten paces, was gold in color, and that the marks and signs distinguishing the body of a Buddha shone forth from it clearly. In Hsüan-tsang's time the shadow was rarely seen, and what appeared when it was visible was only a feeble likeness.

To the west of this cave was the stone where the Buddha spread his robe after washing it; the stone still bore the cloth's imprint. Not far from the cave were three stūpas, two marking where the Buddha taught, and the third containing hair and nail relics. In Fa-hien's time a monastery here housed seven hundred monks, but Hsüan-tsang does not mention this monastery. In this district where Fa-hien saw nearly a thousand stūpas in honor of Arhats and Pratyekabuddhas, Hsüan-tsang makes no reference to such monuments.

While modern Jalalabad (Jalalakot) fits the general location of Nagarahāra, ruins of several ancient towns in the area render exact identification of Nagarahāra problematic. The remains of monasteries and stūpas are extensive: At least fourteen sites have been identified, many of them associated with finds of relics. The most important sites appear to be at Chahar Bāgh, Bīmarān, Dauranta, and Haḍḍa.

Remains of a large stūpa approximately eighteen hundred feet in circumference have been found at a place known as Khwaja Lahoree. Remains of six stūpas were discovered at Chahar Bāgh, four of which contained relics. In recent years additional ruins have been found at Chahar Bāgh: the base of a stūpa about three hundred feet in circumference and the remains of eleven monasteries, unearthed from the mounds dotting the nearby fields. Excavations of these sites are incomplete; coins found here date the site to the time of Maues and Kaniṣka (first to second centuries C.E. (HBA 53–54)

Additional relic stūpas have been discovered at Sultanpur and on a hill at Barabad; mounds near the stūpa at Barabad may be ruins of a vihāra. Although stūpas once stood at Nandara, Deh-Rahman, and other such sites, the stūpas of Bīmarān appear to have had a special importance. Four stūpas were opened here in the nineteenth century, and three were found to contain relics. An inscription indicates that one round relic box, made of gold set with rubies and encircled with a repoussé design of the Buddha and other figures, was donated by Śivarakṣita, son of Muñjavat. The art on the box identifies it as related to the Mahāyāna tradition. Coins found near the box date from the time of Azes (early first century C.E.) and refer to Azes as a Dharma king.

As at Bāmiyān, monasteries and individual dwellings were carved out of the faces of hills and cliffs at Dauranta, Kajitulu, Siah-Kok, and Allahnazar, all sites within about thirty-five miles of Jalalabad. A sixth site, Baswal, where 150 caves have been counted, is the most extensive. Even though blackened with soot after centuries of use by nomads, the Baswal caves bear faint traces of exquisitely painted frescos. The location of the caves on the banks of the Kābul River or its tributaries provided the Buddhist communities there with an abundant water supply. In the 1960s a Japanese expedition, exploring the caves of this region, discovered many of them connected by a large tunnel about twelve feet wide. Some of the caves were quite large and finely carved. They appear to have been excavated in stages between the second and early fifth centuries: The Dauranta caves closest to Jalalabad are the most ancient and the Baswal caves, the most distant from the city, are the most recent.

Dauranta, across the Kābul River from Jalalabad, is well-known from the find of a broken tablet containing an edict of Aśoka. The remains of stūpas and cave dwellings here are extensive; many of Dauranta's stūpas were found to contain relics of Arhats, indicating that Dauranta was an important Buddhist center. Each of the relic stūpas is surrounded by smaller votive stūpas. Some scholars associate Dauranta with the word danta, or tooth, pointing out that the tooth relic mentioned by the Chinese travelers may have once been enshrined here. By Hsüan-tsang's time, the tooth relic was gone and only the foundation of the stūpa that may have enshrined it remained. Hsüan-tsang reported other tooth relics at Bāmiyān and at Kapiśa, so it is possible that the tooth relic at Dauranta was moved to one of these locations. The stūpa that once held the tooth may be a ruined stūpa found near the Philakhana caves. (HBA 63)

Above the caves, overlooking the Kābul River, stand the remains of another large stūpa and what appears to be the foundation of a monastery. A square niche in the stūpa, about fifteen to twenty feet high, once housed a standing statue of the Buddha. Opened in the nineteenth century, the stūpa was found to contain precious substances and relics. Nearby, another large niche carved out of the cliff overhanging the Kābul River once held a colossal Buddha-image. (HBA 64)

Haḍḍa

In all of Afghanistan, the site of Haḍḍa, stretching along four miles of hills about five miles south of Jalalabad, is the most widely known. Haḍḍa supplied at least two museums—the Musée Guimet in Paris and the National Museum at Kābul—with large collections of Buddhist art carved in the Bactrian-Indian style. Ruins of stūpas, temples, and monasteries lie scattered across the site, where caves were also used as temples and dwelling-places. There are ruins here of a great stūpa which appears to have been the main monument of Haḍḍa, for centuries a central place of pilgrimage in the Northwest. It is possible that this was the skull-relic stūpa described by the Chinese travelers.

Kapiśa

When Hsüan-tsang visited Kapiśa (the region of modern Begram), a mountain-girt country beneath the Hindu Kush range, he found a land renowned for its turmeric and horses that prospered from its central location on a major trade artery. A branch of the Silk Road, the main caravan route across Asia, ran south and east, linking Kapiśa with Takṣa-śilā. Although the climate was cold and windy, the people fierce, and the language harsh, the Dharma was flourishing in Kapiśa, home to one hundred monasteries and some six thousand monks, mostly adherents of the Mahāyāna. The king of Kapiśa supported the Dharma; each year he made an eighteen-foot-high statue of the Buddha and distributed alms to the poor during the Mokṣa Mahāpariṣad (recitation of the Prātimokṣa). (HT I:55)

At the time of Hsüan-tsang's visit, Kapiśa had just annexed Langhan, a small mountain-encircled pocket of land just north of the pass into India. In this marginally hospitable climate, inhabited by bandits, Hsüan-tsang found ten monasteries housing only a few monks. Most of the monks studied the Mahāyāna teachings.

To the east of the capital, at the foot of a mountain, Hsüan-tsang came upon a monastery housing three hundred Śrāvaka monks. This place, known to Hsüan-tsang as Sha-lo-kia, has been identified with Shotorak, a site near Kapiśa with extensive Buddhist remains, excavated earlier this century. The number of vihāras, temples, and stūpas and the wealth of statues and bas-reliefs found here indicate that Shotorak was a major Buddhist center at the time of Kaniṣka and possibly even earlier. The remains of the monasteries resemble Buddhist buildings at Takṣaśilā. Statues and carvings found arc largely images of the Buddha and scenes from his life (most are now housed in the Kābul Museum).

As the accounts of the Chinese pilgrims testify, the northwest attracted a steady flow of travelers from China between the fifth and seventh centuries. The rulers of northwestern lands, recognizing that their kingdoms were vulnerable to invasion from Central Asia, where China exerted great influence or outright control, built rapprochement by maintaining diplomatic relations with the Chinese court.

These interactions began at an early date. While residing at Kapiśa's Sha-lo-kia Monastery, where he and his companion Prajñākara spent the rainy season, Hsüan-tsang learned that in the early centuries C.E., King Kaniṣka had built this monastery to house hostages he had demanded from tribes east of the T'sung-ling mountains, taken to guarantee peaceful relations. (According to Hwui-li, Hsüan-tsang's biographer, the Sha-lo-kia Monastery was built by a son of the Han emperor who was one of the hostages.) From their likenesses, drawn on the monastery's walls, Hsüan-tsang notes the hostages appeared very Chinese. The local populace treated the hostages, who may well have been Chinese bhikṣus, with the greatest respect.

Long after the hostages returned home, the people of this area remembered them with fasts and prayers for their safety and happiness. By the seventh century, these remembrances had coalesced into a ritual celebration. Other sources verify that the kings of Kapiśa maintained diplomatic relations with China between 619–750 C.E., which helped strengthen religious and cultural contacts between these two Buddhist regions. (HCIP III: 622–623)

A figure of Vaiśravaṇa stood over a hollowed-out spot where the hostages had concealed treasures; further north, above a mountain pass, were more hollowed-out chambers where the hostages practiced meditation. Hsüan-tsang notes that the treasures concealed here were protected by shape-changing yakṣas, and no one dared approach this place. Less than a mile west of the stone chambers, above a great mountain pass, a statue of the Bodhisattva Avalokiteśvara, manifestation of enlightened compassion, looked down in blessing upon travelers passing below. About ten miles southeast of the capital was the vihāra of Rāhula, and next to it the stūpa he had built. Hsüan-tsang relates the story of how the devoted Rāhula, a king's minister, obtained relics for the stūpa, and how the stūpa miraculously closed over him after he had placed the relics within.

Hsüan-tsang's biographer Hwui-li records that the king of Kapiśa was devoted to the Mahāyāna. At one of the Mahāyāna monasteries, he invited Hsüan-tsang to address an assembly of scholars which included Guṇabhadra of the Mahīśāsaka school, Āryavarma of the Sarvāstivādins, and the Tripiṭaka master Manojñāghoṣa. All lived and taught at this monastery, indicating that the Śrāvaka scholarly traditions were still strong in Kapiśa in the seventh century.

Tradition holds that the Buddha himself had traveled to Mount Pilusara in Kapiśa with twelve hundred Arhats at the request of a mountain spirit in the form of an elephant. Aśoka built a stūpa about one hundred feet high on this rock and placed Buddha-relics therein. Several other monasteries in the area were also said to contain relics of the Buddha. Hsüan-tsang mentions that the monastery known as the Monastery of the Old King enshrined a piece of the Buddha's skullbone; another, associated with the king's wife, held relics encased in a hundred-foot-high copper-covered stūpa.

In the last two centuries three sites southeast of Shotorak have yielded many Buddhist artifacts. One may be the site of the Rāhula Vihāra mentioned by Hsüan-tsang. Qala-i-Nader has remains of a large monastery and a stūpa containing ancient relics, probably built at the time of Kaniṣka. Close by is the site known as Tapa Kalan, where remains of another large monastery were found. From artifacts at this last site, it is clear the monastery flourished under the Kuṣāṇas but was probably destroyed by the Hephthalite Huns who ravaged the area in the fifth century. Another site, Paitavā, has been identified as the site of the Pātrārama, the Monastery of the Bowl. This bowl refers to the Buddha's begging bowl, said to have been given as tribute to a Kuṣāṇa king by the Indian king of Pāṭaliputra. The Kuṣāṇa king, most likely Kaniṣka, placed this priceless relic in a stūpa in Kapiśa. Scenes from the Buddha's life were found at this site, including a carving of the Miracle of Śrāvastī.

Still other Buddhist sites exist near Charikar, also in the ancient kingdom of Kapiśa. Well-preserved remains of the stūpa known as Tope Darrah rise more than sixty feet from the level of the valley, where ruins of many monasteries have been found.

Although Buddhist monasteries suffered extensive damage during the fifth-century invasion of the Hephthalite Huns, descendants or successors of these invaders, like the king of Kapiśa in Hsüan-tsang's time, were often strong supporters of Buddhism.

The Dharma was destroyed in Kapiśa not by the Central Asian Huns or Turks, but by Arab armies bent on conversion of the entire area to Islam. Arab attacks began around 650 C.E.; although the early attacks were repulsed, Kapiśa fell to the Arabs led by Ibrahim-bin-Jabul, governor of Zabulistān, in 793. The monks, easily identifiable as religious leaders, were killed; their monasteries were looted and destroyed, their manuscripts burned, and the faces and hands of the images destroyed. Forced conversions to Islam effectively stifled any possibility of Buddhism's recovery, and memory of the Dharma faded from Kapiśa as from all Afghan lands.

Balkh

The fortified city of Balkh, one of Afghanistan's most ancient habitations, was situated northwest of the Hindu Kush range, just south of the Oxus River, at the crossroads of the main trade routes of the ancient world. One of these roads connected Mediterranean lands with Takṣaśilā and India, and the other led to Central Asia and China. Greeks settled in this region after the death of Alexander the Great; eventually Balkh became part of the Greek kingdom of Bactria that took form in the second century B.C.E. Today Balkh is a small town in north central Afghanistan.

Hsüan-tsang mentions that Balkh, far from the Madhyadeśa, was known as "Little Rājagṛha" and was renowned for its numerous sacred relics. Although thinly populated, the region still managed to support one hundred monasteries that housed about three thousand Hīnayāna monks. Outside the city, toward the southwest, was the Navasaṁghārāma, or New Monastery, built by a former king.

According to Hsüan-tsang, the Navasaṁghārāma was a center for Śrāvakayāna and Abhidharma studies, a place where Buddhist writers north of the mountains came to write their commentaries on the scriptures. Hsüan-tsang himself studied the Vaibhāṣika-śāstra for a month while residing here. The Navasaṁghārāma was also a rich monastery; a wash-basin said to have been used by the Buddha dazzled the eyes with its inlay of gold and jewels. The monastery's statue of the Buddha and the temple halls were adorned with gems and precious metals, which were sometimes pillaged by local chiefs. There was also a famous statue of Vaiśravaṇa, who was said to have appeared to a Turkish warlord and thus prevented a devastating attack. The Navasaṁghārāma preserved a tooth of the Buddha and the Buddha's sweeping brush. Those relics, together with the washing basin, were the focus of offerings on the six major fastdays.

To the north of the monastery was a stūpa two hundred feet high that Hsüan-tsang described as covered with plaster hard as a diamond and ornamented with precious substances. To the southwest was an ancient vihāra housing one hundred monks. This monastery appears to have emphasized meditation training and practices; Hsüan-tsang noted a large number of men "with conspicuous talent." It was the custom of the region to build stūpas in honor of the saints who exhibited unusual spiritual powers before their death; hundreds of such stūpas crowded closely together here testified to the attainments of the monastery's practitioners.

In each of the neighboring towns of Ti-wei and Po-li, Hsüan-tsang found a stūpa about thirty feet high. He associates these stūpas with the merchants Trapuṣa and Bhallika, who received hair and nail cuttings from the Buddha, brought them to their native towns in Balkh, and built stūpas in which to enshrine them. A stūpa twenty feet high, said to have been erected in the time of the Buddha Kāśyapa, was located about twelve miles to the west.

Although Balkh, as other cities in this region, suffered from the invasion of the Hephthalite Huns, Buddhism continued to flourish there until the onset of Arab raids, which began in the seventh century shortly after Hsüan-tsang's visit. About 660 C.E., Arabs plundered Balkh and carried away jewels and precious metals stolen from the Navasaṁghārāma. For a time the Arab advance was slowed by non-Muslim Turkish tribes who moved into this area in the late seventh century. But by 715 C.E. Balkh had fallen completely under Arab control. The Navasaṁghārāma was destroyed, its monks slain, and its manuscripts burned.

Today, after centuries of Buddhist activities here, only the ruins of an ancient stūpa and monastery remain. The stūpa, known locally as the Tapa-i-Rustam, or Stūpa of Rustam, still stands sixty feet high. This may have been the two-hundred-foot high stūpa Hsüan-tsang described. Although only the brick foundation of the monastery has survived, the size of the foundation indicates that this monastery was quite large and could well have been the Navasaṁghārāma. To date, Balkh has been but lightly excavated; further research might well yield much more information.

Gaz and Bāmiyān

Hsüan-tsang describes Gaz as the country south of Balkh. The climate was cold and the land hilly and full of stones. Here there were about ten monasteries housing three hundred monks, all of the Sarvāstivādin tradition.

Directly south of Gaz, in the mountains immediately north of the Hajiyak Pass, was the country of Bāmiyān. Its capital city, built on the side of a steep hill and backed by high precipices, overlooked a long valley. Hsüan-tsang describes the climate as rough and the people uncultured in manner, but "remarkable, among all their neighbors, for a love of religion; from the highest form of worship of the Three Jewels (Buddha, Dharma, and Sangha) down to the worship of the hundreds of gods, there is not the least absence of earnestness and the utmost devotion of heart." (HT I:50) He found ten monasteries housing approximately one thousand monks of the Lokottaravādin tradition. The Lokottaravādins, a branch of the Mahāsāṁghika school, maintained centers in Bāmiyān between the second century B.C.E. and the seventh century C.E. This school, which maintained a supramundane understanding of the nature of the Buddha, was famed for the great size of its statues, the largest sculptures known in the Indian cultural sphere.

To the northeast of the city, in a niche carved into the sheer face of a mountain, stood a colossal stone representation of the Buddha, which Hsüan-tsang estimated as being 140 to 150 feet high. "Its golden hue sparkles on every side, and its precious ornaments dazzle the eyes with their brightness." To the east was another monastery and another standing statue of the Buddha one hundred feet high, cast in parts and then joined together. Although damaged, these statues can still be seen here today. The actual height of the large statue is 186 feet, and the height of the smaller statue is 135 feet.

Further east, another monastery enshrined a recumbent figure of the Buddha about to enter Parinirvāṇa, many times greater than lifesize. Hsüan-tsang also describes a remote monastery in the mountains to the east which contained three sacred relics in a golden sealed case: a tooth of the Buddha, another tooth of a Pratyekabuddha, and a great tooth of a cakravartin king. This monastery preserved the Patriarch Śāṇavāsa's almsbowl and his deep red robe woven from hemp.

The robe of Śāṇavāsa, He Who Wears Only Hemp, had a special meaning for Buddhists of Hsüan-tsang's time. It is said in five hundred previous lifetimes Śāṇavāsa wore only clothing made of hemp, and so great were his meritorious actions that in his last lifetime he was born wearing a hemp robe. As Śāṇavāsa grew to maturity, the robe also grew larger. When he was converted to the Dharma by Ānanda, the Buddha's disciple, the hemp robe changed into a religious garment. When he passed into nirvāṇa, however, the robe remained in the world. It is said that this robe of Śāṇavāsa will last as long as the Dharma of Śākyamuni Buddha, and when the Dharma vanishes, the robe will also disappear. (HT I:53)

Bāmiyān today is best known for its two gigantic Buddha statues, which are still the world's largest standing Buddha images. The statues, together with twenty thousand caves carved into the Koh-i-Baba, Hill of Saints, testify to the industry of the Lokottaravādin bhikṣus who inhabited this site for many centuries. The caves range in size from large assembly halls capable of accommodating a hundred people to small individual residences; many of their walls were painted with scenes illustrating the Buddha's teachings. It is possible that Bāmiyān, located on the main route linking India with the Silk Road, was the largest Buddhist center in the northwest, a place where bhikṣus could gather for the rainy season retreat or rest on their journey to Central Asia or China.

More Buddhist caves can be seen in the Foladi Valley, many of which once had painted walls, and still more exist in the valley of Kakhrak, where another large Buddha statue nearly twenty feet high still stands. The frescoes that once covered the walls of these caves are now in the Musée Guimet and the National Museum in Kābul. The art appears to belong to the Mahāyāna or Vajrayāna tradition, but the existence of a Mahāyāna center here is mentioned only by Hui-cha'o, a Korean bhikṣu who visited Bāmiyān in the eighth century. Some paintings depict Vairocana and the Dhyāni Buddhas with their emanations. Large Buddha images painted on the ceilings of the caves are surrounded by medallions containing smaller images of the Buddha, providing the earliest examples of mandalic representations discovered to date. (BCA 301)

Kābul

A large stūpa and monastery have been excavated at a site near Maranjan, on the northwest border of Kābul. This site has yielded nearly perfect images of the Buddha, Bodhisattvas, and donors, all carved in the Gandhāran style; these statues are now in the Kābul Museum. Large coin finds date the site to the fourth century C.E.

Remains of Buddhist monasteries and stūpas have also been found near Shevaki, a village only a few miles south of Kābul. Until recently, two tall pillars, inside columns of a now collapsed monastery, stood on top of the mountain (an earthquake toppled one in 1965). The best preserved stūpa in the region is the Guldara Stūpa, a structure nearly forty feet high. Its Corinthian-style pilasters and large arched niches on the square base of the stūpa are still clearly defined. Nearby are the ruins of a monastery, its walls distinctly discernable. Coins from the time of Maues have been found at Shevaki, dating the site to the first century C.E.

Wardak

Hsüan-tsang called this kingdom Fo-li-shi-sa-t'ang-na, a phonetic rendering of Parśusthāna or Vardasthāna, which was later compressed into Wardak. The capital was Hupiān or Opiān, located a little north of Charikar, a city about fifty miles north of modern Kābul. In his brief description of the area there is only a passing reference to Buddhism. "The climate is icy cold; the men are naturally fierce and impetuous. The king is a Turk. He has profound faith for the three precious objects of worship; he esteems learning and honors virtue (or the virtuous ones, the bhikṣus)." (HT II:285)

Earlier in this century, a reliquary bearing a Prākrit inscription written in the Kharoṣṭhī script was discovered in Wardak, about thirty miles west of Kābul. The inscription dates the reliquary in 179 C.E., during the reign of King

Huviṣka; it indicates that it contained relics of Śākyamuni Buddha and that it was enshrined in a stūpa of the Vagramarigra Vihāra, a Mahāsāṁghika monastery that flourished here through the seventh century.

Fondukistān

A large Buddhist monastery once flourished near Fondukistān, a village in the Ghoraband Valley about midway between Bāmiyān and Kābul. The site of the monastery, at the top of a hill overlooking the river, is said to be the best natural environment for a monastery in all of Afghanistan. The name for the village of Fondukistān may derive from Funduq, meaning a traveler's house or inn, which may have at one time referred to the monastery itself.

The monastery at Fondukistān may have originally been inhabited by a Śrāvaka tradition, but frescoes and statues discovered in the ruins indicate that at some point, probably around the sixth century C.E., the monastery became a Mahāyāna center. Some statues recovered here, found in good condition, are now preserved in the Kābul Museum. The sculpture reflects a fusion of artistic elements deriving from different civilizations: Indian, Central Asian, and Iranian, and perhaps even Chinese. It is likely that the monks who lived here were of many different cultures and that they created the monastery's unusual art and ornamentation. Excavated in 1936 by French archaeologists, the monastery was found to have a large square assembly hall with a stūpa at its center; shrines, monk's residences, and rooms for meditation surrounded the hall itself. Mural paintings, also in mixed artistic styles, covered the wall, and stucco images stood in the niches.

The monastery's remote location in the interior of Afghanistan away from the major routes appears to have protected it from the Huns who wreaked general havoc in this area. However, also probably because of its remoteness, the monastery is not mentioned in any surviving literary record, so its history can be surmised only through the archaeological evidence. It is possible that it began as a solitary meditation retreat site for a few monks, perhaps in the second century C.E., and developed into an important Buddhist center by the seventh century C.E., when this area was ruled by non-Muslim Turks. It was destroyed sometime after the Arab forces of Ibrahim-bin-Jabul sacked Kabul in 743, an event which led to the persecution of the religious orders and the destruction of Buddhism in Afghanistan.

Kandahār

Aśokan inscriptions found near Kandahār, in southern Afghanistan, indicate that the Dharma was probably known here as early as the third century B.C.E. Kandahār is thought to have been founded by Alexander the Great, who may have established an outpost here. Soon afterwards, Kandahār became a border town of the Indian Mauryan Empire, established by Candragupta Maurya and ruled by his grandson Aśoka. The three Aśokan inscriptions found here are written in Greek and Aramaic languages and scripts, confirming the continued presence of Greeks in the region. Thus scholars have speculated that Kandahār, located on the trade route connecting India with Persia, may have been one of the regions visited by Mahārakkhita, the emissary sent to the land of the Yonas during the time of Aśoka.

However, all that is known of Buddhism in this area is by inference. Regional names such as Budhawan spark associations with Buddhism; a man-made cave may be a Buddhist site; small stone mounds in the area, known as Budhawan Darwaza, or Gate of Budhawan, may be the remains of two stūpas. The excavation of mounds at Gurgam and other villages of the region could well yield more conclusive evidence of the scope of Buddhist activities at Kandahār.

The Guldara Stūpa near Kābul

Ghaznī

Ghaznī is only twenty miles south of Wardak, the site of a Mahāsāṁghika center that flourished in the early centuries C.E. Buddhism is thought to have been brought to Ghaznī about the same time as Wardak, although bhikṣus may have settled earlier at Ghaznī. Ghaznī appears to have been within Aśoka's Empire, which would have opened the region to bhikṣus in the third century B.C.E., and Hsüan-tsang observed Aśokan-style stūpas here. Hsüan-tsang describes the countryside of Tsaukūṭa as a succession of mountains and valleys, with the intervening plains fit for cultivation. He mentions two major cities in this region, one of which has been identified as Ghaznī and the other as Guzaristān. Several hundred monasteries housed a thousand or more monks, all of whom followed the Mahāyāna tradition. Hsüan-tsang writes:

"The climate is cold; there are frequent hail and snow storms. The people are naturally light-hearted and impulsive; they are crafty and deceitful. They love learning and the arts, and show considerable skill in magical sentences, but they have no good aim in view. . . . Their writing and language differ from those of other countries . . . . Although they worship many spirits, yet they also greatly reverence the three precious ones (Buddha, Dharma, and Sangha)." (HT II:284)

In recent times, a Buddhist site known as Tapa-i-Sardar or as But-khan (Place of the Buddha) was discovered on a hilltop overlooking the area. Excavation of the top layers revealed a Mahāyāna monastery tentatively dated in the seventh century C.E., but layers as yet uncovered may establish a much earlier date for this site. As other monasteries in the region, Tapa-i-Sardar may have begun as a monastery of a Śrāvaka tradition around the time of Kaniṣka and been later converted into a Mahāyāna center, which would accord with Hsüan-tsang's description. The ruins of vihāras and stūpas uncovered at the site to date indicate that Tapa-i-Sardar was a large monastic complex. Images of the cosmic Buddhas, Bodhisattvas, and Devas have been found here, and manuscript remains unearthed suggest that this monastery may also have been an important center of learning.

Gudul-i-Ahangaran is another Buddhist site discovered near Ghaznī. Although it has yet to be excavated and researched, the site has yielded miniature stūpas and tablets inscribed with the Ye Dharma mantra. The name Ahangaran is thought to derive from Arhantanam, meaning Place of Arhants, the realized ones of the Buddhist Śrāvaka traditions. (HBA 188)

Further out from Ghaznī, on the way to Maqur, is a group of caves housing an ancient Buddhist assembly hall, dwellings for monks, and other types of rooms. As all Buddhist sites in Afghanistan, these monasteries were destroyed by the Arabs who took possession of the land in the eighth and ninth centuries. The ruins of Tapa-i-Sardar still bear signs of burning.

Ghaznī became a strong center for the propagation of Islam. After the Arab occupation came the Muslim Turks. Two of the tribes associated with Ghaznī are the Ghaznavid Turks of the eleventh century and the Ghūrids of the twelfth and thirteenth centuries. Mahmūd of Ghaznī is well known for leading destructive raids on Sārnāth and Vārānasī, and Muhammad of Ghūr and his minion Bhakhtyār Khaljī led the armies that cut a wide swath of destruction through Bihār and Bengal, destroying the Buddhist universities and massacring thousands of monks.

Haibak (Samangan)

Northwest of Kābul, on the road leading to Mazar-i-Sharif, is the village of Haibak, known in ancient times as Samangan. The name Samangan may derive from Samanagāma (Sanskrit Śramaṇagrāma), Village of the Śrāmana (monk). Five Buddhist caves, consisting of a shrine hall, assembly hall, dwellings, living rooms, and baths, have been discovered a short distance from the modern village just below the crest of a hill. Across from the caves, at the top of the hill, is a large monolithic stūpa. The stūpa, carved from solid rock, is approached through an entrance tunnel over fifty feet long. Locally, this site is known as Takht-i-Rustam, or Rustam's Throne. The date of this site, its affiliation, and other aspects of its history are unknown.

Caves known as Hazar Sum (Thousand Caves), were discovered to the southwest of Haibak. About two hundred caves have been found, arranged in groups, with each having one to three rooms. No ornamentation has been found in these caves, which are spartan in style and obviously meant to serve as solitary retreats. Although they were very likely used by Buddhist monks, it is difficult to establish this with certainty. This site may have been sacked and damaged by Huns who invaded the region of Haibak around 460 C.E., but it is likely that Buddhism survived at Haibak until completely driven out by the eighth century Arab invasions.

Kunduz

Buddhism probably came to Kunduz at the time when Kaniṣka ruled northern Afghanistan. Located on the main trade route to Central Asia, Kunduz was probably a major Buddhist center between the second and tenth centuries C.E. According to Hsüan-tsang, who has provided the only early accounts of Kunduz on record, in the seventh century more than ten monasteries housed several hundred monks who practiced both the Śrāvaka and Mahāyāna traditions. Although to date only a few attempts have been made at excavating Buddhist sites, some bas-relief sculptures have been found in the ruins of a monastery that was founded around the second century C.E. The mounds of Angur, Chaqualaq, and Durman near Kunduz are other promising sites.

Part Six

Dharma Centers of South India

KASHMIR
PAKISTAN
TIBET
HIMACHAL PRADESH
PUNJAB
HARYĀNA
UTTAR PRADESH
NEPAL
BHUTAN
RAJASTHAN
SINDH
BANGLA DESH
BIHAR
GUJARAT
WEST BENGAL
MADHYA PRADESH
ORISSA
MAHARASTRA
Jaggayyapeṭa
Maski
Amāravatī
Dhānyakaṭaka
Nāgārjunakoṇḍa
GOA
KARNATAKA
Vanavāsa
Kāñcī
TAMIL NADU
Śrīmūlavāsa
Mālakūṭa
Anurādhapura
SRI LANKA

Dakṣiṇāpatha
The Route South

The Narmadā River on the west and the Vindhya Mountains and Godāvarī River on the east form a natural boundary between North and South India. In ancient times, these geographical features helped shape the course of history and culture, favoring the development of South India as a distinct region. The Buddha's teachings became part of this development, stimulating artistic expression and inspiring some of South India's greatest intellects.

Dakṣiṇāpatha originally referred to the inland trade route that led south from Māhiṣmatī then southeast to the cities near the mouth of the Kṛṣṇa River. Those who first followed this road encountered tribes speaking completely different languages. Where the northerners spoke Indo-Aryan languages akin to Vedic and Sanskrit, the major languages of the south derived from Dravidian, an entirely separate linguistic stock. As the Aitareya Brāhmaṇa records, the people of the north, well aware that the inhabitants of the south were of a different culture, referred to the southerners as Daśyus (non-Āryans).

At the time of the Buddha, most of the peoples south of the Narmadā River still followed pre-Vedic religions and customs. By the time of Aśoka, however, the people of South India were experiencing more sustained contact with the Brahmanic culture of the north. Aśoka gathered into his empire the diverse cultures of north and south; he supported Dharma emissaries to Māhiṣamaṇḍala (probably the region of Mysore) and Vanavāsa (northern Karṇāṭaka) and proclaimed the value of Dharma in a major rock edict in Āndhra and eleven minor rock edicts throughout the southern part of his kingdom. During his reign Buddhism began to take root in South India.

Toward the end of the first century B.C.E., an Āndhran leader named Sīmuka established the Sātavāhana Dynasty which ruled most of the Dakṣiṇāpatha until the third century C.E.. Traditional Indian accounts represent the Sātavāhanas as of mixed Brahmin and Nāga origin, descendants of the priestly class of the north and a powerful warrior tribe of the south. The Sātavāhana rulers and their families were strong supporters of Buddhism, which prospered and proliferated during their rule. During the height of their power, the Sātavāhana kings extended their empire northeast into Berār and Mahākosala (Madhya Pradesh). However, in the third century C.E., the Sātavāhana Dynasty disintegrated, and power passed to local ruling families who carved out kingdoms and established new dynasties.

The two most powerful of these ruling families were the Vākāṭakas and the Ikṣvākus. The Vākāṭaka Dynasty, established by Vindhyaśākti, held sway over Mahārāṣṭra, Berār, and northern Āndhra, while the Ikṣvāku dynasty was centered in the region around Amarāvatī. The founders of the Ikṣvāku Dynasty seemed to have followed the Vedic religion, but inscriptions found at Amarāvatī, Jaggayyapeta, and Nāgārjunakoṇḍa indicate that their successors generously supported Buddhism. (HCIP 3:225) With the end of Sātavāhana rule the western Deccan under the Vākāṭakas and their successors, the Cālukyas and Rāṣṭrakūṭas, was more strongly influenced by Āryan languages and culture. The region that is now Mahārāṣṭra began to take form as a cultural and linguistic unit distinctly different from the Dravidian cultures to the south and southeast. Thus Buddhism in Mahārāṣṭra is included in the section on Western India, while this discussion of Buddhism in South India focuses on the Dravidian cultures of modern Āndhra Pradesh, Tamilnādu, Karṇāṭaka, and Kerala.

Routes of Transmission

The ancient kingdom of Veṅgī, located between the lower extent of the Godāvarī and Kṛṣṇā rivers, was once the central crossroads of the South. Ships from Veṅgī ports regularly sailed for Burma and Śrī Vijaya (Indonesia). Five great roads radiated outward to all parts of India, leading northeast to Kaliṅga, south to Drāviḍa, southwest to Karṇāṭaka, northwest to Mahārāṣṭra, and north to the kingdom of Kosala. All the Buddhist sites and major cities of South India have been found along these five routes.

Many of the ancient cities of the south have yet to be excavated. There are remains of an ancient city at Candraguptapatnam near Śrī Śailam and at Dantavakrakoṭa in Chicacole Talik. Dhānyakaṭaka (Dhāraṇīkoṭa) near Amarāvatī has extensive mounds, and still more mounds have been located at Kaliṅgapatnam. There are also extensive remains at Dendraluru, Pedda Vegi, and Chinna Vegi, which generally date to the epochs of the Śālaṅkāyanas and the Viṣṇikundins (third to mid-seventh centuries C.E.). While excavation of the ancient cities may uncover more Buddhist monuments, monasteries and stūpas in South India were often established at a distance from urban areas in places of great natural beauty, usually on or near mountains that were blessed with an abundance of water. The most extensive Buddhist sites in

South India have been found on the banks of the Kṛṣṇā River and its tributaries.

South India has benefited from its Buddhist heritage. Scholars have noted that the architecture, sculpture, and painting of Āndhra was inspired by Buddhism and developed under the sponsorship of kings and devout Buddhist laypersons. Some Buddhist images and doctrines found their way into the religious movements of the eighth and ninth centuries. In the Tamil country, the Buddha's teachings were expressed in epics early in the history of Tamil literature and the men and women who upheld these teachings were portrayed as heroes. The sons of Tamilnādu made extensive contributions to Buddhist philosophy and logic, and traveled to foreign lands to support Dharma transmission. There are indications that Buddhism has a far longer history in South India than can be traced in the remains of its monuments, and the full extent of this history may never be known. We can only summarize what has come to light at this time and appreciate the knowledge, vision, and beauty these monuments once embodied.

Buddhist Centers of Āndhra

In the river valleys of Āndhra, the Buddha's teachings inspired the creation of large monastic centers and a rich artistic tradition. Even in ruins, the art and monuments of Amarāvatī and the now vanished Nāgārjunakoṇḍa are impressive reminders of transience and a lost heritage.

Hsüan-tsang, in describing the lands of India's southeastern coast, mentions that the Buddha had visited the regions of Āndhra and Dhānyakaṭaka as well as the kingdoms of Coḷa, Drāviḍa, and Malakūṭa which lay to the south. In all of these places Hsüan-tsang found Aśokan stūpas commemorating sites where the Buddha taught the beings who lived there and opened their hearts to the Dharma.

The story of Bavari, a Brahmin ascetic, supports this tradition: While the Buddha was teaching in the Madhyadeśa, Bavari was dwelling with his sixteen disciples in a hermitage near the Godāvarī River, near Alaka in the Assaka country (modern Aurangabad/Nizamabad region). Once, after performing a ritual, Bavari became upset when he was cursed by a second Brahmin who had arrived too late to receive the customary gifts. A deity advised Bavari that only a Buddha could counteract the effects of this curse and such a one was then teaching in Śrāvastī. Bavari sent his sixteen disciples, including Ajita and Tissametteyya, to question the Enlightened One. The disciples traveled from Pratiṣṭhāna (Paithan) on the upper Godāvarī River north through Ujjayinī, Vidiśā, Kauśāmbī, and Sāketa. They finally arrived at Śrāvastī, only to find that the Buddha was then teaching in Rājagṛha. When they heard the Buddha speak in Rājagṛha, all of Bavari's disciples became Arhats except for Bavari's nephew Piṅgiya. No longer attached to worldly concerns, the new Arhats remained in Rājagṛha. Piṅgiya alone returned to his uncle; as he was explaining the Buddha's response to Bavari's questions, the Buddha himself appeared and taught Bavari and Piṅgiya in person.

In the mid-third century B.C.E., the Dharma was propagated in Āndhra by King Aśoka as well as by traveling bhiksus from the Madhyadeśa. Āndhra was part of Aśoka's vast empire; during his reign the king familiarized his subjects in the south with the value of the Buddhist teachings and supported their propagation through edicts inscribed on rocks. His reign joined the smaller kingdoms of North and South India, providing protection for monks traveling south to teach and found Dharma centers. King Aśoka's support for the Dharma set an example of patronage for local kings, and Buddhism began to take root in Āndhra.

The Sātavāhana kings, who came to power with Sīmuka in 230 B.C.E. and ruled Āndhra for 450 years, were generally strong patrons of Buddhism. During their reign, major centers of Buddhism arose along the route south, inland at Jaggayyapeta, and on the banks of the Kṛṣṇā River at Amarāvatī, Dhānyakaṭaka, and Nāgārjunakoṇḍa. These centers were supported not only by royal patronage but also by a prosperous laity, led by merchants who profited in the rich sea trade. Inscriptions on a monument in Jaggayyapeṭa indicate that construction was in progress here during the first century B.C.E. The reliefs on this monument were carved in white marble similar to the white or light green marble used to cover the stūpas and temples of the other centers along the Kṛṣṇā. From the few examples that remain, all of the stūpas and temples in this region appear to have been elegantly carved. Āndhra eventually became internationally famous for its art, its prosperous monasteries, and its accomplished masters.

When Hsüan-tsang traveled in South India during the seventh century, he described the region between the lower Godāvarī and Kṛṣṇā rivers: "The temperature is hot, and the manners of the people fierce and impulsive." In the Āndhra area, he counted twenty monasteries housing approximately three thousand monks. Near Viṅgila (probably the city of Veṅgī, northwest of Elur lake), Hsüan-tsang came to a large monastery with beautifully ornamented towers and balconies. A finely-sculpted figure of the Buddha was enshrined inside this building, and beside it stood a stone stūpa several hundred feet high, said to have been built by the Arhat Acala. An Aśokan stūpa stood to the southwest, marking the place where the Buddha taught the Dharma and converted a great number of people though displaying his spiritual powers.

However, the Dharma was declining in Āndhra at the time of Hsüan-tsang's visit; the momentum for new construction had waned and many monasteries were deserted. Although some activity persisted and pilgrims continued to visit the great stūpa of Amarāvatī, Buddhism rapidly lost ground. Hinduism, revitalized by Śānkara in the early ninth century and carried to passion with the rise of devotional cults, eroded support for Buddhism and absorbed its remains.

In the nineteenth century, both archaeologists and historians began examining the mound-like hills along Āndhra's rivers; to date remains of more than one hundred Buddhist monuments have been found. The main discoveries follow the course of the Kṛṣṇā (Kistna) River: proceeding inland from the eastern coast, the sites include Bhaṭṭiprolu, Gudivāda, Ghaṇṭasālā, Amarāvatī, Jaggayyapeṭa, Nāgārjunakoṇḍa, and Goli. All of the Buddhist centers here appear to date from the second and third centuries C.E., but some of the stūpas appear to have been constructed earlier and then enlarged when centers arose near them.

Recent research has also located Buddhist monuments preserved in their entirety through conversion into Hindu temples, and scholars examining Āndhra's tall Śaivite lingas have found that some are reshapings of pillars that once stood at Buddhist stūpas. Among the temples identified to date as originally Buddhist are the Kopeteśvara temple at Chezarla in the Guntur district, the Trivikrama temple at Ter in the Western Deccan, the Drakṣarāma near Rāmacandrapuram in the East Godāvarī district, and Śrī Śailam in the Nallamalai Hills. Some local customs rooted in Buddhist practices can still be discerned in some parts of Āndhra. (BSI 73–77)

In 1956, the beginnings of a revival of Buddhism in Āndhra was sparked by Dr. Ambedkar's Neo-Buddhist movement and encouraged by the activities of the Bengali monk Sumedha Vimalakṣa. The Buddhist Cultural Organization is working to translate Buddhist teachings into Telugu, and it organizes conferences to connect the efforts of those interested in promoting the revival of Buddhism in the area. From a 1951 count of 230 the number of Buddhists in Āndhra has steadily increased; as of 1981, there were nearly 13,000 people professing adherence to the Buddha's way. (BSI 78–79).

Amarāvatī

By the second century B.C.E., and possibly even earlier, the region between the lower valleys of the Godāvarī and Kṛṣṇā rivers was the home of major Buddhist monasteries.

Amarāvatī, the oldest of these centers, has been identified with modern Amraoti, located about eighteen miles from Guntur, on the southern bank of the Kṛṣṇā River about sixty miles from the ocean, just to the east of Dhāraṇīkoṭa. The Sātavāhana kings supported Amarāvatī and other Buddhist sites in Āndhra; inscriptions at Amarāvatī name as patron the Sātavāhana kings Vaṣiṣṭhiputra Pulumavi (130–159 C.E.), Śiva Śrī (159–166 C.E.), and Yajñaśrī Sātakarṇi (166–196 C.E.), said to have been the patron and friend of Nāgārjuna.

Amarāvatī's main stūpa, estimated as having been 138 feet in diameter and about one hundred feet tall, was once one of the most spectacular stūpas in India. An Aśokan edict found on a pillar at Amarāvatī indicates that a precursor of the great stūpa may first have been erected during Aśoka's reign; tradition (supported by an inscription found at Amarāvatī) ascribes its founding to Mahādeva, the monk sent from Aśoka's capital, Pāṭaliputra, to carry the Dharma to Māhisamaṇḍala. (BSI 35) Second-century inscriptions connect this stūpa and other buildings at Amarāvatī to the Cetiya school, a branch of the Mahāsāṁghika tradition.

Like stūpas in other long-lived Dharma centers, the stūpa of Amāravatī was built up, renovated, and enlarged through the centuries with new casings and ornamental railings, gates, and sculpture. Sculptured slabs appear to have been added around the beginning of the common era, and the stūpa was extensively renovated in the middle of the second century C.E., probably during the reign of Yajñaśrī Sātakarṇi or his two predecessors.

The stūpa was further embellished during the reign of the Ikṣvāku kings who came to power in the third century. When it reached its final form, the great stūpa of Amarāvatī was even larger than the great stūpa at Sāñcī. Its western gate was crowned with a Dharma wheel donated during the reign of Vaṣiṣṭhiputra Pulumavi.

The stūpa of Amarāvatī was especially renowned for its intricately carved white marble casing painted in color. Its base, 435 feet in circumference, was richly ornamented with some of the most beautiful figurative art ever developed in India, modeled in a flowing rhythm, with a subtle and delicate balance of form and space. In the middle of the stūpa's dome was a series of sculptures representing scenes from the Jātakas and Avadānas. Here, as on other Buddhist stūpas, were carvings depicting the whole structure in bas-relief, which provides us today with at least some visual record of how these majestic monuments appeared before their destruction.

In the late Sātavāhana period (second to third centuries C.E.), the stūpa's paved circumambulation pathway, about twelve feet wide, was lined with carved railings illustrating the life of the Buddha, and the stūpa itself was surrounded with Buddha images carved into its white marble facing. The railing was more than twelve feet high and about 175 feet in diameter; archaeologists today estimate its size as consisting of about 244 meters (= 732 feet) of coping resting on 136 pillars and 38 crossbars. (Amar 10; BSI 56) Tradition associates the great master Nāgārjuna with this extensive construction; an inscription at the site mentions the monk Buddharakkhita as having supervised the renovation of the railing. Among the donors for this project was the nun Likhita, Buddharakkhita's disciple; a monk from Pāṭaliputra; three Tamil pilgrims; the people of Dhānyakaṭaka; and a family from Ghantasala. (BSI 52)

The dynamic creativity of Amarāvatī's artistic tradition, closely linked to the Sātavāhana Dynasty, probably waned with Sātavāhana power in the third century C.E. But for centuries thereafter, Amarāvatī's artisans provided a steady stream of exquisite images to Śrī Laṅkā and Southeast Asia, where the graceful and dynamic style of Amarāvatī was emulated by local artisans in those countries. It is possible that Amarāvatī remained an active Buddhist holy place until the tenth century. Images of Avalokiteśvara, Mañjughoṣa, and

Tārā found at the site suggest that the Mahāyāna and possibly also the Vajrayāna traditions flourished here, an assumption supported by Hsüan-tsang's observations. An inscription at Amarāvatī dated 1182 mentions that the great stūpa was still finely decorated with sculptures. An inscription carved at Gadaladeniya, Śrī Laṅkā in 1344 refers to repairs donated by the Śrī Laṅkan pilgrim Dharmakīrti at the two-storied shrine near Amarāvatī's great stūpa.

Loss of Amarāvatī and Modern Excavations

The great stūpa, located seventeen miles west of Bejwada and south of the town of Amarāvatī, was intact in 1796, when the local ruler moved his capital to Amarāvatī. But in the construction that followed, the stūpa was plundered for its treasures; its bricks, covering panels, and carved railings were stripped to provide building materials, and its foundations were converted into a pond. A British archaeologist, Colonel Colin Mackenzie, observed this demolition in progress in 1797, but had no idea of the site's great value.

Years later, in 1816, hearing of the discovery of carvings and sculptures, he investigated the site more thoroughly and recovered some of Amarāvatī's artistic treasures, which were taken to the British Museum in London and to museums in Madras and Calcutta. This site, known locally as Dipāldinne, or the Hill of Lamps, was excavated again in 1816 and 1835, and the ruins of the western gateway were discovered in 1840. British-led excavations continued at Amarāvatī from 1877 through 1908. Most of the sculptures unearthed during this time were taken to the Government Museum in Madras, which now has the largest collection of Amarāvatī's marble sculptures. This museum also preserves 125 inscriptions found at the site, which provide a unique documentation of the devotion of the laity that supported Amarāvatī's development into one of the world's artistic marvels.

In 1958–1959, further excavation at Amarāvatī uncovered still more inscriptions and fragments of sculpture, among many other artifacts. These finds, together with those recovered from excavations made since 1881, were placed in the Archaeological Museum built at the site of the great stūpa.

The Archaeological Museum displays now feature a large standing image of the Buddha, the Bodhisattva Padmapāṇi, and finely-carved drum-slabs depicting stūpas and scenes from the Jātakas. Inscribed steles and fragments of the great stūpa's ornate railings portray scenes from Vaiśālī, Śrāvastī, and other locations important to the life of the Buddha. Scenes on one stele depict the Buddha's last journey and his passing away at Kuśinagara. The museum also holds statues and artifacts recovered from Dhāraṇīkoṭa, Gummadidurru, and other Buddhist sites in the area, including a large sandstone Dharma wheel from Lingarājapalli.

Today, visitors to this site can see the lower part of the inner drum of the stūpa and the circumambulation pathway. A large limestone pillar bearing an inscription stands to the south of the stūpa; other fragments of the frames of buildings are still upright, and remains of monasteries and shrines have been exposed to view. Ruins of other large stūpas have been found around the lower Kṛṣṇā River.

The oldest of these ruins is Bhaṭṭiprolu, which dates to the third century B.C.E., where eleven inscriptions have been found. Five inscriptions were discovered in the ruins of a stūpa at Ghaṇṭaśālā; one connects the Ghaṇṭaśālā Stūpa with the Aparaśaila school, a branch of the Mahāsāṁghika tradition. In recent years some of these sites have been dismantled by scavengers and their bricks recycled into construction projects. Although there are few remains to be seen here today, the mounds awaiting excavation hold out the hope that further research could increase our understanding of the scope and duration of Buddhist activities in the region.

Dhānyakaṭaka (Dhāraṇīkoṭa)

Although the city of Dhānyakaṭaka is well-known in the Tibetan and Chinese Buddhist traditions, its exact location remains problematic. Some scholars have identified it with the ancient city of Vijayavāda (Vijayapurī, modern Bezwada), capital of the Sātavāhana Empire, where ruins of Buddhist monuments and marble images of the Buddha have been found. However, modern archaeological research points to Dhāraṇīkoṭa, where an ancient mound has yielded extensive Buddhist artifacts, as a more likely site. If this is true, Dhānyakaṭaka was only a mile distant from Amarāvatī, and the proximity of these two sites may have led Hsüan-tsang and Tāranātha to refer to them both as Dhānyakaṭaka.

According to the Mañjuśrīmūlakalpa, the great stūpa at Dhānyakaṭaka contained relics of the Buddha. An inscription commemorating the sister of Mahārāja Madhariputra Śrīvira-puruṣadaṭṭa's gift of a pillar to the Sangha also refers to the enshrining of the Buddha's relics here. The presence of the relics elevated Dhānyakaṭaka to the status of a holy place. Inscriptions indicate that this center attracted pilgrims from as far away as Gandhāra, China, Aparānta, Vaṅga, and Laṅkā; donors built temples and monasteries here and dug wells for visiting bhikṣus. Tāranātha adds that the great philosopher Nāgārjuna built the boundary wall of Dhānyakaṭaka Monastery and erected 108 temples inside its compound (Tar 107).

Hsüan-tsang states that the region around Dhānyakaṭaka had a long history of Buddhist activity and was associated with many remarkable events. On hills overlooking the town, Hsüan-tsang found two monasteries donated by a king in former times: the Pūrvaśaila Monastery to the east of Mt. Śaila and the Aparaśaila Monastery to the west. These monasteries were the former home of the Pūrvaśailas and Aparaśailas, subdivisions of the Mahāsāṁghika school. Many historians equate Mt. Śaila with Śrī Parvata, the mountain where Nāgārjuna is said to have spent the last years of his life. The

Mañjuśrīmūlakalpa describes this mountain as a favorable site for Dharma practices.

According to Hsüan-tsang, the king built a road through the valley up into the mountain crags where he created magnificent temples in the mountain caves. He constructed pavilions and galleries and made wide chambers that connected the caves. When this work was completed, a thousand laymen and monks spent the rainy season here each year for a thousand years following the Buddha's Parinirvāṇa. After that time, all who had attained the state of an Arhat rose into the air and went away. Hsüan-tsang cites a tradition that this place is protected by a fearsome shape-changing mountain spirit. For the past hundred years no monks had lived there.

South of Dhānyakaṭaka, Hsüan-tsang explored the large mountain cavern where the master Bhāvaviveka awaits the arrival of Maitreya, the future Buddha. According to traditional accounts, Bhāvaviveka, a learned master in Nāgārjuna's lineage, heard that Dharmapāla Bodhisattva was attracting thousands of disciples in Magadha. Wishing to discuss the Dharma with him, Bhāvaviveka traveled north to Magadha and sent his disciples to arrange a meeting with Dharmapāla. But Dharmapāla replied that he had no time for debate and would not meet with Bhāvaviveka. Returning to his home in the South, Bhāvaviveka lived purely, but still yearned for the opportunity to advance his understanding.

For three years Bhāvaviveka prayed to the Bodhisattva Avalokiteśvara, asking that he endure in his physical body until the enlightenment of Maitreya, the future Buddha, when he could hear the teachings directly from the Great Being. Avalokiteśvara advised him instead to seek rebirth in the Tuṣita Heaven, where the Great Bodhisattva Maitreya was awaiting the time of his final birth. When Bhāvaviveka would not be swayed from his purpose, Avalokiteśvara instructed him to go to Dhānyakaṭaka and meditate in the cave of

Vajrapāṇi. Practicing and reciting the Vajrapāṇi Dhāraṇī, he would obtain his wish.

After Bhāvaviveka had meditated in the cave for three years, Vajrapāṇi appeared to him and gave him the formula for opening the Asura Palace hidden deep within the mountain. There, protected by the Asuras (fierce demigods), he would dwell in unbroken meditation until the enlightenment of the Buddha Maitreya. Then Bhāvaviveka would awaken and be blessed by the Buddha's direct teaching. Bhāvaviveka followed Vajrapāṇi's instructions with single-minded devotion for three more years; then, as promised, the door to the Asura Palace swung open. Bhāvaviveka immediately passed through the door, but only six of all his assembled disciples dared to follow their master into the Asura realm. As the door closed behind Bhāvaviveka and the six disciples, the other disciples watched in dismay, reproaching themselves for having lost this precious opportunity.

Once a thriving Buddhist center, Dhānyakaṭaka was in decline in the seventh century. Hsüan-tsang noted that most of its monasteries were deserted and in ruins. Although about one thousand Mahāyāna monks were residing in twenty monasteries, the Buddhists were far outnumbered by adherents of various non-Buddhist religions. Still they were actively engaged in study and practice. Hsüan-tsang stayed here two months to study the Abhidharma with Subhūti and Sūrya, eminent Tripiṭaka masters of the Mahāsāṁghika school, and taught them the Mahāyāna śāstras in return. (Hwui 137)

Nāgārjunakoṇḍa

A secluded valley west of Amarāvatī and Dhānyakaṭaka was the site of a large and important Dharma center, known today as Nāgārjunakoṇḍa, Nāgārjuna's Hill. Tradition relates that King Sadvaha built a monastery on a mountain in his kingdom for the great master Nāgārjuna. King Sadvaha is usually identified as Yajñaśrī Sātakarṇi, a powerful Sātavāhana king, and the King Jantaka named in Nāgārjuna's Letter to a Friend (Suhṛllekha). The Sātavāhanas, strong supporters of Buddhism, appear to have ruled both Āndhra and Madhya Pradesh between the first century B.C.E. and the third century C.E. The mountain home built for Nāgārjuna is commonly known as Śrī Parvata (Venerable Mountain).

Nāgārjuna is said to have left Amarāvatī after the construction of the railings and retired to Śrī Parvata, which most scholars locate near Nāgārjunakoṇḍa, the site of the Cūḷadhammagiri Monastery. According to Tāranātha and Bu-ston, accounts of Nāgārjuna's later life took place on Śrī Parvata near Dhānyakaṭaka, in the land of the Āndhras, which would place Śrī Parvata in the same region as Nāgārjunakoṇḍa. While Hsüan-tsang locates Śrī Parvata in Mahākosala, modern southeastern Madhya Pradesh, the events he describes are the same as related by Tāranātha and Bu-ston.

It was to Śrī Parvata that the Śrī Laṅkan seeker Āryadeva came to meet Nāgārjuna. Upon hearing of Āryadeva's arrival, Nāgārjuna sent him a cup full of water; Āryadeva cast a needle into the water and sent it back to Nāgārjuna. From this gesture Nāgārjuna understood that Āryadeva wished to penetrate the depths of Nāgārjuna's knowledge. After interviewing Āryadeva, Nāgārjuna accepted him as the disciple most qualified to continue his lineage.

Skilled in the art of medicine, Nāgārjuna greatly extended his own life and also the life of King Sadvaha. The king's son, perceiving that his father showed no signs of aging, asked his mother when he would attain the throne. The mother replied that the king was already two hundred years old; through the power of Nāgārjuna's medicine, he had already outlived several hundred sons and grandsons. Until Nāgārjuna himself perished, the king would not pass from this life. The mother spoke of Nāgārjuna's great generosity and directed her son to ask the Bodhisattva for his head. Approaching Nāgārjuna, the king's son praised the unfailing generosity practiced by those Bodhisattvas who sought to attain the state of a Buddha, and he requested that the great Nāgārjuna emulate their example. Nāgārjuna advised the son to consider the effect of his death on the king and the karma that would result, then picked up a leaf of a dry reed and used it to cut off his own head.

After Nāgārjuna's death, Āryadeva resided on Śrī Parvata, where he wrote commentaries on the master's major works that framed the foundation for the Mādhyamika, one of the four major schools of Buddhist philosophy. At Naṇḍūra, near Nāgārjunakoṇḍa, a container was found that is said to hold Āryadeva's relics.

Although the great stūpa at Nāgārjunakoṇḍa appears to have been built during the reign of the Sātavāhana kings, Buddhism at Nāgārjunakoṇḍa flourished most strongly during the reign of the Ikṣvāku kings, which began around the mid-third century C.E. and probably lasted about a hundred years. A number of inscriptions at Nāgārjunakoṇḍa refer to Śrī Virapuruṣadaṭṭa, the second ruler of this dynasty, as a Buddhist who claimed descent from the lineage of Ikṣvāku, the lineage of the Buddha Śākyamuni. Ehuvula (Cāmtamūla II), his son and successor, was also a Buddhist, as were most of the women of the royal family. Their combined reigns lasted forty-eight years, during which time Buddhism flourished strongly at Nāgārjunakoṇḍa. Third- and fourth-century inscriptions associate Śrī Parvata with Vijayapurī, the capital city of the Ikṣvāku kings; from their names Śrī Parvata (Venerable Mountain) would refer to the mountain range and plateau and Vijayapurī (City of Victory) to the Ikṣvāku capital. In more recent times, this entire region became known as Nāgārjunakoṇḍa.

Inscriptions from the third century C.E. indicate that the Ikṣvāku queens provided generously for construction and support of Buddhist monasteries and shrines in the area. Inscriptions describe the contributions of the patroness Queen

Excavations of Buddhist buildings at Nāgārjunakoṇḍa before the opening of the dam. The site is now under water.

Cāṁtisirī, sister of Cāṁtamūla, founder of the Ikṣvāku kingdom. The Queen supported the construction of the great stūpa of Nāgārjunakoṇḍa, which continued for ten years. The great stūpa enshrined a tooth relic of the Buddha. The laywoman Bodhisirī made at least twelve donations for religious monuments and Bhaṭidevā and Koḍabalisirī of the royal family sponsored the building of monasteries dedicated to the Bahuśrutīya and Mahīśāsaka schools. Substantial support for the Sangha also came from local merchants and craft guilds, which greatly prospered in the maritime trade with Śrī Laṅkā, Southeast Asia, and cities along the overland route to the western coast. In all, fifty-six inscriptions provide invaluable historical information on the monasteries and rulers associated with Nāgārjunakoṇḍa.

During the period ruled by the Ikṣvākus, Nāgārjunakoṇḍa, with more than thirty shrines and monasteries, became the largest Buddhist center in South India. (BSI 45) An inscription near the great stūpa records the donation of a monastery to the Bahuśrūtiya school. Inscriptions found at other monsteries at Nāgārjunakoṇḍa indicate their affiliations with the Aparamahāvinaseliya and Mahīśāsaka schools, and also with the Mahāvihāravāsins, a Śrī Laṅkan order. (The Bahuśrūtiya and Aparamahāvinaseliya schools were related to the Mahā sāṁghika tradition, while the Mahīśāsaka and Mahāvihāravāsins had branched off from the Sthavira tradition.) A stone bearing the footprints of the Buddha was found at the site of the Mahāvihāravāsin monastery.

Inscriptions indicate that Nāgārjunakoṇḍa's monasteries were named for the schools they housed or for the native countries of the bhikṣus who lived there. These monasteries housed bhikṣus from such diverse places as Damila (Tamil) and Vanavāsa in South India, Paluara and Dantapura in the Oḍra-Kaliṅga region, Tosali (Dhauli) in Orissa, and the northern provinces of Kashmīr, Gandhāra, and Vaṅga (Bengal). Nāgārjunakoṇḍa also attracted bhikṣus from Śrī Laṅkā and China. An inscription notes that the patroness Bodhisirī sponsored the construction of the Cuḷadhammagiri Monastery, which was dedicated for the use of Śrī Laṅkan monks; as a result, the monastery was also known as the Siṁhāla Vihāra. Another inscription notes that Śrī Laṅkan monks donated a water tank to the Pūrvaśaila school.

Rediscovery of Nāgārjunakoṇḍa

The expansion of Nāgārjunakoṇḍa ceased with the death of Rudrapuruṣa, presumed to have been the last Ikṣvāku king. Little is known of its subsequent history from Buddhist or secular records. The site appears to have been neglected, then forgotten for centuries. In 1926, a local teacher reported seeing exposed pillars in the area and notified government archaeologists. Excavations began in 1927, a year after an Indian archaeologist discovered the site, and continued until early 1931. The entire valley was intensively excavated between 1954 and 1960, shortly before completion of the huge Nāgārjuna-sagar Dam flooded the entire site.

In six years archaeologists uncovered more than a hundred sites dating from the early stone age to around the sixteenth century. Excavations revealed an extensive complex of Buddhist sites consisting of a central temple and four monasteries belonging to the Aparamahāvinaseliya, Bahuśrūtiya, Cūḷadhammagiri, and Mahīśāsaka schools. Archaeologists also found ruins of a small temple of Harītī, a demoness converted to the Dharma, and another larger shrine.

Nāgārjunakoṇḍa is now an island in the midst of the great reservoir that floods the valley of the Kṛṣṇā River for miles behind the Nagarjunasagar Dam. The ruins of the uncovered sites were salvaged, and nine monuments were reconstructed to replicate their original form. Most of the ruins are still on the island, while those found deeper in the valley were moved to the eastern bank of the reservoir near Anuppu, where they can still be seen. Still, the flooding of this site, termed the Sārnāth of South India by at least one Indian historian, was a tragedy for Buddhists and a great loss to India's cultural heritage. (Nagar 2)

Paṇṇagāma, a small Śrāvakayāna center, has also been located near Nāgārjunakoṇḍa. According to an inscription at the site, members of the Ārya Sangha, preceptors and preachers of the Dīgha and Majjhima Nikāya, once resided here.

Art of Nāgārjunakoṇḍa

The art and artifacts found during the excavations were placed in a museum built to house them, along with miniature replicas of fifty excavated sites. The museum, opened in 1966, is near the main site on the island and can be reached by boat from Anuppu. Among the images it preserves is a reconstruction of a large standing Buddha, nearly ten feet in height. Carvings on beams and slabs salvaged from the ruins of

Nāgārjunakoṇḍa depict the life of the Buddha and scenes from the Jātakas, including the Vessantara Jātaka and the account of King Sibi. Some of the art from earlier periods of excavation was sent to the National Museum in New Delhi, the Government Museum in Madras, and the Indian Museum in Calcutta. The Musée Guimet in Paris and the Metropolitan Museum in New York also obtained some sculptures from Nājārjunakoṇḍa.

The art of Nāgārjunakoṇḍa is very similar to the art of Amarāvatī and other sites in the lower Godāvarī-Krṣṇā river valleys, collectively known as the Andhra artistic tradition, or the Āndhra School, which flourished most strongly between the second and fourth centuries C.E. The artisans of the Nāgārjunakoṇḍa region worked in fine-grained limestone tinged in green and represented similar themes and symbols in a distinctive artistic style. Some historians describe the art of Nāgārjunakoṇḍa as reflecting elements of the Gandhāran and Mathuran traditions as well as indigenous figure-types, all strongly influenced by the graceful flowing style characteristic of Amarāvatī. Bas-reliefs depict scenes from the life of the Buddha, including the Bodhisattva's birth, the home-departure, descent from Tuṣita Heaven, and the Parinirvāṇa, in which the Buddha is represented symbolically as well as in human form. Carvings of Ajātaśatru's procession to visit the Buddha and numerous scenes from the Jātakas were also recovered from this site.

The architecture of Nāgārjunakoṇḍa, which represents the traditions of four Buddhist schools that flourished in the south in the third century C.E., is of particular importance to historians of Buddhism. Here were found stūpas with an inner spoked-wheel structure as well as solid stūpas, and temples and dwellings combined in different ways. Future studies on the architectural elements and art forms favored by each school may shed more light on their distinguishing characteristics. (AAI:179–180)

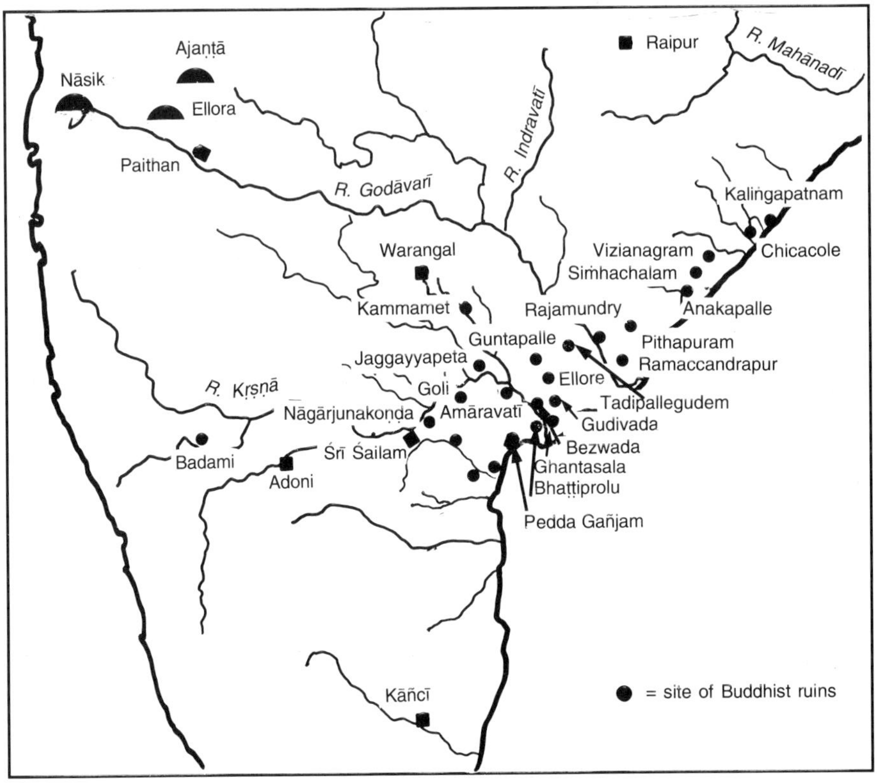

Monuments Around the Great Centers

The great number of sites between the lower Godāvarī and Kṛṣṇā rivers testify to the vitality of Buddhism in this region. At Buddhāni, eighteen miles from Repalle, near the mouth of the Kṛṣṇā River, copper Buddhist images dating from about the fifth century C.E. have been discovered, and stūpas have been located at nearby Gudivāda, Ghaṇṭaśālā, Chejrala, and Goli. Chejrala, site of many stūpa remains, seems to have been a particularly large and thriving Buddhist center.

To the north, inscriptions found at Elluru record land grants to the Pūrvaśailas (one of the Buddhist schools in the area), and a large Buddha image has been discovered here. The ruins of a Buddhist Vihāra were found at Arugolanu, in Tadipalligudem Taluk, in the West Godāvarī District, and a cave dwelling that once housed Buddhist monks has been located at Aripālam, near Anakapalle.

Coin evidence found at the site indicates that the monastery located near Anakapalle, known simply as Saṁghārāma, flourished between the fourth and ninth centuries. C.E. The grounds of Saṁghārāma embrace some of the most ancient shrines and stūpas in Āndhra, including entire hills carved into monolithic stūpas. A two-storied temple carved out of solid rock holds Buddha images and a stūpa. The artistic style indicates that this temple may have been an early Mahāyāna construction.

Marble carvings with inscriptions dating from the third century C.E. were found at Chinna Gañjām, in the Guntur District. Pedda Gañjām, once the capital of ancient Āndhra, was also a Buddhist center in the third century C.E. One mile north of Pedda Gañjām, at Franguladinne, remains of a stūpa were found together with large Buddha images. Kanuparti, six miles north of Pedda Gañjām, is the site of a monastery which was converted into a Hindu temple.

Bhaṭṭiprolu, located near Repalle, is considered one of the earliest Buddhist centers in Āndhra. The great stūpa of Bhaṭṭiprolu was quite large, about 132 feet in diameter. Constructed about the same time as the Bhārhut and Sāñcī stūpas, it held relics of the Buddha which were discovered during excavations in 1891. Inscriptions on the unearthed relic casket identify the relics as those of the Buddha. The Government of India entrusted these precious relics to the care of the Mahābodhi Society. They are now in the Dharmarājika Vihāra, the Mahābodhi Society's center in Calcutta. (BRA 14, 22; BSI 70) Rāmatīrtha, located four miles from Nellimarala, is an ancient Buddhist holy place with many shrines which date to the second century C.E.

Northwest of Amarāvatī, on the northernmost bend of the lower Kṛṣṇā River, stood the monastery of Jaggayyapeṭa, another of Āndhra's early Buddhist centers. Script dating to the second century B.C.E. has been found on the remains of its great stūpa, and a Buddha image dating from the fifth century C.E. was discovered in the ruins of the monastery. During these centuries, Jaggayyapeṭa appears to have been a stopping place for travelers proceeding to or from the western cave temples of Bedsā and Kārli.

Directly north of Jaggayyapeṭa, about six miles from Madura, is Rāmareddipalle, also known as Gummididurru. Rāmareddipalle appears to have been a large Buddhist center as far back as the beginning of the common era, but very little is known of its history. The remains of its main stūpa indicate that its circumference was ornamented with thirty-four marble reliefs in the same style as the sculptures of Amarāvatī.

Many Buddhist remains have been found in the hills of Guntapalle, a virtual treasury of buildings and images dating from the second century B.C.E. Guntapalle, located southeast of Rāmareddipalle in the West Godāvarī District, is the site of monolithic stone stūpas, rock-cut cave temples, and large brick shrines holding limestone images of the Buddha. Cave-dwellings and remains of monasteries and large stūpas have also been found in the hills of Saṅkaran, located in the Vizagapatnam District.

Archaeological research continues to yield information concerning the extent and longevity of Buddhism in Āndhra. According to Ahir, excavations in 1986 located an ancient Buddhist center at Bavikoṇḍa, near Bheemmunipatnam in the district of Viśākhapatnam. Monuments found here included a great stūpa, seven small stūpas, and a monastery containing fifty-one rooms for monks, a large assembly hall, a library, and implements associated with the preparation of medicines. One of the largest stūpas found in South India was recently discovered at Nelakoṇḍapalli in the Khammam district. (BSI 71)

Tamilnādu

Although Buddhist centers on the scale of Amarāvatī and Nāgārjunakoṇḍa have not been found in the land of the Tamils, Buddhism flourished for many centuries in Kāñcī and the prosperous port cities, nurturing distinguished scholars and master teachers who served the Dharma at home and abroad.

The region now known as Tamilnādu lies directly below Āndhra Pradesh and includes the modern cities of Madras, Pondicherry, Tanjore, and Madurāi. In ancient times, this region was formed of kingdoms named after the tribes that inhabited it—primarily the Coḷas in the north and the Pāṇḍyas in the south. Hsüan-tsang, traveling south through the Tamilnādu, identified three countries: Coḷa, northwest of modern Madras; Drāviḍa, the region around Kāñcī; and Malakūṭa, near the southern tip of the Indian peninsula. Of these regions, Kāñcī was the strongest Buddhist center; during the fifth and sixth centuries C.E., this ancient city, the educational center of the Tamil-speaking region, was associated with some of Buddhism's most famous scholars.

Although the Tamilnādu lay outside Aśoka's empire, the Buddha's teachings gradually entered the mainstream of Tamil culture, appearing in Tamil literature between the second and fifth centuries C.E. in the works of the Buddhist poets Ilambodhiyar and Sittalai Sattanar. Sattanar's dramatic poem Maṇimekhalai was a vehicle for expressing Buddhist doctrines and contrasting them with the harsher philosophies of that time. It immortalized the story of Maṇimekhalai, a young girl who became a Buddhist nun under the tutelage of Aravana Adigal, a second-century Tamil master who helped introduce the Dharma in South India. In the fourth century, the Buddhist poet Nagaguttanar based his epic on the story of the nun Kundalakesi, as told in the commentary on the Therīgāthā. (This work is now lost, but it is known through references in Jain works.)

While it is difficult to draw from these examples definite conclusions concerning Buddhism in the Tamil country, it is significant that Maṇimekhalai and Kundalakesi, which focus on Buddhist heroines and strongly convey Buddhist teachings, are two of the five great Tamil epic poems. A third epic, the Valiyapathy, was also by a Buddhist poet, but has not survived to the present day. Still more lost works by Buddhist poets and writers are mentioned in Śaivite and Jain works, including a retelling of the life of King Bimbisāra, devotional poems, and a work on Buddhist philosophy. (BSI 122-123, 146)

References to Buddhist activity in the land of the Tamils gleaned from inscriptions and from literature indicate that Buddhism was a viable part of the Tamil culture at least until the fifth or sixth century. As elsewhere in South India, the seventh-century pilgrim Hsüan-tsang found Buddhism declining in most of the Tamil regions. Only in Kāñcī did he find the Dharma flourishing, supported by contact with Buddhists in Śrī Laṅkā and Śrī Vijaya. The rise of Hindu devotional cults in the eighth and ninth centuries and the incorporation of Buddhist teachings and images into Hindu movements confused distinctions between Hinduism and Buddhism and began a process of absorption. Periods of persecution thinned the ranks of monks and discouraged the laity; vandalism of Buddhist sites increased, with monasteries being robbed of images and other valuables. The growing number of Hindu groups required places of worship; they appropriated the Buddhist monasteries, renovating them for their purpose or salvaging their materials for construction.

Despite these disruptions and pressures, Buddhism persisted in the Tamil lands for many centuries longer. The Mahāyāna monk and grammarian Buddhamitra was teaching and writing in Tamilnādu in the eleventh century under the patronage of the Coḷa king Virarājendra. His work, which incorporated elements of Sanskrit into Tamil grammar, was a lasting contribution to his homeland. Tāranātha mentions that Buddhaśrīmitra, Vajraśī, and many lesser paṇḍitas sought refuge "far to the south" when the monasteries of the north were threatened in the twelfth century. (Tar 319) The scholar Anuruddha was active in South India in the early twelfth century, and inscriptions in 1398, 1533, and 1580 refer respectively to Buddhist logicians, settlements, and a temple in Tanjore. (BCAI 238) Although the evidence is fragmentary, there are clear indications that at least some Buddhist activity persisted far longer in South India than we tend to assume.

The Coḷas

Hsüan-tsang described the Coḷa country, located inland to the southwest of Amarāvatī, as "deserted and wild, a succession of marshes and jungle. The population is very small, and troops of brigands go through the country openly. The climate is hot; the manners of the people dissolute and cruel. The disposition of the men is naturally fierce. . .The monasteries are in ruins and dirty . . ." (HT II:77) An Aśokan stūpa marked the place where the Buddha proclaimed the Dharma here. Hsüan-tsang relates that in a nearby monastery the philoso-

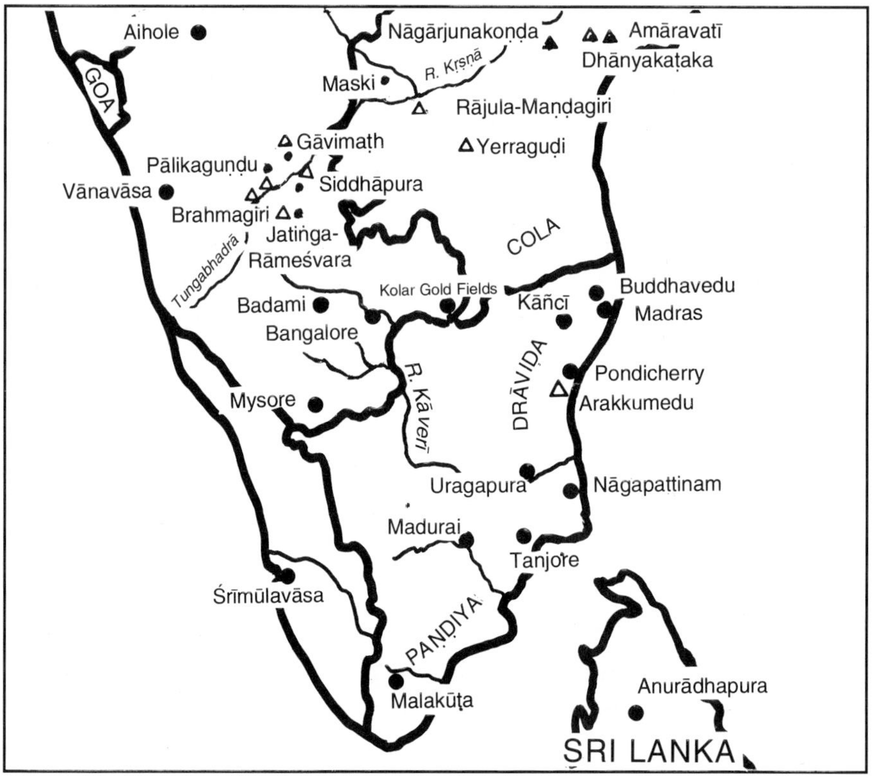

pher Āryadeva had once entered into a discussion with the Arhat Uttara who possessed the six supernatural powers and the eight means of deliverance. At one point, unable to respond to Āryadeva's questions, the Arhat Uttara entered a deep samādhi that enabled him to speak directly with the Great Bodhisattva Maitreya. Upon hearing from Maitreya that Āryadeva would become a Buddha later in this aeon, the Arhat conveyed Maitreya's responses to Āryadeva and offered him homage and praise.

Kāñcī (Kāñcīpura)

Kāñcī, the capital city of Drāviḍa, was the major center of learning in South India. Buddhism came early to Kāñcī, perhaps as early as the third century B.C.E. It is possible that Mahinda stopped here on his way from Vidiśā to Śrī Laṅkā;

Śrī Laṅkā was only a three-day journey from Kāñcī by sea, and Kāñcī had maintained a close connection with Śrī Laṅkā from very early times. Some scholars believe that Mahinda built the first Buddhist vihāra in Paṭṭinappākkam, a port city downriver from Kāñcī; this vihāra is named Indra Vihāra in the Jain epic Silappatikāram. (BIT 23) Several centuries later, the master Āryadeva, disciple of Nāgārjuna, spent his last years at Ranganātha, near Kāñcī. He is said to have died here in meditation, at the hand of a disciple whose master he had defeated in debate.

The Tamil epic Manimekhalai records the name of King Killivalan, who built a Buddhist monastery at Kāñcī for the nun Maṇimekhalai and dedicated a park for the benefit of the Sangha in the second century C.E. Maṇimekhalai's preceptor, the monk Aravan Adigal, lived here after working for the Dharma in Karṇāṭaka and elsewhere in Tamilnādu. In the third century C.E., Skandavarman, the first Pallava king, is said to have patronized Buddhism; history records the names of his sons as Buddhavarman and Buddyaṅkara. (BSI 115)

Buddhist Masters Associated With Kāñcī

Although the historical record is fragmentary, Kāñcī produced a number of famous Buddhist masters during the fifth and sixth centuries C.E., indicating that Buddhism was well-established at that time. Although there is no agreement on the birthplace of Buddhaghosa, the great scholar lived much of his life in Kāñcī, which he calls in one of his writings the center of Pāli Buddhism. (BIT25) At the request of his teacher, Buddhaghosa, who had trained at Bodh Gayā, set sail from Kāñcī in the fifth century to examine the ancient Sinhalese commentaries of the sacred texts. On his voyage, he is said to have met another prominent scholar, Buddhadatta, who was then returning from Śrī Laṅkā. After studying the Sinhalese commentaries at the Mahāvihāra in Śrī Laṅkā and winning the trust of the monks there, Buddhaghosa began to systematize the commentaries and translate them into Pāli, the Prākrit, or spoken dialect adopted by the Sthavira tradition as their canonical language. Buddhaghosa later returned to Kāñcī where he continued his work.

Born at Uragapura, Buddhadatta lived and worked many years at the Bhūtamaṅgala Monastery near Uragapura, south of Kāñcī on the bank of the Kāverī River. It was here that he wrote the Vinaya-viniccaya, a summary of Buddhaghosa's commentaries on the Vinaya teachings, for the sake of promoting knowledge of Buddhaśīla, the Buddhist ethical and moral discipline. He also wrote a major treatise explicating Buddhaghosa's commentaries on Abhidharma and a commentary on the Buddhavamsa. It is possible that these works were written in a vihāra at Paṭṭinappākkam, since they give descriptions of this prosperous port city. (BIT 23)

Buddhaghosa and Buddhadatta are two of the three major editors of the ancient Sinhalese commentaries; the third was the sixth-century master Dhammapāla. According to Hsüan-tsang, Dhammapāla was born in Kāñcī, but other sources mention the city of Tanja, which is probably Tanjore. (BSI 126) It is likely that Dhammapāla spent some time in Śrī Laṅkā at the Mahāvihāra in Anurādhapura reviewing the works of Buddhaghosa. Upon his return to India, he resided for a time at the port of Nāgapattinam in the Dharmāśoka Vihāra, a monastery said to have been built by King Aśoka. (BIT 26) He prepared Pāli editions of the Sinhalese commentaries as yet untranslated as well as a major commentary on Buddhaghosa's Visuddhimagga.

Kāñcī After the Sixth Century

Hsüan-tsang found the Dharma flourishing in the region of Kāñcī (modern Conjeevaram), located on the Pālār River forty-three miles southwest of modern Madras. The city of Kāñcī was then about five miles in circumference. Hsüan-tsang described the land as fertile and regularly cultivated, producing abundant grain, flowers, and fruits, as well as precious gems. "The climate is hot, the character of the people courageous. They are deeply attached to the principles of honesty and truth, and highly esteem learning." (HT II:229) According to Hsüan-tsang, the Buddha had visited this area often, and there still stood a number of Aśokan stūpas marking places where the Buddha had taught. At the time of Hsüan-tsang's visit, there were more than a hundred monasteries here housing over ten thousand Sthavira monks.

Many Kāñcī Buddhist centers had close ties with Dharma communities in Śrī Laṅkā. During Hsüan-tsang's visit, three hundred monks from Śrī Laṅkā arrived in Kāñcī to seek relief from a famine then gripping the island kingdom. This incident testifies to the close ties that still linked the Buddhists of Kāñcī with those of Śrī Laṅkā.

The Pallavas ruled the region of Kāñcī from c. 500 to at least 750 C.E. During their reign, new devotional Śaivite and Vaiṣṇavite movements rose like a tide in South India and gradually supplanted the Buddhist and Jain traditions. However, Buddhism appears to have persisted longer in Kāñcī than elsewhere in the south. Saroruha, one of the eighty-four mahāsiddhas, was a prince of Kāñcī and attained realization nearby; another siddha, Līlapa, was from South India, which often referred to the region of Kāñcī. A Javanese poet mentions that Buddhist monks were still in Kāñcī in 1362. (HISI 195) The prolonged vitality of Buddhism at Kāñcī was supported by Śrī Laṅkā: the general of King Bhuvanaikabahu IV of Śrī Laṅkā (fourteenth century) had a monastery built at Kāñcī. (KTA 238)

Since Buddhist monasteries were generally taken over by Hindu groups, either as they stood or pulled down and reconstructed, archaeologists have only located one Buddhist site—the remains of a single stūpa—to be excavated in Kāñcī. However, a large number of images have been preserved within Hindu temples. Some are quite large, indicating that the temples that house them probably began their existence as Buddhist shrines. The Kamakṣi Amman temple in Kāñcī, which held five Buddha images, is considered to have been a Mahāyāna temple dedicated to Tārā. (BSI 144–145) To date, statues found range in date from the seventh to the fourteenth centuries; further research will probably uncover many more. (BSI 136–138)

Buddhavedu

Tradition associates the small village of Buddhavedu, near Madras, with the physical presence of the Buddha. Although little is known of Buddhavedu's ancient history, archaeologists have unearthed the remains of a monastery here; a Buddha image and a Bodhi tree were found near the monastery, and an inscription at the site records that the Coḷa king who ruled here in the tenth century dedicated the village to the Buddhist Sangha, ensuring the monastery a source of support. A Buddha image found in the ruins of Arukkumedu, once a flourishing commercial center near Pondicherry, has led to speculation that Buddhist centers may have been founded in that city also.

Nāgapattinam

South of the Kāverī (Cauvery) River, in the ancient land of the Paṇḍiyas, is the seaport city of Nāgapattinam, where Buddhaghosa, Buddhadatta, and Dhammapāla embarked for Śrī Laṅkā. In the sixth century, Dhammapāla composed the commentary on the Netti-pakaraṇa at the Dharmāśoka Vihāra in Nāgapattinam. In the eighth century a monastery was built for Chinese merchants who traded through this port. (Chinese records and inscriptions in Burma note that this monastery was active as late as the fifteenth century.) South India's trade with the empire of Śrī Vijaya (modern Indonesia) also passed through Nāgapattinam. An eleventh-century copper-plate inscription records that King Māravijayottuṅga of Śrī Vijaya donated a shrine at the Cūḍāmaṇivarma Monastery and the Coḷa king Rājarāja I (985–1014 C.E.) donated the income from one of his villages for this shrine's maintenance. Patronized by the Coḷa kings who ruled this area between 850 and 1200 C.E. and watched over by the kings of Śrī Vijaya, Buddhism became well established in Nāgapattinam.

The monasteries of Nāgapattinam were well-known for their rich collection of Buddhist images. In recent times large statues, including representations of a standing Buddha and a standing Avalokiteśvara, have been discovered in Nāgapattinam. Since these statues were brought here after 1600 C.E., it is likely that the practice of Buddhism persisted up to the seventeenth century. When Nāgapattinam's last Buddhist structure was demolished by Christian missionaries in 1867 and replaced by a church, five Buddha images were found buried at the site and donated to the British governor. Since that time excavations of Nāgapattinam's monasteries have yielded more than 350 bronze images dating from the ninth to thirteenth centuries.

Although Buddhist centers on the scale of Amarāvatī or Nāgārjunakoṇḍa have not been found in Tamilnādu, this region produced a number of outstanding masters whose contributions benefited the Dharma and Sangha far beyond their home country. In addition to Buddhaghosa, Buddhadatta, and Dhammapāla—the three great luminaries who rendered the Sinhalese commentaries into Pāli—the Tamilnādu was the homeland of a distinguished line of Mahāyāna masters, who set down their treatises in Sanskrit.

Mahāyāna Masters of Tamilnādu

Siṁhavakra, near Kāñcī, was the birthplace of the fifth century logician Dignāga, who developed the science of logic known as Pramāṇa. According to Tāranātha, Dignāga became a monk in the Vatsīputrīya tradition, but was expelled when he questioned his teacher on a point of doctrine. Dissatisfied, Dignāga went north where he met the great master Vasubandhu and became his disciple. Excelling in philosophy, Dignāga specialized in discerning valid proofs of knowledge and became famous for his skill in debate. His work, the Pramāṇasamuccaya, provided an essential guide for philosophical inquiry and became the foundation for a lineage of outstanding logicians.

Dignāga's work was continued by his brilliant countryman Dharmakīrti, whose writings became an integral part of the philosophy programs of India's great universities as well as the educational centers of Tibet. According to Tāranātha, Dharmakīrti was born in Trimalaya in South India and mastered the Vedas early in life. He went to the prestigious university of Nālandā, where he was ordained by the South Indian scholar Dharmapāla and studied under Dignāga's disciple Iśvarasena. Impressed with Dharmakīrti's understanding of Dignāga's Pramāṇasamuccaya, Iśvarasena declared Dharmakīrti Dignāga's true disciple. In seven major treatises, headed by the Pramāṇavarttika, Dharmakīrti expanded and refined the science of knowledge.

Dharmapāla, the master of Hsüan-tsang's own teacher Śīlabhadra, was born the son of a king's minister in Kāñcī. According to Hsüan-tsang, Dharmapāla could not refuse a marriage arranged for him by the royal family yet he yearned to be free to study the Dharma. So great was his sincerity that he was miraculously transported to a distant monastery, where he became a monk. Applying himself to study, he developed into a great scholar and won fame through his brilliance in debate. He later served as head teacher of Nālandā.

Bodhidharma, who introduced the meditative Ch'an tradition to China, was born into a noble family of Kāñcī. He learned the principles of dhyāna, or meditation, from his preceptor Prajñātāra and transmitted them in India. In 526 C.E. he went to China, where he made his way to the Shao-lin Monastery near the translation center of Lo-yang. Under Bodhidharma's guidance, Shao-lin became the center of the Ch'an tradition which soon took root also in Korea and Japan.

Bodhiruci, a seventh century Tamil monk, traveled to China, where he studied the Dharma with the Mahāyāna master Yaśaghoṣa. After several years of intensive study, he began working with a translation team to translate Sanskrit texts into Chinese. Continuing this work until his death in 727 C.E., he produced a total of fifty-three translations.

Vajrabodhi, a Mahāyāna master learned in the Vajrayāna, was born in 661 C.E., either in Kāñcī or further south, in the country of the Paṇḍyas. After studying at Nālandā and serving in Śrī Laṅkā, he went to China, accompanied by his disciple Amoghavajra. Together they founded the Chen-yen school, the only Vajrayāna tradition established in China, and Vajrabodhi translated many Sanskrit texts into Chinese.

In 736, Bodhisena, a monk/scholar of Madurāi, traveled to Japan at the invitation of the emperor and performed the consecration ceremony for the gigantic statue of Vairocana installed in the Tōdai Monastery at Nara. The first Indian monk to teach in Japan, Bodhisena worked for the Dharma in Japan until he passed away in 760.

Malakūṭa

Further south, in the region of modern Madurāi, was the kingdom of Malakūṭa, renowned for its abundance of gems. Although it is not clear that Hsüan-tsang actually traveled here, he describes an Aśokan stūpa marking the place where the Tathāgata once visited and mentions an old monastery built by Mahendra. To the south of Malakūṭa was Malayagiri, or Mt. Malaya, traditionally considered one of the sites of the Buddha's Third Turning teachings. To the east of the Malaya hills lay Mount Potala, considered the dwelling-place of the Bodhisattva Avalokiteśvara.

"The passes of this mountain are very dangerous; its sides are precipitous, and its valleys rugged. On the top of the mountain is a lake; its waters are clear as a mirror. From a hollow proceeds a great river which encircles the mountain as it flows down twenty times and then enters the southern sea. By the side of the lake is a rock-palace of the devas. Here Avalokiteśvara in coming and going takes his abode. Those who strongly desire to see this Bodhisattva do not regard their lives, but, crossing the water, climb the mountain forgetful of its difficulties and dangers; of those who make the attempt there are very few who reach the summit. But even to those who dwell below the mountain, if they earnestly pray to behold Avalokiteśvara, sometimes he appears as Iśvaradeva, sometimes in the form of a yogi; he addresses them with benevolent words and then they obtain their wishes according to their desires." (HT II:233) This site described by Hsüan-tsang has been identified as the shrine of Balaji, an incarnation of Viṣṇu, located at Tirupati, where an image of the Bodhisattva Avalokiteśvara has been converted into a representation of Balaji. (BSI 75–76)

Kerala and Karṇāṭaka

Of all the Indian states, Buddhism in Kerala is the most difficult to trace to an early date. The Vinaya and early chronicles make no mention of this region, which, like the Tamil country, lay outside Aśoka's empire. Buddhism came earlier to Karṇāṭaka, where Aśokan edicts have been found.

Some of the earliest references to Buddhism in Kerala appear in the Tamil epic Maṇimekhalai, which mentions that Aravan Adigal, a Buddhist monk who lived in the second century C.E., had propagated the Dharma in Vañji, an ancient capital. Jayasiṁha Perumal, who ruled this region in the first century B.C.E., may have been a Buddhist, but the first confirmed Buddhist king did not reign until four centuries later. This king, who ruled in the late third century C.E., was Bana Perumal, also known as Baudha Perumal. His reign was short-lived; according to the Keralotpatti, a seventeenth century chronicle, Bana Perumal was overthrown by Brahmins opposed to Buddhism and the Buddhists of Kerala were persecuted and expelled. Additional persecutions occurred in the eighth century at the instigation of two Brahmin teachers, Kumārila Bhatta and Śānkara.

Buddhism fared better during the ninth century, when the Buddhist king Vikramāditya Varaguṇa of the Varadu Dynasty ruled in central Kerala. His capital was Śrīmūlavāsam, near modern Alwaye. (BSI 98) An inscription ordered by this king, dated c. 868 C.E., documents an extensive grant of land to the Mūlavāsa Monastery, a Buddhist center. The Mūlavāsa Monastery appears to have been so widely known that a manifestation of Avalokiteśvara bears its name. An inscription found on such a statue in Gandhāra identifies the image as Dakṣiṇāpatha Mūlavāsa Lokanātha.

The Mūlavāsa Monastery survived if only in memory as late as the eleventh or twelfth century, when it was mentioned in the Mūṣikavaṁsa, a Sanskrit dramatic poem. The Mūṣikavaṁsa relates how Vikramarāma, king of the Mūṣikas, saved the Buddhist temple at Mūlavāsa from the ocean by throwing large blocks of stones into the beachhead to strengthen the shore. The poem also relates that Valabha, another Mūṣika king, visited the Mūlavāsa Vihāra, paid homage to the lord of the temple, and received blessings. The location of Śrīmūlavāsa has recently been traced to the Alleppy district, where finely detailed Buddha images have been found.

The search for additional traces of Buddhism in Kerala has produced only fragments of information. Many place names here incorporate the word 'palli,' which once referred to Buddhist shrines. The use of this term in place names may well reflect a distant memory of Buddhist sites. Scholars consider that a number of present-day Hindu temples, including the Sabarimala, an Ayyappa shrine, were originally built to be Buddhist places of worship. Kerala also has caves that once served as living quarters for Buddhist monks or as reliquaries. (BSI 100–101) A movement to revive Buddhism in Kerala was begun by C. Krishnan in the 1920s and supported by the Mahābodhi Society of India. Buddhist vihāras established in Calicut in 1927 and 1937 continue to serve a small Sangha of Buddhist practitioners.

Buddhism in Karṇāṭaka

In the center of South India, the north-flowing Tuṅgabhadrā River, originating in the Malaya mountain range, joins the Kṛṣṇā River in its eastward flow to the Bay of Bengal. About halfway along its route, Aśoka had edicts carved at the towns of Brahmagiri, Pālikguṇḍu, Jatinga-Rāmeśvara, Siddhāpura, and Gāvimaṭh. Aśokan edicts have also been found at Rājula-Maṇḍagiri, where the Tuṅgabhadrā joins the Kṛṣṇā, and at Maski, a short distance upriver. Only a few Buddhist remains have been found in this region, but an inscription associates the town of Kampil (modern Kampili, on the southern bank of the Tuṅgabhadrā) with a Buddhist monastery, in support of which King Dantivarma granted the income from one of his villages.

South Indian scholars hold that the Pañcapāṇḍya Malai, mountain caves of the Pāṇḍya country, date from the third century B.C.E., making them the oldest known residences of Buddhist monks in South India. Remains of Buddhist monuments have also been found near the village of Arithapatti, in the Kalugumalai range.

Koṅkanapura

Concerning this area, Hsüan-tsang wrote: "The land is rich and fertile; it is regularly cultivated and produces large crops. The climate is hot and the disposition of the people ardent and quick. Their complexion is black and their manners fierce and uncultivated. They love learning and esteem virtue and talent." (HT II:254) At Koṅkanapura, Hsüan-tsang counted one hundred monasteries and about ten thousand monks of the Śrāvakayāna and Mahāyāna traditions. A large monastery with about three hundred monks stood beside the royal palace; its temple was over a hundred feet high. In this temple was a jeweled tiara said to belong to the prince Sarvārthasidda (the Buddha's name before his enlightenment).

Outside the city was another large monastery about fifty feet high, which held a sandalwood image of Maitreya Bodhisattva said to have been carved by the Arhat Śroṇaviṁśatikoṭi, a disciple of the Buddha and son of a wealthy merchant of Campā. At King Bimbisāra's invitation, Śroṇaviṁśatikoṭi traveled to Rājagṛha to meet the Buddha and entered the Sangha soon after. Various archaeologists have suggested Vanavāsa, Annagundhi, and Kokanur as possible sites of the ancient Koṅkanapura; the most recent writings on the subject identify Vanavāsa with Koṅkanapura.

Vanavāsa

Vanavāsa was the destination of the Thera Rakkhita, when Mogalliputta Tissa sent out nine missions to all parts of India after the council at Pāṭaliputra. At Vanavāsa, Rakkhita, rising in the air, proclaimed the Anamatagga Saṁyutta and converted sixty thousand persons to the Dharma. As a result of this teaching, thirty or thirty-seven thousand people joined the Sangha and fifty monasteries were established.

Vanavāsa is mentioned in the Mahāvaṁsa as one of the monasteries flourishing during the Śuṅga Dynasty (c. 186–173 B.C.E.). During this period Vanavāsa sent a delegation of eighty thousand bhikṣus under the leadership of Candagutta to attend ceremonies consecrating the Mahāthūpa of Anurādhapura. An inscription found in the largest cave temple at Kārlī, records that this temple, excavated during the first century C.E., was sponsored by a Buddhist merchant of Vaijayanti (Vanavāsī).

Although Vanavāsa (Vanavāsī) was named as a Buddhist center in inscriptions as well as in Sanskrit and Pāli texts, only recently have physical remains of its existence been located. Ancient Vanavāsa is generally equated with modern Banavāsi, which in turn is associated with Vaijayanti, the early capital of the Kadambas. Banavāsi is located in the northern Kanara district on the Varadā River, east of the Tuṅgabhadrā River. An inscription found there dates from the Caṭukula-Sātakarṇi Dynasty. (Lüders 1186) Recent excavations at Banavāsi have unearthed the remains of a Buddhist stūpa, revealing a base with the radiating spokes of a Dharmacakra, similar to stūpas found in Nāgārjunakoṇḍa.

Aihole

The most complete Buddhist monument found to date in Karṇāṭaka is a two-storied temple located at Aihole on the Meguti Hill. The lower part of the structure has been excavated from the rock and the upper story erected through construction. The temple, the oldest structure at Aihole, appears to date from the first part of the sixth century C.E.; its ceilings and doors are carved with scenes of the life of the Buddha and episodes from the Jātakas. A large sculpture of a Bodhisattva stands near the entrance to the hill.

Badami and Dambal

A Buddhist cave dating to the sixth century C.E. has been located at Badami, the capital of the Cālukya kings, as has an image of the Bodhisattva Padmapāṇi. At Dambal, in the Dharwar District, an inscription carved in 1095 C.E. records that sixteen merchants erected a monastery and a temple dedicated to Tārā here during the reign of Lakṣmīdevī, queen of Vikramāditya VI. A second shrine or temple to Tārā was sponsored at Dambal by Sangaramaya of Lokkigundi.

Goa

The Portuguese protectorate of Goa, situated on the western coast just above the state of Karṇāṭaka, appears to have supported a Buddhist community. Aśnikita, king of the Bhojas who occupied this area in the sixth century C.E., donated land for a Buddhist vihāra here, and sculptures from a later date have been found in the village of Muśir.

Buddhism in Modern Karṇāṭaka

In recent times, scholars researching Karṇāṭaka's religious history have pointed out instances where Hindu cults arose around figures that were actually Bodhisattvas. Both Avalokiteśvara and Mañjuśrī appear to have been at some point accepted as Śaivite deities. Additional remnants of Buddhism can be seen in certain religious movements that arose in medieval Karṇāṭaka, most noticeably in the teachings of Basava in the twelfth century. (BSI 90–91)

New Buddhist movements began to form in Karṇāṭaka as early as 1900, when the South India Buddhist Association of Madras undertook missionary work among the Tamil laborers of the Kolar Gold Fields and founded the Buddha Vihāra at Champion Reef. Since then, the Mahābodhi Society of India has established a Buddha Vihāra in Bangalore, which developed into an active center under the Ācārya Buddharakkhita. The Aśoka Vihāra, in the city of Mysore, is another recently established Buddhist center.

Since 1959, when Tibetans fled their homeland, Tibetan settlements have been established in Bylakuppe, near Mysore; in Mundgod, in the North Kanara district; in Cauvery Valley; and in Kollegal. With them the Tibetans brought their knowledge and strong devotion to Buddhism, and have worked diligently to reestablish their cultural and religious traditions. Among the Tibetan monasteries established to date, the largest are Thegchay Ling and Namgoling. Both of these Tibetan centers are located in Bylakuppe.

Part Seven

Prācya
The Eastern Kingdoms

TIBET
Kathmandu
UTTAR PRADESH
NEPAL
SIKKIM
BHUTAN
ARUNCHAL PRADESH
ASSAM
NAGALAND
Dinajpur
Rangpur
MEGHALAYA
Patna
Monghyur
Bhagalpur
Somapurī
BIHAR
Campā
Kajughira
Karṇasuvarṇa
BANGLA DESH
MANIPURA
TRIPURA
Comilla
MIZORAM
WEST BENGAL
MADHYA PRADESH
Rangamati
Tāmralipti
Chittagong
BURMA
Raipur
ORISSA
Ratnagiri
Bhubaneswar
Puri
Caritrapura
Gañjam
Udayagiri
Warangal
Kaliṅganagara
Sālihuṇḍam
ANDHRA PRADESH
Amāravatī
Nāgārjunakoṇḍa
BAY OF BENGAL

Vaṅga and Kaliṅga

The lands of eastern India have distinctive cultures and customs that transcend political boundaries. At the time of the Buddha, these lands took their name from the independent tribes that inhabited them. The Vaṅgas occupied the southern part of West Bengal and the Kaliṅgas lived in modern Orissa and northern Āndhra. Although Buddhism took root here a little later than in other regions of India, the Dharma flourished in these lands for many centuries.

Prācya, the Eastern Region, refers to all the lands east and southeast of the Madhyadeśa; it includes the modern states of West Bengal, Assam, Tripura, and Orissa, as well as the country of Bangladesh. This Eastern Region embraced people of widely diverse cultures, from those in the Brahmanic fold who entered this area from the west to the indigenous cultural groups who had come into eastern India from the north and southeast, largely through Nepal and Burma. At the time of the Buddha, most of the provinces east of the Ganges were populated by aboriginal hill tribes with their own range of cultures, customs, and languages.

In contrast to the west and northwest, where the Dharma took root quickly, Buddhism developed slowly in the eastern lands. The Jain religion, founded by Mahāvīra, a contemporary of the Buddha, spread more rapidly in the east and enjoyed the support of many eastern rulers. Although the early patriarch Dhītika worked for the Dharma in the east, Buddhism did not take hold here until the time of Aśoka.

For clarity, the lands discussed in this section are grouped into units that share a similar Buddhist heritage: Vaṅga and Kaliṅga, now West Bengal and Orissa; Puṇḍravardhana and Samataṭa, modern Bangladesh; and Assam and Tripura, both states of India to the east of Bangladesh.

Vaṅga and Kaliṅga

Although Bengal is now divided into west (India) and east (Bangladesh), historically, two major kingdoms—Vaṅga in the south and Gauḍa in the north—were merged to form the state of Bengal. The ancient kingdom of Vaṅga roughly corresponded to the southern half of modern West Bengal, and the kingdom of Kalinga occupied the area now known as Orissa. The boundaries of the old kingdoms shifted over the centuries. At various times northern Kaliṅga became known as Utkala, Oḍra, and Orissa, while southern Kaliṅga, the land between the Mahānadī and Godāvarī rivers, retained its original name. Most of ancient Kaliṅga is now part of the modern state of Orissa and its southernmost region is part of the state of Āndhra Pradesh. The Buddhist sites of India's eastern coast will be presented here as if traveling from north to south, beginning with Vaṅga (West Bengal) and proceeding south through Utkala (northern Orissa) and Kaliṅga (southern Orissa and northern Āndhra).

Flowing eastward from the great cities of the Madhyadeśa, the Ganges River gave traveling bhikṣus ready access to the lands in its path. Reaching the coastal city of Tāmralipti (modern Tamluk, southwest of Calcutta) bhikṣus traveled south along the coastline, making inland detours through nearly impassable jungles. From the coast of Kaliṅga one could travel, as Hsüan-tsang did, inland to Mahākosala (also known as Dakṣiṇa-kosala). But the east was not always hospitable to travelers; the climate was tropical, the terrain often difficult, and the people belonged to a wide range of cultures with different customs and languages. Brigands roamed the countryside, waylaying unwary travelers.

The eastern lands were relatively isolated from the Madhyadeśa until the middle of the third century B.C.E., when Aśoka annexed Vaṅga and subjugated Kaliṅga in a devastating invasion. Perhaps to heal the sufferings of the Kaliṅgans, Aśoka ruled Kaliṅga benevolently. His reign linked Kaliṅga with the Madhyadeśa and his support of Buddhism gave bhikṣus easier access to this once remote region.

Aśoka's successors, the later Mauryan kings, were supplanted by the rulers of the Śuṅga Dynasty. By the time Śuṅga power waned around 50 B.C.E., Kaliṅga and its southern neighbor, Āndhra, had become major centers of Buddhism on India's eastern coast. As the kings of the Madhyadeśa lost their hold on the eastern regions, the main current of the Dharma began to flow from the south: Bhikṣus from Āndhra and Śrī Laṅkā sent monks to the coastal cities of Kaliṅganagara and Tāmralipti to support the growth of the Dharma. An inscription at Nāgārjunakoṇḍa relates that Sinhalese bhikṣus had also converted the Kaliṅgan cities of Tosalī and Palura. Vaṅga, Orissa, and Kaliṅga became relatively autonomous until the third century C.E. Between 385–413 C.E., Kaliṅga paid tribute to the kings of the Gupta empire, but otherwise maintained its independence.

Although Kaliṅga remained free from the influence of northern rulers, in the eighth century, the Bengali leaders united under Gopāla to form the Pāla Empire, bringing all of Vaṅga and the northern parts of Orissa under a single government. Thus strengthened, the Pāla Empire soon extended as far east as Vārāṇasī and embraced the entire Ganges Valley from Vārāṇasī to the Bay of Bengal. The Buddhist communities of Vaṅga and Orissa, connected directly to the Sanghas and universities of the Madhyadeśa, flourished under the Buddhist Pāla kings' umbrella of protection and support. The Mahāyāna traditions in particular benefited from this connection. The study and practice of Vajrayāna became especially strong in the hill monasteries and remote retreats of Orissa.

From the eighth to the twelfth century, the Pāla kings continued to patronize the great Buddhist monasteries in their realm. They established new universities and sponsored the artistic masterpieces for which the Pāla Empire became famous throughout the Buddhist world. In supporting religion, literature, and the arts, the Pālas forged the Bengali peoples into a strong cultural unity. Among the distinguished centers to arise in their empire was the Traikūṭaka Monastery, where Haribhadra, disciple of Śāntarakṣita, composed his commentary on the Aṣṭasāhasrika-prajñāpāramitā. The Traikūṭaka Monastery is thought to have been located in the Rāḍha country of modern West Bengal.

Bengal was the home of the seventh-century master Candragomin, renowned as the greatest lay scholar of India, and of Atīśa, Vikramaśīla's outstanding paṇḍita who assisted the second transmission of the Dharma to Tibet in the early eleventh century. Its reputation for excellence in Mantrayāna studies was well established in the tenth century, when Ānandagarbha, after his studies at Vikramaśīla, went to Bengal to study the Yoga Tantras with Prakāśacandra, king of siddhas, and the master Subhūtipālita. His fame attracted Prajñāpālita from Magadha and very likely others as well. (Tar 285-286)

The siddhas appeared to have flourished in Bengal from the eighth century onward. According to Abhayadatta, who compiled biographies of the siddhas in the eleventh or early twelfth century, the siddha Jayānanda was a Bengali king's minister; the long-lived siddha Putali was a Bengali, as was the siddha Mekhopa, a foodseller. Gorakṣa the herdsman,

Caurāṅgi the mutilated prince, and Thagana, who attained siddhi from meditating on falsehood, were all from eastern India, most likely from Bengal.

The Sena kings who supplanted the Pālas in the twelfth century revived the Hindu traditions and withdrew support from the Buddhist centers. Unable to protect the remains of the empire, the Senas retreated into the southern part of Bengal, where their lineage came to an end in the mid-thirteenth century. While most monastic centers appear to have been destroyed in the thirteenth century, it is likely that the Mantrayāna tradition, which did not rely so strongly on central institutions, continued in the east long after the destruction of the great monastic universities. Between Vaṅga and Kaliṅga, the possibilities for survival were greatest in Kaliṅga, which remained free from Muslim occupation.

Tāmralipti

The city of Tāmralipti (modern Tamluk) was located in what is now the Midnapur District of West Bengal. However, in ancient times, the name Tāmralipti applied not only to the thriving seaport that served the region as its capital city, but to the whole of the southwestern part of the Ganges Delta as well. Known to Ptolemy as Tamalites and to Pliny as Taluctoe, Tāmralipti was a prosperous international center of commerce linked by sea routes to Śrī Laṅkā, Burma, China, and the empire of Śrī Vijaya (modern Indonesia). It was known to Mahāsāṁghika bhikṣus from Āndhra, to the south, who propagated the Dharma in Tāmralipti between the second and fifth centuries C.E. From the port itself, they sailed to southeast Asia, even to the coast of China, although this was known to be a long and dangerous journey.

The Dharma probably reached its height in Tāmralipti in the fifth century, when Fa-hien, who stayed in the area two years copying Dharma texts before sailing to Śrī Laṅkā, counted twenty-four active monasteries. In the seventh century, Hsüan-tsang noted ten monasteries with about one thousand monks. Modern excavations on the sites of Kurahar and Bulandibagh have revealed the remains of a pillared hall dating to Mauryan times, as well as the Arogya Vihāra and remains of other monasteries.

Kaliṅga/Orissa

At its fullest extent, the kingdom of Kaliṅga extended along the east coast of India from the Ganges Delta to the Godāvarī River. The Mahavagga, a Pāli Vinaya text, indicates that the province of Ukkala occupied the northern part of this region, although the Mahāvastu, a Mahāsāṁghika text, places Utkala in the northern region of Uttarāpatha. By Hsüan-tsang's time, the lands north of the Mahānadī River were known as Oḍra, or Orissa, and Kaliṅga stretched along the eastern coast from the Mahānādī south to the Godāvarī River. Inland from the eastern coast kingdoms was the land known as Dakṣiṇakosala (southern Kosala) or Mahākosala (greater Kosala), which is now part of Madhya Pradesh.

In Aśoka's time, Kaliṅga roughly comprised what is now the modern Purī and Gañjām districts and part of the Cuttack District of Orissa. Its fiercely independent people resisted the influence of outside cultures and maintained their autonomy until forced to yield to Aśoka. Aśoka's war with Kaliṅga, in which hundreds of thousands were slain, affected Aśoka so greatly that he renounced all form of aggression from that time onward. After the war, Aśoka took a special interest in this region. Fourteen Aśokan rock edicts and two special edicts have been found in the hills near the village of Dhauli, a few miles southwest of Bhuvaneśwar. (Dhauli has been identified with ancient Tosalī, where Śrī Laṅkan bhikkhus once propagated the Dharma.) Aśokan edicts have also been found at Jaugadha, in the Gañjām District of modern Orissa. According to Hsüan-tsang, Aśoka built ten stūpas commemorating sites where the Buddha taught the Dharma and erected additional stūpas commemorating visits of the four previous Buddhas. Kaliṅga received a tooth relic of the Buddha, which was enshrined in a stūpa at Dantapura. (Dantapura means Fort or City of the Tooth; it is likely that the city was named for this event.)

Before Aśoka, the greater part of Kaliṅga's populace followed the Jain tradition; after Aśoka joined Kaliṅga to his empire, Buddhism took hold strongly. The commentary on the Theragāthā (Aṭṭhakatha) records that Aśoka's brother Mogalliputta Tissa retired to the land of the Kaliṅgas, where Aśoka built him the Bhojakagiri Monastery. According to Buddhaghosa's Samantapāsādikā, eight families of Kaliṅga were in the retinue of Aśoka's daughter, the nun Sanghamittā, when she took a branch of the Bodhi Tree from India to Śrī Laṅkā. For centuries thereafter, Buddhism in Kaliṅga was closely connected with Śrī Laṅkā. According to an inscription found at Nāgārjunakoṇḍa, Sinhalese monks established monasteries in the Kaliṅgan cities of Tosalī and Palura, as well as in Tāmralipti to the north.

In the centuries after Aśoka's reign, the Dharma became well-established in northern Kaliṅga. Tāranātha relates that during the reign of Aśoka's grandson Vigatāśoka. the wealthy Brahmin Raghava, who had become a Buddhist, asked the Arhat Posada to convene a great assembly of Arhats. Posada invited the Arhats and Raghava provided for their sustenance for three years. (Tar 78)

After the end of the Śuṅga Dynasty around 75 B.C.E., Kaliṅga was probably autonomous for a time, although little is actually known of that historical period. Around 50 B.C.E., Khāravela, a warrior of the Ceḍi clan, became king and forged Kaliṅga into a major power. In Indian histories, Khāravela is famed for encouraging the spread of Indian culture overseas, particularly in Suvarṇadvīpa, the golden land of southern Burma. For a time, Khāravela was a threat to the rulers of northern Indian kingdoms. Extending his influence into the Madhyadeśa, he attacked Rājagṛha around 50 B.C.E. He defeated the Pandya king in the far south and entered the lands of the Sātavāhanas to the west.

Although Khāravela was a patron of all religious traditions, he appears to have been a devout Jain and was known as the 'Bhikṣu King.' The rulers of Kaliṅga from 350 C.E. onward appear to have been strong followers of the Jain and Brahmanic traditions, and after the seventh century the rulers were all Jains. Buddhism co-existed with Jainism and the Brahmanic traditions throughout its history in Kaliṅga.

Hsüan-tsang describes Oḍra (Orissa) and Kaliṅga as separate kingdoms. At the time of Hsüan-tsang's visit in the mid-seventh century, King Harṣa's rule extended over most of north India. Although Orissa was technically within his empire, the Orissan Śailodbhava kings continued to rule, and Kaliṅga maintained its autonomy. Hsüan-tsang notes that although the people, the culture, and the language of Orissa differed significantly from those of Vaṅga to the north, many applied themselves diligently to knowledge, and most of the people of this region were Buddhists.

Although in the kingdom of Orissa Hsüan-tsang found only ten stūpas dating from Aśokan times, he reports that the Dharma was flourishing at the time of his visit. There were one hundred monasteries and ten thousand monks in Orissa alone, and all were associated with the Mahāyāna. Several centuries earlier, the Mahāyāna traditions had begun to develop strongly in Orissa. Nāgārjuna and Vasubandhu, a fourth or fifth century Mahāyāna philosopher, are both said to have founded temples in Orissa.

Orissa, remote from the currents of north Indian empires, appears to have long been considered a place of retreat: the master logician Dignāga (c. fifth century C.E.) retired to Orissa to meditate and to write his great treatise, the Pramāṇasamuccaya. Hsüan-tsang describes the Puṣpagiri, or Flower Mountain Monastery, as the site of a stūpa renown for its wonders; this was a popular gathering place of the Buddhist laypeople, who came to offer flowers and incense.

According to Tāranātha, there were upheavals in both Bengal and Orissa in the early eighth century just before Gopāla, the first Pāla king, founded his empire. The Kara kings came to power in Orissa about the same time as Gopāla became king of Bengal. Since the Kara kings considered themselves descended from an 'earth lineage' (as distinct from the Brahmanic solar and lunar lineages), they called themselves Bhaumas, 'of the earth', and are often referred to as Bhaumakaras. The first three Bhaumakara kings strongly supported Buddhist communities, constructed monasteries, and sponsored extensive art projects. Jajpur, their capital city, was a flourishing Buddhist center during the reign of the later Gupta and Bhaumakara kings. Mahāyāna images dating from the eighth century have been found here. Among them was a sixteen foot-high image of the Bodhisattva Padmapāṇi and an image of Vajrasattva found at Salempur. Further south, on the northern bank of the Virūpa (Birupa) River, images of Prajñāpāramitā and Avalokiteśvara were discovered in the ruins of the city of Cauduar. (BCAI 207)

Tāranātha's *History*, Abhayadatta's *Lives of the Eighty-four Great Siddhas,* and other sources mention Orissa as the home of many great siddhas, including Luyi-pa and Darika, who was once an Orissan king. From the tenth century onward, Orissa attracted masters from Tibet seeking to obtain the siddha's knowledge and lineages. Archaeological finds in the Āsia Hill range indicate that the Mahāyāna flourished here between the eighth and twelfth centuries, when the intensive practice of Vajrayāna made this area an important place in the transmission of the Tantras. Further study of Buddhist sites in Orissa promises to yield valuable information on the later development of the Mahāyāna in India.

The Āsia Hills: Ratnagiri, Udayagiri, and Lalitagiri

Mahāyāna Buddhism flourished for centuries in the Āsia Hills along the Virūpa River, where extensive ruins of three major centers have been unearthed at Ratnagiri, Lalitagiri, and Udayagiri. Collectively, these monasteries appear to have been an important center for study and practice of the Vajrayāna. Located northeast of modern Cuttack, Ratnagiri was a major Buddhist center dating from the fifth century C.E. or possibly earlier. The script in use during Gupta times has been found on several stone slabs there, one bearing the image of Avalokiteśvara and others inscribed with the text of the Pratītyasamutpāda-sūtra. The Ratnagiri Mahāvihāra and a second monastery were built on the western side of the hill, and stūpas were erected on the eastern side. The Ratnagiri Mahāvihāra, clearly identified on terracotta seals found at the site, is nearly square, measuring 181½ × 180 feet, while the second monastery is somewhat smaller, about ninety-five feet on each side. Remains of sculptures found here are all related to the Mahāyāna and Vajrayāna traditions.

Tradition records that Bodhiśrī, Nāropa, and other great siddhas lived and practiced on Ratnagiri, the Hill of Jewels. Later, after the destruction of the great universities of the Madhyadeśa, this area probably provided a last refuge for Buddhist scholars and practitioners. The museum in Bhubaneśwar now houses seven Buddhist sculptures found in Orissan sites—representations of the Buddha, Avalokiteśvara, Mañjuśrī, Vajrapāṇi, and Tārā that have partially survived the centuries. Additional images found in Orissa were sent to Calcutta's Indian Museum and elsewhere in India.

The main stūpa of Ratnagiri, built around the eighth century, appears to have been erected over the ruins of an earlier stūpa, possibly constructed as early as the fifth century. Ruins of a large number of smaller stūpas were ornamented with carvings of images of the Buddha, Avalokiteśvara, and Tārā, as well as of specifically Vajrayāna representations.

Ruins of a monastery at Ratnagiri

Hundreds of small votive stūpas ornamented with carved Vajrayāna symbols and deities, together with plaques inscribed with Dhāraṇīs, were found near the main stūpa.

Additional remains of Buddhist monuments and buildings have been found on a hill at Lalitagiri, which was known to have been an important Mahāyāna center. Mounds nearby have yielded statues of the Buddha and the Great Bodhisattvas, tentatively dated from the eighth century.

Udayagiri, the southernmost of the three sites, may have been a center of Vajrayāna Buddhism. Hsüan-tsang described two stūpas in this region erected on sites where miraculous events occurred. One was at the monastery of Puṣpagiri, and the other on a hill to the northwest. This description could have referred to the Udayagiri and Khaṇḍagiri hills, which lie close together, separated by a decline that serves as the roadbed of the route linking Bhubaneśwar and Chandka. Remains of a number of statues of Buddhas and Bodhisattvas, including a twelve-armed representation of Prajñāpāramitā and an eight-armed sculpture of the protectress Mārīcī, have been found on Udayagiri. The Udayagiri and Khaṇḍagiri hills are the site of two large cave complexes associated with King

Khāravela—the Hāthi Gumphā and the Rāṇi Gumphā. However, it is not certain whether these caves were affiliated with the Buddhist or Jain traditions.

Caritrapura

Hsüan-tsang describes the walled seaport of Caritra as teeming with traders from foreign lands. Outside the city he found a cluster of five monasteries "of lofty structure and with very artistic images." He writes that from the high points of the coast he could see, toward the island of Sinhāla, the stone of the tooth-relic stūpa "brilliantly shining and scintillating as a bright torch burning in the air." (HT II:206) Caritrapura appears to have been close to modern Purī, home of the Jagganātha temple, which some scholars believe may have originally been the site of a Buddhist center. (BCAI 204)

Kaliṅganagara

Several great masters of the Mahāyāna are associated with the Kaliṅgan capital of Kaliṅganagara and regions south of the Mahānadī River. The fifth-century Mādhyamika scholar Buddhapālita is said to have taught the Dharma in Dantapurī; Dharmakīrti built a temple in Kaliṅga in the seventh century, and the eighth century master Śāntideva lived near Kaliṅganagara after leaving Nālandā University. All three masters are said to have passed away in the land of Kaliṅga.

The route southwest to Kaliṅganagara led through desert, jungle, and forest, "the trees of which mount to heaven and hide the sun." Hsüan-tsang notes that "the climate is burning; the disposition of the people vehement and impetuous." (HT II:207–208) The small towns in this coastal region between the the Mahānadī and Godāvarī rivers were lightly populated, and there were few practicing Buddhists. Most of the people belonged to religions other than Buddhism, particularly Jainism. Ten monasteries housed about five hundred monks who studied the Mahāyāna according to the teaching of the Sthavira school. South of Kaliṅganagara, Hsüan-tsang saw an Aśokan stūpa one hundred feet tall, built to commemorate the visit of the four past Buddhas of the Bhadrakalpa. Excavation of the numerous mounds in this area that may some day yield clues to the growth of the Sangha along India's eastern coast.

Sālihuṇḍam

To the north of Kaliṅganagara, Hsüan-tsang described a stone stūpa about a hundred feet high on top of a mountain precipice. "Here, at the beginning of the kalpa, when the years of men's lives were boundless, a Pratyekabuddha attained nirvāṇa." (HT II:209) This site has been tentatively identified as Mt. Sālihuṇḍam, located in the Gañjām district, on the south bank of the Vaṁṣadhārā River and six miles west of Kaliṅgapatnam. A whole complex of Buddhist monuments was discovered and explored here between 1943 and 1947. An inscription on pottery found at the site, dated in the second century C.E., records that the pottery belonged to the Kaṭṭahārāma, a monastery endowed by the descendants of the Rāṣṭrapālaka Haṁkudeyika. (HIB 343) Ruins of stūpas, statues, and brick vihāras found here and in the region of the village of Sālihuṇḍam include representations of Tārā and Māricī, indicating that this was a center of Mahāyāna and Vajrayāna traditions. It appears to have flourished at least until the seventh century.

Caskets found in the remains of the stūpa of Sālihuṇḍam contained three crystal stūpas. One stūpa was rounded, like the ancient stūpa of Sāñcī; the second was bell-shaped; and the third was more elongated in shape, surrounded with elegantly carved railings. It is thought that these crystal stūpas represent three stages of the Sālihuṇḍam Stūpa's growth: the original construction and two renovations, resulting in its final appearance, which closely resembled the great stūpas of Amarāvatī and Nāgārjunakoṇḍa.

Inland: Mahākosala (Dakṣiṇakosala)

Northwest, in the interior, between the Mahānadī and Godāvarī rivers, Hsuan-tsang came to the land of Mahākosala, which probably refers to southeastern Madhya Pradesh. Mahākosala is also called Dakṣiṇakosala, or South Kosala, to distinguish it from the kingdom of Kosala in the Madhyadeśa. Hsüan-tsang describes this mountain-girt region as being eighteen hundred li or at least three hundred miles inland to the northwest of Kaliṅganagara, An Aśokan stūpa marked the place where the Buddha demonstrated his powers so the Dharma could thrive unhindered in this region. In the seventh century, Mahākosala was a strong Mahāyāna center with a hundred monasteries housing ten thousand monks.

Hsüan-tsang relates that the Brahmaragiri Mountain, located about fifty miles to the southwest, was where King Sadvaha, at great cost, had tunneled out a magnificent monastery in the rock for Nāgārjuna. In each of the monastery's five stories were four halls connected by a vihāra, and in each vihāra a gold lifesize image of the Buddha ornamented with precious stones. Small streams flowed down through the five levels, and light from holes venting to the top of the cave illuminated the interior.

The king assembled one thousand monks to dwell in this monastery, and Nāgārjuna collected all the Buddha's teachings, the explanatory works of the Bodhisattvas, and the miscellaneous writings, and placed them on the uppermost level. On the lowest level lived Brahmins who attended to the monastery, and on the second to fourth levels lived the monks and their disciples. At some point the monks quarreled; when they left the cave to present their disagreements before the king for resolution, the Brahmins took advantage of this opportunity to destroy the monastery and barricade it against the monks' return. According to Hsüan-tsang, after that the Brahmins have allowed no one to see the route in or out of this region.

The site of Hsüan-tsang's Mahākosala has proven elusive; some scholars associate it with Warangal, a city about the right distance inland and northwest of Kaliṇganagara. However, no Buddhist sites have been found there, leading other scholars to adjust the pilgrim's directions to the southwest, and equate Mahākosala with Amāravatī or Nāgārjunakoṇḍa, sites more often associated with the great master Nāgārjuna.

However, Buddhist art and the remains of temples have been found inland along the Mahānadī River near Śrīpura (modern Sirpur, near Raipur, in southeastern Madhya Pradesh). A large stone image of the Buddha was found in the ruins of one of the monasteries here. Inscriptions indicate that the Śaivite king of this area, Mahāśivagupta Balārjuna, was an important patron of Buddhism, and it is likely that the temples and monasteries of Śrīpura were built during his reign. But the great number of cast metal images found here indicate a longer period of royal patronage beginning around the late seventh or eighth century. These images are very similar to seventh- through ninth-century images found at Nālandā, suggesting a close connection between Buddhists of Mahākosala and Magadha. (AAI:418)

Mahāśivagupta Balārjuna's mother was from the Maukari Dynasty that ruled Magadha before the rise of the Pālas, which very likely contributed to Magadha's influence on this region's artistic tradition. An exquisite metal image of Tārā seated on a lion-throne and attended by two of her manifestations, together with similar finds, indicate that the Mahāyāna was strong in this area. Here, protected from the upheavals of the Muslim invasions, Buddhism could well have survived through the twelfth century or even longer. Further explorations in the Śrīpura region may extend knowledge of the last centuries of the Dharma in India. (AAI:419)

Puṇḍravardhana and Samataṭa

Although Buddhist texts and histories name some famous monasteries of eastern Bengal, it is only in this century that archaeological excavations have revealed the size and extent of the Buddhist centers that once flourished here.

The ancient provinces of Puṇḍravardhana (north), and Samataṭa (south) encompassed the area roughly equivalent to modern Bangladesh and the bordering districts of India. A third province is sometimes delineated in the center to accommodate the independent city-state of Karṇasuvarṇa. In ancient times the entryway to the entire eastern region was through the city of Kajughira (also known as Kajaṅgala), located on the Ganges River at the point where the great waterway begins to subdivide into the many arms of its huge delta. To the north, between the Ganges and Brahmaputra rivers, was Puṇḍravardhana, the land of the Puṇḍra tribe. Southeast, on the lower Ganges Delta, lay the area known as Samataṭa, the Level Country, named for its flat flood plain that rose to an equal height on each side of the river. Samataṭa included the modern district of Chittagong, a strip of coastal land that arcs southeast to northern Burma.

Hsüan-tsang's records provide the most complete first-hand account of Buddhism in India's easternmost region. Additional information can be found in Tāranātha's *History of Buddhism in India* and gleaned from modern archaeological research. It is a great misfortune that the tides of political change and the scarcity of funds have impeded efforts to recover the heritage of ancient Bangladesh. Since the use of archaeological sites cannot be governed by the interests of science, an incredible wealth of ruins have been destroyed in modern times, often within view of the scientists who appreciated their cultural value. What has been preserved and identified to date verifies that the Buddhist centers flourished in Bangladesh through the twelfth century. Long past that date, the Buddha's teachings continued to inspire the many laypeople here who continued to rely on the Buddhist teachings as a support and guide for their lives.

The Buddhist texts record that the Buddha visited these eastern lands. In teaching the Dharma in Samataṭa and Karṇasuvarṇa for seven days and in the land of the Puṇḍras for three months, he blessed this region as a future home of the Dharma. For several centuries, little more is known of how Buddhism developed in these regions; it is possible that it did not advance far beyond the city of Kajughira, gateway to the eastern provinces and the Bay of Bengal, until after the time of Aśoka, since none of the nine missions sent out in Aśoka's time to propagate the Dharma appear to have settled here. In later years the Chinese travelers noted only a few Aśokan stūpas in Karṇasuvarṇa and one each in the kingdoms of Puṇḍravardhana and Samataṭa.

In the fifth century C.E., and possibly earlier, pilgrims arriving by sea from China, Śrī Vijaya (modern Indonesia), Śrī Laṅkā, and Burma were disembarking at Tāmralipti and passing through Kajughira on their way to the holy sites of Bodh Gayā and Sārnāth. The monastery of Nālandā, which became a major university in the fifth century, began to attract an ever-increasing number of students from countries outside India. Many traveled the route from Tāmralipti to Kajughira, stopping at monasteries along the way. In the seventh century Hsüan-tsang and I-tsing both traveled extensively in the region watered by the Ganges Delta. The number of Buddhists living in the east or arriving here from foreign lands may have been a factor in locating Somapurī, Vikramaśīla, and other large monasteries east of Nālandā.

Kajughira (Kajaṅgala)

Hsüan-tsang describes the land between Kajughira (near modern Rājmahal) and Samataṭa as rich and productive, endowed with a warm climate, and populated by hospitable people who honored learning and the arts. At the time of Hsüan-tsang's visit, the royal line of Kajughira had died out, and the kingdom was being administered by a neighboring state; the towns were nearly deserted, and most of the populace resided in villages. Wild elephants roamed the southern frontiers. Hsüan-tsang notes six or seven monasteries with about three hundred monks and at least ten temples of various Brahmanic sects, but he gives no further details as to the affiliations or history of the monasteries. Near the Ganges he saw a great stūpa made of bricks and stone, with sculptured figures of devas, Buddhas, and Brahmanic saints in its niches.

Karṇasuvarṇa

Hsüan-tsang describes Karṇasuvarṇa, east of Kajughira, as a prosperous country populated by people who supported learning. In its environs were ten monasteries housing two thousand monks of the Saṁmitīya tradition, together with three monasteries that still followed the rules of the religious order established by the Buddha's cousin Devadatta. Raktaviti, a large monastery with multistoried towers, was at this time a celebrated center where the most distinguished and learned Buddhist masters assembled to engage in dialogue and exchange views. This custom was established after a debate between two men who came to Karṇasuvarṇa from South India: a tīrthika (non-Buddhist) philosopher and a learned Buddhist śramaṇa (monk).

The tīrthika master went about beating on copper plates he had attached to his body, challenging all the learned men of that place to debate with him. But none dared accept the challenge. Finally one scholar remembered a śramaṇa who had been living in the area in silence and obscurity. The śramaṇa agreed to a debate on the condition that, if he won, the king would build a monastery and invite monks to establish a center there. The śramaṇa defeated the heretic with his knowledge and skill in logic; impressed, the king founded the monastery of Raktaviti as he had promised and supported the teaching of the Dharma in his kingdom. In recent years ruins of an ancient city were discovered at Raṅgamāṭi in the Murshidabad District of West Bengal. This site, identified as ancient Karṇasuvarṇa, has yielded some Buddhist images.

Puṇḍravardhana

According to Hsüan-tsang, Puṇḍravardhana, the Sugarcane Country, was located about one hundred miles east of Kajughira. As mentioned above, the Buddha taught the Dharma at Puṇḍravardhana for three months during an unusually long stay outside the Madhyadeśa. The Sumāgadhāvadāna relates that the Buddha visited Puṇḍravardhana at the request of Sumāgadha, daughter of Anāthapiṇḍada, generous patron of the Sangha. Married to a merchant of Puṇḍravardhana, Sumāgadha was distressed at the beliefs and customs of her husband's family, and prayed to the Buddha to bring the Dharma to her new home. In response to her prayers, the

Buddha came with his disciples and turned the wheel of the Dharma in this remote land.

Inscriptions at Sāñcī dated around the time of the Śuṅga Dynasty (c. 187–75 B.C.E.) mention donations received from laypeople of Puṇḍravardhana, indicating that the Dharma was known and venerated in this region in the early centuries B.C.E. Hsüan-tsang describes Puṇḍravardhana as a prosperous kingdom with about twenty monasteries housing a total of three thousand monks who studied within both the Śrāvaka and Mahāyāna teachings.

West of Puṇḍranagara, Puṇḍravardhana's main city, was the large Po-chi-p'o (Brightness of Fire) Monastery, variously translated as Vaśibhasaṁghārāma, Bhasa Vihāra, or Vasu Bihār. At the time of Hsüan-tsang's visit this spacious monastery housed seven hundred Mahāyāna monks, including many renowned monks from eastern India. Nearby was the Aśokan stūpa commemorating the place where the Buddha gave teachings at Puṇḍravardhana. Occasionally the stūpa was seen to emit a bright light. A neighboring vihāra housed a statue of Avalokiteśvara, which was visited by travelers from far and near.

From the eighth century onward, most of Puṇḍravardhana came under the rule of the Pāla kings, who supported the building and maintenance of major Buddhist centers in this province for centuries after Hsüan-tsang's visit. At least three major sites have been located to date in ancient Puṇḍravardhana: the Bhasa Vihāra described by Hsüan-tsang, the great vihāra of Somapurī, and the Sitakot Monastery.

Bhasa Vihāra

In 1879, Cunningham located the ruins of Bhasa Vihāra four miles northwest of the railway station of Mahāsthān in the vicinity of the Shibganj Police Station of Bogra District. Excavations revealed two monasteries and a central temple, a large number of mounds and extensive ruins of the city of Puṇḍranagara and its environs. The Mahāsthān Museum was built in the center of the site, which radiates out four miles in each direction. The monastery grounds, which measured eight hundred by seven hundred feet, encompassed three large mounds and two small ones; before excavation the height of the tallest mound was thirty-one feet. Excavation revealed a moat-like depression around the monastery, indicating the presence of a man-made lake. Among the forty-two large bronze images found here were representations of the Buddhas Śākyamuni and Akṣobhya, and the Bodhisattvas Padmapāṇi, Vajrapāṇi, Mañjuśrī, and Tārā. Ninety inscribed terracotta sealings, thirty-seven terracotta plaques, and sixty bronze votive images were also recovered during excavation. (BArch 1975)

Somapurī

The monastic university of Somapurī, City of the Moon, was located far to the east, in an area remote from the urban centers of its time. Somapurī is now identified with the impressive site discovered near Pāhārpur in the Rājshāhi District of Bangladesh and excavated in 1936. The discovery earlier this century of a copper-plate inscription dated c. 478 C.E. links this site with a grant of land for the building of a Jain vihāra. Another inscription found in the ruins indicates that the Jain vihāra later became the site of the Buddhist monastery of Somapurī and associates King Dharmapāla with its construction. The origins of Somapurī can thus be traced to the eighth century.

The maintenance of such a large monastery in this remote region required substantial resources and patronage, linking the fortunes of Somapurī directly to the success of the Pāla kings and the prosperity of the region in general. The presence of Somapurī and other major Buddhist sites in the area indicates that the Dharma flourished strongly in the eastern lands between the eighth and twelfth centuries. The late eleventh or twelfth century master Abhayadatta refers to Somapurī as "a Dharma circle with thousands of monks, a veritable ocean of them." (BL 27)

Although few names of Somapurī's paṇḍitas have come down to us, Abhayadatta, chronicler of India's great siddhas, notes that two famous masters, Kṛṣṇācārya and Virūpa, lived at Somapurī, probably in the eighth century. Kṛṣṇācārya, also known as the siddha Kṛṣṇa-pa or Kānhapa, was initiated into the practice of Hevajra at Somapurī by his guru Jālandhari. Kṛṣṇācārya was a noted Mantrayāna scholar; at least seventy-two of his works were translated into Tibetan and preserved in the bsTan-'gyur. Virūpa, famous siddha and vidyādhara of the Hevajra lineage, began his religious life as a monk at Somapurī and attained siddhi through his practice at that monastery.

The Pāla Empire, seriously weakened in the tenth century, was revitalized by Mahipāla later in the same century. A devout Buddhist, Mahipāla supported thousands of monks and scholars at Odantapurī in Bihār and sponsored ceremonies at Nālandā and Somapurī. During his reign, or shortly thereafter, Somapurī's main temple was completely renovated and votive stūpas were built in its shrine to Tārā.

After the reign of Mahipāla and his son Nayapāla, successive invasions by the Ceḍi king Karṇa of Central India, by the Coḷa king Rājendra in the south, and by a local chief named Divya weakened Pāla rule once again. Somapurī may have sustained further damage during these disruptions; although Rāmapāla reestablished Pāla rule in the last quarter of the eleventh century, the great monastery never fully recovered its former glory.

Somapurī declined further under the rule of the Sena kings who replaced the Pālas in the twelfth century; it may also have been damaged by the Varmans, a strongly Hindu

The ruins of Somapurī, one of the largest monastic complexes ever built in India, showing the temple entrance and the main mound

Kṣatriya clan that ruled a small kingdom to the south. But it is likely that Somapurī remained an active Buddhist center until the Muslim armies under Muhammad Bhakhtyār Khaljī invaded this region in 1204. As the largest and highest structure for miles around, Somapurī would have been a prime target for destruction. The temple and monastery were probably completely abandoned shortly thereafter.

In the nineteenth century, a large mound was discovered near Pāhārpur about twenty-nine miles northwest of Mahāsthān (the modern name for the ancient capital, Puṇḍranagara). The mound adjoins a small village which is still called Dharmapurī. This village is thought to have grown up with the great monastic university and to have been named for its sponsor, King Dharmapāla.

At the time of its discovery, the Pāhārpur mound was an immense heap of bricks standing eighty feet above the surrounding fields. Completely covered with brush and crowned by a great spreading banyan tree, the mound was the haunt of leopards and other wild animals. Early examinations were inconclusive, but in 1919 the mound came under the protection of the Ancient Monuments Preservation Act, and responsibility for its excavation passed to the Archaeological Department. The first excavations were made in 1923 by archaeologists from Calcutta University and the Varendra Research Society. This work revealed a few rooms at one corner of the monastery. When the work was continued in 1925–1926, the main staircase and lower area was cleared. Thereafter, a series of annual excavations removed layer after layer of earth and debris. The remains of Somapurī's great central temple gradually emerged as if by magic from the amorphous brush-covered mound.

The monastery of Somapurī, which measures 919 × 922 feet, is considered the largest single monastery ever built on Indian soil. The outside walls, over twelve feet tall, were actually a square rim of 177 rooms that enclosed a spacious courtyard. The temple stood in the center of the compound, with the main entryway to the courtyard on the north side. Ornamental pedestals stood in the center of ninety-two of the 'rim structure's' rooms; these were not part of Dharmapāla's original construction but appear to have been built during a later period of renovation. These pedestals, which may have held images important in ceremonial or devotional practices, were unknown in monasteries unearthed in India, but they have also been found in Buddhist ruins further south.

The main temple of Somapurī was constructed in the form of a viśvavajra, a cross with arms projecting at equal distances from the center. From a basically square floor plan, the temple rose vertically to a substantial height, with the upper floors probably expanded after the main construction. The temple

hall; the northern wing had eight dwelling-rooms and the southern and western wings each had eleven dwelling rooms. The outer wall of the compound was more than eight feet at its thickest part, and the entire compound measured 139 × 135 feet. Two bronze images, one of Padmapāṇi and the other of Mañjuṣrī, were recovered from the site and placed in the Dinajpur Museum. These, together with other bronze images found in Bangladesh, have since been lost.

Devīkoṭa

The ruins of the city of Devīkoṭa, mentioned in Abhayadatta's *Lives of the Eighty-four Great Siddhas,* have been discovered in northern West Bengal near Baṅgarh, a village about eighteen miles south of the town of Dinajpur. The monastery of Koṭivarṣa once flourished nearby. Devīkoṭa was the home of the sisters Mekhalā and Kanakhalā, who attained realization of Mahāmudrā through following the teachings of Kāṅhapa, and as siddhas benefited the people of Devīkoṭa for many years. The siddha Udheli was a rich nobleman of Devīkoṭa who attained the power of flight through the teachings of Karṇaripa.

Jagaddala

The Jagaddala Mahāvihāra was founded by King Rāmapāla of the Pāla Dynasty, who ruled the kingdom of Varendra from his capital of Rāmavatī from approximately 1084 to 1130 C.E. Although Tibetan sources locate the Jagaddala Monastery in Orissa, its connection with Rāmapāla and his capital Rāmavatī favor placing it in Varendra, as northern Bengal was known during his time. From the description of the Jagaddala Monastery by Nandī, Rāmapāla's court poet, it appears that Buddhism was flourishing in Varendra in the early twelfth century. The monastery, located near Rāmāvatī on the banks of the Ganges and Karotoyā rivers, was the largest Dharma center in Varendra.

Jagaddala attracted some of the greatest masters of that time, including the logician Mokṣākaragupta and Śākyaśrī-bhadra, the Kashmiri paṇḍita who served as Vikramaśīla's last abbot and sought refuge in Jagaddala when Vikramaśīla was destroyed. According to the colophon of the Tarkabhāṣa, a treatise on logic, Mokṣākaragupta wrote this text while residing at Jagaddala. Śākyaśrī, together with his disciples Vibhūticandra and Dānaśīla, translated many texts into Tibetan; eventually all three masters went from Jagaddala to Nepal and from there to Tibet, just ahead of the forces of Muhammad Khaljī, who had destroyed the great centers of Magadha and were marching east toward Varendra.

The Muslim invaders ravaged the city of Rāmavatī, but it is not known if they also destroyed Jagaddala or if it declined as a result of their destruction of neighboring Buddhist centers. It appears that the city of Rāmavatī was resettled after the Muslim invasion and continued to be inhabited through the fifteenth or sixteenth centuries.

Samataṭa

Traveling south through Samataṭa, on the way to the coast, Hsüan-tsang counted about thirty monasteries housing about two thousand monks of the Sthavira tradition. In one monastery, he saw an eight-foot-tall statue of the Buddha shaped from green jade, said to possess great spiritual power. He relates that several bhikṣus from this region, together with members of wealthy families, had pursued higher studies at Nālandā. Among them was Hsüan-tsang's own teacher Śīla-bhadra, a scion of Samataṭa's royal family who was abbot of Nālandā during Hsüan-tsang's visit. This region was also home to a large number of Jain ascetics, and there were about a hundred temples of various Brahmanic traditions.

Today, extensive ruins testify that when Hsüan-tsang visited, Buddhism in Samataṭa was yet to reach its full potential. Most of the monasteries found to date were built in the eighth to twelfth centuries, a period of history that for southern Bangladesh is fragmentary at best. Until this century, the very existence of a monastery at Paṭṭikerā was known only through a mention in the colophon of a manuscript of the Aṣṭasāhasrikā-prajñāpāramitā preserved in the Cambridge University library and from references in Burmese records. Although archaeologists have long been aware that jungle-engulfed mounds near Comilla probably concealed much of Bangladesh's history, the country, ravaged by political upheavals and economic problems, has only recently begun to support systematic excavations.

The rock of this region is not well-suited for carving, and few stone sculptures have been found here. But some images in soft shale and some lifesize figures in black basalt have been unearthed from sites near Comilla, together with a number of bronze images ranging from under three inches to fourteen inches in height. However, many examples of this art, including thirty-six of the finest bronze images, have been lost or stolen. Since the art found here is said to be unlike any other Buddhist art, future finds may help determine the nature of Buddhist practices here as well as trace this later form of the Buddhist artistic traditions.

Paṭṭikerā (Paṭṭikerakā)

Burmese chronicles indicate that in the twelfth century, Burma maintained a close relationship with the city-kingdom of Paṭṭikerā. While Paṭṭikerā has long been associated with Samataṭa, its precise location was unknown until the discovery of a copper plaque near the city of Comilla, east of Dacca on the border of Bangladesh and Assam. This plaque, named the Copperplate of Bhavadeva, bears an inscription recording a grant of land given by Raṇavaṅkamalla Śrī Hārikāladeva for a Buddhist vihāra in Paṭṭikerā in the year 1220. The inscription referred to Paṭṭikerā as a great city adorned with forts and monasteries; it also named the kings of the Khadga and Deva Dynasties that had ruled this region from the seventh to thirteenth centuries, restoring to Bangladesh a missing part of their history.

The Copperplate of Bhavadeva had been found on the Lalmai-Maināmatī ridge in the Tippera District, about six miles from Comilla, where in 1875 roadbuilding activities had cut through jungle growth and accidentally discovered potentially rich archaeological sites. Excavations on the Maināmatī ridge, begun in 1955, have unearthed remains of the Salban and Ānandarāja Vihāras and found potentially rich sites in mounds at Rūpban-Kanyā and Rūpban Murā. Excavators have described the Maināmatī complex of sites as comparable in size and magnitude to Takṣaśīla and Nālandā.

The first Buddhist monument uncovered here was the Salban Vihāra, which appears to have been founded before Somapurī and to have flourished between the seventh through twelfth centuries. A large number of seals bearing the name Salban Vihāra were found at the site. From the ruins, archaeologists could detect four distinct phases of building and repair. All the buildings and stūpas here were made of bricks. During the third phase, a large temple similar to the temple of Somapurī Monastery had been constructed in its center. The Salban temple, like the temple of Somapurī, was laid out in a cruciform shape. A complex of three stūpas was located nearby at Kutila Mura. It is possible that these three stūpas honor the Buddha, Dharma, and Sangha, and that this complex is the Ratnatraya (Three Jewels) shrine known from the Burmese chronicles to have been near Samataṭa's capital. The site of the capital, however, has not been confirmed.

The largest of the Maināmatī discoveries to date is the Ānandarāja Vihāra, which was located in a mound with an area of six square miles. This site, now variously named after

Ānandadeva, the third king of the Deva Dynasty, or his son Bhavadeva, may be the monastery of Paṭṭikerā referred to on the Bhavadeva Copperplate. The monastery enclosed a large central shrine which was probably similar to the architecture of Somapurī. Nearby was a dried-up water tank with unusually high banks, capable of holding a large quantity of water. The architecture of the ruins, together with the sculpture and terracotta plaques of the Buddha and Padmapāṇi found in the mound, indicate that the monastery was built during the Pāla Dynasty, around the eighth to the tenth centuries C.E.

Close by the Paṭṭikerā site are other large mounds, two of which had been excavated as of 1982. One mound, about four hundred feet square and fifteen feet tall, is known as Rūpban-Kanyā. When discovered, the mound held the well-preserved ruins of a square brick monastery with pillared halls surrounding a central shrine. This mound, as many others in Bangladesh, was torn down in the interests of military construction, with no time allotted for archaeological research. Photography was prohibited and the site was bulldozed, with dismayed archaeologists watching the destruction from a distance. The only artifact salvaged was a large bronze bell over three feet tall, which is now in the Maināmatī Museum.

Rūpban Murā, a much larger mound six miles to the south, contains a cruciform structure richly adorned with carved plaques and moldings, similar in plan and decorative motifs to the Somapurī excavations at Pāhārpur. Here were found many small images of the Buddha seated in vajrāsana inscribed with the Ye Dharma mantra. Smaller mounds on the site may contain the remains of votive stūpas. Little more is known of this monastery, which is thought to have been constructed between the ninth and eleventh centuries.

Nearby, from the dry bed of a water-storage pond, archaeologists recovered two larger images, one related to the Dhyāni Buddhas and the other a representation of Mañjuvajra, a form of the Bodhisattva Mañjuśrī. Further excavation of the Maināmatī and surrounding hills will reveal the full magnitude of Samataṭa's Buddhist sites and may help fill the missing spaces in the ancient history of Bangladesh.

Caṭṭagrāma

According to Tibetan sources, Paṇḍita Vihāra, a great Tantric center associated with the siddha Tailapāda, teacher of Nāḍapāda, flourished in southeastern Bengal. The Paṇḍita Vihāra is now thought to have been near Jhewari, located in the Chittagong Hills. In recent times, images found around Caṭṭagrāma, in the Chittagong District of Bangladesh, indicate that this region was a center of Mahāyāna Buddhism long after other centers were destroyed or had declined. Little else is known of the history of Buddhism in this remote area.

However, it is now clear that Buddhism never completely vanished from the Chittagong District. The Thera Saṁgarāja Sāramitta of Arakan came to Caṭṭagrāma in the eighteenth century and reformed the Buddhist community here. The Borua Buddhist Monastery of Chittagong is the primary center for the Boruas, a community of ethnic Bengalis, and the Chakma tribe of the Chittagong Hill Tracts adheres to its Buddhist heritage. Although recent reports indicate that the Chakma tribe is experiencing severe government harassment and repression of their culture, the Chakmas have maintained the Chakma Raj Vihar, their center at Rangamati, and continue to revere and implement the Buddha's teachings in their daily lives. As of 1984, Sādhana Mahāsthavir, also known as Bana Bhante, the Forest Monk, was sustaining the practice of the Chakma community from his island home in the jungle. (GDF 120–121)

Tripura and Kāmarūpa

Although Kāmarūpa is linked to Dhītika, fifth patriarch of the Dharma, no solid evidence has yet been found to confirm the existence of a Buddhist tradition here. But sculptures found in Tripura to the south indicate that Mahāyāna Buddhism was practiced for centuries in this remote land.

Tripura, once the eastern frontier of Puṇḍravardhana, is now a hill-province governed by India, situated between Bangladesh and Assam. Buddhist centers appear to have existed in the southern region of Tripura bordering on Comilla and Chittagong from the sixth century onward, with less activity in the heavily forested and sparsely populated north. The Buddhists of Tripura appear to have been influenced and nurtured by the Ānandarāja and Paṇḍita Monasteries, as well as other centers in the Comilla and Chittagong regions.

According to a copper-plate inscription, in the sixth century land in southern Tripura was granted for building a Buddhist center dedicated to Avalokiteśvara, and Buddhist sculptures found in Pilak and Jolaibari appear to date between the ninth and twelfth centuries. An intricately carved statue of Hevajra discovered at Dharmanagar indicates that Vajrayāna Buddhism reached as far as the remote northern tip of Tripura. According to Abhayadatta, Virūpa, a famous siddha and vidyādhara of the Hevajra teachings, was born in Tripura, "the city of King Devapāla."

To date, Pilak, which may have been known to the rulers of Arakan in the eighth century, is the only site in this area to have been even partially excavated by archaeologists. A brick shrine was unearthed at Pilak together with images of the Mahāyāna and Vajrayāna traditions. Pāla and Sena art styles reflected in images found in Tripura connect Tripuran Buddhism with such sites as the Paṇḍita Vihāra in Chittagong and the Ānandarāja Monastery at Maināmatī.

Kāmarūpa

The fifth patriarch, Dhītika, disciple of Upagupta, was the only one of the seven patriarchs to be associated with the eastern region. According to Tāranātha, upon Dhītika's miraculous arrival in Kāmarūpa, a wealthy Brahmin named Siddha, mistaking him for the sun-god, paid him homage. When Dhītika presented himself as a follower of the Buddha's teachings, Siddha built him the Mahācaitya, which means a great shrine or monastery.

Hsüan-tsang describes the country of Kāmārūpa as being about 1,600 miles in circumference. He found few Buddhists in Kāmarūpa, which the patriarch Dhītika had visited perhaps around the third century B.C.E., and no evidence that there was ever a monastery built in that area. Kāmarūpa had long been outside the boundaries of Indian suzerainty, but its capital Pragjyotiṣka was the overland link between Burma and the Ganges Basin—a difficult and dangerous route, but profitable for trade in the gems and precious jewels of Southeast Asia. Worship of non-Buddhist deities prevailed; according to Hsüan-tsang, what Buddhists there were in the area practiced in secret. Still, Kumārarāja, also known as Bhāskaravarman, was a friend and ally of King Harṣa and fond of learning. Impressed that a bhikṣu from China should travel so far to his country, Bhāskaravarman sent a messenger to Nālandā, where Hsüan-tsang was then residing, and invited him to visit Kāmārūpa.

Hsüan-tsang's preceptor Śīlabhadra, perceiving that the pilgrim was reluctant to undertake this journey, advised him, "We judge from this that he (Bhāskaravarman) is changing his principles and desires to acquire merit to benefit others. You formerly conceived a great heart and made a vow with yourself to travel alone through different lands regardless of life, to seek for the Dharma for the good of the world. Forgetful of your own country, you should be ready to meet death; indifferent to renown or failure, you should labor to open the door for the spread of the holy doctrine, to lead onwards the crowds who are deceived by false teaching; to consider others first, yourself afterwards; forgetful of renown, to think only of expanding the Dharma." Hsüan-tsang then made his way to Kāmarūpa. Bhāskaravarman received him warmly and invited the pilgrim to accompany him to King Harṣa's court.

Bhāskaravarman also appears in Tibetan history as an ally of the Tibetan king Srong-bstan-sgam-po. Ruler of a vast empire that stretched deep into Central Asia and China, Srong-btsan-sgam-po exerted great influence in Kāmarūpa and Nepal, which may actually have formed part of his empire. Nourished by the efforts of outstanding Vajrayāna masters and Mahāyāna paṇḍitas from Uḍḍiyāna, India, and Kashmir, Buddhism gained a strong foothold in Tibet during the eighth century. Although persecution and political upheavals in the ninth century caused much destruction, the critical Vinaya and Vajrayāna lineages were preserved unbroken. When order was restored, Buddhism again flourished openly; Tibetans traveled to India seeking texts and teachings from the Buddhist masters of Bihār and eastern India, initiating a second period of Dharma transmission.

Kāmarūpa was the home of the great siddhas Rāhula and Mīnapa. Rāhula met his teacher in a cemetery, where he had gone to die after enduring ridicule for suffering the infirmities of old age. His teacher showed him how to draw concepts into the orb of the moon, then to eclipse them with the Rāhu of non-dual experience (Rāhu is the deity who devours the moon during an eclipse). After practicing in this way for sixteen years, the old man obtained the siddhi of Mahāmudrā. From his practice he took the name of Rāhula and trained the living beings of Kāmarūpa. Mīnapa was a fisherman of Kāmarūpa; he heard the Dharma while living in the belly of a great fish who had swallowed him alive. After meditating in the fish's belly for twelve years, he attained realization.

Little is known of the practice of Buddhism in Kāmarūpa after the seventh century. However, the traditions that took root in Tibet supported the Dharma traditions of Bhutan and Sikkim, Kāmarūpa's northern neighbors, from the eleventh century to modern times. If Buddhism had survived in Kāmarūpa, it is likely that this would have been noted by their Buddhist neighbors.

The Waning of Buddhism in the East

Through the last half of the twelfth century, after the Pāla Empire disintegrated, the east was ruled by the Sena kings who had little interest in Buddhism. When the Muslim armies swept into Magadha and systematically destroyed the great universities of Nālandā, Vikramaśīla, and Odantapurī, the Sena king Lakṣmaṇasena, famed for his military prowess, did nothing to protect them. As the Muslim army advanced east toward the Brahmaputra River, Lakṣmaṇasena took refuge in Vaṅga, which he and his descendants were able to hold.

Many of the paṇḍitas who escaped the destruction in Magadha sought refuge in the monastic centers of the east. But as the Muslim armies advanced eastward, the paṇḍitas fled north to Nepal and south to Orissa and Āndhra. Even with the loss of the paṇḍitas and great Vajrācāryas, teachers of the Vajrayāna traditions, Buddhist communities persisted in remote areas of the east. Madhusena, a Buddhist king, ruled in some part of eastern Bengal in 1289, and Buddhism appears to have survived much longer in the kingdom of Paṭṭikerā. In the seventeenth century, the Tibetan pilgrim Buddhagupta Tathāgatanātha reported that Buddhists were active not only in Bengal and Orissa, but also in Trilinga, Vidyānagara, Karṇāṭaka, and elsewhere in South India.

Although the history of Buddhism in India may never be completely recovered, so long did the Buddha's teachings prosper in India that despite centuries of neglect and destruction, the monuments and art they inspired are such an integral part of the land that even time may not completely eradicate their traces. May the search continue for places where generations of Buddhist practitioners preserved the light of liberation, and may efforts to regenerate the sacred sites open new vistas of understanding throughout the ten directions.

Sarva Maṅgalaṁ

May all beings be happy.

Travel Information

The increased interest in Buddhist holy places has stimulated the building of facilities for pilgrims and tourists. Many of the modern temples near the major holy places accommodate guests, and the Government of India administers tourist bungalows or rest houses at many of the sites. Tours to nearby sites can be arranged through the offices of the Indian Tourism Development Corporation located in major cities, and the larger hotels in Vārāṇasī, Patna, and Aurangabad can recommend more possibilities for chartering buses for a more extended tour. Patna is a central location for many of the pilgrimage sites: Nālandā, Rajgir, Bodh Gaya, Vārāṇasī, and Vaiśalī are all within 125 miles of the city.

Accommodation and travel details are constantly changing, and prospective travelers will want to consult the updated editions of major travel guides for current information. However, travel between two points that appear close on a map can take much longer in India than one might expect. The following information can serve as a brief introduction to transportation usually available and to possible itineraries.

Lumbinī can be reached by air from Kathmandu, Nepal or by bus or train from India. The flight from Kathmandu lands at Siddarthanagar, about thirteen miles east of Lumbinī. Bus tours from India can be arranged through major Indian travel companies in Vārāṇasī, New Delhi, and Patna, or travelers can take the Gonda-Gorakhpur Railway to the Naugarh station and travel the rest of the way (about twenty-two miles) by bus. From Lumbinī, travelers can tour Tilaurakot (the Nepalese Kapilavastu) and other Nepali villages with Buddhist ruins as well as Piprahwa (the Indian Kapilavastu) by hired car or bus.

Bodh Gayā can be reached most easily by train from New Delhi, Vārāṇasī, and Calcutta, or by bus from Patna. From Gayā, the nearest rail station, travelers can take a taxi, bus, or motorized rickshaw to the village of Bodh Gayā. Most pilgrims will wish to lodge at Bodh Gayā, but accommodations are also available at Gayā. Bodh Gayā is the single most popular pilgrimage destination for Buddhists of all nationalities. It is also a holy place for Hindus. The most comfortable time to visit Bodh Gayā is during the cool season from December to March.

Sārnāth is easily reached by taxi or bus from Vārāṇasī. Although most visitors stay in Vārāṇāsi hotels, some lodging is available in Sārnāth in government bungalows or in monastery guest quarters. A tour of the central grounds, the Chaukhandi mound, and the Sārnāth Museum can take a full afternoon. Visitors may also wish to see the modern temples and institutes near the site.

Kuśinagara. Many visitors to Kuśinagara travel to Gorakhpur by air or by train, then to Kuśinagara, a distance of about thirty-two miles, by bus or taxi. Accommodations are available at lodges and rest houses or at several of Kuśinagara's modern monasteries. The site is quiet and peaceful. Pilgrims may wish to stop here overnight and spend time in reflection and meditation.

Śrāvastī. Travelers can reach Saheṭh-Maheṭh, the site of ancient Śrāvastī, by train from Lucknow or other major cities to Balrampur, then from Balrampur by road to the site itself, a distance of about eleven miles. Excavations have revealed extensive remains of the Jetavana and other monasteries and shrines of this important site. The Burmese and Chinese temples have rest houses for travelers and there are government-run Inspection Houses at the site and in nearby towns.

Sāṁkāśya, modern Sankissa, is the most remote of all the eight major holy places. From Delhi or Agra, pilgrims can take the Northern Railway as far as Pakhna and travel by horse carriage the rest of the distance (about seven miles). There is a government-run Inspection House at Sankissa and several hotels at Farrukhabad, but for those interested in Buddhism there is little here to be seen.

Rājagṛha, modern Rajgir, is about two hours by road from Bodh Gayā, and cars or busses can be chartered in Bodh Gayā for a one or two day excursion from the site of the enlightenment. In two days, the pilgrim can tour Nālandā, visit the Bamboo Grove, climb the Vulture Peak, and continue on to the modern Viśvaśānti shrine. Most of Rājagṛha's special places are readily accessible, although many will wish to linger a while at sites described in the Buddha's teachings.

Vaiśālī can easily be reached by road from the major city of Patna, less than fifty miles away, or from Muzzafarpur or Hajipur, a distance of less than twenty-five miles. There are two tourist bungalows near the grounds of Vaiśālī, and many visitors stay at the modern hotels in Patna. A tour of Vaiśālī and its museum, with some time for reflection, can be completed within a few hours.

Sañcī, located in Madhya Pradesh about twenty-seven miles from Bhopal, can be reached by train from Delhi or Vārāṇasī. For visitors wishing to spend time at the site, there are overnight accommodations at Sañcī and major hotels in

Bhopal. From Bhopal, travelers can usually reach Sañcī by train or by taxi within an hour.

Ajaṇṭā. Trains from Delhi and Calcutta pass through Bhopal daily on the way to Bombay. From Bhopal, one can travel by train to Jalgaon and then by taxi to Ajaṇṭā. The caves are normally open to visitors between nine AM and five PM, and touring all the caves usually takes around three hours, although many will wish to spend more time near the caves that rank among the world's great marvels. There are guest accommodations at Fardapur, less than two miles from the caves. A road leads from Fardapur to Aurangabad, the usual point of departure for viewing the caves of Ellora, but transport from Ajaṇṭā to Aurangabad can be problematic. Groups may wish to charter a bus from Vārāṇasī or Bhopal for more flexible travel among the caves of Mahārāṣṭra. When traveling from Ajaṇṭā south to Aurangabad, watch for the scenic viewing place opposite the Ajaṇṭā caves. This is the place where the British hunting party first sighted the Ajaṇṭā cave temples.

The Ellora caves are normally reached on a day tour from Aurangabad. Some travelers may wish to fly directly into Aurangabad from Vārāṇasī or Delhi and visit Ajaṇṭā and Ellora on buses that travel daily from Aurangabad's railway station. However, Ajaṇṭā is about sixty-seven miles north of Aurangabad and the trip shortens the time available for viewing the caves.

Pronouncing Sanskrit

In contrast to the English alphabet of twenty-six letters, Sanskrit is a syllabic language with fourteen vowels and thirty-three basic consonants. In transcribing Sanskrit words, English-speaking scholars developed a system of diacritical marks to indicate the precise Sanskrit letter used in forming the words. The system formalized by Sir Monier Monier-Williams in *A Sanskrit-English Dictionary* (first published in 1899) became the standard used by English and American scholars. Although some scholars have recently introduced simplifications intended to assist the general reader, these are not entirely satisfactory. The editors of this book have adhered to the standard used by the Library of Congress and most scholarly publications.

Unlike English sounds, the sounds of Sanskrit syllables are regular and vary little from word to word. Although a student of Indian languages will need to learn and practice the distinct nuances of each sound to communicate with native speakers, most English speakers can learn the essential pronunciation of Dharma words by remembering a few simple guidelines.

Most of the consonants in the Sanskrit terms in this book can be pronounced as they would sound in English. The major points to remember is that *c* is always pronounced *ch,* and *ś* and *ṣ* are pronounced *sh*. As an added refinement, the dot under t, d, and n indicates that this sound is made with the tongue curled under against the palate (retroflexive), as opposed to the unmarked t, d, and n, which are sounded with the tongue touching or slightly protruding between the teeth, producing a dental sound. The h often added to k, g, c, j, t, d, p, and b simply indicates that the consonant is aspirated, as the English dh in adhere is aspirated. Since the average English speaker does not associate retroflexive and dental or aspirate and unaspirated consonants with differences in meaning, most readers will not find it necessary to develop this particular skill. Some attention to syllabic emphasis and vowel sounds, however, can greatly improve one's pronunciation.

Syllabic emphasis: Sanskrit has no system of accented or stressed syllables. Syllables do, however, have short and long properties which English speakers may hear as accented syllables. For best results, beginners are advised to practice pronouncing each syllable as evenly (unstressed) as possible. This minimizes distortion and facilitates the refinement process. Vowels are the most critical factor in correct pronunciation. The most common vowels and their sounds are:

vowels	sounds	vowels	sounds
a	as in mica	ṛ	as in merrily
ā	as in father	ḷ	as in revelry
i	as in fill	e	as in there
ī	as in police	ai	as in aisle
u	as in full	o	as in go
ū	as in rude	au	as in haus (German)

Abbreviations

AAI	Susan and John Huntington, *Art of Ancient India: Buddhist, Hindu, Jain.* New York: Weatherhill, 1985.
Amar	H. Sarkar and S. P. Nainar, *Amāravatī.* New Delhi: Archaeological Survey of India, 1972.
AN	Anguttara Nikāya
ASI	Alexander Cunningham, *Archaeological Survey of India. Report 1862–1865.* Volume I. Simla: 1871.
AT	Yeshe De Research Project, *Ancient Tibet.* Berkeley: Dharma Publishing, 1986.
BA	*The Blue Annals,* translated by George N. Roerich. Second edition, Delhi: Motilal Banarsidass, 1976.
BArch	*Bangladesh Archaeology* 1975 vol. 1:1, edited by Dr. Nazimuddin Ahmed. Govt. of Bangladesh, Dacca.
BCAI	Binayendra Nath Chaudhury, *Buddhist Centres in Ancient India.* Calcutta: Sanskrit College, 1982.
BGT	Dipak K. Barua, *Bodh Gaya Temple: Its History.* Buddha Gaya: Buddha Gaya Temple Management Committee, 1981.

BiogD *Biography of Dharmasvamin*, translated by George Roerich. Patna, 1959.

BIT Shu Hikosaka, *Buddhism in Tamil Nadu*. Madras: Institute of Asian Studies, 1989.

BK F. M. Hassnain, *Buddhist Kashmir*. New Delhi: Light & Life Publishers, 1973.

BL *Buddha's Lions*, translated by James Robinson. Berkeley: Dharma Publishing, 1979.

Bodh *Bodh Gaya: The Site of Enlightenment*, edited by Janice Leoshko. Bombay: Marg Publications, 1988.

BRA K. R. Subramanian, *Buddhist Remains in South India and Early Andhra History, 225 A.D. to 610 A.D.* New Delhi: Cosmo Publications, 1981.

BSI D. C. Ahir, *Buddhism in South India*. Delhi: Sri Satguru Publications, 1992.

DR bDud-'joms 'Jigs-bral-ye-śes-rdo-rje, *The Nyingma School of Tibetan Buddhism*. Boston: Wisdom Publications, 1991.

EI *Epigraphica Indica*. Calcutta.

GDF Tim Ward, *The Great Dragon's Fleas*. Berkeley: Celestial Arts, 1993.

GES Domenico Faccenna, *A Guide to the Excavations in Swat (Pakistan), 1956–1962*. Rome: Scuolo Grafico Salesiana, 1964.

GT John Marshall, *A Guide to Taxila*. Calcutta, 1918.

HBA C. S. Upasak, *History of Buddhism in Afghanistan*. Sarnath: Central Institute of Highter Tibetan Studies, 1990.

HCIP *History and Culture of the Indian People*, edited by R. C. Majumdar. Volumes III–V. London: George Alwin & Unwin, 1951–1955.

HIB Étienne Lamotte, *History of Buddhism from the Origins to the Śaka Era*, translated from the French by Sara Boin-Webb. Louvain: Peeters Press, 1988.

HIBS Hirakawa Akira, *A History of Indian Buddhism From Śākyamuni to Early Mahāyāna,* translated and edited by Paul Groner. Honolulu: University of Hawaii Press, 1990. (Asian Studies at Hawaii, 36).

HISI Sewett, *Historical Inscriptions of South India*

HT Hsüan-tsang. *Si-Yu-Ki: Buddhist Records of the Western World,* translated by Samuel Beal. Reprint edition. Delhi: Motilal Banarsidas, 1981.

Hwui Shaman Hwui Li, *The Life of Hiuen-tsiang,* translated by Samuel Beal. Reprint edition, Delhi: Munshiram Manoharlal, 1973. First published London, 1911.

JBRS *Journal of the Bihar Research Society.*

JRAS *Journal of the Royal Asiatic Society.*

KTA C. R. Srinavasin, *Kanchipuram Through the Ages.* Delhi, 1979.

Luders H. Luders, *A List of Brāhmī Inscriptions from the Earliest Times to about A.D. 400* (Epigraphia Indica, X).

Math John Huntington, "Mathurā Evidence for the Early Teachings of Mahāyāna,"in *Mathurā: The Cultural Heritage,* edited by Doris Meth Srinivasan. New Delhi: American Institute of Tibetan Studies, 1989.

Nagar K. Krishna Murthy, *Nāgārjunakoṇḍā: A Cultural Study.* Delhi: Concept Publishing Company, 1977. pp. 1–17.

Nau Jean Naudou, *Buddhists of Kaśmir.* First English edition, Delhi: Agram Kala Prakashan, 1980.

Tar Tāranātha, *History of Buddhism in India,* translated by Lama Chimpa and Alaka Chattopadhyaya. Atlantic Highlands, NJ: Humanities Press, 1981.

Tax John Marshall, *Taxila.* 3 volumes. Cambridge, 1951.

Bibliography

Abhayadatta. *Buddha's Lions: Lives of the Eighty-four Siddhas,* translated by James Robinson. Berkeley, California: Dharma Publishing, 1979

Adikaram, E. W. *Early History of Buddhism in Ceylon.* Migoda: Puswella, 1946.

Alexander, P. C. *Buddhism in Kerala.* Annamalainager: Annamalai University, 1949.

Ahir, D.C. *Buddhism in South India.* Delhi: Satguru Publications, 1992.

Ansari, Abdul Quddoos. *Archaeological Remains of Bodhgaya.* Delhi: Ramanand Vidya Bhawan, 1990.

Aśoka. *The Edicts of Aśoka.* Edited and translated by N.A. Nikam and Richard P. McKeon. Chicago: University of Chicago Press, 1958.

Aśokāvadāna. *The Legend of King Aśoka. A Study and Translation of the Aśokāvadāna,* by J. Strong. Princeton, University Press, 1983.

Banerjee, Anukul Chandra. *Sarvāstivāda Literature.* Calcutta: The World Press Private Limited, 1979.

Bangladesh Archaeology 1975:1, edited by Dr. Nazimuddin Ahmed, Department of Archaeology and Museums. Dacca: Ministry of Sports and Culture, Government of Bangladesh.

Barua, B. M. *Gaya and Buddhist Gaya: Early History of the Holy Land.* Calcutta, 1931.

Barua, Dipak K. *Buddha Gaya Temple: Its History.* Buddha Gaya: Buddha Gaya Temple Management Committee, 1975. Second revised edition, 1981.

Basham, A. L. *The Wonder That Was India: A Survey of the Culture of the Indian Sub-continent Before the Coming of the Muslims.* New York: Grove Press, 1959.

Beal, Samuel. *A Catena of Buddhist Scriptures from the Chinese.* London: Trübner & Co., 1871.

Bhadrakalpika-sūtra. *The Fortunate Aeon: How the Thousand Buddhas Become Enlightened.* Berkeley: Dharma Publishing, 1986.

Buddha-Dharma. New English Edition. Berkeley: Numata Center for Translation and Research, 1984. Second edition, 1987.

Buddhaghosa. *The Path of Purification (Visuddhimagga),* translated by Bhikkhu Ñāṇamoli. Second ed. Colombo: A. Semage, 1964.

Burgess, James. *The Buddhist Stūpas of Amarāvatī and Jaggayyapeṭa.* Varanasi: Indological Book House, 1970.

Bu-ston Rinpoche. *History of Buddhism,* translated by E. Obermiller. Heidelberg: Institut für Buddhismuskunde, 1931. (Materialien zur Kunde des Buddhismus 18)

Chaudhury, B.N. *Buddhist Centres in Ancient India.* Calcutta: Sanskrit College, 1969.

Crystal Mirror VI. Berkeley: Dharma Publishing, 1984.

Csoma Korosi, Alexander. "Analysis of the bKa'-'gyur," in *Asiatic Researches* XX:2 (1829), pp. 393–552.

Cunningham, Sir Alexander. *The Ancient Geography of India, Vol. I: The Buddhist Period,* London: Trübner, 1871. New enlarged edition; reprinted Varanasi: Indological Book House, 1975.

Cunningham, Sir Alexander. *Archaologic Survey of India, Four Reports Made During the Years 1862–65*. vol. I, Simla, 1871.

Davies, C. Collin. *An Historical Atlas of the Indian Peninsula*. Second edition. Oxford University Press (Indian Branch), 1959.

Dikshit, Kashinath Narayan. *Excavations at Paharpur, Bengal*. Delhi: Manager of Publications, 1938. (Memoirs of the Archaeological Society of India, 55)

Dīpavaṁsa. Chronicle of the Island of Ceylon, translated by B. C. Law. Ceylon: Saman Press, 1959.

Dudjom Rinpoche. *The Nyingma School of Tibetan Buddhism: Its Fundamentals and History*. 2 volumes. Boston: Wisdom Publications, 1991.

Elliot, M. *The History of India as Told by Its Own Historians: The Muhammadan Period, by Sir H. M. Elliott. Vol. II*. London: Trübner and Co., 1869.

Emmerick, R. E. *Tibetan Texts Concerning Khotan*. London, 1967.

Faccenna, Domenico. *A Guide to the Excavations in Swat (Pakistan) 1957–1962*. Rome: Scuolo Grafico Salesiana, 1964.

Filliozat, Jean. *Political History of India from the Earliest Times* to *the 7th Century A. D.* Calcutta, 1957. (L'Inde Classique, 2)

'Gos lo-tsa-ba. *The Blue Annals,* translated by George N. Roerich. Second edition. Delhi: Motilal Banarsidass, 1976.

Hanifi, Manzoor Ahmad. *A Short History of Muslim Rule in Indo-Pakistan*. Dacca: Ideal Library, 1964.

Hassnain, F. M. *Buddhist Kashmir*. New Delhi: Light & Life Publishers, 1973.

Hirakawa Akira. *A History of Indian Buddhism From Śākyamuni* to *Early Mahāyāna,* translated and edited by Paul Groner. Honolulu: University of Hawaii Press, 1990. (Asian Studies at Hawaii, 36)

Hirosaka, Shu. *Buddhism in Tamil Nadu*. Madras: Institute of Asian Studies, 1989.

Hsüan-tsang. *Si-Yu-Ki: Buddhist Records of the Western World,* translated by Samuel Beal. London: Trübner, 1884. Reprint, Delhi: Motilal Banarsidass, 1981.

Huntington, Susan L. and John L. Huntington. *The Art of Ancient India: Buddhist, Jain, Hindu.* New York: Weatherhill, 1985.

Hwui Li. *The Life of Hiuen-tsiang,* translated by Samuel Beal. Second edition. New Delhi: Manoshiram Manoharlal Publishers, 1973.

I-tsing. *A Record of the Buddhist Religion as Practised in India and the Malay Archipelago (A.D. 671–695),* translated by J. Takakusu. Delhi: Munshiram Manoharlal, 1966. (first published Oxford, 1896)

Jātakatthavaṇṇanā. Buddhist Birth Stories, or Jataka Tales, translated by T. W. Rhys-Davids. Volume I. London: Trübner, 1880.

Kumar, Dilip. *Archaeology of Vaishali.* New Delhi: Ramanand Vidya Bhawan, 1986.

Lalitavistara. *The Voice of the Buddha: The Beauty of Compassion,* translated by Gwendolyn Bays. Berkeley: Dharma Publishing, 1983.

Lamotte, Étienne. *History of Buddhism from the Origins to the Śaka Era,* translated from the French by Sara Boin-Webb. Louvain: Peeters Press, 1988.

Law, Bimala Churn. *Kauśāmbī in Ancient Literature.* Delhi, 1939. (Memoirs of the Archaeological Survey of India, 60)

——. *The Life and Work of Buddhaghosa.* Delhi: Nag Publishers, 1923.

——. Rājagṛha in Ancient Literature. Delhi, 1938. (Memoirs of the Archaeological Survey of India, 58)

——. *Śrāvastī in Indian Literature.* Delhi 1935. (Memoirs of the Archaeological Survey of India, 50)

——. *Tribes of Ancient India.* 2nd ed. Poona, 1973. (Bhandarkar Oriental Series, 4)

Leoshko, Janice, ed. *Bodh Gaya: The Site of Enlightenment.* Bombay: Marg Publications, 1988.

Light of Liberation. Berkeley: Dharma Publishing, 1992. (Crystal Mirror Series, VIII)

Lineage of Diamond Light. Revised edition. Berkeley: Dharma Publishing, 1991. (Crystal Mirror Series, V)

Mahajan, Vidya Dhar. *Muslim Rule in India.* Second edition. Delhi: S. Chand & Co., 1965.

The Mahāvaṁsa, or The Great Chronicle of Ceylon, translated by Wilhelm Geiger. First Published 1912. Reprinted Colombo: Ceylon Government Information Department, 1950. New Delhi: Asian Educational Services, 1986.

Mahāvastu, translated by J. J. Jones. London: Luzac, 1948–1956. (Sacred Books of the Buddhists, vols. 16, 18, 19)

The Mahayana Mahaparinirvana-Sutra, translated by Kosho Yamamoto. 3 vols. Ube City, Japan, 1973–1975. (Karin Buddhological Series, 5)

Majumdar, R. C., ed. *History and Culture of the Indian People.* Volume I, *The Vedic Age.* London: George Alwin & Unwin, 1951,

——. Volume II, *The Age of Imperial Unity.* Bombay: Bharatiya Vidya Bhavan, 1951.

——. Volume III, *The Classical Age.* Bombay: Bharatiya Vidya Bhavan, 1954.

——. Volume IV, *The Age of Imperial Kanauj.* Bombay: Bharatiya Vidya Bhavan, 1955.

——. Volume V. *The Age of Imperial Unity.* Bombay: Bharatiya Vidya Bhavan, 1951.

Marshall, John. *A Guide to Sanchi.* Calcutta: Superintendent Government Printing, 1918. Reprint ed., New Delhi: New Society Publications, 1980.

——. *A Guide to Taxila.* Calcutta, 1918. Reprint ed., Karachi, 1960.

——. *Taxila.* 3 volumes. Cambridge, 1951.

Mizuno Kōgen. *The Beginnings of Buddhism,* translated by Richard L. Gage. Tokyo: Kōsei Publishing Co., 1980.

Mookerji, Radha Kumud. "The University of Nālandā," in *Journal of the Bihar Research Society* 30 (1944), pp. 126–159.

Mukherji, Purna Chandra. *A Report on a Tour of Exploration of the Antiquities of Kapilavastu, Tarai of Nepal, During February* and *March, 1899.* Delhi, Indological Book House, 1969.

Mullik, C. C. *Nālandā Sculptures: Their Bearing on Indonesian Sculptures.* Delhi: Pratibha Prakashan, 1991.

Murthy, K. Krishna. *Nāgārjunakoṇḍa: A Cultural Study.* Delhi: Concept Publishing Company, 1977. pp. 1–17.

Nakamura Hajime. *Gotama Buddha.* Los Angeles, 1977.

Ñānamoli, Bhikkhu. *The Life of the Buddha as it Appears in the Pāli Canon.* Kandy: Buddhist Publication Society, 1972.

Naudou, Jean. *Buddhists of Kaśmīr,* translated by Brereton and Picron. First English edition. Delhi: Agam Kala Prakashan, 1980.

Paramārtha. *The Life of Vasu-bandhu,* translated by J. Takakusu, in T'oung Pao, Serie II, vol. V (1904), pp. 269–466.

Prasad, Ram Chandra. *Archaeology of Champā and Vikramaśīla.* Delhi: Ramanand Vidya Bhawan, 1987.

Puri, B.N. "Central Asia and its Peoples' Role in Ancient Indian History," in *Prolegomena to the Sources of the History of Pre-Islamic Central Asia,* edited by J. Harmatta, pp. 181–186. Budapest: Akadémiai Kiado. 1979.

Puri, B.N. *Buddhism in Central Asia.* Delhi: Motilal Banarsidass, 1987.

Rockhill, W. Woodville. *The Life of the Buddha and the Early History of His Order,* derived from Tibetan works in the bKah-hgyur and bsTan-hgyur. London: Kegan Paul, Trench, Trübner & Co., 1884.

Roerich, George N., tr. *Biography of Dharmasvamin.* Patna: K.P. Jayaswal Research Institute, 1959.

Sahu, N. K. *Buddhism in Orissa.* Cuttack, Utkal University, 1958.

Sankhalia, Hasmukh D. *The University of Nālandā.* G. Paul and Co., 1934.

Sarkar, H. and S. P. Nainar. *Amaravati.* New Delhi: Director General Archaeological Survey of India, 1972.

Sarkar, H., and B. N. Misra. *Nagarjunakonda.* New Delhi: Director General Archaeological Survey of India, 1972.

Saunders, Kenneth J. *Epochs in Buddhist History.* Chicago, 1924. (The Haskell Lectures, 1921)

Singh, Jai Prakash and Gautam Sengupta, eds. *Archaeology of North-Eastern India.* Delhi: Vikas Publishing House, 1991.

Srinivasin, C. R. *Kanchipuram Through the Ages.* Delhi, 1979.

Srinivasin, Doris Meth. *Mathurā: The Cultural Heritage.* New Delhi: American Institute of Tibetan Studies, 1989

Subramanian, K. R. *Buddhist Remains in South India and Early Andhra History, 225 A.D. to 610 A.D.* New Delhi: Cosmo Publications, 1981.

Tāranātha. *History of Buddhism in India,* translated by Lama Chimpa and Alaka Chattopadhyaya. Simla: Indian Institute of Advanced Study, 1970.

Thomas, E. J. *The Life of Buddha as Legend and History.* London, Routledge & Kegan Paul, 1927. 3rd ed. (revised) 1949.

Upasak, C. S. *History of Buddhism in Afghanistan.* Sarnath: Central Institute of Higher Tibetan Studies, 1990.

Ward, Tim. *The Great Dragon's Fleas.* Berkeley: Celestial Arts, 1993.

Warder, A. K. *Indian Buddhism.* Second revised edition. Delhi: Motilal Banarsidass, 1980.

World Peace Ceremony, Bodh Gaya. Berkeley: Dharma Publishing, 1994.

Index

Sita-Cintāmaṇi Mahākāla

Tarthang Tulku

About Tarthang Tulku: A Note from the Staff of Dharma Publishing

The general editor for the *Crystal Mirror Series* is Tarthang Tulku, an accomplished Tibetan lama who has made his home in the United States for the past twenty-three years. Since his arrival in India in 1959, Rinpoche has worked with complete dedication for the transmission of the Dharma. As his students, we have learned to find inspiration in his tireless devotion and profound respect for the Dharma.

For seven years while he was living in India, Rinpoche taught at Sanskrit University in Varanasi, establishing an international reputation as a scholar. During this time he founded Dharma Mudranalaya and began publishing texts from the Tibetan Buddhist tradition. He has continued this work in America for over twenty years. Today books by Dharma Publishing, including a number of translations of important Buddhist texts, have been adopted for use in more than five hundred colleges and universities throughout the world.

In addition to his work as a scholar and publisher, Rinpoche has been active as an author and educator. He has written nine books presenting teachings for the modern world, produced two translations, and served as editor of the Nyingma Edition of the Tibetan Buddhist Canon, the Research Catalogue of the Nyingma Edition, and the Guide to the Nyingma Edition. He is founder and president of the Nyingma Institute in Berkeley and its affiliated centers, where several thousand students have come in contact with the Dharma.

In the midst of all these activities, Rinpoche has also found time to serve in the traditional role of teacher for a growing community of Western students. Always willing to experiment, he has established a form of practice for his students in which their work on behalf of the Dharma becomes a path to realization. Many of his students do not have frequent direct contact with Rinpoche, but through the institutions he has established, they are able to grow in wisdom and understanding, while developing practical skills that enable them to make their way in the world. Above all, Rinpoche has devoted much of his energy to the creation of Odiyan, a country center that he hopes will one day change the basis for Dharma practice in the West.

Because of the incredible range of activities in which Rinpoche engages during a single day, it has not been possible for him to verify the accuracy of every element of the books we have produced under his direction. As a result, there may be mistakes in some of the material presented here, for which we take full responsibility. We only hope that on balance we have been successful in transmitting some elements of the Dharma tradition.

Those of us who have had the opportunity to work under Rinpoche in the production of Dharma Publishing books are deeply grateful for the example he has set us. His dedication and reliable knowledge, his steady, untiring efforts, his competence, and his caring allow us to direct our energy with complete confidence that despite our own imperfections, our work can be of benefit to others.